Great Holiness Classics

Volume 5

GREAT HOLINESS CLASSICS

in Six Volumes

Volume 1

Holiness Teaching—New Testament Times to Wesley

Volume 2

The Wesley Century

Volume 3

Leading Wesleyan Thinkers

Volume 4

The 19th-Century Holiness Movement

Volume 5

Holiness Preachers and Preaching

Volume 6

Holiness Teaching Today

* GREAT HOLINESS CLASSICS *

VOLUME 5

Holiness Preachers and Preaching

Edited by
W. E. McCumber

Volume Advisors:
Dennis Kinlaw
Mark R. Moore

BEACON HILL PRESS OF KANSAS CITY
KANSAS CITY, MISSOURI

Beacon Hill Press of Kansas City

ISBN: 083-411-2892

083-410-9093 series

Printed in the United States of America

10 9 8 7 6 5 4 3 2 1

Contents

Foreword

John Wesley is acknowledged and acclaimed as the chief architect of the doctrine of entire sanctification or Christian perfection as understood within the Holiness Movement. However, the truth this tenet expresses derives from the very heart of Scripture, and the experience and life it enshrines have been known and exemplified by the saints of every age.

Nor did Wesley give final and complete formulation of this truth. Theology is an ongoing process; it endeavors to interpret truth in language and thought-forms relevant to each succeeding generation. The creativity of the Spirit is evident in the unfolding of the doctrine from Wesley to the present. The truth of Christian holiness is so grand it defies any finality of expression.

Furthermore, since saints within every Christian tradition have found this Kingdom treasure, their witness to holiness reflects the variety of these traditions. The truth of perfect love is like a sparkling diamond—to appreciate its full beauty and brilliance we must view it from many angles.

This series of classics is designed to provide the modern reader a compact library of holiness literature. Herein you will find, along with appropriate editorial introductions and comments, many of the significant primary documents of the Holiness Movement. I commend these volumes as a devotional treasure for those who seek spiritual enrichment as well as a resource library for teachers and preachers who would deepen and enlarge their understanding of this central truth of Scripture.

—WILLIAM M. GREATHOUSE
General Superintendent
Church of the Nazarene

Understanding the Great Holiness Classics

Holiness

Christian holiness is a scriptural teaching to be understood and a relationship with God to be experienced. God is a holy God, and He asks His people to be like Him in this respect.

In the Old Testament we read, "Ye shall be holy: for I the Lord your God am holy" (Lev. 19:2). In teaching us about our responsibilities to God, Jesus summarized the first chapter of the Sermon on the Mount with the admonition: "Be ye therefore perfect, even as your Father which is in heaven is perfect" (Matt. 5:48).

Every sincere Christian wants to know what it means to be as holy as God asks us to be. Every follower of Christ feels at times yearnings to be more Christlike, to somehow realize the Christian perfection Jesus sets before us.

It is this ideal and goal taught in the Scriptures that has, across the centuries, stirred every devout Christian who has sought and experienced God's sanctifying grace. In John Wesley's *Plain Account of Christian Perfection* he records his own experience of discovering this truth: "I tell you, as plain as I can speak, where and when I found this. I found it in the oracles of God, in the Old and New Testament, when I read them with no other view or desire, but to save my own soul" (*Works,* 11:444).

The Holiness Classics

Following in the tradition of Wesley and other devout persons who have sought and preached Christian holiness, the publishers conceived and launched this series of six volumes of *Great Holiness Classics.* The desire and purpose was, in Wesley's words, to "spread scriptural holiness over these lands" in the 20th century.

The commission given to the editors states that desire.

> To provide a representative compilation of the best holiness literature in a format readily accessible to the average minister, thus providing: (1) the preservation of the essential elements of our holiness heritage; (2) an overview of the broad scope of the holi-

ness message; (3) a norm for holiness theology, proclamation, and practice; (4) a succinct reference work on holiness; and (5) a revival of the best of the out-of-print holiness classics.

What Is a Classic?

A classic work comes from the past, but simply being old does not make it classic. To be classic, a work must have enduring excellence. Its content must be so true and persuasive that succeeding generations read it and are moved to accept the truth and to shape their lives by it. Seeking after holiness as taught in a classic, one finds the truths verified both in Scripture and in his own experience with God. A work is classic because its truths are central to revealed and to experiential Christianity.

It is this verifying of previous experience that keeps a classic alive in the consciousness of the Christian community. There is here a principle somewhat parallel to the scientific method. In science we accept as true an experiment that can be repeated under similar conditions with the same results.

Because a holiness classic represents such a verifiable and biblical promise of spiritual fulfillment, it becomes a typical example of true teaching and a dependable model of Christian experience. Other persons who ponder the Scripture and perform the experiment report comparable experiences of God. The accumulating testimony verifies the classic nature of the document.

A classic thus becomes an authoritative commentary on scriptural truth. It contains guidance that can be depended on to result in sound action and blessed results. The work therefore becomes a norm for future generations. It affirms to the reader, "If you approach God as I did and respond to Him, as by His Word and Spirit He led me to respond, you will discover that He works in your life as I testify He has worked in mine."

In a letter to Dr. Middleton, Wesley cites this appeal to holy living as characteristic of the Christian fathers: "What the Scripture promises, I enjoy. Come and see what Christianity has done here; and acknowledge it is of God" (*Works,* 10:79).

Selection of Materials

The editors have been guided by these concepts of classic holiness writings. Works that have spoken to succeeding generations have endured; therefore, we have included them. Writings that present views widely held by other holiness writers are to be considered classic. A work that stimulates the reader to try the grand experiment is classical. In Christian literature, writings that most faithfully reflect biblical teachings are classical in the best sense of being truly Christian norms.

The materials here selected as classic, then, (1) reflect accurately the teachings of the Bible, (2) have a broad and common base of Christian testimony, (3) and are in line with the best thinking of Christian leaders who have enjoyed the experience of God's sanctifying grace.

What we have chosen, we believe, gives a true account of God's plan for holy living. These writings offer a norm for Christian life that reflects God's will for His children. They lead to the greatest personal fulfillment and inspire believers to make their most effective contribution to the extension of God's kingdom.

Truth with Tolerance

Not all sincere Christians understand Bible holiness in the same way. What is here reflected is generally called the Wesleyan interpretation of entire sanctification. Even within the circle of those who follow Wesley there are some differences of interpretation. The statement of "Concepts and Identifying Terms" was drawn up as a way to reflect the widely accepted positions of the Wesleyan, Methodist tradition.

We recognize and appreciate guides to holy living from other traditions as in the Moravian, Quaker, Mennonite, and modern Keswick movements. Much of what is here included crosses all denominational boundaries. It will therefore speak to the spirits of evangelical Christians from most of the historic orthodox communions.

In order to avoid being too restrictive in our selections, we have sought the advice of a broad group of nearly 50 Bible scholars and churchmen whose names appear in the lists of editors, and of members of the editorial advisory boards. These persons have all been involved in a continuing consultation on the choice of materials to be included. We trust that the broad consensus further assures our choice of truly classic materials.

Editorial Policy

The editors were instructed to select writings "judged by the quality of the material and its ability to speak to this generation." Because many of the holiness classics, especially in the first two volumes, come from an earlier period of writing, we were further given "the right to excerpt and edit the materials, updating archaic usage as needed."

Our goal has been, insofar as is possible, to let the writers speak for themselves. In excerpting we have tried to be completely faithful to the writer's views, deleting only dated, irrelevant, or duplicated materials. Our concern has always been to present as clearly as possible what the writer believed, experienced, and taught about Christian holiness.

In order to make our selections as clear as possible for today's reader we have: (1) modernized some spelling and punctuation, (2) divided some long paragraphs for greater ease in reading, (3) prepared brief introductions and analyses of the writings included, and (4) inserted center heads, side heads, and cut-in headings as brief indications of content in order to guide the reader who is looking for specific aspects of holiness teaching.

For the historical scholar who wishes to follow in our footsteps and form his own judgment of our accuracy, we have: (1) indicated our sources by title, date, edition, and page numbers from which the selection is taken (where relevant for accuracy, we have used the earliest editions of the text); (2) retained original paragraph numbers to aid the reader in locating the source of our quotations; (3) used ellipses to indicate where material has been omitted; and (4) retained italics that appear in the originals, to show what the writers sought to emphasize.

To help the reader more easily distinguish editorial comment from the classic materials quoted, we have printed the editor's additions in a slightly darker type.

Our Prayer

The prayer of the editors and publishers is that all who read these classics of holy living may come to understand "the way of God more perfectly" (Acts 18:26).

We pray "that Christ may dwell in your hearts by faith; that ye, being rooted and grounded in love, may be able to comprehend with all saints what is the breadth, and length, and depth, and height; and to know the love of Christ, which passeth knowledge, that ye might be filled with all the fulness of God.

"Now unto him that is able to do exceeding abundantly above all that we ask or think, according to the power that worketh in us, unto him be glory in the church by Christ Jesus throughout all ages, world without end. Amen" (Eph. 3:17-21).

—A. F. HARPER
Executive Editor

Concepts and Identifying Terms

At the beginning of the project the editors were mandated to "strive for balance, reflecting the various facets of holiness—crisis and process, practice and proclamation, etc."

In order to guide us and to test the inclusiveness and balance of materials chosen, it seemed necessary to devise an instrument for reminder and measurement. We therefore developed the following list of concepts and identifying terms.

The statements are designed to indicate the teachings of the church. The identifying terms are planned as a kind of shorthand device for highlighting these truths throughout the set and in the indexes.

We believe the statements faithfully reflect what the Bible teaches and what the Church has believed and taught across the centuries. The terms are biblical and/or classical in the sense that they represent the language the Church has used to describe the various facets of the experience of God's sanctifying grace.

For convenient reference, we have used these code words as cut-in heads on pages where the related concepts are explored.

A. Doctrinal

1. The requirement of entire sanctification is rooted in God's holiness. — **God's Holiness**
2. The need for entire sanctification is seen in the remaining presence of inbred sin, or carnality, in believers. The experience of entire sanctification includes cleansing from this original sin. — **Carnality/ Cleansing**
3. Entire sanctification is a gift of God's grace. — **Grace**
4. God provides the gift in the atonement of Christ. — **Atonement**

5. To be sanctified wholly means to receive grace to love God with your whole heart and to love your neighbor as yourself. **Perfect Love**
6. At conversion, Christians receive God's Holy Spirit in regeneration, sometimes described as initial sanctification. To be sanctified wholly means to be baptized, or filled with the Holy Spirit, as happened to the disciples in the Upper Room. **Holy Spirit**
7. To be filled with the Holy Spirit brings added power to conquer sin, to love others, and to witness for Christ. **Power**[1]
8. God offers the ministry of the indwelling Holy Spirit to make us more Christlike. **Christ-likeness**
9. We believe the doctrine of entire sanctification is taught in the Bible and is consistent with other salvation truths of Scripture. **Scriptural**
10. Entire sanctification is God's call to all Christians. **For All Christians**
11. Entire sanctification is experienced as a second blessing of grace subsequent to regeneration. **Second Blessing**
12. Because entire sanctification is God's gift in response to faith, it occurs in a moment of time, just as God's forgiveness comes in an instant. **In a Moment**
13. Entire sanctification is also known as Christian perfection, perfect love, heart purity, the baptism with the Holy Spirit, being filled with the Spirit, the fullness of the blessing, full salvation, the deeper life, Christian holiness, scriptural holiness, the rest of faith, and the promise of the Father. **Names**

B. Steps to Seeking and Finding

14. The new birth is a prerequisite to entire sanctification. **New Birth**

---

1. Item 7 was omitted from the first printing of volumes 2 and 3. It will appear in subsequent editions of all volumes in the series.

15. Conviction of need is a condition for the personal quest after holiness. — **Hunger**
16. Full consecration is both a precondition and a gracious fruit of entire sanctification. — **Consecration**
17. Faith grounded on the full-orbed purpose of Christ's death, and the fullest consecration of which we are capable, is the human condition for entire sanctification. — **Faith**
18. God gives the witness of His Spirit when we are sanctified wholly. — **Assurance**

C. Living the Life of Holiness

19. Christians grow in likeness to Christ, both before and after entire sanctification. Successful growth requires obedience, trust, deep devotion, and personal discipline. — **Growth**
20. Being filled with the Spirit makes a difference in a Christian's attitudes. — **Attitudes**
21. Holiness tends toward fulfillment of life and wholeness of human personality. — **Wholeness**
22. Though sanctified wholly, men and women are still limited by their imperfections in judgment, personality, and conduct; they are still subject to all sorts of temptation. — **Humanity**
23. Dangers to which the sanctified are especially vulnerable include spiritual pride and setting standards too high. — **Dangers**

D. Proclamation—Witnessing

24. Testifying to God's work of entire sanctification honors God and spreads the truth. — **Witnessing**
25. The truth of entire sanctification and a holy life is to be proclaimed through preaching. — **Preaching**
26. Understanding of the truth of Christian holiness and hunger for the experience are communicated through teaching. — **Teaching**
27. The truth of Christian holiness is spread through written testimony, exposition, and exhortation. — **Writing**
28. We document and prove holiness by living holy lives and by Christian ethical behavior. — **Ethics**

Acknowledgments

Grateful acknowledgment is given to the following publishers for their permission to reprint sermons in this collection:

Beacon Hill Press of Kansas City:

Myron F. Boyd and Merne A. Harris, compilers, *Projecting Our Heritage*

James B. Chapman, *Christian Living in a Modern World*

General Superintendents (1985-89), *Sanctify Them . . . That the World May Know*

James McGraw, compiler, *The Holiness Pulpit* and *The Holiness Pulpit No. 2*

Wesley D. Tracy, editor, *The Redeemed Will Walk There*

John Wesley, *The Works of John Wesley*, 3rd edition

H. Orton Wiley, *The Harps of God and Other Sermons*

Wm. B. Eerdmans Publishing Company:

Paul S. Rees, *Stand Up in Praise to God.*

Editor's Introduction to Volume 5

Making a collection of sermons is almost as sure to displease as to please. Limitations of space do not allow the inclusion of many sermons that are clearly as good or better than some of those selected.

The sermons collected here are from preachers living and dead. They represent a time span from Wesley's day to the present. Sermons by preachers now deceased were the easiest to select and prepare. Their contemporaries could not reproach me for ignoring other deserving preachers and sermons. My contemporaries, however, can register scores of justifiable protests, should they wish to do so.

The process of selection is inescapably subjective. I can only plead that, so far as possible, I have been guided by the advices and recommendations of the committee chosen to offer guidance. Where personal choice has intruded, I have honestly attempted to secure and include the choicest material available to me in the too-limited time and means for research at my disposal. I could not find published sermons from some preachers I had hoped to include. Some preachers who were invited to contribute sermons did not do so, for whatever reasons.

The preachers and sermons presented herein are, without denying their individuality, fairly representative of their generations.

Editing has been done in some of these sermons, always in the interest of brevity and clarity. In addition to my own editing I have tried to be amenable to and cooperative with the executive editor.

Reading hundreds of sermons, and almost as many pages of history, was beneficial to me. My own appreciation for those men and women who have labored faithfully to proclaim the message of full salvation has been increased, and my own resolution to pursue a worthy though inferior place among them has been strengthened.

Quoting Gen. 1:3, Ronald L. Willingham commented, "God spoke creation into existence. That day speech created light; today speech creates *enlightenment.*" This is the first aim of holiness preaching, to focus light upon the subject. The second aim is to persuade, that the church may experience and express what God has willed, Christ has provided, and the Holy Spirit is available to execute.

—W. E. McCumber

1

THE DOCTRINE OF HOLINESS

C. William Fisher
(1916—)

An evangelist is often a pastor between charges, looking for a place to locate. C. William Fisher is an evangelist by calling. His entire ministry has been devoted to evangelism. In revival meetings throughout the United States and around the world, God has used his anointed music and preaching to bring thousands to Christ and to revive the hearts of flagging Christians.

Reared in Oklahoma, he united with the Church of the Nazarene in his youth, graduated from one of its colleges, and devoted his life to its ministry. For many years his summer months have been devoted to home mission areas, and many churches and districts have benefited enormously from his generous labors.

Thousands who never saw him have been touched by his ministry through radio and print media. His books have sold widely, and for eight years he was speaker for "Showers of Blessing," the radio voice of the Church of the Nazarene. His messages, models of organized, clear, and impassioned thought, were carried on more than 700 stations across his nation and around the world.

I first heard C. William Fisher preach at a district assembly in Florida when I was a young Christian and a novice minister. His message affirmed the expendability of Christians as soldiers of the Cross, and it made a profound impression on my heart. I could see why he was in such demand as a revivalist. Years later it was my privilege, as a pastor, to have him conduct revival services in the church I served. I found him to be in private what he was in public, a man committed to the will and Word of God.

"Free at Last!" sets forth the full measure of freedom from sin that we can presently experience through the blood of Jesus Christ and the power of the Holy Spirit. This freedom is expounded in language that ordinary people can understand and is illustrated in ways that capture heart and mind in the same grasp. Loaded with biblical content, but wearing its theology in overalls, it is a choice sample of how to preach to the vast majority of congregations a minister is likely to address.

Fisher is not an advocate of "cheap grace." He makes it clear that any personal experience of this liberation from sin will cost the believer nothing less than a full and hearty submission to the will of God.

Free at Last!*

If the Son therefore shall make you free, ye shall be free indeed (John 8:36).

The editors of *Life* magazine commissioned Margaret Bourke-White to do a picture essay on India, primarily to see what changes, if any, had taken place in that vast country since independence. The pictures, along with her own text, appeared in the magazine as a series.

When Miss Bourke-White returned to America, she wrote a book and titled it *Halfway to Freedom.* That was her evaluation of the people of India after independence. They had come to certain measures of freedom but were only about halfway to full freedom.

As I sat in a public library one afternoon, reading Miss Bourke-White's book, it came to me that her very title was an all-too-adequate description of the spiritual pilgrimage of thousands of Christians, men and women and young people who had come to know Christ in a measure of valid freedom but who were, in reality, only halfway to the . . . enjoyment of full freedom in Christ. They had heard the "Emancipation Proclamation" announced from Calvary's cross and had come to know Christ in the

I. *Freedom from the Guilt of Sins*

And that is real freedom. Weighted down by the chains of evil habits, evil thoughts, evil attitudes, and evil pleasures, thousands of

---

*Source: Sermon manuscript.

. . . fettered men and women have made their pilgrimage to the foot of the cross of Christ. And there, bowed down by the weight of their chains, they have looked up and dared to believe that the proclamation meant what it said. Weary of their shackles . . . they have asked, "What must I do to enjoy this freedom? What must I do to get rid of these chains? What must I do to be freed of this guilt?"

THERE IS FORGIVENESS

And Jesus has answered, "Repent and believe. Tell Me that you are sorry for your sins. Tell Me that you are tired enough of those chains that bind you that you will forsake everything that has forged them about you. Tell Me that you will live in My freedom from this hour on." In that moment of repentance and faith, as they look up in expectancy and trust, Jesus reaches down with His redemptive power, breaks every chain . . . and sets the prisoner free. The tyranny of guilt is gone . . . and the soul that was shackled is now free. He is not only freed *from* sins but also freed *to* a new life, a released life, an authentic life in Christ.

There are those . . . who say that no one can experience instantaneous freedom. "What you have to do," they say, "is to take hold of each link in the chain that binds you and through great struggle and effort break that link. Then take hold of another link and through great effort break that link, and so on."

But in spite of what *anyone* says—be he an atheist who says that none of it is possible, be he an agnostic who says that you couldn't know it even if it did happen, be he a liberal theologian who ridicules the whole personal encounter, be he a skeptic who sneers at the whole Blood-bought plan of redemption—I still believe that

There is a fountain filled with blood
Drawn from Immanuel's veins;
And sinners, plunged beneath that flood,
Lose all their guilty stains.

Thank God, will you, for the freedom a chained and fettered sinner can find at the foot of the cross of Jesus! He may have learned only part of the definition, but that is far better than not knowing the word at all. He may be only halfway to full freedom, but that is so much better than being a slave to his sins. Even partial freedom is better than slavery.

But in Christ there is not only freedom from the guilt of outward sins but also

II. *Freedom from the Bondage of Inward Sin*

We now identify ourselves with those who have been forgiven and freed from their own sins, and we are having a wonderful time as new creatures in Christ. Old things have passed away and, behold, all things have become new in Him (2 Cor. 5:17). And it is a marvelous experience and relationship. Thank God, no one needs to minimize the reality and glory of conversion when he preaches holiness, for it is only the truly converted who can be entirely sanctified.

Suppose someone should come up to us in those days or weeks or months of newfound joy and say, "Now it is wonderful what you have allowed God to do for you, but there is a deeper experience that He has for you. He can give you freedom on a deeper level. He can liberate you at the very center of the self."

A DEEPER EXPERIENCE

Well, we wouldn't argue about it, but we might say, "I don't really know what more God could do for . . . me. I was on my way to hell, and now I'm on my way to heaven. Some things I once thought I *had* to have for my life to be happy and fulfilled I no longer find necessary at all. And those things that I once couldn't see any value in I now find to be of supreme value. I just don't know what God could do for me that He hasn't already done."

We are happy in this newfound relationship with Christ, and we have a right to be, for we are new creatures, we know the joy of forgiveness, we have been liberated from the tyranny of the guilt of past sins. Life for the first time is purposeful and significant.

But then, one day, *something* happens. Some provocation, some challenge, some tragedy, some personal affront, some shattering experience, some overwhelming temptation hits us, and we are caught off guard. We respond in such a disappointing, contradictory way that we are robbed of that edge of victory and that dimension of joy that we had known. We realize that we are not as free as we thought we were because we have become conscious of a bondage at the center of the self. There is revealed a bound condition at the core of being, and we are perplexed and disturbed about it. We say, "Surely God can do more for me than this. Surely He can make me more adequate for such a life situation."

MADE AWARE OF OUR NEED

So, in our disturbed state, we go to God's Word to find help. As we read we come to this: "The carnal mind is enmity against God: for it is not subject to the law of God, neither indeed can be" (Rom. 8:7). We look up the word "enmity" and find that it means "contrary to, in contradiction with." Well, at least we know what to call that which arose within us. God says it is the carnal mind, the carnal nature, the devil's nature still within me, even though I have been forgiven of my own sins.

As we continue to read, we come to this: "For God hath not called us unto uncleanness, but unto holiness" (1 Thess. 4:7). "And the very God of peace sanctify you wholly; and I pray God your whole spirit and soul and body be preserved blameless unto the coming of our Lord Jesus Christ. Faithful is he that calleth you, who also will do it" (5:23-24).

We say to ourselves, Well, I don't understand all that those scriptures mean, but it does look like God is trying to get me to see that He has a work for me that I have not experienced as yet. He has not called

WHOLENESS

me to inner conflict, inner fragmentation, inner contrariness, but unto holiness—wholeness, integration, inner unity, inner focus. And there begins a hunger for this relationship with God that knows no inner pullback, no inner contradiction, no inner conflict with His will,

III. *A Hunger That Leads to Hope*

Then one day we read how that even the disciples of Jesus were vacillating in their allegiance to Christ, and fluctuating in their commitment to His cause. When the heat was really turned on and the pressure was exerted, every last one of those disciples fled or failed Him. Peter, who a few short hours before had professed his love so loudly, played the coward and denied his Lord.

But wait; read on to where it tells of those same disciples on the Day of Pentecost and afterward. Now they were saturated with a new reality and power. Even though they endured far greater and more

TRANSFORMED AT PENTECOST

intense pressure *after* Pentecost than they ever had *before,* they were now strong, poised, and victorious. Obviously they had received *something* on the Day of Pentecost they had never experienced before, something that even three years of fellowship with Christ in His ministry had not given them. Whatever it was they received, it made *the* difference between victory and defeat, between success and failure in their lives.

As the hunger for more of God, for this "wholeness," for this liberation at the center becomes more intense, we read on in God's Word more avidly.

"Oh, I wish God had an experience for me similar to that of the disciples on the Day of Pentecost," we say. "I need something like that so badly. Things come up at home that I am simply not adequate to meet victoriously. Things come up at work or at school or at church, and I pop off, which just makes me embarrassed, chagrined, and defeated." And I think, What a fine Christian you turned out to be! Oh, how I wish God had an experience that would do for me what that experience those disciples received on the Day of Pentecost did for them. But I suppose that is too much to expect. I guess I'll just have to muddle through the best I can.

But the longing for such an experience lingers until one day we come to this: "For this is the will of God, even your sanctification" (1 Thess. 4:3). That word "your" seems to leap right out of God's Word into our waiting hearts, and we say, "Why, it *is* for me! It is God's will that *I* be sanctified!" And there is now hope to go along with the hunger.

HOPE IN GOD'S WORD

But along with the hunger and hope comes the question, "How can I experience this liberation at the center, this inner wholeness and victory?" Again we find the answer in God's Word: "Wherefore Jesus also, that he might sanctify the people with his own blood, suffered without the gate" (Heb. 13:12).

So we look again to Calvary and ask, "Jesus, do You mean that You can not only forgive my sins but also cleanse my heart? Do You mean that You can do more than break the chains of the sins I have committed and free me from the guilt of those transgressions? Can You melt and dissolve the inner shackles of the carnal mind, the bondage at the center, and set me completely free? Is that what You mean?"

FULL SALVATION

In that incredulous moment Jesus replies, "Yes, I can do all of that for you. For when I died on this Cross, I didn't die to give men half answers for their problems; I died to give men an adequate answer for their deepest sin problem. I can give you an answer to your inner cry for freedom. Come."

In response to that promise, the true child of God does not hesitate or refuse, saying, "Well, I don't understand all about it"; or, "Well, I'm living a very good life as it is"; or, "Well, if this is really true, why don't *all* churches preach it?" (But then again, why don't all churches preach the initial experience of repentance and the new birth?) The true child of God doesn't stand back and give out with the excuses; his attitude is, If this is for me, I want it—and I want it now!

So we make our way to the foot of the Cross again—yes, thank God for a second crisis experience, for a full realization of the word "freedom." As we kneel there, we ask, "What am I to do to enjoy this freedom?" And God answers, "You must consecrate; you must surrender your all; you must turn over *everything;* for if I am to do a liberating work at the center of the self, you must *yield* at the center."

CONSECRATION

So we begin to consecrate. We put *things* on the altar; we put *circumstances* on the altar; we put *people* on the altar; we put cantankerous *kinfolk* on the altar. Finally, we put *self* on the altar—and that is what God has been insisting upon all along. For if He has the self, He has everything the self has. In that moment of full and complete surrender, we reach up in faith and embrace the promise, "If the Son therefore shall make you free, ye shall be free indeed" (John 8:36).

IV. *A Liberating Freedom*

In response to our surrender and faith, God applies the liberating merits of the blood of Jesus to our innermost being. There is a freeing up, a release, a melting of the chains of the carnal mind, a dissolving of the bondage of the selfish self, and an infilling with the power of the Holy Spirit. To this the Spirit gives witness. "For by one offering he hath perfected for ever them that are sanctified. Whereof the Holy Ghost also is a witness to us" (Heb. 10:14-15).

Along with this witness there may be ecstasy, but there may not be. In any case, the ecstasy is not the important thing; the important thing is that we have entered into a new and deeper relationship with God. For in that moment, God purges from the heart that inner defilement, that inner contamination. In that moment the inner pullback is canceled out, the inner contrariness is removed, the inner conflict is resolved. The heart is now pure, clean, freed—not only *from* sins but also *for* a life of holiness and victory and unity and integration and wholeness and effective witness.

ASSURANCE

You can't find that kind of freedom at the United Nations, in the White House, or in the halls of any congress or parliament. But you *can* find that kind of freedom at the foot of the cross of Jesus Christ. There is only one place in this universe where one can find the full definition of the word "freedom," and that is at Jesus' feet. For "if the Son therefore shall make you free, ye shall be free indeed." *Free at last!*

I came to a new dimension of appreciation for this word "freedom" in our visit to Berlin. As we passed "Checkpoint Charlie," the guide and the driver of our tour bus got off, and a Communist guide and driver got on. After touring in East Berlin, seeing the haunted look on the faces of the people in that tragic sector of the city, and seeing the incredible contrasts between East and West Berlin, we returned to the checkpoint, where our original guide and bus driver got back on. As our guide stood in the front of the bus, he said, "Everybody take a deep breath." I suppose everyone did; I did. Then he said, "Now, honestly, doesn't freedom even *taste* better!" And it did seem to.

After a tour of the wall, that unbelievable, tragic wall of separation between East and West Berlin, we returned to our starting point. Before the guide let us out of the bus, he said, "Ladies and gentlemen, you may have thought I was too emotional on parts of this trip, especially when I spoke of that wall. But I'll tell you why I feel deeply about it: My father and mother live on the other side, in East Berlin. I would give everything I have if I knew of a way to bring them over to freedom."

We filed out of the bus, and as I was walking down the sidewalk, my heart filled with gratitude to God. This guide had said that he would give everything he had if he knew of a way to bring his mother and father over to political freedom. But I have had the privilege through these years to stand up openly and proclaim that I knew of a way to spiritual freedom for every bound . . . and imprisoned soul. That way leads directly and inescapably to the foot of the cross of Jesus Christ!

How grateful and humbled I felt that afternoon as I thought of the incalculable privilege that had been mine to proclaim—in many countries, and to those of different cultures and colors—that at the foot of the cross of Christ they could find more than political freedom, economic freedom, or psychological freedom. They could find freedom from the fetters of their own sins and freedom from the bondage of inward sin until they were truly free, free to live life to the full—abundantly, happily, purposefully, and in glad and grateful obedience to God's will!

What will this freedom cost you? It will cost you everything you have. But if you will give God *your* all, He will give you *His* all. You will find that what God can give will make you adequate to meet whatever you have to meet in life and to meet it victoriously.

And through it all you will be able to exclaim, with a spiritual certainty that is infinitely more profound and meaningful than any political, racial, or economic reality, "Free at last! Thank God, in *Christ*, I'm free at last!"

Adam Clarke

(1762[?]-1832)

Adam Clarke was early Methodism's outstanding scholar. His chief legacy to the Church was his *Commentary on the Holy Scriptures,* on which he labored for 40 years. It remains in daily use today, combining to an unusual degree massive learning with intense devotion.

Clarke excelled also as a preacher. Wesley Tracy appropriately titled a study of his preaching, *When Adam Clarke Preached, People Listened.* One who listened was Mrs. Pawson, wife of a minister with whom Clarke labored in Liverpool. In her diary she wrote, "Brother Clarke is, in my estimation, an extraordinary preacher; and his learning confers great luster on his talents: he makes it subservient to grace. His discourses are highly evangelical: he never loses sight of Christ. In regard of pardon and holiness, he offers a present salvation. His address is lively, animated, and very encouraging to the seekers of salvation."

Clarke was born in Ireland and converted in his youth under Methodist preaching. At the urging of John Wesley, he began his ministry in 1782, growing rapidly and steadily in the esteem of his fellow Methodists and the learned public. Before his death from cholera, in 1832, he had been honored with degrees from the University of Aberdeen and by election to a number of Royal Societies of learned men. These honors, a biographer wrote, "did not turn his head or chill his heart."

While learning did not turn his head, an angry papist once split Clarke's head with a huge stone. The assassination attempt nearly succeeded. The Church owes a great debt to Clarke's hat, which somewhat cushioned the blow.

His sermon "The Doctrine of Holiness" recalls Mrs. Pawson's assessment. Here is learning "subservient to grace" and the offer of "a present salvation." It comes from a minister who combined highly energetic preaching with deep concern for souls.

The sermon also verifies Samuel Dunn's evaluation: "Dr. Clarke's preaching was chiefly expository. He endeavored to explain the terms in his text; to ascertain the precise meaning [intended by] the Holy Ghost; and then to apply to the understandings and consciences of his hearers the hallowing truths thus discovered."

The Doctrine of Holiness*

> *Create in me a clean heart, O God; and renew a right spirit within me. Cast me not away from thy presence; and take not thy holy spirit from me. Restore unto me the joy of thy salvation; and uphold me with thy free spirit* (Ps. 51:10-12).

It is not possible to conceive anything more solemn or important than . . . a sinner bowing in the presence of his Creator and Judge; and it is impossible to conceive any subject that can more deeply impress the heart or interest the feelings of the man than this. It is a matter in which his present comfort and eternal blessedness are concerned. And we are not to suppose, friends, that these things are prime matters of consideration merely with such persons as are mentioned in this book . . . they concern us as much as they did them. We also may say, "We have sinned and come short of God's glory. Against us, because of our offenses, is the wrath of the Lord kindled: and it is impossible to expect comfort in this [world], or blessedness in another world, unless the fierceness of the divine justice is turned away from us."

We are not only interested to get our state changed, but our

---

*Source: Adam Clarke, *Discourses on Various Subjects Relative to the Being and Attributes of God and His Work in Creation, Providence, and Grace,* vol. 4. London: William Tegg, 1868.

nature also. Having transgressed God's law, it proves there is in us an evil principle . . . for the transgression of the law in the life is only the external manifestation of what is in the heart; and, as man acts from inward feelings, an unrighteous act sufficiently [indicates] an unrighteous principle. . . .

CARNALITY/ CLEANSING

Consider the absolute necessity there is, that sin should be forgiven in order that we may not bear the punishment denounced against the transgressors of that law. There is also a necessity of having the heart purified, that we may be prepared to enjoy God in glory through eternity. These two things should deeply impress and ever occupy our minds . . .

The verses which you have heard read contain these important points. In the psalm is shown us a man in the presence of God, struggling for salvation, and wrestling with God for the redemption of his soul . . . So occupied was he with the state of his soul, that he makes no preface. He falls at once before his Judge, and his distress dictates immediately to him the prayer: "Have mercy upon me, O God, according to thy lovingkindness; according unto the multitude of thy tender mercies blot out my transgressions . . ." (vv. 1 ff.).

Hear what the Psalmist says, "Create in me a clean heart, O God." . . . He offers to God the feelings of his own heart; and doubtless, with a conviction that God, who had produced the desire in his heart, was ready to satisfy that desire. He says, "Create in me a clean heart, O God; and renew a right spirit within me." Does not the Psalmist refer to his *soul,* his judgment, understanding, and will, in the first clause; and to his *affections* and passions, as being irregular, unholy, and impure in the second?

CLEANSING

I conceive him to have these two things in view: First, his mind, with its faculties and operations; secondly, his passions, with their attachments and irregularities. . . .

The person who offered up the prayer was convinced that the whole state of his nature was out of its due course, and that his spirit was wrong. Hence, he says, "Create in me a clean *heart,* . . . and renew a right *spirit* within me." Again, he might apply this, referring to the state of purity and holiness in which he was formed by God. [God] created man in His own image and likeness; and now, feeling that he is miscreated . . . and convinced that the God who created him at first in righteousness and true holiness can bring him back into that state; and conscious that it is as great an act of almighty power thus to restore him, as it was in the beginning to make him; hence, he says

. . . "Create in me a clean heart." By this expression he shows us that the thing which he expected to be done for him could be done only by the living God. . . .

There are very few that . . . contradict the doctrine common in the Church of God . . . that man is not *now* what God made him; that he is fallen, and . . . he comes into the world with a perverted nature . . . There is not a man on the face of the earth that is not a proof of it; and the man who rises up to oppose it gives one of the most convincing proofs of the truth of it. It is impossible that an infinitely righteous and holy God could have made the soul as it now appears . . . God can make nothing opposed to His own nature . . . We are informed that He intended to make man in His image and likeness, for it is expressly said, "Let us make man in *our* image, after *our* likeness" (Gen. 1:26); . . . as He intended thus to create him, thus He did create him.

We might have been at a loss concerning the meaning of those words, "the image and likeness of God," if another inspired writer had not interpreted them. He tells us, the image of God consists in righteousness and true holiness . . . pointing out the principle that actuated all the powers of the human being. The effect of the working of that principle is always true inward holiness; such holiness as comes from God himself; a principle working in all the powers of the human mind, and a principle producing righteousness; everything conformed to God's will and nature. . . .

Not only must the mind have been made holy and pure, but all the lower powers and faculties; for as the body came immediately from the hand of God, as well as the soul, there was nothing imperfect in the body, any more than in the mind. He "formed man of the dust . . . and breathed into [him] the breath of [lives]" (Gen. 2:7). God was the Creator of the one as well as of the other: the former manifested the skill of God; the latter, His purity. The body was a proper place for the soul to dwell in. . . . Yet we find in this wonderful system enough to convince us that it is not in the state in which it was made: for though we are not able, in many cases, immediately to detect the appearance of disease, yet it is evident, in human life, that there is the seed of evil in the body, which brings about death in various forms, and secures the accomplishment of that great purpose of the Almighty, expressed in those words, "Dust thou art, and unto dust shalt thou return" (3:19).

DEATH DUE TO THE FALL

We see it is impossible for men to escape death. Death is an imperfection in the works of God, and disgraceful to the human being; and I know of nothing more so, on this side of eternal damnation. It is a proof, then, that God's justice has assigned it to this period, and that God in the beginning could not have made this body with an intention thus to destroy it.

But when we look into the mind of man, we find more there to convince us of our fall and imperfection. We generally . . . say, in [the soul] we mark understanding, judgment, and will; and we say of the understanding, it is the place where the ideas are fixed; of the judgment, it is a certain power by which man is enabled to determine about things presented to the understanding; and of the will, it is another certain power by which man determined to act in reference to what the judgment has decreed. I see something else in the soul of man, which may be properly called imagination; the place where the images of things are first engendered, and from which the understanding receives those images.

Now if this place, where the images or forms of things are engendered . . . be disordered . . . then all becomes false. . . . Thus it is with everything that passes into this power of the human mind: everything is distorted. We have not, except from the immediate influence of God himself, right images of any thing spiritual or divine presented before this power or faculty of the human soul; or if any image correct and pure is presented before it, on being received, the image is distorted: hence, we find, there is not a correct notion of God in the universe, but what has been received from revelation, or from the influence of God himself. . . . Hence the endless forms of the Divine Being, which have been contrived by men, and set up as objects of worship: and we find among them, not only those forms which are most pleasing to man (as taken from the best of his own species), but forms the most fantastic have been used to represent the Being of infinite perfection.

DISTORTION DUE TO SIN

This has not been the case merely with heathen nations. When we consider ourselves, what strange notions have we formed of God. Till the time when divine light shone upon our minds, what did we know of God? What strange notions did we form of His omnipotence? How often did we seek for privacy to cover transgressions immediately against God's law! How often did we suppose, that though God was a witness of our actions, yet that He was so merciful He would pass our transgressions

DEPRAVED UNDERSTANDING

by. Hence the mind became cold, and in consequence of this, it walked in its own darkness.

When we come to look into the understanding, we find it has given as little evidence of perfection as the imagination. What do we know? What do we understand from the things presented to us? Nothing, consequently, right. The result has been that our whole conduct has been broken in pieces. When our minds appeared [to be] directed right, notwithstanding this, we have in a few hours taken a wrong path; the act has showed a contrary direction to that indicated in the beginning.

Look at the judgment; see how it has comported itself. We find light put in the place of darkness, and darkness in the place of light. We find that crooked has been called straight, and straight crooked; that wrong judgment has been formed in general. This has shown us . . . an obliquity which was not accidental, but had, in its nature, opposition to God. What we determined to do was in general what God commanded us not to do. . . . Then the will comes in, to consummate the determination [of the judgment] by bringing it into action. When we consider the actions of the heart, all these were originally right; the soul was helped by those meaner powers; but these are now . . . averse from those things which God has commanded us to be attached to. We have loved that which we should have hated, and hated that which we should have loved. We have feared where there was no cause for fear: and where there was cause, we have not feared. In short, wayward, and unholy, and impure has been the whole system of our actions and affections.

OPPOSITION TO GOD

A man, looking into his soul and, by the light of God, seeing his sins, more enormous than tongue can paint them, would offer up this prayer: "Create in me a clean heart, O God; and renew a right spirit within me."

Brethren, let us apply this prayer to our own hearts. What do your hearts feel that is honorable to God? What attachments have you? What affections springing up there? How have you glorified God? Do you feel power so to do? No, you feel a heart deceitful and desperately wicked. You have struggled and found the struggle vain; still it was deceitful and desperately wicked. You have been sometimes so confounded at this, that you have despaired of heaven, because you found that you could not bring a clean thing out of an unclean.

Have you not thought of God in this way? Yes, you have; you have thought of Him as a loving God, and that He had a right to your obedience, to your affectionate obedience, which from you He has not received. Have you never in such a case thought of Jesus? Have you not heard that "God *so* loved the world, that he gave his only begotten Son, that whosoever believeth in him should not perish, but have everlasting life" (John 3:16)? Yes, you have; but you have thought yourselves too vile, too unholy, to have part in His merits, or to attract His notice.

JESUS CAME TO DESTROY SIN

Have you not heard that He died for sinners . . . for sinners of all kinds? Have you not heard that He came to put away sin by the sacrifice of himself? And have you not heard that word (may God write it on your hearts!), that He came to "destroy the works of the devil" (1 John 3:8)? Jesus came to . . . counterwork the devil's work: this is the meaning. The devil has been at work: Jesus came into the world to confound him. Satan has his foundation: Jesus came to destroy that, and to lay another foundation, and build you on it. All that the devil has laid, as a foundation, [Jesus] comes to destroy; to pull down, in order that He may build you up, as you were in the beginning, and make you a proper habitation of God through the eternal Spirit.

But you have thought again, you were too perverted; you felt the darkness of your understandings. The images which have been represented—the distortions of divine things when brought into the imagination—have sometimes struck you with horror, and you supposed, in consequence, that your case was beyond cure. Did you never consider the creative energy of God; that He has all power in heaven and in earth; that all other energies are inferior to His; and that, if He undertook to counterwork any energy, it must be counterworked? His power is the same as when He created you; and though you are miscreated, yet the God of heaven can recreate you. And has not God produced in you the convictions you feel? You see you cannot save yourselves . . . that no being that God has formed can change your mind—make your mind a right mind, and make your heart a right heart: then you are obliged to have recourse to God.

GRACE AND POWER

But to be convinced of His ability would be small relief, if you could not see a reason why God should exercise His power to purify your soul and forgive your sins. But this you can see, through the atonement made by Jesus Christ. Here is an infinite reason why God should do it: Jesus died for you. Here comes in now the creative energy of God, manifested through Jesus Christ. Offer up the sacrificial death of Jesus as the reason why your impure

ATONEMENT

hearts should be cleansed, why your unholy souls should be purified: and as you are led to depend on His almighty power, you will find that all things are possible to them that believe. . . .

GOD CAN DO IT

We *can be* saved, but saved only by the living God. We can be purified, but by no less a power than that which created the heavens and the earth. You know that power can create you anew; and you know, too, that the depth of your impurity is no argument, so long as the eternal mercy of God through Jesus Christ comes in. I wish this view were more generally received. I come to the Almighty God to be saved. I have this reason why I should come—Jesus died for me: the depth of mine iniquity, or the greatness of my crimes, are no absolute reasons against pardon or purity, because the sacrificial death of Jesus has infinite merit, and power unlimited. Hence all the wretched arguments, that are brought against cleansing the soul from sin, are blown away by the Spirit of God, as is every other cloud brought by the devil in order to obscure God's eternal mercy.

CARNALITY

The Psalmist says, "Renew a right spirit," or, as the margin reads, a *constant* spirit. . . . My old spirit must be made new; mending will not do here; improving will not do here. As there was a creation in the first case, there must be a creation in the latter case. The mind here is represented as old and worn out . . . It cannot perform those acts which are proper for an immortal spirit. It is like an instrument out of tune, incapable of doing the work it formerly was capable of performing. All is old and passing away. Jesus Christ comes in here.

Fickleness is the character of man next to sinfulness . . . if he is constant to anything in the world, it is to his unsteadiness to his own purposes; full of good purposes to live to God; changing these purposes almost immediately, and living to the devil; forming friendships and alliances, which appear formed only to be broken; hence, variations and contentions among men . . . The Psalmist felt this and prays to have a *constant* spirit. Let me have . . . a spirit which can at all times recognize three things: First, *God,* the object at which I must aim; secondly, the *soul,* the great subject employed in aiming at God; and thirdly, the *line* marked out by divine revelation, which leads to God, in whom the soul finds rest.

Let us pray to God for this fixedness and certainty of character. There was never a greater word used than that word: "My heart is fixed, O God, my heart is fixed: I will sing and give praise" (Ps. 57:7).

It is a good thing that the heart be established by grace. He that can say his heart is fixed, and continues with his fixed heart to give praise to God, is a man whose heart is created anew. . . .

He goes on, and says, "Restore unto me the joy of thy salvation; and uphold me with thy free spirit." He sees that the state in which God had formed him was a state of happiness. . . . "Oh!" says he, "restore me this joy!" Bring me again to this state of happiness. What is misery among men? . . . It is sin. . . . There could not have been misery if there had not been sin. The misery of man is the sin of man; and misery continues while sin remains . . . To take away from man his mental misery . . . the power of guilt must be broken, the impurity of sin must be purged away. In short, the man, according to God's promise and purpose, must be created anew. . . . And then, says the Psalmist, "Uphold me with thy free spirit." I am still as much dependent on His grace for the continuance of salvation, as I was on His mercy for the reception of that salvation; and . . . here [is] where the doctrine of perseverance is properly considered. We retain what we have received. . . . By being upheld by the Almighty, we are kept in continual [contact] with the Almighty. . . .

FULLNESS OF LIFE

It is only by being created anew, by being brought into the image of God, by being filled with God, that we can have any expectation of persevering. It is only by being thus changed that we are brought into the way which leads to heaven; and it is only by being upheld by the free Spirit of God that we continue in that way; and we cannot be upheld thus except we abide in the truth. Hence the necessity of abiding in a state of purity; without this there is no hope of perseverance. Perseverance is a mere fable without it.

FILLED WITH GOD

In reference to this, the Psalmist offers up that other petition, "Cast me not away from thy presence!" Let me never be out of Thy sight. Let me walk with Thee as Enoch "walked with God" (Gen. 5:22, 24). The heart seems to feel a kind of horror lest it should be cast out of His presence, where there is fullness of joy. He is not here speaking of a state of glorification, which some have supposed, but of the state of believers on earth.

And not only that, but says he, "Take not thy holy spirit from me." There may be cases in which we give cause for God to take away His Spirit, by leaving undone what we should perform, and doing what we ought to have left undone. There may be in me many things contrary to Thy infinite holiness, but, O my God,

HOLY SPIRIT

"Cast me not away from thy presence; and take not thy holy spirit from me." Hence arise two important considerations: First, Man goes safely to heaven while he walks in the presence of God; secondly . . . to walk in the presence of God, [man] must have the Spirit of God.

"Uphold me with thy free spirit." The original word, which seems to be here used as a metaphor, signifies the shore or prop of a building. A building will stand a thousand years—only shore it up. Here, a person feels he is nothing but what he is in his God; that as all creatures are bent to destruction and decay, he shall fall if not upheld by his Maker. He, therefore, leans on his Maker and leans confidently. "Uphold me by thy free spirit," or, as some translate the word, "noble" (and very properly); "Uphold me by thy noble spirit"; for I am uncertain, fickle, vile, except as supported by Thy divine Spirit. . . . O my God, "Uphold me by thy noble spirit"; give me a spirit that will not condescend to sink into sin, that I may act up to the dignity I am called to . . . showing forth by a holy life and conversation . . . that which distinguishes the nobility and excellence of the Spirit of God. Amen.

Jesse T. Peck

(1811-83)

In his study, *The Holiness Revival of the Nineteenth Century,* Melvin Dieter reminds us that "the Methodist Episcopal General Conference of 1872 elected eight new bishops, six of them were friendly with the holiness cause." One of the six was Jesse T. Peck, who 16 years earlier had published *The Central Idea of Christianity.* The central idea was, of course, personal holiness as a second work of grace.

Jesse Peck, however, did not give immediate and hearty endorsement to those who adopted the strategy of special meetings and methods for the promotion of holiness. He opposed, for example, the Tuesday Meetings of Phoebe Palmer, fearing they would encourage tendencies toward schism.

He so far overcame his fears as to participate in such meetings, however. This particular sermon was preached in the third of the great national camp meetings, at Round Lake, N.Y., in 1869. Timothy Smith implies, in *Revivalism and Social Reform,* that the holiness revival that had been gathering momentum for a couple of decades was what swept Peck "into the bishop's chair" in 1872.

Peck's influence for holiness extended beyond his pulpit ministry through his writings, especially as a contributor to such periodicals as the popular *Guide to Holiness.* He minced no words in addressing the problem of increasing worldliness in the churches, and spared no effort in advocating the experience of holiness as its antidote.

The sermon presented here is a poor model in one respect—

the preacher never expounded the text he announced. The text merely introduced the subject, which was certainly biblical, but the text itself was not developed and applied in the ensuing message. Peck's obvious purpose was to affirm, as strongly as possible, God's provision to satisfy the Christian's hunger for inner purity here and now. His strategy for achieving that purpose was to describe a rich variety of terms and symbols by which Scripture sets forth the possibility of present deliverance from all sin.

In those national camp meetings a preacher seldom got the pulpit more than once or twice. You can discern in many of the sermons an effort to crowd as much holiness doctrine into each sermon as possible. The present one is no exception. This may not be the soundest homiletical approach, but given the urgency they felt in a decisively limited opportunity, it is understandable.

God's Provision for Man's Holiness*

Follow peace with all men, and holiness, without which no man shall see the Lord (Heb. 12:14).

Whence are the criticisms which stern Christians are disposed to bring upon themselves? . . . I have an idea that the searching criticisms we practice upon ourselves are based upon actual depravity, and are illustrated to us by the light kindly vouchsafed by the Holy Ghost. That this is the reason why we are searching ourselves, that God gives us the light of the Holy Spirit, the promptings of divine influence to induce that search, I have no doubt. . . . The heart yearnings which we have [for] the power which will relieve us from our felt depravity are from God. He himself pervades and moves hearts, that men may long to be saved from what they feel to be inward depravity. I raise the question, in connection with these searching criticisms and heart yearnings, *What answer is given to them from God in the Holy Bible?*

INWARD DEPRAVITY

There is a logical probability that the things which, under the searching of God's Spirit, we condemn in ourselves are to be resisted, overpowered, and exterminated by the power of the Holy Spirit. That

*Source: A. McLean and J. W. Eaton, eds., *Penuel; or Face to Face with God.* New York: W. C. Palmer, Jr., Publisher, 1870.

logical probability . . . [is seen] in the fact . . . that the Holy Spirit points out . . . the depraved state of the soul. Conviction is a part of the great plan of redemption . . . and if it were not God's plan to condemn and remove these depraved states, and supply their place with what was right and holy, then the judicial dispensation would supersede redemption, and then only punishment would follow, and that would be connected with despair, and not with hope.

GOD GIVES HUNGER

The answer we should expect to prayers that God himself inspires—such as David uttered, when in self-scrutiny he lifted up his heart . . . and prayed, "Create in me a clean heart, O God; and renew a right spirit within me" (Ps. 51:10)—is to be found in some provision or arrangement of God . . . clearly delineated in the gospel. As an illustration of the certainty that there is a remedial response from God to these yearnings of ours, I would introduce the saying of Jesus: "Blessed are they which do hunger and thirst after righteousness: for they shall be filled" (Matt. 5:6).

I. Consider one fact: *Inspiration uses exhaustive terms to describe the supply of these wants.*

[These terms] are selected, it would seem, to express this supply in the strongest manner possible; and it seems to me that in this effort Inspiration labored under the burden of inexpressible thought. Hence the change of expression, and the adoption of one kind and another, in order to reach and convince the human understanding of truths which are too large for language.

The *exhaustive character* of this language is to be considered. Take a few specimens from the Scriptures. . . .

CHRISTIAN PERFECTION

"Be ye therefore perfect" (Matt. 5:48). This was uttered as the completeness of an idea; and it could not be increased in strength, and requires elimination, if it be applied to the work of piety in general. It seems as if God had selected a word to try, if possible, to get out the idea that the yearnings after Christian perfection were provided for. I need not tell you that we are only pleased with what is perfect in itself. That is one reason why we are not pleased with ourselves; since, if we accept not the gospel provision, we inevitably fall below a proper standard.

We have also the word "sanctify," which radically means to make whole, and was so employed at first; but in the subsequent use of the word an inferior sense was attached to it, and it was graded downward, and, therefore, could not exactly embody the idea embraced in the prayer of the apostle—"Sanctify you wholly" (1 Thess. 5:23); the emphasis being on the word "wholly," as much as to say, The ordinary use of the word "sanctify" has become less than the truth and, therefore, requires an exhaustive epithet, and hence the word "wholly" is added.

SANCTIFIED WHOLLY

If you take the word "faith," you find that in its ordinary acceptations it is not strong enough to employ in regard to these intense heart yearnings; and hence, in such a connection, it is "most holy faith" (Jude 20), a kind of faith which reaches to the clearest and broadest privileges.

Take the term "love"—it is a very precious word . . . but when you come to use it for God's preparations and our heart yearnings, it is not strong enough, and you have "perfect love" (1 John 4:18). It was a short . . . word to render adequately the great sum of the law—"Thou shalt love the Lord thy God with all thy heart, and with all thy soul, and with all thy mind, and with all thy strength" (Mark 12:30; cf. Matt. 22:37; Luke 10:27). In this commandment there seems to be a strong effort of Inspiration to get everything in, and to make the inventory perfect. . . . The language setting forth Christian privilege . . . employs as high, comprehensive, and intense words as possible. . . .

PERFECT LOVE

II. Now, secondly, consider *the scope of the terms used in answer to our heart yearnings.*

I will mention three things.

First, the scope is against all sin. The condemnation of sin in the Bible reaches to every form and degree of it. . . . No man can put his finger on a law that condemns outward sin but allows it in the heart. The law is everywhere searching; it goes down into the thoughts and intents of the heart. . . . There is no form of sin that is covered or tolerated by the law, and for the good reason that God's legal government is a unit, and His sovereignty is a unity. God never intended sin should enter the universe. He made angels and men without it. It is an infringement of His plan and a disturbing element.

FREEDOM FROM SIN

Second . . . every provision of the gospel scheme points to heart purity or holiness. God has sent His Son into the world to save His people from their sins . . . and you understand [this salvation] to mean nothing less than the . . . satisfaction of those yearnings [for holiness].

HEART PURITY

The great doctrine of justification by faith is illustrative, and we ask, "Why must we be pardoned?" Evidently because our sins are in the way of holiness; pardon is preliminary to holiness. The whole gospel of the Bible is for the purpose of making men holy, and its every provision points to nothing else. . . . You take out the very vitality of the gospel when you take out holiness. I can see nothing left if you take out "The blood of Jesus Christ his Son cleanseth us from all sin" (1 John 1:7). . . .

If the covenant of the Bible means anything, it means that provision has been made for our holiness, and therefore we hold to the doctrine of the Wesleys, that the gospel is completely adapted to satisfy the heart yearnings of the Christian for purity. There can never be anything in its stead. If an angel should come down from heaven and tell us, "After you are regenerated and made living Christians, even though you find in your hearts the remains of depravity, you should be satisfied, for there is nothing beyond it, no arrangements to make your recovery from sin entire," we are authorized by Scripture to reject it. And if an apostle should rise from the dead and preach to us that "there is no blood that can cleanse from all sin," that apostle is to be rejected. . . .

SECOND BLESSING

Our position, that the scope of the gospel does respond to our entire wants, is the old position, the sound position, the revealed position, and not exceptional, as some would have you believe. . . . Beyond a question, Christian history shows that a poor, simple-hearted brother who prays, "Create in me a clean heart," is perfectly orthodox. The man who says, "The blood of Jesus Christ his Son cleanseth us from all sin," . . . is perfectly sound in the old theology. There has never been any other orthodoxy, and any contrary teaching is less than the gospel. . . . The strength of this argument is in its truth, and in the Holy Spirit's mighty power to satisfy your longings for purity.

III. Notice, now, *the symbolism of holiness.*

I have selected three symbols.

First, *the blood symbol.*

In the old dispensation they took the blood of bulls and goats and sprinkled the Book of the Law and all the people, saying, "This is the blood of the testament which God hath enjoined unto you." . . . "And almost all things are by the law purged with blood; and without shedding of blood is no remission" (Heb. 9:20, 22).

Now that startling word "blood" would be the last one man would select for a symbol of peace or purity. There are no two things more unlike each other than blood and love, or blood and salvation. . . . Yet the symbol is selected by Inspiration, for here it is: "Almost all things are by the law purged with blood." . . . You connect blood with unholy strife and with the death penalty. We can see its application in connection with man's demerit and destruction, but why is it connected with his salvation?

By it we are conducted to one thing and one only, "the Lamb of God, which taketh away the sin of the world" (John 1:29). . . . The

ATONEMENT

sacrificial lamb was a part of the great idea of being made holy through Christ. "For if the blood of bulls and of goats, and the ashes of an heifer sprinkling the unclean, sanctifieth to the purifying of the flesh: how much more shall the blood of Christ . . . purge your conscience from dead works to serve the living God?" (Heb. 9:13-14). . . .

Blood [actually] stains, it does not purify anything; but in the symbolism of the gospel, it is the most thoroughly purifying influence in the universe . . . and I don't know how any creature could utter a more momentous truth than is heard in the song of the redeemed: "Unto him that loved us, and washed us from our sins in his own blood, and hath made us kings and priests unto God and his Father; to him be glory and dominion for ever and ever" (Rev. 1:5-6). . . . While [physical] blood would render whatever it touches impure, it is the only thing that takes away the stains of sin. You go up till you get to the drapery of heaven, and it is white, and made white in the blood of the Lamb. This underlies all the efficiency of the work of grace; there is blood everywhere.

Second, let us look at *the water symbol.*

See how washing was employed. There was washing of pots and kettles . . . and garments. When any man did a wrong, he was to wash

CLEANSING

his hands and remain unclean till evening. Washing is appointed and spoken of in the Scriptures to show us the necessity of spiritual washing. "Then will I sprinkle clean water upon you, and ye shall be clean" (Ezek. 36:25). In the use of the water symbol you reach baptism, and the word translated "wash" is baptize, and means the symbolic use of water . . . that it may teach us that our souls may be washed and made clean.

It is said, "I will sprinkle clean water upon you," and then, "I will pour out my Spirit upon you" (cf. Joel 2:28; Acts 2:17). Here is the double baptism of water and the Holy Ghost, and that is indicative of the thorough and practical power which God will employ to make us clean in His sight. I showed you the blood symbol, now I introduce the water baptism as pointing to the power of the Holy Ghost in renovating the soul from all sin. Men were very vile, and it was to be kept in remembrance that the Church, composed of those who were once like all other sinners, had been made clean, and here is the testimony: "And such were some of you: but ye are washed, but ye are sanctified, but ye are justified in the name of the Lord Jesus, and by the Spirit of our God" (1 Cor. 6:11).

HOLY SPIRIT

Third, I pass to speak of *the fire symbol.*

[It is] a most expressive and powerful help to interpret the language of divine revelation. You remember . . . there was a burning bush, and a voice spoke out of the fire . . . teaching His people that they were to be saved as by fire. When the children of Israel came out of Egypt the fire symbol was chosen, and it guided them. . . . Elijah went to heaven in a chariot of fire and symbolized that everything that could not rise up in flame would not enter heaven. . . .

Isaiah had a vision of the Lord sitting upon a throne, high and lifted up, and His train filled the temple, and the [seraphim] stood above Him, and they began to cry, "Holy, holy, holy, is the Lord of hosts." The prophet saw in the light of that holiness that he was impure, and he cried out, "Woe is me! for I am undone; because I am a man of unclean lips, and I dwell in the midst of a people of unclean lips: for mine eyes have seen the King, the Lord of hosts" (Isa. 6:3, 5).

What was the man to do? Why, one [seraph] flew away having a live coal in his hand, which he had taken with the tongs from off the altar; and he laid it upon his mouth and said, "Lo, this hath touched thy lips; and thine iniquity is taken away, and thy sin purged." Immediately the power of cleansing by fire was realized. The great problem of prophetic ministry was settled by fire. There was no missionary power in him until God had taken fire from the altar, and with it touched his lips, and then he said, "Here am I; send me" (vv. 7-8).

CLEANSING FIRE

The power of the fire symbol explains the plan of salvation. Zechariah heard from the Lord that in all the land two parts of the people should be cut off and die, but, "I will bring the third part through the fire, and will refine them as silver is refined, and will try them as gold is tried." And what shall happen when they are refined? "They shall call upon my name, and I will hear them: I will say, It is my people: and they shall say, The Lord is my God" (13:9). The fire tried them and burned out all the dross from their souls, and then they went on their way rejoicing. . . .

BAPTIZED WITH THE HOLY SPIRIT

You remember [that] John said, "I indeed baptize you with water unto repentance," which is the symbol of the weakest power, "but he that cometh after me is mightier than I . . . he shall baptize you with the Holy Ghost, and with fire," which shall come down as the result of the Atonement (Matt. 3:11; cf. Mark 1:7-8; Luke 3:16). When the fire came down at Pentecost, it . . . sat upon them like cloven tongues. Everything that cannot stand the fire shall be burned up.

IN A MOMENT

As I close, I want you to realize two or three things that I hold to be of great practical importance in these relations. . . . Not one of the symbols that have seemingly struggled to get the great idea of purification out applies to growth. . . . All our dear friends who think they supersede the necessity of being purified speedily by the idea of growth fall outside of the entire terminology of the divine system. . . . It is a serious mistake to trust to growing into the state of purity. God has exhausted the Bible symbols to get before us this idea . . . that sin can be really taken out, and this is the reason why we are urging you to have it done today. In this we glory, that whatever hinders our growth can be taken away now, by faith in Jesus. . . .

When I think about the young minister, as he may be clothed with power to shake the kingdom of Satan, and to bring down the throne of Dagon; when I think of the very important work he is going out to do, it seems to me that he should almost desire that neither sun, moon, nor star should arise until he had been filled with the power and might of the Spirit. . . . Oh! whatever else you neglect, do not neglect the Blood; do not lack the baptism of fire. . . . God bless you and help you to realize the purifying grace.

F. Watson Hannan, D.D.

(1866-1929)

In 1907, when Drew Theological Seminary became 40 years old, it published its first volume of sermons based on the Golden Texts of the International Sunday School Lessons. These sermons were prepared by seminary professors and over 40 of the "devoted graduates."

In this first volume occurs the sermon "Jesus Cleanses the Temple," by F. Watson Hannan. At the time, Hannan was pastor of the Bushwick Avenue Methodist Episcopal Church in Brooklyn.

Based upon Ps. 93:5, Hannan's sermon is virtually a compendium of holiness doctrine. The structure and language are simple, and the sermon is delightfully readable.

Hannan strikes his most telling blow when he comes to the fourth and final point of his outline: "The Possibility of Holiness." No stammering, no equivocation marks his forthright insistence that "We can be holy when God dwells in us. Then indeed we are the Lord's house. It is not only expedient that we be holy, it is imperative. That life can be lived. The Holy Spirit is here to sanctify us wholly. . . . The domination of the Holy Spirit fits us to maintain the holiness of the Lord's house forever and brings to us the purity and power that enable us to live in the will of God."

When thousands plead for Baal, and other thousands defer the possibility of holiness to the next world, we could wish that such clear and convincing advocacy of present holiness marked pulpits everywhere, even the pulpits of the modern holiness movement.

The sermon is a worthy model for preachers. It demonstrates the value of (1) simple organization, (2) positive proclamation, and (3) fervent application.

A word of explanation: Like some other sermons in the volume, the title and content seem slightly disconnected. That is because the sermons were based on the Golden Texts but took the titles of the Sunday School lessons. This one belonged to a series on the life and ministry of Christ in the Gospel of John.

Jesus Cleanses the Temple*

Holiness becometh thine house, O Lord, for ever (Ps. 93:5).

The text introduces us at once to the subject of personal holiness, for there cannot long be sanctity to a place without there [being] holiness of the people. The 93rd psalm is a declaration of the might and majesty of God, and of the permanence of all that He has established. The house of the Lord is for His people, and its holiness is complexioned by the holiness of His people; and holiness being the perfect wholeness, or health, of the soul, it is the mark of the soul's permanence in the house of the Lord.

WHOLENESS

We shall consider at this time not the abstract holiness of a place, but the practical holiness of a people. If we ourselves are holy, the sanctity of the house of the Lord will easily be preserved inviolate. Note

I. *The Call to Be Holy*

There are many calls to vocations—some are called to the ministry, some to medicine, some to teaching, some to music, some to art. . . . God calls men and women to these various vocations by the very aptitudes . . . with which He endows them. But the call to be holy is not a call to vocation but to character, and to every one this call comes. We are all called to be saints, which is a call to holiness; and there is no life, however crude or obscure, to whom that high calling of God does not come.

FOR ALL CHRISTIANS

This call comes to all because holiness is fundamental to our

---

*Source: Ezra Squier Tipple, ed., *Drew Sermons on the Golden Texts for 1908*. New York: Eaton and Mains; Cincinnati: Jennings and Graham, 1907.

eternal fellowship with God. If we are to dwell in the house of the Lord all the days of our life, we must be like Him in character: therefore God makes that demand of us. Holiness is the nature of God. . . . We are called up to this transparent nature, and the most important work of our life, whatever our occupation may be, is to realize our calling in terms of personal experience.

GOD'S HOLINESS

The call to be holy is clearly a call to separation. The Old Testament conception of holiness was that of separation. That is the way God first taught the idea of holiness. Separation in space from the unclean was a symbol of separation in quality from the unholy. The cleanliness required for body and garment was a symbol of the purity required for character and conduct. The Tabernacle, in the very structure as well as its use, taught the idea of the separation of holiness.

That separation remained until our great High Priest offered himself once for all an atoning sacrifice for the sin of the world, and the veil was rent in twain from top to bottom, and every soul had access into the holy of holies without the intervention of any human priest. The Temple was modeled after the Tabernacle, to perpetuate the idea of holiness. A holy God in a holy place, to be worshiped by a holy people. God directed Moses to build for Him a holy place, but He also commanded him to sanctify the people. Repeatedly in the Old Testament is the command to some leader to sanctify the people, and for the people to sanctify themselves, for only thus could they approach God. Separation in space was used to teach separation in character.

The idea of separation was twofold. First, it was separation from sin, from everything that defiled. In order to deepen and make clear that idea, the ceremonial law of cleanness was practiced. Meddling with what God calls unclean is dangerous business; and those who try to justify their living in contact with the world by the example of Jesus must be very sure that they are motivated to it as Jesus was. He did not come to compliment, cajole, or make capital of sinners, but to save them. His sociability was always complexioned by His evangelism. Whatever may be our necessary physical and social contact with the world, we must be separate from it, in the quality of our character. In that sense God's people must be a separate people.

SEPARATION FROM SIN

But this separation, in the second place, has a positive side. It is separation to all that is Christlike in character and service. "Be ye holy" is a call to the life adjusted to the will of God. By every experience of joy or sorrow, or doing or enduring, God is calling us up into His own likeness. Separation to all that is holy and Christlike in character and conduct is sanctification. "Holiness becometh thine house, O Lord, for ever," means that a sanctified people shall enjoy its privileges, conduct its worship, and administer its affairs. God calls us to holiness.

SEPARATION TO CHRISTLIKENESS

II. *The Obligation to Holiness*

It is not a matter of convenience whether we shall be holy or not; there is a divine obligation on us, binding us to it. That obligation is grounded, first, in the reasonableness of holiness. It is impossible to unify moral incompatibles. The heavenly hosts are holy; heaven is holy; God is holy. What fellowship could the half consecrated and moderately righteous have with them? But we are to have fellowship with God here. God says, "Be ye holy; for I am holy" (1 Pet. 1:16). His holiness is a reason for ours. "How can two walk together, except they be agreed?" (cf. Amos 3:3).

GOD'S HOLINESS

Second. The obligation to be holy is grounded in God's right to demand it. Creatorship carries with it the right to designate the thing created to a specific purpose. The principle underlying copyright and patent is that author and inventor have a right to the things they produce. God can lay upon us the obligation to be holy. We belong to Him. He made us.

Redemption emphasizes the right of Creatorship. Man by sin repudiated his obligation to be what God made him, and delayed God's purpose in him, and destroyed himself. Then, at infinite cost, God redeemed him back to his original purpose. By the cost of the blood of God man is under obligation to realize the purpose of redemption.

Third. Our obligation to be holy lies deeper than either the Creatorship or redemption of God, namely, in God's Fatherhood. We are more than redeemed creatures; we are redeemed sons. Sin is ungrateful, unreasonable, and unfilial. A son is, by the very fact of sonship, under obligation to be in character like his good father. The family honor requires it. The family protection and provision, education and privilege, make it imperative. As children of God redeemed from sin, and disciplined to do God's perfect will, and to enjoy His bounty, share His home, participate in the rule of His kingdom, and be in His fellowship forever, we are under obligation by every reason and right to be holy. . . . "Holiness becometh thine house, O Lord, for ever" carries with it as its corollary, "Be ye holy; for I am holy."

III. *The Content of Holiness*

Only a word can here be said on a great subject that would require a volume worthily to set it forth. It may seem trite to say that holiness is soul soundness, wholeness, or health. But we must realize this in experience before holiness will be either sanely lived or taught. Nothing is less self-conscious or more sympathetic and active than health. No one in perfect health would think of belaboring an invalid. No more would holiness belabor one whose spiritual health was subnormal. The effort of both, through warm sympathy, is to help the weak brother up to physical or spiritual health. Perfect health expresses the right relation of the body to the laws of God. Holiness expresses the right relation of the soul to God himself.

WHOLENESS

Of course, we recognize that our holiness here in the body is not the perfect and unconditioned holiness of God, nor of perfect spiritual beings who never knew sin. Nor does it lift us out of the realm of temptation. We cannot expect a higher plane of spiritual living than Jesus had. He had His temptations, swift, subtle, and strong. When men have reached a state where they no longer have temptations, that state is not moral mastery but spiritual insensibility. The devil never lets any man alone except the one who is of no use to God.

HUMANITY

The holiness which we find everywhere emphasized in the New Testament, and exemplified in the life of Jesus Christ, is that state of spiritual life where sin is shunned and hated; where goodness is loved for its own sake; where the will is perfectly homed in the will of God; where the Holy Spirit dominates the life in motive, affection, and action. We may be beset with temptations, but we have the mastery over them. We love Christ supremely and for His own sake. We have a passion to extend His kingdom to the ends of the earth; to see every soul for whom Christ died brought to a knowledge of the truth. We are not free from errors of judgment, or from the failures of weakness and ignorance; but the objective of our life is to do the will of God.

Grouping together the last eight words in the New Testament which are translated "holy" or "holiness," we get this broad meaning for holiness—strong, reverent, pious, godly, worthy, pure, holy. The life that attains to these will surely be at its best and will realize the purpose of God.

IV. *The Possibility of Holiness*

Neither call nor obligation can ever extend to the impossible. Christ said, "Follow me." God says, "Be holy." Again, Christ says, "Be ye perfect." Indeed, space would not permit the citation of even the most prominent passages that bear directly on what may be taken for granted as the possibility of holiness. It is nowhere intimated that this high requirement cannot be met. To require what could not be done would be arbitrary and unreasonable, moral tyranny.

A GLORIOUS POSSIBILITY

There are some high human attainments which only the favored few ever may reach; as Ruskin said of the great painter Turner, "There is but one Turner in 500 years, and God decides without any admission of auxiliary cabal what piece of clay His soul is to be put into." But God is every day lifting the scum of the city up to the Light of the World. The Holy Spirit is not a respecter of what piece of clay He shall enter; but into whatever souls that long to know and do the perfect will of God, He comes with sanctifying power.

FOR ALL CHRISTIANS

We are predestined to be conformed into the image of the Son of God, and every help necessary thereto is at the disposal of faith and obedience. Our subtlest and most dangerous temptations are not to gross and vulgar sins, but to defeat, by neglect, the purpose of God in our lives—to fail to come into the likeness of Christ. We are the real temples of the Holy Spirit. That realized in experience is the possibility of our holiness. "If a man love me, he will keep my words: and my Father will love him, and we will come unto him, and make our abode with him" (John 14:23).

We can be holy when God dwells in us. Then indeed we are the Lord's house. It is not only expedient that we be holy, it is imperative. That life can be lived. The Holy Spirit is here to sanctify us wholly. This life of holiness which is possible, reasonable, and imperative is ours for the living of it. The domination of the Holy Spirit fits us to maintain the holiness of the Lord's house forever and brings to us the purity and power that enable us to live in the will of God. "Now unto him that is able to keep you from falling, and to present you faultless before the presence of his glory with exceeding joy, to the only wise God our Saviour, be glory and majesty, dominion and power, both now and ever. Amen" (Jude 24-25).

HOLY SPIRIT

W. T. Hogue
(1852-1920)

Wilson T. Hogue was one of the foremost scholars of the Free Methodist church. He provided a history of his denomination and authored several other books, including a volume on homiletics and pastoral theology that was widely used in holiness circles. At the time he preached this sermon (1901) he was serving as editor of *The Free Methodist*, the official organ of his church, described by him as "a clean journal, adapted to the family, and for holiness throughout."

This sermon was preached at the historic General Holiness Assembly in Chicago, a 10-day meeting that brought together leaders of the holiness movement from various denominations. Their objectives were large and exciting, including a modern Pentecost and an "opportunity to again publish to the world the true mission and object of the holiness movement . . . and so, as far as possible, remove prejudice that comes from misunderstanding or has resulted from extreme, erroneous, and fanatical positions assumed by some so-called holiness workers." They aimed at the proclamation and demonstration of sane, earnest, biblical holiness. As host pastor, J. P. Brushingham, of the First Methodist Episcopal Church, Chicago, said, "We are not here simply for dress parade."

Hogue's sermon reflects that identification of entire sanctification with the baptism with the Holy Spirit, which had become staple theology in the holiness movement. It rings the changes on the essential understanding of that baptism as (1) a second work of grace; (2) with cleansing, illuminating, and energizing effects; (3) to be sought through earnest, persistent prayer; (4) based upon the supreme promise of the new covenant; (5) and available to every believer who will meet the conditions.

Like other leaders of this dynamic movement, Hogue saw the baptism with the Holy Spirit as the fountain of that purity, stability, and unity needed to cement the disparate grorupstogether as a force for the renewal and expansion of Christianity.

Hogue was himself the product of such a spiritual force. He was converted in a camp meeting just 40 years before he delivered this sermon. In those four decades he had become one of the pillars, not only of his denomination but of the entire holiness movement. His voice and pen had placed several generations in his debt, and his influence is still felt today.

The Pentecostal Baptism*

And when the day of Pentecost was fully come, they were all with one accord in one place. And suddenly there came a sound from heaven as of a rushing mighty wind, and it filled all the house where they were sitting. And there appeared unto them cloven tongues like as of fire, and it sat upon each of them. And they were all filled with the Holy Ghost, and began to speak with other tongues, as the Spirit gave them utterance (Acts 2:1-4).

That was the birthday of the Christian Church. It was the birthday of Christianity itself. The Christian Church . . . was born of the Holy Spirit. . . . It takes the Holy Spirit to constitute it a living organism in the beginning—to preserve it as a living organism to the end. Nothing short of such a baptism and empowerment . . . can put and keep that Church in a normal condition, and make it the proper representative of Jesus Christ and constitute it the Body of Christ in the spiritual sense.

It becomes very important therefore to know something about the Holy Spirit and His operations. . . . The Spirit of God is the very

---

*Source: S. B. Shaw, ed., *Echoes of the General Holiness Assembly.* Chicago: S. B. Shaw, Publisher, 1901.

soul of the Church, as [He] is of every individual spiritual life. I am sorry the Church of this period has found it necessary to look back to the primitive Pentecost as though the like were never to be expected again on earth. As I understand it, that was but one instance or illustration of what ought to prevail with God's people always and everywhere. . . .

FOR ALL CHRISTIANS

I am glad to be assured that what the disciples got in the Upper Room, the wonderful manifestation and fullness of divine light, love, grace, power, and victory that came to them on that memorable day—is for God's people through all time. It is not because God is straitened or limited that some fail to get it now. It is because they fail to meet the conditions. If we measure up fully to the conditions, we may have Pentecost repeated. . . . The important thing on that occasion was not the sound from heaven, not the fiery manifestations, but the thing spoken of in the last verse of my text—"They were all filled with the Holy Ghost." That is what we ought all to recognize; and the moral and spiritual results ordained by God will invariably follow if we get and retain this blessed fullness provided for us in Christ.

I want to call your attention to several things connected with the Pentecostal baptism with the Holy Ghost.

I remark, in the first place, that

I. *The original Pentecostal baptism with the Spirit was a second work of grace.*

I mean by this that the disciples who received it had already experienced the preliminary operations of the Spirit in regeneration; that they were already men of God. Some tell us that the . . . disciples did not receive their conversion until the baptism with the Holy Spirit on that day. Let me call your attention to what Jesus said about them long before the Day of Pentecost.

THE BAPTISM IS FOR CHRISTIANS

Turn to John 15:19. Here I read, "If ye were of the world, the world would love his own: but because ye are not of the world, but I have chosen you out of the world, therefore the world hateth you." I cannot conceive of Jesus Christ talking that way to unconverted men. They were so distinct from the world that the world hated them. . . .

You will also remember that as Jesus met Peter and the other apostles in the coasts of Caesarea Philippi, He said, "Whom do men say that I the Son of man am?" Peter answered: "Thou art the Christ, the Son of the living God. And Jesus answered and said unto him, Blessed art thou, Simon Bar-jona: for flesh and blood hath not revealed it unto thee, but my Father which is in heaven" (Matt. 16:13, 16-17). There had been a revelation of Christ to one of these disciples, at least, just such as constitutes a real and radical conversion. St. Paul tells us that "no man can say that Jesus is the Lord, but by the Holy Ghost" (1 Cor. 12:3). No man can say it in a true and spiritual and experimental sense, unless it has been divinely revealed unto him in his own salvation.

Some tell us this baptism was simply a gift of miracle-working power. . . . [But] these disciples had the power of miracle working before the Day of Pentecost. In sending out His apostles on their mission to the lost sheep of the house of Israel, He said, "As ye go, preach, saying, The kingdom of heaven is at hand. Heal the sick, . . . cast out devils: freely ye have received, freely give" (Matt. 10:7-8). Thus they were empowered to heal the sick, cast out devils, and perform various miracles in His name before the Day of Pentecost. . . .

SECOND BLESSING

Note again that before He left them, our Lord told those followers of His, who had been . . . under His own instruction for three years or more, and who had walked in personal fellowship with Him, to tarry in Jerusalem for something further. As the time of His ascension drew near, "They asked of him, saying, Lord, wilt thou at this time restore again the kingdom to Israel? And he said unto them, It is not for you to know the times or the seasons, which the Father hath put in his own power. But ye shall receive power, after that the Holy Ghost is come upon you: and ye shall be witnesses unto me both in Jerusalem, and in all Judaea, and in Samaria, and unto the uttermost part of the earth" (Acts 1:6-8). He told them to wait for it, and they did. The text tells us the result. . . .

FOR ALL CHRISTIANS

There is a second installment of the Holy Spirit for all believers. His preliminary office work is accomplished in our conversion and justification. In the Pentecostal baptism, He comes in abiding fullness to dwell in us as our abiding Comforter, Illuminator, Sanctifier, Guide, and Stand-by. The original word translated "Comforter" means a Stand-by. Blessed be God! You can stand anything if you have that "Stand-by" enthroned within you always.

I call you to notice, in the second place, that

II. *This Pentecostal baptism was the fulfillment of a supreme promise.*

Of all the glorious promises of former dispensations, that which referred to the bestowment and dispensation of the Holy Spirit was of supreme excellence—the climax and glory of the whole. It is called emphatically "The promise of the Father" (Acts 1:4; cf. Luke 24:49), just as though it were the only promise He had given. This is because it contains the sum of all the rest.

SCRIPTURAL

Go back to the prophetic age and see this verified. The prophets sang in wondrous raptures concerning the coming of Christ to redeem this world, and with the deepest pathos they described His humiliation and sufferings. But in more enrapturing and inspiring strains they sang of the future outpouring of the Holy Spirit. Of the Spirit-filled messengers of the new dispensation, Isaiah sang, "The wilderness and the solitary place shall be glad for them; and the desert shall rejoice, and blossom as the rose. It shall blossom abundantly, and rejoice even with joy and singing: the glory of Lebanon shall be given unto it, the excellency of Carmel and Sharon, they shall see the glory of the Lord, and the excellency of our God" (35:1-2). Isaiah further speaks of it as floods poured out on the dry ground, and rivers upon the thirsty land (v. 7; 44:3). . . .

The Psalmist tells us that when God's people go through dry places, they shall "make it a well; the rain also filleth the pools" (84:6). Ezekiel . . . foresaw the glorious dispensation of the Holy Spirit. He likened it to a river beginning with the issuing of waters out from under the sanctuary. Mere droppings . . . flowed together and, without any visible tributary from without, increased in depth and volume until it became a mighty and impassable river. . . . It was also said that everything should live whithersoever this river should come, and by it even the waters of the Dead Sea were healed (47:1-9).

Note this peculiarity about that river. It was characterized by a perpetually accumulating flow. In this it symbolized the law of the bestowment of the Spirit. Instead of looking backward to Pentecost for the greatest manifestation of the Holy Spirit, we . . . ought to have Pentecost repeated and augmented today. . . .

The supreme promise in the ministry of John the Baptist related to the gift of the Holy Ghost. He preached the twofold work of grace. First, he preached Christ as the Atoner for sin, by whom we come to God. He cried, "Behold the Lamb of God, which taketh away the sin of the world" (John 1:29). Having acquainted them with Him as the atoning Lamb, he began to tell them about a "mightier than I, whose shoes I am not worthy to bear," and added, "He shall baptize you with the Holy Ghost, and with fire" (Matt. 3:11; cf. Mark 1:7-8; Luke 3:16). His supreme mission was to point to Jesus Christ as the Baptizer with the Holy Spirit. To preach Christ fully we must present Him in both of these offices—as the great Atoner for the sins of the world and the Baptizer of believers with the Holy Spirit. To preach Him as the Atoner only is to preach but half the gospel.

Coming now to the ministry of Jesus, we find that He also preached the twofold work of grace. First, He taught His disciples . . .

TWOFOLD WORK OF GRACE

concerning the mystery of the death He was to accomplish on the Cross. He said to them, "Except ye eat [my] flesh . . . , and drink [my] blood, ye have no life in you" (John 6:53). Later, however, He proclaimed to them the gospel and mission of the Comforter. . . . "Nevertheless I tell you the truth; It is expedient for you that I go away: for if I go not away, the Comforter will not come unto you; but if I depart, I will send him unto you" (16:7).

That was the promise of something better than to be favored with His visible presence and to listen to the gracious words that proceeded from His lips. It is better to have an indwelling, though invisible, Comforter than to have with us the visible Jesus. He must depart, but He was to send another Comforter, Advocate, Intercessor, which meant the gift of the Spirit . . . to all believers for all time. . . . The culminating and supreme thing in the ministry of Jesus Christ was to be this bestowment of the Comforter. . . .

I call your attention next to the fact that

III. *The baptism of the Holy Ghost was received in answer to prayer.*

In Acts 1:9 we read, "And when he had spoken these things, while they beheld, he was taken up; and a cloud received him out of their sight." They stood and gazed until two men in white apparel appeared and said: "Why stand ye gazing up into heaven? this same Jesus, which is taken up from you into heaven, shall so come in like manner as ye have seen him go into heaven." Then they went back to the Upper Room, where "all continued with one accord in prayer and supplication . . ." (vv. 11, 14). They prayed. They all prayed. They all continued to pray. Ten days were spent chiefly in this exercise. "And when the Day of Pentecost was fully come, they were all with one accord in one place," and suddenly came the sound from heaven, and the fiery emanations, "and they were all filled with the Holy Ghost." This wonderful baptism and enduement with power came upon the infant Church in answer to prayer.

And yet there are many people who . . . say it is an insult to God himself to pray for a baptism with the Spirit. They tell us that when the Holy Spirit came at Pentecost, He came to stay, hence, we err in praying for His coming again. That may be true as to His coming to the Church at large but not as to personal experience. Jesus taught that we should ask the Father for the gift of the Holy Spirit. . . .

PRAY TO BE FILLED

We must cry to God for the fullness of the Spirit. David cried unto the Lord for heart cleansing, and the Lord gave it to him. He said, "Create in me a clean heart, O God; and renew a right spirit within me" (Ps. 51:10). . . . We need to seek Him earnestly, as on the Day of Pentecost, where they were all in one place with one accord, most earnestly praying to God, and not praying at each other. . . . There was no jar, no discord, no disturbing vibrations, but all was in perfect harmony. That is what we need here. It is good and blessed for brethren to dwell together in unity. I never knew a marked degree of the Holy Ghost to come down where there was discord manifested among the brethren.

I remember in 1861 when God sanctified my mother and converted me on the Allegheny Campground in western New York. During those days very few professed it unless they got it; it cost so much. I remember how they prayed too. They would pray all night. They prayed through and the Pentecostal power and fire came. Just so there is no better way to seek the Pentecostal baptism now than that of earnestly and persistently crying unto God for it.

Again, I remark that

IV. *The primitive baptism with the Spirit was given at a peculiarly appropriate season*—"when the Day of Pentecost was fully come."

Pentecost was the anniversary of the giving of that law which originally was written in the tables of stone by the finger of God. The law under the Old Testament was outward and objective—a set of rigorous, external exactions. The distinguishing characteristic of the new covenant is the promise that under its provisions the law is to be written on the mind and heart. It is the work of the Holy Spirit to do this. Baptism with the Holy Spirit baptized the very essence of the law into the mind and heart. It is not the abolition of the law, but a new promulgation of it. It does not release from obligation to keep the law, but makes us all the more sensible of that obligation. At the same time it puts within us the constant disposition and ability to keep the divine requirements. Blessed be God!

LOVING GOD'S WILL

There is a sense in which a sanctified believer is not under the law. He doesn't obey the law . . . any longer in a servile spirit, or from feeling "I must." Of course he has to recognize the law. The law is not taken away. The law is put into the heart, however, and so becomes his thought, desire, will, and activity. It is this that makes it a kind of second nature . . . to do the things required by the law, and so to delight in it as to say, "O, how love I thy law! it is my meditation all the day" (Ps. 119:97).

WALKING WITH THE SPIRIT

Some people seem to be fond of living in the seventh chapter of Romans, where they are ever in a vain struggle to keep the law. Paul, in this chapter, says: "O wretched man that I am! who shall deliver me from the body of this death?" (v. 24). I don't see how anyone can want to live where there is nothing but wretchedness, where they have always to say, "The good that I would I do not: but the evil which I would not, that I do" (v. 19). . . . Thank God there is a more excellent way. Paul, in the eighth chapter of Romans, tells of another law which counterworks this law in the members which enslaves us. He says: "There is therefore now no condemnation to them which are in Christ Jesus, who walk not after the flesh, but after the Spirit" (v. 1).

Holding this book in my hand, I let it go. According to the law of gravity, it goes down. But I have the ability to bring in the operation of another law and thereby to overcome the operation of that downward law and send the book heavenward. If my ability were infinite, I could send it upward forever. God is able by His Spirit to reverse the downward law of our depraved natures [so] as to bring our wills, affections, and affinities to perfect harmony with himself, and to keep them there forever. Moreover, He will do this when we meet the conditions. . . . Thus, by the sanctifying baptism of the Spirit the law is written on fleshly tablets of the heart. . . . As the New Testament Pentecost signifies this new writing and promulgation of the law, how fitting that its inauguration took place at Pentecost, the anniversary of the original publication of the law.

I call you to notice, further, that

V. *The outpouring of the Spirit was attended by peculiar and significant phenomena*—a [noise] like a rushing mighty wind and cloven tongues like as of fire.

These phenomena were symbols of the Holy Spirit's operations. As the Divine Breath swept down upon that Upper Room assembly, there was a sound as of a rushing mighty wind. Wind is a symbol of the Spirit. It is independent in its operations. "Thou . . . canst not tell whence it cometh, and whither it goeth: so is every one that is born of the Spirit" (John 3:8). You must let Him come in His own way. He will submit to no dictation, to no formula of yours or mine.

A pastor prayed, "O Lord, we beseech Thee to send us the Holy Spirit, send Him upon us very graciously. Send Him upon us very quietly, send Him upon us very beautifully." Do you suppose He came? By no means. He was insulted to His face. I like the old Methodist way of putting it better, as when we sing, "Come as Thou wilt, but Holy Spirit, come."

Wind is also a reviving, inspiring, and purifying agent, and in all these respects is a symbol of the Holy Spirit.

Then came the fiery manifestation. Fire has ever been the symbol of [the] Divine Presence. It is a symbol of ardor. It is illuminating, inspiring, refining, purifying, and penetrating. Dr. Parker says that what is received by each is to be communicated to the whole world. It is always for unity that the Holy Spirit is given. If God gives the Spirit to you, it is that you may be His agent to convey it [Him] to others.

I call you to observe, finally, that

VI. *This Pentecostal baptism with the Spirit was a universal bestowment.*

FOR ALL CHRISTIANS

"They were all filled with the Holy Spirit." How glorious it must have been! I have often thought I would like to live to see one church of whose membership it could be truly said, "They were all filled with the Spirit." Brethren, this sanctifying baptism is for us all—ministers, laymen, old and young, learned and unlearned, rich and poor. It is for all. Moreover, all ought to have it. . . . We need whole churches that are sanctified and Spirit-filled to overcome the opposition of the world.

What marvelous results follow when God's people are filled with the Holy Spirit! What a change it effects in their own hearts and lives!

How much God wrought through those who were filled with the Spirit at Pentecost.

Spectators mocking said, "These men are full of new wine!" But Peter said, "These are not drunken, as ye suppose, seeing it is but the third hour of the day" (Acts 2:13, 15). Then he began telling in a simple way their experience: how God had raised Jesus from the dead, who had shed forth upon them the Holy Spirit as foretold by the prophet Joel. He charged upon them the murder of Christ and fervently exhorted them to repentance toward God and faith in our Lord Jesus Christ.

Three thousand were cut to the heart, and cried, "Men and brethren, what shall we do?" (v. 37). Peter exhorted them to repent and be baptized in the name of Jesus. They did so, and there were added to the disciples that day about 3,000 souls. Following this, there came permanent revival, and the Lord added to the church daily such as should be saved.

My friends, if you are without this baptism, seek it now. You can afford to forego eating and sleeping . . . and give yourself in prayer until God baptizes you with the Holy Spirit. To seek it successfully, however, you will need to hunger and thirst after righteousness. You will have to be in accord with spiritual people and love your neighbors. If you are indulging any hard feelings against anyone, you cannot get the Holy Ghost. He cannot endorse anything of that kind. . . .

Pray for the blessing. Pray until the heavens part and distill their blessings upon your head. There is such a thing as praying through and touching the arm that moves the world. God grant us to see Pentecost repeated at this Holiness Assembly. Amen!

Henry Clay Morrison
(1857-1942)

Henry Clay Morrison, orphaned as a boy, was reared by grandparents who surrounded him with godly influences.

A lifelong Methodist, he was converted during a revival meeting in the country church his family attended.

While serving as a pastor, and engaging in great revivals, he entered into the experience of entire sanctification. The Holy Spirit fell upon him in overwhelming power. "I felt my heart was cleansed from all sin," he wrote later.

In his ignorance, however, he listened to those who advised him to live holiness but not profess it. As a consequence, he quenched the Spirit and forfeited the abiding peace, purity, and power he could have enjoyed.

Some three years later the Lord renewed the sense of cleansing; Morrison humbly but promptly testified to it, and "pressed forward in the highway of holiness" for the rest of his life.

In addition to a fruitful preaching ministry in revivals and camp meetings, Morrison founded a holiness paper, called at first the *Old Methodist* and later the *Pentecostal Herald.*

Morrison was twice president of Asbury College, the first term for 15 years, the second for 11 years.

He was a gifted orator, with a singular power to move his listeners. Such gifts are easily abused to the detriment of the church and the destruction of souls. But Morrison was a man of unimpeachable character, and none of the excesses bordering on

fanaticism that marked the work of some holiness warriors ever marred his labors.

"The Obedience of Love" is a sermon he often preached as an evangelist. It accents the truth closest to his heart, that "the religion of Jesus Christ is love," love that inspires obedience to God and delights in service to mankind.

The sermon is not formally structured, but the outline and progress of thought is readily apparent: (1) "On the keeping of His commandments all else depends." (2) "The fulfilling of the high law of love is impossible without the rich grace offered in the gospel." (3) "The provisions of the gospel are equal to the requirements of the law." The atoning grace of Christ makes possible our obedience to the love command of Christ. "Actual sins must be forgiven, and the carnal nature must be eliminated. But all of this is provided for in the plan of redemption."

Few voices ever raised in advocacy of holiness were so eloquent and fruitful as that of H. C. Morrison. When he died in 1942, "a great tree fell in the forest."

The Obedience of Love*

> *If ye keep my commandments, ye shall abide in my love; even as I have kept my Father's commandments, and abide in his love* (John 15:10).

These words were spoken by our Lord to His disciples the evening of His betrayal. It was a most memorable occasion. The clock of destiny on the tower of time was striking the hour that marked the close of the old dispensation and ushered in the new.

It was on this never-to-be-forgotten evening that Christ celebrated with His disciples the feast of the Passover for the last time and instituted with them that new feast, *the Lord's Supper.* It was on this evening that He told them plainly of the coming separation, of the cruel death which awaited Him. [He then] comforted their troubled hearts with the assurance that having prepared a place for them, He would come again to receive them unto himself.

---

*Source: H. C. Morrison, *Life Sketches and Sermons.* Louisville, Ky.: Pentecostal Publishing Co., 1903.

He taught them humility and love for one another by washing their feet, and promised them the coming and abiding of the Holy Ghost forever. He taught them that they must be His witnesses, showed them that they must suffer for His sake, illustrated to them with the vine, its branches, and the husbandman, the close and dependent relation existing between them, himself, and the Father. He prayed for their deliverance from the evil one, for their *sanctification,* and oneness.

The text is the key to the entire situation. On the keeping of His commandments all else depends. It matters not what grace is given, or what promise is made, all fails if His commandments are neglected or violated. The gift of the Holy Ghost is conditioned on the keeping of His commandments. "If ye love me, keep my commandments. And I will pray the Father, and he shall give you another Comforter, that he may abide with you for ever" (John 14:15-16).

OBEDIENCE ESSENTIAL

The religion of Jesus Christ is not an ordinance, it is not a profession, it is not speaking like an angel, foreseeing like a prophet, giving all of one's goods to feed the poor, or one's body to be burned. The religion of Jesus Christ is love, not a mere sentiment or affection. It is not simply a lofty admiration for His spotless character, His sinless life, His compassionate and merciful attitude toward lost men. It is something far deeper and higher than this.

It is a holy love for Christ that fills the heart with adoration, praise, and *obedience.* It enables the soul to find its higher joy in *keeping His commandments.* One of the distinguishing qualities of this unselfish, holy love is that *it delights in service.* This keeping of His commandments is the one supreme test of true discipleship. "And hereby we do know that we know him, if we keep his commandments. He that saith, I know him, and keepeth not his commandments, is a liar, and the truth is not in him. But whoso keepeth his word, in him verily is the love of God perfected; hereby know we that we are in him. He that saith he abideth in him ought himself also so to walk, even as he walked" (1 John 2:3-6).

It will be readily admitted that this high standard is very far above human nature as we find it. But God's provisions are easily equal to His requirements. The fulfilling of the high law of love is impossible without the rich grace offered in the gospel.

GRACE ENABLES LOVE

To use a figure of speech, there is a wide stretch of country between the state of the natural man described by the apostle in Rom. 3:10-18, and the new, or spiritual, man described in Col. 3:10-17. Let us contrast these scriptures here: "As it is written, There is none righteous, no, not one: There is none that understandeth, there is none that seeketh after God. They are all gone out of the way, they are together become unprofitable: there is none that doeth good, no, not one. Their throat is an open sepulchre; with their tongues they have used deceit; the poison of asps is under their lips: whose mouth is full of cursing and bitterness: their feet are swift to shed blood: destruction and misery are in their ways: and the way of peace have they not known: there is no fear of God before their eyes" (Rom. 3:10-18).

If the daily papers which bring us the news of the fearful murders and nameless crimes which are of daily occurrence in the very centers of our civilization are at all reliable, this picture of fallen humanity is not overdrawn. Fearful as it is, we must admit it true to life. Who will question it who, under the light of the Holy Spirit, has looked into the depths of his own heart?

Now, behold the wonderful transition in this same degraded and sinful nature. "And have put on the new man, which is renewed in knowledge after the image of him that created him: where there is neither Greek nor Jew, circumcision nor uncircumcision, Barbarian, Scythian, bond nor free: but Christ is all, and in all. Put on therefore, as the elect of God, holy and beloved, bowels of mercies, kindness, humbleness of mind, meekness, longsuffering; forbearing one another, and forgiving one another, if any man have a quarrel against any: even as Christ forgave you, so also do ye. And above all these things put on charity, which is the bond of perfectness. And let the peace of God rule in your hearts, to the which also ye are called in one body; and be ye thankful. Let the word of Christ dwell in you richly in all wisdom; teaching and admonishing one another in psalms and hymns and spiritual songs, singing with grace in your hearts to the Lord. And whatsoever ye do in word or deed, do all in the name of the Lord Jesus, giving thanks to God and the Father by him" (Col. 3:10-17).

FORGIVENESS AND CLEANSING

Wide as the contrast is between the natural man here portrayed in Rom. 3:10-18, and the new man in Christ, described in Col. 3:10-17; yet it is possible, by the forgiveness of sins and the cleansing of the blood of Christ, to make the journey across from the land of bondage to the Canaan of perfect love. Not only is this possibility taught in the Scriptures, but it has been graciously verified in many lives. John Bunyan made this wonderful journey. There he was, a degraded, profane, vulgar Sabbath desecrater. But the power and grace of God found way into his heart, and he not only forsakes all of his sins but rejoices to suffer persecution for Christ's sake. There never were uttered braver words than those spoken by him when he said to his persecutors who offered to release him from prison, in which they had kept him long years, if he would cease preaching: "Rather than give up the privilege of preaching the gospel, I will remain in this prison until the moss be grown upon my forehead like my eyebrows. But you turn me out today, and I will preach Christ tomorrow." The commandments of Christ are impossible to those who do not love Him, but the love of Christ makes the heart delight in obedience.

GOSPEL PROVISIONS

We reflect that the provisions of the gospel are equal to the requirements of the law. "Where sin abounded, grace did much more abound" (Rom. 5:20). And when the abounding grace blots out all the transgressions, and cleanseth away all unrighteousness, the soul rejoices in the truth of that saying of John, "His commandments are not grievous" (1 John 5:3). To keep the *high law of love*—is the first and *great* commandment, that is "*the fulfilling of the law*" (Rom. 13:10). To keep the high law of love, to "love the Lord thy God with all thy heart, and with all thy soul, and with all thy mind, and with all thy strength . . . [and to] love thy neighbour as thyself" (Mark 12:30-31), and to love thine enemies, and love all men with a pure heart fervently, to keep this high law of love, the heart must be perfected in love. Actual sins must be forgiven, and the carnal nature must be eliminated. But all of this is provided for in the plan of redemption.

"Whereby are given unto us exceeding great and precious promises: that by these ye might be partakers of the divine nature, having escaped the corruption that is in the world through lust" (2 Pet. 1:4).

CLEANSING/ CARNALITY

Let us not complain of the weakness of our human nature, and the height of the standard our Lord has set up. Rather let us rejoice that the carnal nature can be cleansed away, and that we may, in its stead, have the *love of God* shed abroad in our hearts by the Holy Ghost, thus having been made partakers of the divine nature.

The power of the Atonement is not exhausted in providing forgiveness for those who have violated the law; it is abundantly able to bring these same violators of law into such perfect harmony with Him who fixed the law that they can say with the Psalmist, "O [God,] how love I thy law!" (119:97).

"This is the covenant that I will make with them after those days, saith the Lord, I will put my laws into their hearts, and in their minds will I write them" (Heb. 10:16).

There is an exceeding great and precious promise in 2 Cor. 6:16: "Ye are the temple of the living God; as God hath said, I will dwell in them, and walk in them; and I will be their God, and they shall be my people."

It is not the business of the Christian to strive in his own strength to keep the high law of love. It is not to be kept by binding oneself with rigid rules. The legalist is at best a slave. The hermits and monks have made a mistake in forgetting the spirit and striving after the letter of the law. They have shut themselves away from men and tortured their flesh. Their motives have been good, perhaps, but their methods have been contrary to the entire philosophy of the plan of redemption.

We are saved by grace. *He has suffered, "the just for the unjust"* (1 Pet. 3:18). Infinite mercy has solved the sin problem. God has discovered a plan by which He may remain just, in the justification of the ungodly. He found a sinless man who was willing to bear our sins in His own body on the Cross. *"With his stripes we are healed."* "All we like sheep have gone astray . . . and the Lord hath laid on him the iniquity of us all" (Isa. 53:5-6).

ATONEMENT

Through the sufferings and death of Jesus Christ there is *opened up a fountain for sin and uncleanness.* His blood cleanseth from all sin. The Holy Ghost coming into the soul brings with Him and inaugurates the reign of the high law of love.

Then let us, trusting in the full atonement of Jesus' blood, seek the baptism with the Holy Ghost. Filled with Him we will be able to keep His commandments and abide in His love, even as He has kept the Father's commandments and abides in His Father's love. Amen.

Milton S. Agnew

(1905—)

Milton Agnew is a retired colonel in the Salvation Army. A graduate of the University of Chicago and of Northern Baptist Seminary, he spent a number of years in the Army's educational work, helping to train their young people for officership and ministry.

Convinced that training to live is a crucial part of training to serve, Agnew has been a major advocate of the experience and life of holiness, both within Army ranks and throughout the evangelical community. His preaching and writing have kept the truth of holiness before the people of God, placing the entire holiness movement in his debt.

His sermons and articles contain strong exegetical elements. He concentrates upon the meaning of biblical words and phrases, the tenses of verbs employed by the writers of Scripture, together with their application to human life. These ingredients, more than any others, furnish the spine and heart of his preaching and teaching ministry.

A sermon like "God's Pattern for Perfection" may be faulted by some for its style. Literary elements are not dominant. But the preacher is involved here with something more significant than rhetoric or eloquence; his concern is clarity and urgency. Truth made plain, with its power to take captive the minds and lives of God's people, seems to be his goal.

The divisions of the sermon are supplied naturally from the text, where three verbs dominate and control the message of this

verse of Scripture. These verbs also give the sermon its logical direction—from past adoption to present cleansing to future maturation. Each crisis and process in the spiritual lives of God's people is the result of faith in Him as Provider and Promiser of all needed grace, grace that accepts, cleanses, and perfects those who come to Him.

God's Pattern for Perfection*

> *Having therefore these promises, dearly beloved, let us cleanse ourselves from all filthiness of the flesh and spirit, perfecting holiness in the fear of God* (2 Cor. 7:1).

Among Paul's various writings on the subject, none seems to be more positive and enlightening regarding the matter of perfection than [the text].

This message will center on three verbs: "Having," "cleanse," and "perfecting"—their meaning, their order, their type of action, and their relationship as to subjects and predicates.

I. *The phrase "**Having** therefore these promises" leads us at once to examine the nature of these promises which are already possessed, which have already been acquired.*

The *substance* of these promises is adoption or sonship, as given in the preceding verses: "I will receive you, and will be a Father unto you, and ye shall be my sons and daughters, saith the Lord Almighty" (2 Cor. 6:17-18). Now in rejoicing over such a heritage we need first to beware of the so-called universal fatherhood of God. In a generic sense this is true. Paul declares, "There is one body, and one Spirit, even as ye are called in one hope of your calling: one Lord, one faith, one baptism, one God and Father of all, who is above all, and through all, and in you all" (Eph. 4:4-6). To the men of Athens, in connection with his talk regarding the altar "to the Unknown God," he states, "For in him we live, and move, and have our being; as certain also of your own poets have said, For we are also his offspring. . . . we are the offspring of God" (Acts 17:28-29).

---

*Source: James McGraw, comp., *The Holiness Pulpit No. 2*. Kansas City: Beacon Hill Press of Kansas City, 1974.

But in a spiritual sense this is not so. Paul said to the Ephesians: "We all . . . were by nature the children of wrath . . . dead in sins" (Eph. 2:3, 5). Jesus boldly accused the unbelievers, "Ye are of your father the devil, and the lusts of your father ye will do" (John 8:44). No, we cannot subscribe to the popular idea of the universal fatherhood of God and brotherhood of man—in a spiritual sense. It is simply not so.

But we can rejoice in the possibility of owning these promises. John announces, "But as many as received him, to them gave he power to become the sons of God, even to them that believe on his name" (John 1:12); while Paul declares to the Corinthians, "Therefore if any man be in Christ, he is a new creature" (2 Cor. 5:17), and proclaims to the people of Rome, "Ye have received the Spirit of adoption, whereby we cry, Abba, Father" (Rom. 8:15). Yes, such promises are available to all.

Now Paul makes it clear that the *condition* of these promises is separation. In the preceding chapter he has exhorted the people of Corinth, "Wherefore come out from among them, and be ye separate, saith the Lord, and touch not the unclean thing; and I will receive you" (2 Cor. 6:17). Again he had pleaded, "Be ye not unequally yoked together with unbelievers: for what fellowship hath righteousness with unrighteousness? and what communion hath light with darkness?" (2 Cor. 6:14).

Was this not true with the Israelites? To be acknowledged as God's people—as His children—they were required to come out from Egypt, separate themselves, and leave the unclean things of the land. *Then,* and not until then, could God own them.

NEW BIRTH

Let us not sell short this matter of becoming a child of God, of being saved, of regeneration. God expects all His children to be separate from sin, separate from the world, separate from the unclean things of godlessness. There are too many who expect God to own them as His own—in Egypt, in their worldliness—"unseparated Christians" (if there can be such a term). That, decidedly, is not God's plan. "Thou shalt call his name JESUS: for he shall save his people from [not in] their sins" (Matt. 1:21).

Of course this matter of being separate from the world must be kept within context. A pressing of this beyond reason has resulted in some people becoming monks and hermits. Possibly the pinnacle of this absurdity was achieved when one, Simeon Stylites, a monk who died in A.D. 459, remained for 35 years on a small platform on top of a 50-foot stone pillar near Aleppo, Syria, in order to be "separate from the world." For this feat, he was made a saint. No, we must remember the petition our Lord uttered for His disciples (John 17:15), "I pray not that thou shouldest take them out of the world, but that thou shouldest keep them from the evil" (keep the world out of them).

The *privileges* of these promises are great. The guest of a king may be welcomed graciously and remain for the period of his invitation, only to leave the palace with the proud memory of having been an honored guest. The servant of the king may abide in the household, be often in the presence of the king, and serve him well. But he is only a servant. However, the son of the king needs no invitation, no introduction, no friendly courtesies. He is the son. And he is also the heir. For the king is his father. The son calls him by the tender name, "Abba, Father."

II. *To those, then, who possess these promises—who are sons or daughters of the Father—Paul continues, "Let us* **cleanse** *ourselves from all filthiness of the flesh and spirit."*

Now this "filthiness" does not mean limitations in skills; it is not shortcomings in manners, in courtesies, or in thoughtfulness; it is not weakness, or even infirmities. The word is *molusmos, . . .* variously translated as "defilement," as "pollution," as "contamination." When I was a boy, my brother became ill with typhoid fever. Investigation showed that our well was contaminated. This condition had to be corrected or we might all have become ill. We "cleaned out the well." So Paul says there is, in the soul of him who is a child of the King, a contamination of the flesh and spirit.

Did not the children of Israel exhibit such a contamination after their separation from Egypt? This was evidenced by their spirit in their murmuring, their criticism, their jealousy; as to the flesh, in their lusting after the leeks, the garlic, the onions of Egypt. Oh, no, they did not want to return to Egypt to be slaves—only to enjoy again the "fruits of the land." It was not until they entered the Promised Land, and found delightful food of milk and honey and grapes, that they realized there was something better than the old life.

CARNALITY CONTAMINATES

How like the Israelites are many Christians! Not desiring by any means the slavery again of sin, they hanker after some of the pleasures of the world. They indulge in some of the "fruits of sin"; they complain, gossip, are touchy, uncharitable.

This is the sin principle, inherited from Adam, for which the child of God is not responsible and therefore for which he cannot be *forgiven.* This requires a different work of grace. This is pictured by Samuel Hodges in his song:

Tell me what to do to be pure
In the sight of the all-seeing Eyes.
Tell me, is there no thorough cure,
No escape from the sin I despise?
Tell me, can I never be free
From this terrible bondage within?
Is there no deliverance for me
From the thraldom of indwelling sin?

The answer, of course, is *cleansing.* This is a cleansing that is *promised:* "Then will I sprinkle clean water upon you, and ye shall be clean: from all your filthiness, and from all your idols, will I cleanse you" (Ezek. 36:25).

It is a cleansing that is *longed for:* "Who can understand his errors? cleanse thou me from secret faults" (Ps. 19:12); "Wash me throughly from mine iniquity, and cleanse me from my sin. . . . Purge me with hyssop, and I shall be clean: wash me, and I shall be whiter than snow" (Ps. 51:2, 7).

It is a cleansing that is *provided:* "Christ also loved the church, and gave himself for it; that he might sanctify and cleanse it with the washing of water by the word" (Eph. 5:25-26).

This cleansing is the *crisis act* of entire sanctification. That this is a crisis act is indicated by the aorist tense of a defined act, as contrasted to the present tense of a continued action.

IN A MOMENT

These two tenses are nicely illustrated in verse 17 of the preceding chapter: "Wherefore come out [as a crisis act] from among them, and be ye separate [as a continuing life practice], saith the Lord." . . . "Let us cleanse" is the invitation to an act of the moment.

And the action is to include *all* filthiness, *all* defilement, *all* pollution, *all* contamination—not part. It is a sanctification that is entire.

Well may we sing in confidence with the hymn writer: "Beautiful river, flowing to cleanse and keep me from sin."

III. *The third verb is* **perfecting**—*"perfecting holiness in the fear of God."*

This is not a parallel clause that calls for an "and," as indicated in the unfortunate translations of NEB and RSV: "And in the fear of God complete [perfect] . . ." There is no *and* in the original. Rather it is a present participial clause indicating *subsequent* continuous action. It is not "*thus* perfecting holiness," but rather "*then* perfecting holiness." As Daniel Steele puts it: "Hence the duty enjoined in 2 Cor. 7:1, of perfecting holiness, is a progressive work, realizing, or carrying into practice, that cleansing from all filthiness . . . [which is] instantaneously wrought within."

Nor is perfecting "our *consecration,*" as in the NEB, Amplified, and Moffatt translations. Rather it is "perfecting *holiness*" as in ASV, RSV, and Weymouth. The first edition of the RSV carried "consecrate" here and elsewhere. It was Dr. John A. Huffman and others who protested to the translation committee that *hagiazō* carried, in many places, the concept of sanctify and, in noun form, of holiness, both by theology and by etymology. The committee took his protest under advisement, recognized the validity of his argument, and in the 1946 edition changed the word here and in many other places to *holiness* and *sanctify.*

The *process* of perfection is supported by the present tense. Bishop Moule is credited with the statement that "sanctification is a crisis with a view to a process; or a process succeeding a crisis." Thus "cleanse" is a crisis, "perfecting" a process.

BOTH CRISIS AND PROCESS

Was that not so with the Israelites? Moses had said, "He brought us out . . . that he might bring us in" (Deut. 6:23). Thus was accomplished, in typology, the two crisis experiences of salvation and sanctification. But it must be remembered that, even after the Israelites had been in the land for some time, it was Joshua who challenged them, "How long are ye slack to go to possess the land, which the Lord God of your fathers hath given you?" (Josh. 18:3). If coming into the land was the act of a defined day, the possessing of the land was a process of many years. Thus it is with the experience and life of holiness.

Consider the exact meaning of the word "perfecting," *epiteleō.* It is essentially twofold. As declared by Dr. Steele, it means first to carry into practice, to realize, to execute fully, to perform. It is instructive to note how this same verb is used in Phil. 1:6, "Being confident of this very thing, that he which hath begun a good work in you *will perform* it until the day of Jesus Christ." This puts holiness into every part of the life, into every ambition, into every standard. It puts holiness into the workshop, the home, the school, into friendship, industry, vocation. It assures that true holiness is truly practical, that it relates to everyday life.

But the word also means to mature, to bring to full stature, to complete. Purity is subtraction, and it is instantaneously accomplished. Maturity is addition. It is the result of experience, trial, conflict, nutrition. In my youth I watched the workmen, at a given time in the spring, spray the peach trees to kill the insects, the worms, the "impurity." But it took many weeks of warm sunshine to produce the luscious, ripe peaches.

GROWTH

Thus entire sanctification is not merely the negative goodness of a cleansing of the heart wrought at the moment of faith, but it is also the aggressive and progressive living, growing, maturing; the applying of the principles of Christian ethics to every part of the life, "till we all come in the unity of the faith, and of the knowledge of the Son of God, unto a perfect man, unto the measure of the stature of the fulness of Christ" (Eph. 4:13).

A steamship line carries the slogan "Half the fun is getting there." Half the fun of heaven can be "getting there" with a life of holiness down here.

2

IMPORTANT HOLINESS EMPHASES

Richard Watson
(1781-1833)

Richard Watson became Methodism's first systematic theologian. His *Christian Institutes,* appearing in 1823, are still valuable for study. He was a brilliant scholar, possessing "the reasoning power of a philosopher and the imagination of a poet."

Watson was born in 1781 in Barton-on-Humber. Shortly after his conversion he was called to the Wesleyan ministry and began preaching at 16. He dropped out of the conference in 1801, his orthodoxy suspected. In 1812 he returned, to become one of their notable leaders.

Theology, missions, and social reform, especially the abolition of slavery, were his consuming interests.

His death at the age of 52 enriched heaven but deprived the church of one of its outstanding thinkers, writers, and preachers.

His published sermons breathe the seriousness characteristic of early Methodism. Methodist preachers, like their founding father, Wesley, were "out of breath pursuing souls." Never trivial, never entertaining, their preaching aimed at converting sinners to Christ and establishing believers in holiness.

"The Inheritance of the Saints" expounds "light" as an appropriate figure for heaven's (1) splendor, (2) purity, (3) felicity, and (4) knowledge. Then it proclaims the "meetness which is wrought by God in the hearts of all" who will enjoy the inheritance. God prepares them for heaven by (1) a relative meetness, adopting them as "heirs," and by (2) a personal meetness, making them "saints." Only the holy can enjoy heaven, and we are made holy on earth: "Before I see God in heaven, He must manifest himself to me here. I must, in a word, be a man sanctified, hallowed to God, before I can ever approach that holy Being. . . . To produce in us this meetness is the work of God. His grace only can mortify the evils of our nature and make us partakers of His holiness. That grace is freely offered to you."

Watson's messages to the church were offers of the sanctifying grace of God. They are systematic and exegetic, flashing with light and burning with energy. To read them is to become a better person and an abler preacher.

The Inheritance of the Saints*

> *Giving thanks unto the Father, which hath made us meet to be partakers of the inheritance of the saints in light* (Col. 1:12).

The darkness of paganism . . . changed the character of earth by making it the only hope and home of man; and thus left him no care beyond that of multiplying his present enjoyments.

What paganism did by its darkness . . . worldliness does by its spirit. It shuts out another state . . . and, "What shall I eat? what shall I drink? and wherewithal shall I be clothed?" becomes the sole care of man. For this he forfeits immortal life; and his last hour drags him unprepared to the seat of judgment.

LIVING FOR GOD

What external Christianity effects in doctrine, inward and vital Christianity effects in the habit and tendencies of the mind. It connects time with eternity, and earth with heaven. Gladly does every true Christian confess himself to be a stranger and pilgrim upon the earth; and "they that say such things declare plainly that they seek a country" (Heb. 11:14). They still seek it. Whatever advantages may be on earth, whatever their religious improvement and fellowship with God may be; still they seek a country. All things are subordinated to that; and they feel that they cannot, must not, rest until they attain it.

Such was the connection established between the hearts and lives

---

*Source: Richard Watson, *Sermons and Sketches of Sermons,* Vol. 1. New York: B. Waugh and T. Mason, 1836.

of the first Christians and a future world, by the glorious ministry of the apostles; and at the review of it the apostle gives thanks to the Father. Such is that connection of tendency, hope, and effort which may be established between us and the same immortality. Let us aim at the cultivation of it; and let the topics which our text contains be suffered to promote the great result in all our hearts. We have,

I. *An interesting view of the future world, as it is inherited by believers:* "The inheritance of the saints in light" (Col. 1:12).

Various are the views of that glorious immortality which is exhibited to our faith and hope in the gospel; and each of them is found in Scripture to have some special points of interest. That before us is full of delightful instruction. The saints in a better life are said to be "in light."

1. They are so in respect to the *place.*

It is a place of splendor. We may take this literally. Since the inhabitants are surrounded by material objects, light is not excluded. It arrays all nature with beauty; cheers it with vigor; and inspires it, so to speak, with feeling. But the term suggests the idea of ceaseless activity. Night and sleep are related to each other. The reason of night is the frailty of man, needing repose; but when it is said, "No night is in heaven," that very expression indicates an activity which never wearies; a buoyancy of spirit which never grows languid; noble exercises which never cease; and an entire employment of time, even when eternity shall carry on its distinctions and divisions, if any, forever.

2. The saints in heaven are in light as it respects *purity.*

HOLINESS AND HEAVEN

Darkness is an emblem of sin; light [an emblem] of holiness. . . . Evil covets darkness; it shuns detection; it covers itself with veils, often painted and shining, but veils still. It courts error, in order to stifle conscience, which will work when in the light. A soul panting after holiness comes to the light, that its deeds, if evil remains, may be reproved and corrected; and its works, if good, be manifested that they are wrought in God. The light of truth leads the way through every successive step of holiness.

Light may, therefore, well stand for holiness, the element from which it springs, and in which it delights. Into that light we are brought here, but often by a slow process through our own fault; and even to the end of life it is connected with infirmities; but in heaven the Church has neither spot, nor wrinkle, nor any such thing. There thou shalt never sin through ignorance; nor fail of the perfection of duty through weakness; nor offend thy brother through mistake; nor be a stumbling block to others. All hearts there are open to each other as to God; and the perfect image of the supreme light of purity itself shall be fully and visibly reflected from every one.

3. They are said to be in light in respect of the *permanency of their felicity.*

Night is an emblem of affliction; light, of gladness. Sorrow courts the gloom . . . joy expands in bright and cheerful skies. . . . Nor are the vicissitudes of day and night without their emblematic meaning in the present state. Our blessings often have their dawn, their noon, and their setting; our afflictions deepen from the dark of evening to the gloom of midnight, and then the morning breaks with some new comfort. Such are the alternations of the present state. . . .

But there the saints of God are in eternal light. No sickness blasts, no death devours; no families are broken up . . . no injustice grinds; no tongue wounds, nor do losses grieve. And there, as to spiritual enjoyments, no depression of the body abates their ardor; no temptation throws a dark cloud before the sun of heavenly manifestations; no fears that "I shall one day fall by the hand of my enemy" (cf. 1 Sam. 27:1) chill the exultation of a past victory. They are in light. It is the permanency of holiness that gives permanency to bliss. . . .

4. They are in light as it respects *knowledge.*

We come, it is true, "out of darkness into . . . marvellous light"; but still "we see through a glass, darkly" (1 Pet. 2:9; 1 Cor. 13:12). We are sure that brighter discoveries are objects of hope, because St. Paul, after all his high illumination, anticipated with so much joy the removal of the dim medium, that he might "see . . . face to face." In this respect we are not yet in the light. The illuminated circle about us is surrounded with haze. The prominent parts of things, like the tops of hills, catch the beams of the day which is breaking from eternity; while the valley and the distance lie hid in shade. Of many a mysterious individual providence we would know more; but the reason of the case is yet unexplained.

Into the mightier plans of God even piety would humbly pry; but . . . they are "dreadful"; and . . . are complicated. . . .

Into the difficulties of some great doctrines of revelation we are sometimes urged to look. We dare not question the truth of what God has revealed; and we adore the depth of the divine counsels even when our minds fail adequately to comprehend them. . . . And yet these are "things" which we, as well as angels, "desire to look into" (1 Pet. 1:12).

In this blessed Book how many texts are obscure? Nay, is there one, the clearest, of which we see the full length, and breadth, and depth, and height?

Ah! who would not have the mystery of his little life unfolded, that he may know more fully the wisdom which has guided him; the love which has watched over him; the unwearied but invisible hand which has restrained him from evil, and supplied all his wants?

Who would not see all prophecy converted into history? all the complexity of the world's government converted into one bright manifestation of wisdom, power, holiness, and goodness? Who would not see every page of this Book brightening under his gaze? And, above all, who would not rise to a nearer vision of Him, the Eternal, the infinite Essence, the Source of all, the Perfection of all; "of whom . . . are all things," and to whom glory and honor are forever due (Rom. 11:36)?

THE HOPE OF THE SAINTS

This has been the crowning hope of good men in all ages. Job expressed a joyful assurance that in his flesh he should see God; and St. John exultingly exclaims, "We shall see him as he is" (1 John 3:2). It shall be done. The saints are "in light." And—to refer to the former illustration—though now the light strikes only upon the prominent hills, and leaves the vale and the distance in darkness, breaking the connection and relation of things by interposing shadows; yet as the sun ascends, and shines down in brighter rays, the light sinks into every valley, dissolves every mist, and throws one vast scheme before us . . . one boundless harmony.

In the text we have,

II. *The meetness which is wrought by God in the hearts of all who are raised to the enjoyment of this inheritance.*

This meetness, or fitness, is expressed in two terms in the text. One is relative, and the other personal.

1. The relative meetness is expressed by the word "inheritance." It is assigned to "heirs."

Our natural heirship is forfeited by sin. Redemption has brought back the inheritance; but we become heirs by becoming children; and we are made the children of God by the faith which secures to us the blessing of justification. Till this blessing is obtained, there is no meetness of relation. The inheritance is not mine, and I am forbidden to hope for it. If I die under the delusion of finding admission into heaven while my sin is unforgiven, I shall be awfully disappointed. My name is not in the book of life till my guilt is canceled, and my person adopted; for it is only when we are "justified by his grace" that we are "made heirs according to the hope of eternal life" (Titus 3:7). Where, then, is your evidence of this heirship? Is it within you, in the witness and fruit of the Spirit?

JUSTIFICATION

2. The second term indicates the personal meetness. It is the term "saints."

The word signifies hallowed, sanctified persons. Mark, my brethren, the correspondence, the fitness, between a hallowed state and heaven. Shall I illustrate this by contrast? Dwell, then, for a moment upon it. Here is a man that has a distaste to God's service. It is a weariness to him. He avails himself of every pretext to neglect it; and when he does engage in it, he is restless and unhappy. Is he meet to be employed in the worship of God day and night forever? Would heaven to him be a place of rest and joy?

SANCTIFICATION

Here is another, who shuns the full light of truth lest he should be reproved. Can he go into that pure and searching element which shall set his secret sins in the full light of his countenance forever? Would he voluntarily choose such a place as . . . his inheritance?

Here is a third. So enervated is his heart, that nothing spiritual or eternal lays hold upon a single affection. What shall meet the gross taste of this man in the spiritualities of that world of light?

Take a fourth. He is a trifling lover of pleasure, or a sensualist.

Take a fifth. He is cankered with envy, fumes in anger, glowers with revenge, swells with pride, or is contracted with selfishness. You see no meetness here. Let no man deceive himself. It cannot be that persons with these dispositions should have any inheritance in the kingdom of Christ and of God. Before I can enter that light, it must shine into my heart, to give the knowledge of the glory of God in the face of Jesus Christ. Before I join that society, love and charity must ameliorate my temper. Before I enter upon those hallowed meditations, my meditation upon Him must be sweet on earth. Before I see God in heaven, He must manifest himself to me here. I must, in a word, be a man sanctified, hallowed to God, before I can ever approach that holy Being, those saints in light, that holy heaven. "Blessed are the pure in heart: for they shall see God"; but

ATTITUDES

"without [holiness] no man shall see the Lord" (Matt. 5:6; Heb. 12:14).

FOR ALL CHRISTIANS

To produce in us this meetness is the work of God. His grace only can mortify the evils of our nature and make us partakers of His holiness. That grace is freely offered to you. Already it has been vouchsafed to you; for in its first communications it waiteth not for the call of man. It will increase by your diligence; for to him that hath . . . shall be given. "He giveth more grace" (James 4:6); grace to lead you from repentance to pardon, and to that perfect love which casteth out all fear. Make it your business to go on unto perfection, and to be filled with all the fullness of God.

Give thanks to the Father for those who are made meet for the heavenly inheritance. You see the work in their heavenly-mindedness, their devotional spirit and habits, and in their pure and upright walk. Glorify God [because of] them.

Give thanks to God if the work be begun in yourselves. If it is not begun, give thanks that you are spared to this day; and now aspire to the prize of your high calling of God in Christ Jesus.

Asbury Lowrey

(1816-98)

This sermon was preached at the National Camp Meeting for the Promotion of Holiness in 1873. According to the reporter for that camp meeting, an "almost breathless attention" was given to the preacher, and faces were suffused with "gleams of intelligent appreciation" as "longstanding difficulties, to a clear understanding and personal exercise of faith, suddenly gave way." Following the sermon many sought and found the experience of entire sanctification.

Asbury Lowrey was then a pastor in the Methodist Episcopal church and one of the most active leaders of a national movement to promote holiness by special meetings and literature. Earlier that same year he had engaged John Inskip and William McDonald for a meeting in his church, which drew great crowds and also drew heavy fire from critics within Methodism opposed to the renewed emphasis on personal holiness.

Lowrey's answer to the criticism is labeled by Melvin Dieter "a classic example of the many apologies which were made by the movement's defenders." Lowrey's pen was often busy as an apologist for holiness, indicting the worldliness of the church in general, and defending the propriety of special efforts and methods to promote heart holiness. He pleaded with the church he loved not to reject the very task for which it had been thrust into the world, according to its sainted founder.

Lowrey served two holiness publications as editor for a number of years, *Christian Standard* and *Divine Life.* He is best known

to later generations of holiness people for his book *Possibilities of Grace*, published in 1884.

John Wesley's "rediscovery" of sanctification by faith was as distressing to many churchmen as Luther's rediscovery of justification by faith. But Wesley's teaching provided the stimulus for such sermons as this one by Lowrey. The simple outline and the urgent application indicate the prevailing motive of the preacher —truth for life's sake, *saving* faith! Faith is guarded from abstraction by being anchored to the atonement of Christ and the promises of Scripture. "Such promises, underlaid by the Atonement, meet us everywhere and challenge our faith."

While much of what Lowrey says about faith has the broadest possible application, throughout the sermon he keeps light focused upon the possibility of immediate entry by faith into the experience of entire sanctification.

Have Faith in God*

Have faith in God (Mark 11:22).

The New Testament is extensively a treatise on faith; an exposition of the doctrine, duty, and results of faith. The scheme of redemption is penetrated in every part by the conditionality of faith. The life of a Christian is a life of faith in opposition to a life of sense and groveling materialism. Faith enters into all the heights and depths and complexities of Christian experience. It is not only instrumental but substantive. It is essential to the nature, vital to the existence, and indispensable to the growth of spiritual life. It has both invigorating and nutritive properties. By it the texture of the inner man is built up and developed into completeness and maturity.

Allow us to engage your attention with the nature, origin, object, and uses of faith.

I. *The Nature of Faith*

Faith, as used in the Scriptures, is an equivocal term. With belief as its reigning idea, it has different shades of meaning. In its lowest

---

*Source: Adam Wallace, ed., *A Modern Pentecost*. Philadelphia: Methodist Home Journal Publishing House, 1873.

sense, it implies only a cold intellectual assent to religious truth, independent of good works. For example: "What doth it profit, my brethren, though a man say he hath faith, and have not works? can faith save him?" (James 2:14). That is, can the mere faith of credence, or the foreboding faith of trembling devils, save a man?

Faith is sometimes put for the entire code of gospel precepts, as in the text: "A great company of the priests were obedient to the faith"; that is, they submitted to the general requirements of the gospel (Acts 6:7). Faith is also used as a symbol of Christianity or a title of believers. For instance, "As we have therefore opportunity, let us do good unto all men, especially unto them who are of the household of faith"; that is, the family of believers, called "the household of faith," are to have the precedence in our charities (Gal. 6:10). . . .

Literally, and according to the meaning of the original word *(pistis),* faith imports persuasion, confidence, and trust. Parkhurst, in defining the Greek term, says: "It generally implies such knowledge of, assent to, and confidence in certain divine truths, especially those of the gospel, as produce good works." Dr. Dwight says: "The faith of the gospel is that emotion of the mind which is called trust or confidence exercised towards the moral character of God, and particularly of the Savior." We accept their statements as good general definitions. According to them, the first thing necessary to evangelical faith is religious instruction. The second is a convinced judgment; the third is a confiding motion of the heart and mind called trust, by which we renounce every other refuge and shut ourselves up to the merits of Christ for salvation.

As Dr. Bunting justly remarks, "It is such a hearty concurrence of the will and affections with the plan of salvation, as implies a renunciation of every other refuge, and an actual trust in the Savior and personal apprehension of His merits." Such a belief of the gospel and such a reliance on the Atonement as leads us to come to Christ, to receive Christ, and to commit the keeping of our souls into His hands in humble confidence of His power and willingness to save. . . .

SAVING FAITH

Now faith in the sense of trust, which is peculiar to gospel belief, is necessary to spiritual life. Many persons have been sufficiently instructed in religion, and also convinced of its truths, who remain unhealed of sin. Perhaps I now address a multitude who believe in the being of God; the inspiration of the Scriptures; the divinity and Messiahship of Christ; the necessity and virtue of the Atonement; the possibility and indispensableness of pardon and the new birth; the gift and offices of the Holy Ghost . . . and yet, with this large and true faith they remain dead in trespasses and sin. What is the matter? . . . It is not the want of faith, but the want of that property of faith which alone appropriates—the property of trust—the property of reliance. It is that desperate self-renunciation, and universal abandonment of every other refuge, which, looking up to Jesus, says:

Other refuge have I none;
Hangs my helpless soul on Thee.

Could my tears forever flow,
Could my zeal no languor know,
These for sin could not atone;
Thou must save, and Thou alone.
In my hand no price I bring;
Simply to Thy cross I cling.

Some, however, use another subterfuge in order to quiet the uneasy and painful sensations of the mind, and obscure the fearful events and responsibilities of eternity. They preposterously assert that they do trust in Christ and have, as others, hope of salvation. And yet they never shed a penitential tear, nor breathe a prayer for mercy, nor quit their cherished sins. They may not be steeped in depravity, but the ungodliness to which they are constitutionally prone, they allow, and love, and practice.

Now life and death are not more widely separated and incompatible than this faith differs from that of a living Christian or true penitent. It is the faith of presumption, a trust that Christ will save them in their sins without saving them from their sins. It is a conceit, a delusion which seeks to accomplish an absurdity, a moral impossibility. It makes Jesus, not a Savior from sin, but a mere warrantee against hell and misery, in defiance of sin, and in harmony with sin. This cannot be, for: "What communion hath light with darkness? And what concord hath Christ with Belial?" (2 Cor. 6:14-15).

That faith which is connected with salvation lets light in upon the corruptions of the heart, produces penitential tenderness, and creates aversion to sin. Then it puts us upon the pursuit of salvation. It feels after saving merits and healing virtues. It looks up to Jesus, takes hold of His promises, leans hard on His atonement, makes fast the fingers of its confidence in the gory wounds of

FAITH IN CHRIST

His side, and finally settles down upon the conviction that Christ has become to him wisdom, righteousness, sanctification, and redemption. Now faith is to him "the substance of things hoped for, the evidence of things not seen" (Heb. 11:1).

II. *The Origin of Faith*

There are always two opposite beliefs on this point. Some men have taken the position that faith is an exclusive and arbitrary gift of God. Others, by consequence, have leaned to the opposite extreme, and represented faith as the independent act of man. . . . The truth lies at the mean distance between these polemic poles. The Scriptures clearly teach that faith is in part the gift of God, and in part the exercise of a free and responsible agent. The power to believe is of God, the appropriation and use of that power is the work of the suppliant, whether penitent sinner or seeker of holiness.

That there is a sense in which faith is the gift of God is sufficiently manifest from the following texts: "Looking unto Jesus the author and finisher of our faith" (Heb. 12:2). "And the apostles said unto the Lord, Increase our faith" (Luke 17:5). These passages evince that God is concerned in the origin, increase, and perfecting of our faith. And it is quite evident that without the inspiration of power, giving to the mind believing biases, no man would and no man could reverse the unbelieving tendencies of his nature and have faith in God in the sense of the text. He might have the faith of a Deist, which is cold as a moonbeam and bounded by the icebergs of materialism; but the faith of a Christian, which pulsates with life and love, and mantles itself with the leaves, and flowers, and fruitage of usefulness, he cannot have without divine help inspiring him with Godward inclinations and trustful dispositions.

FAITH IS GOD'S GIFT

But other considerations clearly show that the exercise of the power to believe is the act of man. And this exercise is not necessitated. Whether we will believe or not is a contingency that hinges upon our volitions. The first proof of this position is the serious fact that we are made responsible for our faith. To believe is a duty positively commanded of all men. Not to believe is a punishable offense. "He that believeth and is baptized shall be saved; but he that believeth not shall be damned" (Mark 16:16). The acts of God are [not subject to judgment]; but the acts of men are either rewardable or punishable, according to their moral character. Hence as believing is to be rewarded with salvation, and

FAITH IS MAN'S CHOICE

unbelief is punishable with damnation, it must be man's own proper and responsible act.

Another evidence is founded upon the conditionality of salvation. According to the Scriptures, faith is the sole condition of salvation. Paul says, "Therefore we conclude that a man is justified by faith without the deeds of the law" (Rom. 3:28). Now if faith is exclusively the gift of God, then salvation is tendered to us on a condition which God himself performs, or necessitates us to perform. That is, He makes justification conditional and unconditional at the same time, which is a bold absurdity. We reach then this conclusion, that faith is a joint work. The power to believe is given to us of God; the employment of that power, styled belief, is required of us on the part of God. And while God freely inspires the power, yet He will no more believe for us than He will repent or pray for us.

FAITH IS A JOINT WORK

And having bestowed the ability, He will not hold any man guiltless, nor suffer him to go unpunished, who lives or dies in unbelief. And the assumption is not improbable that we all have vastly more power to believe than we use. It is, with us, a buried talent—a wasted force. . . . But should there be a lack of power, it may be supplemented at any time by an appeal to God. Lord, I believe; help Thou my unbelief. . . . We must recollect, however, that prayer for more power to believe is but solemn mockery if we do not use what we have. God helps those who help themselves. It was only when the handful of meal in the barrel and the little oil in the cruse were freely used according to the Lord's direction, that He pledged himself to the poor widow of tried faith, saying, "The barrel of meal shall not waste, neither shall the cruse of oil fail, until the day that the Lord sendeth rain upon the earth" (1 Kings 17:14). The power of belief must be stretched to its utmost tension before He will increase it.

III. *The Object of Faith*

God is presented in the text as the Object of faith. In His all-comprising fullness and supremacy He is set before us to challenge faith. It is in His being, unity, spirituality, natural and moral attributes, and especially in His redemptive work, that we are invited and required to focalize trust. God here represents every star of hope, every gleam of light, every healing virtue, every festive joy, every beatific prospect. Faith in God comprises so many points that we cannot notice them in detail. We must confine ourselves to those truths which more especially enter into evangelical faith.

At bottom . . . saving faith in God implies trust in the sacrificial and propitiatory offering of Christ. We cannot separate between God and His Son, nor can we ignore the Atonement, and exercise a life-restoring faith in God directly and immediately. God does not, and cannot, allow himself to be approached by the sinner in his own name and proper person. To do so would involve connivance at sin, and introduce anarchy into the moral government of God. The emphatic words of Christ are these: "I am the way, the truth, and the life: no man cometh unto the Father, but by me" (John 14:6). A mediator must come between us and God . . . as an intercessor . . . and substitute—not pleading for pardon on the basis of unsatisfied clemency; but bearing in his hands a full and satisfactory indemnity for the impairment done to the holy order of the universe by human sin. . . .

TRUST IN CHRIST

There was an irreconcilable clash between human crime and the holiness of heaven, which could only be adjusted by satisfaction. . . . It was not only an advocate, with eloquent voice and powers of persuasion, that we needed, but a priest as well, to offer gifts and sacrifices—a priest with crimson temple and gory side and hands all dripping with atoning blood. Even the power of Christ to save is confined within the limit of His mediation and sacrifice. "Wherefore he is able also to save them to the uttermost that come unto God by him, seeing he ever liveth to make intercession for them" (Heb. 7:25).

Indeed, all the possibilities and encouraging certainties of salvation spring out of the blood of expiation. . . . "For if the blood of bulls and of goats, and the ashes of an heifer sprinkling the unclean, sanctifieth to the purifying of the flesh: how much more shall the blood of Christ, who through the eternal Spirit offered himself without spot to God, purge your conscience from dead works to serve the living God?" (Heb. 9:13-14). There is to be an eternal recognition of the Blood as the procuring cause of holiness. Those who have gone to heaven, we are told, washed their robes and made them white in the blood of the Lamb. Those who sing in heaven adopt the chorus, "Unto him that loved us, and washed us from our sins in his own blood" (Rev. 1:5). It is only when we take fast hold upon the Atonement that we get down among the primary rocks of our faith. . . .

ATONEMENT

Faith in God implies faith in His promises and covenant engagements. God has not only provided saving merits, and healing virtues, and cleansing fountains, but He has pledged himself to appropriate these efficacies on the most easy and practical conditions. These unmerited promises . . . are given to us . . . that by them we might be partakers of the divine nature, having escaped the corruption that is in the world through lust.

FAITH IN GOD'S PROMISE

The Lord has entered into a solemn contract with the sinning race—a contract to save us fully and forever through Christ; and now He condescends to make use of means to inspire confidence and hope in the fulfillment of His testimonial engagement. He has required its continual reassertion from the pulpit. He has ratified it with two sacraments, and finally confirmed it by an oath. . . . He has even put His fidelity and justice at stake to assure us that there shall be no failure in the fulfillment of His self-assured obligations. Therefore it is said, "If we confess our sins, he is faithful and just to forgive us our sins, and to cleanse us from all unrighteousness" (1 John 1:9). Here the Lord directly commits himself to work pardon and holiness on the sole condition of what is comprehended in the confession of sin. . . .

Such promises, underlaid by the Atonement, meet us everywhere and challenge our faith. If we are not fully saved, then the sin must lie at our door, and the failure must be charged up to our own account. Indeed, when we look at the ground and facilities of faith from this standpoint, we cannot be surprised that unbelief has been ranked among the hell-deserving crimes.

FULLY SAVED

But what is it to believe the promises of God? Is it merely to credit the truth and sincerity of God? Is it the limit of faith to rely even confidently on the future indefinite verification of the utterances of God? If this is all, then impenitent sinners may be true believers. It is not enough to believe God is able and willing to save. Nor is it enough to believe that He is able and willing to save to the uttermost, and to save us now. It is not impossible for a well-instructed, clever sinner to believe all this. We must advance a step further and include in our trust the . . . actual saving work of God. We must think of Him as never allowing a promise to go to protest, as never forgetting the date of its maturity, as never asking an extension of time. We must think of believing and receiving as coetaneous and inseparable. . . .

SAVED TO THE UTTERMOST

The Lord seems to delight in seeing His children defy improbabilities. All the bold and daring instances of faith on record are most commended by the Savior. The case of the centurion, whose servant was sick of the palsy, was a type of faith most pleasing to Jesus. Christ, being solicited, said, "I will come and heal him." But the centurion answered . . . "Lord, I am not worthy that thou shouldest come under my roof: but speak the word only, and my servant shall be healed. For I am a man under authority, having soldiers under me: and I say to this man, Go, and he goeth; . . . and to my servant, Do this, and he doeth it." When Jesus heard it, He marveled and said, "I have not found so great faith, no, not in Israel." Then Jesus said to the centurion, "Go thy way; and as thou hast believed, so be it done unto thee." And his servant was healed in the selfsame hour (Matt. 8:5-13; cf. Luke 7:1-10).

This was a crucial case. The disease was incurable, the subject a mere servant, the suppliant unworthy, the means to be employed was a simple word in the absence of the subject. The cure, such was the nature of the case, must be instantaneous and entire, or prove a manifest failure. But as the faith of the centurion measured up to the sublime urgencies of the case, the mighty work of healing was done in the selfsame hour. The faith was the exact measure of the cure, and the two acts were inseparable. Jesus spoke, the man was every whit whole.

So it is with us. Faith brings just those blessings in kind and quantity which are made its specific object. If it is pardon, it brings pardon and the peace of reconciliation. If it is limited salvation, or change of heart, it brings regeneration. If it is a perfect cure, it brings, under proper conditions, full redemption, a pure heart, entire sanctification.

FAITH FOR SANCTIFICATION

"Have faith in God." It will cancel your guilt, disburden your soul, put a new song in your mouth, and give you beauty for ashes, the oil of joy for mourning, and the garment of praise for the spirit of heaviness.

"Have faith in God." It will bring the cleansing Blood and the quickening Spirit into contact with thy heart. It will deliver you from sin, and all that frets, and wastes, and burns, and rankles, and festers, and ulcerates within. It will put your soul to rest in God—a rest that no storm can break. . . .

"Have faith in God." It will graft you into Jesus and send back His life currents into all the avenues, and channels, and capacities of your being. It will give to your practical life, thrift, and bloom, and fruitage, crowned with a large culture of Christlike development.

"Have faith in God." And it will give you to be rooted and

grounded in love—energizing the forces of your nature with an invincible stability.

"*Have faith in God.*" And it will lift you above the world—above its tumult and strife, above its sordid pursuits and dissipations, above its sins, sorrows, and debasements—and finally it will send you sweeping through the gates washed in the blood of the Lamb; and then it will set you to singing on and on forever, "Unto him that loved us, and washed us from our sins in his own blood . . . to him be glory and dominion for ever and ever" (Rev. 1:5-6).

Oswald Chambers

(1874-1917)

Oswald Chambers is best known for *My Utmost for His Highest,* a devotional book that God has blessed for the growth and guidance of thousands of Christians.

Son of a Baptist pastor in Aberdeen, Scotland, Chambers experienced his personal conversion under the preaching of Charles H. Spurgeon.

During his college years he hungered desperately to be filled with the Spirit, and in "a little meeting held in Dunoon," he stood doggedly by faith, in the absence of any feeling, upon the promise of the Heavenly Father to give the Holy Spirit to those who asked (Luke 11:13). As the consequence, a Presence and power possessed him that revolutionized his experience and his ministry. He once summarized the experience in these words of praise: "Glory be to God, the last aching abyss of the human heart is filled to overflowing with the love of God."

Chambers' ministry of Bible teaching was cut short by death when he was 42. His last ministry was to army troops stationed in Egypt in 1917.

He has been called an "evangelical mystic," but his was the mysticism of Paul—centered in Christ and anchored to Scripture.

The message titled "Which?" is taken from *Facing Reality,* a volume of what Chambers calls "nothing more than suggestions thrown out." It would be correct to say that "Which?" is an extended outline. Nevertheless, it has been included because it expresses so clearly and potently the radical holiness proclaimed and taught by Chambers.

The crucified life is the authentic Christian life. Such a life is possible only through the death of the world-befriending ego. To Chambers, "Love is the beginning, love is the middle, and love is the end" of gospel experience and ministry. And that love is possible because the Lord "takes out that old carnal nature, root and branch and ramification, and lives inside."

The either-or character of the gospel and of Christian experience is powerfully affirmed in these somewhat sketchy lines.

Oswald Chambers is a probing reminder that true life is measured by quality, not by quantity. His brief years were packed with service and influence that continue to bear fruit today. His secret is simple: "Not myself, but my Master."

Which?*

God forbid that I should glory, save in the cross of our Lord Jesus Christ, by whom the world is crucified unto me, and I unto the world (Gal. 6:14).

God or sin must die in me. The one elementary Bible truth we are in danger of forgetting is that the gospel of God is addressed to men as sinners, and nothing else. In tracing the experimental line of church history, one notices a significant thing—whenever a voice has been raised, like John Wesley's, on behalf of God's great power to deliver from sin, instantly a reacting wave of piety occurs. It takes the form of devotion and sentimental religious activity while the real message of the gospel is lost by obliteration. After John Wesley's teaching, a protest was lodged strongly against his emphasis on a second definite work of grace, and the consequence was a revival of sentimental higher life not rooted and grounded in a changed life by God's grace.

I. *Christ or Barabbas?*

"And they crucified him" (Matt. 27:35).

Christ *versus* Barabbas—we have to choose. For a long while we can ignore sin and dwell on the fact that God is our Father, but if we

---

*Source: Oswald Chambers, *Facing Reality*. London: Simpkin Marshall, n.d.

mean by that that He forgives sin because He is loving, we make the

GOD'S HOLINESS

Atonement a huge blunder and Calvary a mistake. What does Barabbas represent? The expedient to Jesus Christ, something less radical, less emphatic, less against what we want. What is the "Barabbas" in your life and mine? Shall we give our vote for Christ or Barabbas to be crucified? Most of us have voted at one time in our history . . . against Christ. The choice is always put when we are in the ascendant, when we are not being overswayed either by Christ or Barabbas, but when we are in full possession of our powers; then God's providence puts the choice suddenly in front of us—Christ or Barabbas?

II. *Christ or the Old Man?*

"Knowing this, that our old man is crucified with him" (Rom. 6:6).

What is our "old man"? The disposition of sin in us discovered by the incoming Spirit of God when we are born from above. A Christian experiencing the first work of God's regenerating grace begins to discern this disposition, and the issue is clear that the old disposition must be crucified or the Spirit of Christ must be crucified; the two cannot remain long together. Paul states triumphantly, "Knowing this, that our old man is crucified with him . . ."

CARNALITY CRUCIFIED

It was not a divine anticipation on the part of the apostle Paul, it was a very radical, definite experience. Are those of us who have experienced God's regenerating grace prepared to go the whole length with Jesus Christ? Are we prepared to let the Holy Spirit search us until we know what the disposition of sin is, the thing that rules and works in its own way, that lusts against the Spirit of God that is in us? Will we agree with God's verdict that that disposition should be identified with the death of Jesus? If so, then thank God, it will be as dead in us as the dead Christ was as a crucified body. Beware of going on the line of "I am reckoning myself to be dead indeed unto sin" unless you have been through the radical issue of will with God. Are we willing to be so identified with the death of Jesus Christ that we know with no apology that our old man was crucified with Him?

III. *Christ or I?*

"I have been crucified with Christ; and it is no longer I . . . but Christ [that] liveth in me" (Gal. 2:20, ASV).

Christ or "I"? I mean the religious "I," the spiritual "I," the pride of spiritual possession. Have we learned the glorious, unmistakable privilege of being crucified with Christ until all that is left is Christ's flesh and Christ's blood in our flesh and in our blood where once the world, the flesh, and the devil had their way? These are tremendous things to say in the light of the way the modern mind looks at things, but not too tremendous in the light of the gospel.

IV. *Christ or the World?*

"By whom the world is crucified unto me, and I unto the world" (Gal. 6:14).

What is the world? The set of people with the ambitions, religious or otherwise, that are not identified with the Lord Jesus Christ. Paul says, "I am crucified to that world, and that world is crucified to me." When the world comes before us with its fascination and its power, it finds us dead to it, if we have agreed with God on His judgment about sin and the world.

These are not only statements made in God's Book, they are meant to be real, definite experiences in our lives. If the issue is put before you in your own life just now—Barabbas or Christ—you can no longer debate the question, you must decide; but let me plead with you to decide for Christ and have "Barabbas" crucified.

If you have been born from above and the Spirit of God is discerning in you the "old man," the disposition of sin, then make it an issue of will with Him, tell Him that you want to be identified with the death of Christ until you know that your "old man" is crucified with Christ.

If you have gone through that issue of will, then stand clear for Christ and Christ only, until "I have been crucified with Christ" is not a sentiment but a sensible fact in daily living, walk, and conversation, stamped with the otherworldliness of the life hid with Christ in God.

Samuel Chadwick

(1860-1932)

The most influential holiness preacher in England since John Wesley may well have been Samuel Chadwick. He became a fixture at the Southport Convention. He was for years the president of Cliff College. He was elected to "John Wesley's chair" as president of the Methodist Conference. He was editor of *Joyful News*. In all these capacities his avowed aim was to spread scriptural holiness.

Chadwick was the son of honest, faithful, hardworking Methodists. He was converted at age 10 and began to preach at age 16. As a lay evangelist he experienced some great revivals.

Received into the Methodist Conference, Chadwick was ordained in 1890. Until his death in 1932, at the age of 72, he remained unswervingly loyal to his Lord and his church.

"The Extra Mile" is one of the few sermons Chadwick ever published. His best-known work, *The Way to Pentecost,* was published shortly after he died and has been a powerful influence for holiness. It was one of the few books that exercised a radical effect upon my own life and work, and for it I will be eternally grateful.

Chadwick loved to preach. Norman Dunning, his biographer, quotes him as saying, "I would rather pay to preach than to be paid not to preach." His intensely evangelistic preaching was undergirded by constant prayer. "He prayed as one who lived in intimate fellowship with the Eternal."

His ministry was well received by all classes of society. Lloyd

George heard him preach at Brighton and became his friend for life. Chadwick was especially loved and heard by the working classes, who found in him a man who understood their struggles and valued their souls.

"The Extra Mile" is Chadwick at his finest, powerfully combining sound exposition with pointed application. Like the Sermon on the Mount, from which it is drawn, the message sets forth the life of holiness as love exceeding law. "The measured mile made the Pharisee; it is the extra mile that makes the Christian. The yardstick is broken in the kingdom of heaven; its religion is that which revels in the excess of legal demands, and delights in obedience without measure." His closing sentence is a nail-clincher: "This is the only religion that either God or man believes in; and the only religion by which the world can be saved."

The Extra Mile*

> *Ye have heard that it was said, An eye for an eye, and a tooth for a tooth: but I say unto you, Resist not him that is evil: but whosoever smiteth thee on thy right cheek, turn to him the other also. And if any man would go to law with thee, and take away thy coat, let him have thy cloke also. And whosoever shall compel thee to go one mile, go with him twain. Give to him that asketh thee, and from him that would borrow of thee turn not thou away* (Matt. 5:38-42, ERV).

These sayings of Jesus have been the cause of much difficulty to the Christian conscience. No man obeys them; and yet no earnest Christian is quite at ease in ignoring them. In the estimation of Christ they are of vital importance, for they are the very qualities that give proof of sonship and distinguish His followers from the rest of the world. Christians are to be known by the things in their life that are in excess of the claims of law, civilization, and duty.

Others demand restitution, recognition, and appreciation. The Christian resists not wrong, returns good for evil, and reflects the divine character in the persistence of unappreciated goodness. These

---

*Source: Samuel Chadwick, *Humanity and God.* Reprint. Salem, Ohio: Schmul Publishing Co., 1982.

"extras" are the distinguishing marks of Christianity and declare men to be sons of the Father which is in heaven. If this is the estimate Christ puts upon these things, no follower of Christ can ignore them, and it is important we should understand and obey them.

St. Matthew's Gospel is the Gospel of the Kingdom. The Sermon on the Mount is the manifesto of the King. It first sets forth the character of the citizen and then proceeds to adjust the old order to the new life. We understand perfectly His treatment of the old law. There He teaches us that obedience to the letter is not enough. Sin is a question of spirit rather than action. Its offense is in the motive, not in the transgression; in the attitude, not in the act. Hatred is murder, a lustful look is adultery, and extravagance of speech is of the evil one. God judges by the heart. That is clear.

ATTITUDES

Then we come to those precepts which are in excess of law, and set forth the Christian's spirit in social life, and define his attitude to social wrongs. Resist not evil; turn the other cheek to the smiter; submit to injustice rather than go to law; yield to the oppressor even in excess of his demand; give to the beggar, and to the borrower, lend; love your enemies; pray for persecutors; and do good to the evil and unthankful. Everything short of this is common civility and natural obligation. For those who are sons of God, the way of perfection is in the things that exceed the natural moralities of men, and the common civilities of polite society. It is the extras that make the Christian. . . .

Now, we are asked, did Jesus mean what He said? If He did, where are the Christians? If He did not, then what did He mean?

I. *The Interpretation of the Christian Extra*

There is no doubt that the literal interpretation is the easiest and simplest. There is no real difficulty about turning the other cheek, giving your cloak to the man who steals your coat, going a second mile with the man who compels you to go the first. . . . The occasions for obedience in these things are exceedingly rare. Face-slapping, robbery, and compulsion are not common in a free country. Most people would go through life without ever being required to turn the other cheek. Even in giving and lending, literal obedience to the letter would not be difficult. Christian people would gladly surrender every possession if assured it was the will of God; but when they had given all, they would have placed themselves beyond the possibility of obedience. Men would still ask, and they would have nothing left to give.

It is not the desire to shirk a difficult task that has led to the rejection of a literal interpretation of these words. The Master has just been insisting upon obedience, not to the letter but to the spirit of the law. Does He take away one letter to establish another? Is it not still an insistence upon the true spirit, beyond the region of the law in the realm of social duty? Just as obedience to law must go beyond the letter to motive, affection, and desire, so our recognition of social duty must go beyond the exactions of society, the compulsions of necessity, and the civilities of custom. The Christian must be peaceable, inoffensive, meek, benevolent, trustful.

CHRISTLIKENESS

The difficulty of a literal interpretation is its inconsistency with Christ's other teaching and His own example. He gave explicit directions to His disciples concerning their duty to people who wronged them; "and if thy brother sin against thee, go, shew him his fault between thee and him alone: if he hear thee, thou hast gained thy brother. But if he hear thee not, take with thee one or two more, that at the mouth of two witnesses or three every word may be established. And if he refuse to hear them, tell it unto the church: and if he refuse to hear the church also, let him be unto thee as the Gentile and the publican" (Matt. 18:15-17, ERV).

Obedience to these instructions would save the church much heart-burning and strife; but such obedience is very definite resistance of evil. It challenges the wrongdoer, examines the offense, and punishes the offender. There are more ways of resistance than by force; and in these directions of Christ the whole weight of the influence and authority of the church is brought to bear upon the wrongdoer.

It is contrary to Christ's own example. He resisted evil, attacked wrongdoers, and when smitten did not turn the other cheek. When He went up to Jerusalem, He found the House of Prayer turned into a house of merchandise and a den of thieves (John 2:16). He made a scourge of small cords and cast all out of the Temple, both sheep and oxen. He scattered the money of the traffickers and overthrew their tables. On another occasion He drove them out, stopped the service, and refused to let any man carry a vessel through the Temple. That is more than passive resistance; it is a vigorous aggression.

In the Judgment Hall of Caiaphas one of the officers "struck Jesus with his hand, saying, Answerest thou the high priest so?" Jesus did not turn the other cheek. He challenged the smiter. "If I have spoken evil, bear witness of the evil: but if well, why smitest thou me?" (John 18:22-23, ERV). He did not answer force with force, blow with blow, but He exposed and rebuked the wrong, and certainly did not fulfill the letter of His own saying.

The true interpretation is found in Christ's method of teaching. He taught by metaphor, allegory, parable, and proverb; and each of these methods has its own law of interpretation. The command to cut off the right hand and pluck out the offending eye is manifestly metaphorical. It is a strong figure of speech, by which He teaches that nothing is to be spared to bring misused faculties into subjection to righteousness and holiness. When surgery is essential to life, there must be no hesitation. From metaphor He passes to proverb, and gives short proverbial directions on the Christian's manner of life in the presence of the wrongs and needs of the world. Resist not evil is the general principle, and it is followed by specific occasions which illustrate its application.

Proverbs have a province and method all their own. "They embody," says Bishop Gore, "a principle of common, but not universal application, in an absolute and extreme form." Consequently they have an appearance of mutual contradiction. Every proverb may be challenged by another proverb that flatly contradicts it, and yet both are true. Look at one or two. "Take care of the pence, and the pounds will take care of themselves." Be mindful of the trifles, and the great things will not need much attention. But in caring for pence, men lose the capacity for dealing with pounds. They become pettifogging, absorbed in trifles, and ingenious in things of no value. So there come such proverbs as: "Penny-wise and pound-foolish," and "Spoiling a ship for a pen'orth of paint." Settle the great fundamentals and broad principles, and leave details to fall naturally into place.

Take another proverb: "Look before you leap," which means, Never try to jump a ditch till you have measured it; never undertake anything till you have calculated all the forces and countered all the difficulties. Very good advice; but the people who are always measuring ditches never jump any. It is wonderful what critics they become, but they lose their capacity for initiative and enterprise. They can discover impossibilities, but they never accomplish anything. So the proverb "Nothing venture, nothing have" goes right in the teeth of this prudent wisdom. Instead of stopping to measure the ditch, shut your eyes and jump. Better miss your jump than lose the capacity for daring. . . .

This contradictoriness of proverbs is due to their limitation of truth and absoluteness of form. They state a general, but not universal, principle as if it were the whole truth. Each speaks with authority, making no allowance for limitation or exception.

Christ's proverbs are no exception to this peculiarity. What does He say? "Resist not evil." That is simple, absolute, complete. It recognizes no limitations and makes no allowance for exceptions. Yet Christ's own teaching and example show us that there are both limitations and exceptions. It is a principle of general but not universal application; and it is necessary to determine the extent of its obligation. To deduce from it a doctrine of absolute and universal nonresistance is to pervert its teaching and to exalt the letter above the spirit.

So long as the wrong is personal and private, it is a Christian's duty to bear it in the spirit of meekness; but when it is wrong done to others for whom we are responsible, resistance becomes a duty. If a man's child is in peril through the mad freak of human fiends, is he to stand by with placid patience and see it outraged and murdered? Is it not his duty to strike for his child? If nonresistance were absolute, there would be an end of discipline, civilization, and organized life: anarchy would be rampant and destruction inevitable.

The prohibition against going to law is a sound rule of life. It is a man's wisdom, generally speaking, to keep clear of litigation. St. Paul condemns the Corinthians because they took their contentions before the civil court. But is a man never to resort to law? Can we live and enjoy the social and civic privileges of a community, and ignore its obligations? Even though we may forgive an offense against our own property, have we not responsibility to our neighbors? Are we at liberty to turn loose upon society men who will plunder its property and imperil its security? There are times when the plain duty of the Christian is to hand a lawbreaker over to law.

Does the command to give and to lend impose indiscriminate charity as a Christian duty? Ought we to give to everyone that asks, and lend to every man that would borrow? One of the curses of the land is the indiscriminate charity of good people. The scriptural rule is, "If any will not work, neither let him eat" (2 Thess. 3:10, ERV), and it is no part of a Christian's duty to provide for men too lazy to work. What it does mean is that possessions are to be held in stewardship for God, and at the disposal of a brother's need. "Whoso hath the world's goods, and beholdeth his brother in need, and shutteth up his compassion from him, how doth the love of God abide in him?" (1 John 3:17, ERV).

Exceptions do not excuse a rule but prove it. Care must be taken lest in turning from the letter, we lose also the spirit. These commands are binding. The follower of Christ must be a man of peace, meekly enduring wrong, suffering loss, enduring hardship, full of compassion and simple faith. A contentious spirit, full of wrangling, always on the defense, is not Christian. Going to law as a rule is neither seemly nor wise. Good must be returned for evil, for only by good can evil be overcome, and our business is not the punishment of sinners but their salvation. Our service must not be grudgingly rendered, but cheerfully, and in excess of necessity. Our stewardship must be a reality, and the needs of the unfortunate supplied, hoping for all and despairing of none. Such was the life of our Lord, and such also must be ours.

COMMANDS OF JESUS BINDING

II. *The Example of the Extra Mile*

Let us look at the command concerning the extra mile as an example of the spirit of the Christian life. "Whosoever shall compel thee to go one mile, go with him twain." The reference is to public transport service. Roman troops had power to requisition able-bodied men. Marching through a district, they could compel a man to act as porter or guide within a certain area or limit. Such service was not popular. The government was alien and hated. Often the demand was inconvenient as well as laborious and was apt to be rendered in a reluctant and complaining spirit. Christ's command is that even when service is compulsory and unreasonable, it should not be rendered in a sullen and slavish spirit, but readily, cheerfully, and in excess of the demand.

Such compulsions are happily far removed from the modern conditions of life. There remain but few occasions when we can be impressed into unwilling service in the interests of the state. But compulsory service is still with us. In every life there are circumstances that force us to unwelcome tasks. Every man has duties that are undertaken not of choice but of necessity. They are the measured mile we are compelled to travel, and the Master says they are not to be undertaken in a spirit of angry rebellion or sullen repining, to be growled at and groaned under, but in a spirit of cheerfulness that is ready to give double the demand. Compulsions are to be regarded as opportunities. . . . The bitterness of the first mile is to be cured by adding a second.

ACCEPTING THE UNPLEASANT

The Christian religion is not the religion of the measured mile.

It was the religion of the Pharisee. With him everything was measured, and with scrupulous care he sought to meet its exact demands. It was a religion of law expressed in hard and fast regulations, to which he gave a cold and calculating obedience down to the utmost minutiae of life. Jesus hated the Pharisee's religion. He abhorred its slavish spirit, its mechanical exactness, its measured precision, and said of it: "Except your righteousness shall exceed the righteousness of the scribes and Pharisees, ye shall in no wise enter into the kingdom of heaven" (Matt. 5:20, ERV). The measured mile made the Pharisee; it is the extra mile that makes the Christian. The yardstick is broken in the kingdom of heaven; its religion is that which revels in excess of legal demands, and delights in obedience without measure.

All virtue begins with the excess of necessity.

DUTY FREELY CHOSEN

There can be no virtue in compulsory obedience. If a thing is done because it cannot be helped, what reward is there? If obedience is yielded only to force, what merit is there in obedience? If the march is at the point of a bayonet, there is no room to boast over the marching. . . . The value and preciousness of virtue are in its voluntariness. There is no virtue in necessity, no religion in compulsion, no credit in obedience that has no choice. That principle underlies all the relationships of life. There is nothing precious anywhere till the region beyond necessity and compulsion has been reached. In service it is the extra that tells. So long as service scrupulously measures its mile, its wages are its reward. . . . It is the service not in the contract that makes it precious; service rendered not for pay, but under the inspiration of love. The sacredness of toil begins where the compulsion of wages ends.

It is the same in friendship. There is a measured mile of propriety, self-respect, and social obligation. It is regulated by the demands of society, for civility, courtesy, and etiquette. The less real the friendliness, the more frigid and careful is the observance of its rules. We never take liberties with strangers. Friendship that is always exact and under constraint has neither worth nor soul. True friendship begins where the compulsion of propriety ends, and conventionalities are lost in the freedom of mutual enthusiasm and affection. Second-mile friendship is the most precious thing in the world. It does not consider exactions, but leaps with joy to every opportunity of service. *Must* is lost in *may*, and sacrifice is its highest joy.

If this be true in things human, how much more must it be true in things divine? In religion, above all, it is true that its value and preciousness are in its freedom and spontaneity. So long as ought and must are the forces behind our worship and service, it is profitless to us and an abomination to God. While God is regarded as a hard Master, exacting His due with merciless precision, we shall find in religion neither joy nor power. The test is in the extra mile. Many keep their religion at the irreducible minimum. They pray as much as they must to escape being lost, go to worship as much as they are obliged for the maintenance of their religious respectability, and give no more than is necessary to save their reputation.

CHRISTIAN LOVE BRINGS JOY

God hates the irreducible minimum and scorns the gift brought out of necessity and for the sake of reputation. He keeps His eye on the extra. He loves hilarity in worship and service. The grudging spirit and compulsory service He will not have. Temple treading, studied attitudes, and polished platitudes He abominates as mockery and hypocrisy. He seeks soul, not machinery; the love of sons, not the cringing obedience of slaves.

There is no way of reaching the second mile except over the first. We cannot begin at the second; it is a continuation of the first, and the first must be done before the second can be begun. Spontaneity and delight are reached through fidelity to the compulsions and necessities of duty. The servants in the parable of the talents did not enter into the joy of their Lord until they had proved their faithfulness to the obligations of their trust. They had toiled with no other incentive than a good conscience, and the hope of commendation when their Lord should return (Matt. 25:14-23). The way to the paradise of joy is by the rugged path of duty. It is the reward of discipline and perseverance.

RIGHTEOUSNESS INVOLVES DUTY

It is so in everything. There is often a toilsome stage of drudgery about halfway across the measured mile. When Joash, king of Israel, came to see the dying prophet, he was commanded to shoot out of the window facing eastward; then he was commanded to take the arrows and smite upon the ground. "He smote thrice, and stayed." The dying Elisha was wroth with him for stopping at the third stroke instead of going on to the sixth (2 Kings 13:14-19).

We are not told how many strokes are necessary for complete conquest, but we usually manage to stop halfway. One [blow] is struck with enthusiasm; two, from a sense of duty; three, of necessity; and then we seek an excuse to stop. Most people fail about halfway; they stop short of mastery and never find the ease and joy of efficiency sustained by enthusiasm. Who does not know the drudgery stage in music, where unmusical scales have to be practiced by the hour? In languages there is the dreary toil of irregular forms and the technique of idioms. The artist and the nurse, the tradesman and the professor, the soldier and the scholar, have all to go over the measurements, regulations, and compulsions of the initiatory mile.

DUTY IS NOT ENOUGH

The religion of the Pharisee was good as far as it went; its fault was that it did not go far enough. "Ye tithe mint and anise and cummin, and have left undone the weightier matters of the law, judgement, and mercy, and faith: but these ye ought to have done, and not to have left the other undone" (Matt. 23:23, ERV).

Never shirk an irksome task. "The surest way to escape a difficulty is to face it plump." The man who will not master the things that are hard to him can never come to skill and delight in his task. It is through the compulsions of the first mile we reach the joys of the second. We must learn to obey law if we would be free, and to serve if we would be fit to rule. Duty is the first word, though it is not the last.

The spirit in which the first mile is traveled will decide whether we ever walk the second. If the mile of necessity is accomplished at the point of the bayonet, the moment the point is withdrawn the march will end. The traveler that is rebellious and reluctant will never go on an extra yard.

The second mile is reached by doubling the first. Whatever the exaction of a difficult or irksome task, double it. If it demands an hour as a minimum, give it two; if three strokes will just do it, give it six. One day I sat reading in the corner of a room where a girl was brought, pouting, for her music practice. She was compelled to play for an hour every day. The piano was opened, after much trouble the stool was adjusted, and, limp and listless, she began her task. Every few minutes she stopped to look at the clock, and twice went to see if it had not stopped. The moment the hour struck, bang went the piano and away she scampered. Clerks and workmen leave their tasks often with a similar sigh of relief. Such never get to the second mile. They spend all their days in the incompetence and joyless drudgery of the first.

The same rule holds in religion and morals. Perfection, power, and joy are found in the voluntary excess of legal exaction. The man who doubles what is generally acknowledged to be sufficient is the man who discovers the secret of holy and happy religion. If for prayer and meditation an hour is necessary, add a second and you shall have power with God and prevail. If giving a tenth is duty that taxes the generous instincts of the soul, double it, and giving will become a delight. By exceeding the measure the sense of exaction is lost. Adding the voluntary to the compulsory delivers the soul from the necessity for compulsion. That is the way to lose the duty in the joy.

GIVING ALL BRINGS JOY

In this way the spirit of the second mile is anticipated in the first. Hard work done for pleasure is never a burden. Recreation would be toil if it were compulsory. By the same law compulsion may become delight, and drudgery a pleasure, if undertaken in a free spirit, and inspired by a great motive. The spirit of consecration that accepts all duties as in the Father's will, all drudgery as opportunity, and all exaction as privilege, will turn repining into gladness, and set the Decalogue to music.

This is the spirit of the children of God. Not a resentful, contentious spirit, striving for its rights, and repining over its wrongs; not a mechanical or grudging obedience to the exactions of unwelcome duty, without exhilaration, graciousness, or power; not a hard, unsympathetic, unbelieving greed in the presence of misfortune and want; but a spirit that suffers meekly, serves cheerfully, and ministers joyfully is the spirit of the Christian life. This is the only religion that either God or man believes in; and the only religion by which the world can be saved.

HOLINESS IS LOVE EXCEEDING LAW

Andrew Johnson

(1876-1959)

Andrew N. Johnson was described after his death in 1959 as "one of the very brilliant graduates of Asbury College." Following his graduation there in 1903, he received graduate degrees from other schools, including a Ph.D. from Milton University.

An elder in the Kentucky Conference of the Methodist Episcopal Church, South, Johnson labored as an evangelist throughout the United States and in Canada and Mexico. The memoirs section of the Journal of the Kentucky Conference for 1960 says, "He preached in brush arbors, schoolhouses, missions, small churches, tent and camp meetings, and in large churches with great ease and effectiveness." His zeal for Christ often carried him to the streets where he would exhort passersby to come to Christ. W. L. Clark, who conducted Johnson's funeral, said, "At the Annual Conference he often held street meetings in which the saints were blessed and sinners made to tremble."

Andrew Johnson was a fighter. A special target of his crusading zeal was the liquor industry. John Paul, writing in *The Herald* after Johnson's death, said, "He was one of the great temperance champions, opposing liquor and the liquor traffic." Energetic opposition to the liquor industry was almost a hallmark of the holiness movement in those days, and Johnson could always be found at the front of the battle.

"A Scriptural Putting" reflects the controversy that was red-hot in Johnson's day between "eradicationists" and "gradualists," the former contending for an instantaneous deliverance from in-

bred sin, the latter for deliverance by degrees across a period, usually one's life span, of time. Andrew Johnson makes his case for instantaneous cleansing by an appeal to the meaning and tenses of the verbs employed in the Greek New Testament. Some listeners must have found this heavy going, but if they couldn't always follow his discussion, they had no doubt about his conclusion.

The sermon also reflects the controversy between the "eradicationists" and the "suppressionists." Again, Johnson makes his point emphatically and clearly. What is "put off" is carnality, what is "put under" is humanity. Bodily appetites are suppressed, but sin is destroyed.

A Scriptural Putting*

That ye put off . . . the old man . . . that ye put on the new man, which after God is created in righteousness and true holiness (Eph. 4:22, 24).

Since man by nature is wrong, being tainted and corrupted by the Fall, it is the glorious work of grace to bring him back to original righteousness. The fact that he has been utterly deprived of divine life necessitates the entire reconstruction in every phase and feature of the intellect, sensibilities, and will. Hence the plan of salvation in the scheme of redemption was devised with reference to the restoration of a lost and fallen race.

Poets have written, philosophers have reasoned, and theologians have argued concerning this theme of themes. Angels have desired to look into its mysteries, and flaming evangels have proclaimed it to the ends of the earth. The greatest and most logical of all the apostles thoroughly analyzed the subject. Let us observe, therefore, how beautifully and tactfully he presents the matter in his Epistles to the churches.

I. *Put On.*

In Eph. 4:22-24 he exhorts them to put off the old man and put on the new man. In Galatians he declared that so many as had been

---

*Source: *Twentieth Century Holiness Sermons.* Louisville, Ky.: Pentecostal Publishing Co., n.d.

baptized into Christ had put on Christ (3:27). The Romans were admonished to put on the Lord Jesus Christ and not to make provisions for the flesh (13:14). These teach that some superior and extraneous force must be brought into requisition. When the earth, for instance, was a nebulous mass of chaos, it was entirely impossible for it to evolve itself, under the action of the centripetal and centrifugal forces, into cosmic symmetry and beauty. The application of an outside or external agency was necessary.

GOD ACTS FIRST

Just so the Eternal Spirit of God must move upon or over the lost soul. A divine element evidently must be introduced, the heavenly exotic must be planted, life from God must be imparted. Even physical life as we know it came not, as some agnostics would have us believe, from the sparks of impinging worlds, or the fortuitous concourse of atoms, but through the principle of biogenesis—life from preceding life.

The human body, with all its organic functions and skillful arrangements, cannot extend its existence without constant supplies of rich nourishment appropriated from the external realm. The mind itself must receive instruction and information by external perception. The body would dwarf and die and the mental life fail of development left to themselves. Food for the former and truth for the latter . . . supplied by the intervention of externalities is the law of extended existence in the physical and metaphysical world.

BORN FROM ABOVE

This rule . . . applies with double force in regard to the salvation and preservation of the soul. Everywhere in the Bible we are besought to look beyond and above ourselves for the help that was laid upon One that was mighty. Ye must be born from above is the sine qua non of entrance into the Kingdom. Every fluttering bird, struggling beast, and sprinkling priest in the old dispensation, representing the necessity of external agency, point to Jesus, the antitype by whom and through whom alone we are to receive life and life more abundantly. The dry bones of the valley in Ezekiel's vision rattled, rose, and came together at the voice of prophecy, and were bound with sinew and clothed with flesh; and yet all this was effected by an external force, as was the finishing touch, the gust from the winds of heaven that gave them life.

Again, it is necessary that the new man (a real principle of divine life) be put on. Formal works and ritualistic services, which are often furnished as substitutes, are not sufficient to regenerate. "Not by works of righteousness which we have done, but according to his mercy he saved us, by the washing of regeneration, and renewing of the Holy Ghost" (Titus 3:5). The sculptor may, with chisel and hammer, bring the perfection of form from the rough block of crude marble, but he cannot add to the polished piece of statuary, however beautiful he may make it, that indefinable and inestimable boon of real life. . . . Yet the creative genius of the "immortal" artist could as easily and nearly superinduce the essential element of life to his specimens as the priest or preacher could impart divine life around the Communion rail or at the baptistery. Forms and ceremonies can never impart the grace which they, in the divine economy, are used to signify. Nothing short of a personal and appropriate contact with divinity will enliven the soul, kindle holy fire upon the altar of the heart, and establish within the individual the principle of life. . . .

II. *Put Under.*

HUMANITY DISCIPLINED

"I keep under my body, and bring it into subjection: lest that by any means, when I have preached to others, I myself should be a castaway" (1 Cor. 9:27). Here is the scripture that teaches the true doctrine of suppression. *What* we are to suppress or keep under is the question. The new man is to be put on, and the outward man is to be put under, suppressed. What wholesome advice this. There are natural appetites that must be guarded, physical infirmities that need to be watched, and legitimate desires to be kept in bounds of temperance. It is the greatest of fallacies to call these things sin, for it is plainly stated in the Bible that every sin that a man doeth is without the body. Our physical members are to be yielded as servants of righteousness unto holiness. The body itself is to be presented a holy sacrifice in order to prove the good, acceptable, and perfect will of God.

It takes more than the physical and chemical elements that . . . make up the external . . . part of the human organization to constitute sin. The intelligence, motive, and will must be brought into play, and in them are invested the power to willfully transgress a known law—to commit sin. "The soul that sinneth, it shall die" (Ezek. 18:4, 20). How absurd, then, that antinomian view that after regeneration the *soul* cannot sin, but the *body* sins constantly and necessarily.

There are other teachers who, while they do not claim that the body per se commits actual sin, yet contend that sin (inbred) dwells in the flesh (body). According to this theory the Atonement is insufficient, [and] the mission of Christ who came to destroy the works of the devil is a failure. If Satan could inject sin in the body and Christ could not take it out, the whole plan of salvation would come to a halt, and . . . hell would shout the victory over the Lamb.

Such is not possible, for the keys of death and hell and the grave are hanging to the girdle of the King of Kings and Lord of Lords. Besides, the term "flesh" as used in these connections means the carnal mind. Hence there is no reason in the universe why we should not know the truth which makes us free indeed—free from sin—and gives us fruit unto holiness.

Let us then, as Paul, keep our bodies under and bring them into subjection; in other words let us "suppress" them and by so doing impress the world around us that there is a reality in the holiness which we profess. We will have plenty to occupy us in warding off the enemy, and subjugating and regulating the outer man, without keeping a little supply of sin in some remote corner of our existence, the "suppression" of which is thought to be necessary to give us employment and keep us humble. Therefore put the body under and be not a castaway.

III. *Put Off.*

"That ye put off concerning the former conversation the old man" (Eph. 4:22). "Knowing this, that our old man is crucified . . . that the body of sin might be destroyed" (Rom. 6:6). The Greek word for "put off" is *apothesthai* and the one for "destroyed" in the passage quoted is *katargeō.* The meanings of these words respectively . . . are first, to *thrust away, to reject.* The second one, *to make idle, to render inoperative, to bring to naught.*

In order that we may understand the strength, intensity, and nature of these words . . let us . . . see how the divinely inspired writers employed them. Acts 7:27: "But he that did his neighbour wrong thrust him away *[apōsato].*" Acts 13:46: "It was necessary that the word of God should first have been spoken to you: but seeing ye put it from *[apōtheisthe]* you, . . . we turn to the Gentiles." Rom. 11:1: "I say then, Hath God cast away *[apōsato]* his people? God forbid." 1 Tim. 1:19: "Holding faith, and a good conscience; which some having put away *[apōsamenoi]* concerning faith have made shipwreck." Rom. 3:3: "Shall their unbelief make the faith of God without effect *[katargēsei]?*" 1 Cor. 1:28: "And things which are not, to bring to nought *[katargēsē]* things that are." 1 Cor. 2:6: "Nor of the princes of this world, that come to nought" *[katargoumenōn].*

These instances reveal the potency of the word for *put off* and also *destroy.* The man who thrust away Moses certainly did not desire to "suppress" him as a slave, but with all the earnestness of an irritated soul he wished to get rid of him or to banish him from his presence or absolutely have nothing in common with him. The same is true in regard to the Jews' attitude toward the gospel of Christ delivered to them. They utterly ignored it and rejected it with such emphasis and decision as to cause the apostle to leave them and turn to the Gentiles. This is a case of complete antipathy toward and entire separation from something.

DECISIVE ACTION

When the question was asked, "Has God cast away his people?" the same word was employed. Here it can mean nothing else than perfect separation from—every bond of union, every cord of attachment forever severed. Of course the reply was negative, but the meaning of the verb could have been no stronger had such been the attitude toward His people. The shipwreck of Hymenaeus and Alexander doesn't favor the theory of the suppressionists very much, if the old man is to be scuttled, twisted, torn, and smashed like lightning, wind, and wave demolish a ship.

The term destroy speaks for itself. If the old man is crucified that the body of sin might be destroyed, it begins to look as though there is a faint possibility of getting rid of this troublesome "nature." The references from Corinthians are easily understood and are decidedly on the side of the eradicationist. The strongest word, probably, is the one used in Col. 2:11: "In whom also ye are circumcised with the circumcision made without hands, in putting off the body of the sins of the flesh by the circumcision of Christ." It is *apekdusei,* found . . . only in this passage. *Apo* means "from" and *ek* also means "from," both united means "sure enough" from. So if language stands for anything, we can be completely cleansed and entirely delivered from the old man or inbred sin in this life and throughout eternity. Praise God! . . .

CLEANSED IN THIS LIFE

Since the "old man" can and must be put off in this life, at what particular time . . . may this work be accomplished?

As this sin principle . . . cannot be repented of, forgiven, adopted, or regenerated, it is safe, reasonable, scriptural, in harmony with experience, and consistent with the various creeds of Christendom to say that our complete riddance therefrom is not effected in, by, or at the moment of conversion. Nor will it do to deny the existence of original sin when it is so plainly taught, largely admitted, and sensibly felt.

SECOND BLESSING

Granting, for the sake of argument, that there is no native depravity, how then can we account for the universality of guilt, the universality of death, and the universality of the Atonement? . . . Paul, in the third chapter of 1 Corinthians, calls it carnality. "I, brethren, could not speak unto you as unto spiritual, but as unto carnal, even as unto babes in Christ. I have fed you with milk, and not with meat: for hitherto ye were not able to bear it, neither yet now are ye able. For ye are yet carnal" (vv. 1-3). They were babes in Christ, certainly regenerated, still they were carnal. . . .

Once more, it is claimed that if people can be cleansed from all inbred sin in this life, their posterity would be born pure. If the parents are holy, the children will not be possessed with the inbred sin. That may sound plausible, but there is more sound than sense in it. "But wilt thou know, O vain man," that superinduced qualities are not transmitted by natural generation? . . . Holiness in the parents of the child was acquired by a special act of faith on the part of the individual and is not transferable. The presence of this holiness in their hearts expels sin. Holiness is not extended in this form to the child, hence there is nothing of the acquired nature of holiness in its heart. The absence of holiness therein opens the gate for the presence of inbred sin, as all must have one or the other. . . . The genealogical inheritance of the child accrues from a more remote ancestry, even from Adam.

The new man, therefore, must be put on, the outward man must be put under, the inward man put right, and the old man put off; hence *the scriptural putting.*

H. Orton Wiley
(1877-1961)

Just before the turn of the century pharmacist H. Orton Wiley was called to preach. In 1906 he was ordained by Phineas F. Bresee and was destined to become the leading theological influence in the Church of the Nazarene for several generations.

A native of Nebraska, he grew up in Oregon and California. His career was in the western United States, chiefly as an educator but also as a pastor. He served as president of Northwest Nazarene College in Idaho for 10 years and twice as president of Pasadena College in Pasadena, Calif. For 8 years he edited the *Herald of Holiness.*

His influence as a writer reached its climax with the publication of his three-volume *Christian Theology.* It has furnished holiness people, especially preachers, a definitive and comprehensive discussion of systematic theology. Wiley never stammered in his advocacy of Wesleyan holiness theology. Nevertheless, his spirit was irenic and teachable, and he learned from all historic and contemporary streams of theological thought. His major work reflects this breadth of mind and depth of love.

In pulpits, classrooms, and camp meetings Dr. Wiley wielded a gently powerful influence over the thinking and living of multitudes. His exegesis of Scripture, formulation of theology, and preaching of the gospel were reinforced by a manner and lifestyle that endeared him to classes and congregations wherever he served.

Wiley's death in 1961 had almost the character of the closing

of an era in holiness circles. We have been awaiting another theological opus that will do for present and future learners what Wiley's careful but fervent theology did for other grateful generations.

"God's Plan for His Church" was preached at Berkeley, Calif., Church of the Nazarene. Wiley had gone there in 1916 to serve as pastor while pursuing graduate studies at Pacific School of Religion. He makes large use of Scripture, drawing from the experiences of Moses and Israel those principles and methods that he intended to use to assure revival, outreach, and growth in the church he pastored.

He did not expect the church to prosper without sacrifice, labor, and faith. All human endeavor, however, would be unavailing apart from the power of the Holy Spirit. That power was available to make prophets of all the Lord's people.

God's Plan for His Church*

Enviest thou for my sake? would God that all the Lord's people were prophets, and that the Lord would put his spirit upon them! (Num. 11:29).

The children of Israel were on their way to Canaan. They had escaped the cruel bondage of Egypt and had made their way . . . to Kadesh-barnea, where they were to enter upon the inheritance which God had sworn to their father Abraham would be theirs. But they were fearful and unbelieving and for their doubt were turned back into the wilderness to wander for 40 long years, until the carcasses of those who were disobedient should fall in the wilderness. . . .

No greater task ever came to a man than the task which was given to Moses—that of leading 3 million people out of bondage into a new country. How often he was in communion with heaven, and yet how often he was pressed almost out of measure!

At the time of the event of which our text forms a part, this great company were in the wilderness . . . tenting from place to place and living upon the manna which fell from day to day. As far as the eye

---

*Source: H. Orton Wiley, *The Harps of God and Other Sermons,* comp. and ed. Ross E. Price. Kansas City: Beacon Hill Press of Kansas City, 1971.

could see, there was nothing but desert sand and dwarfed shrubs with an occasional oasis. It was a great contrast to the fertile fields of Goshen with their bounteous harvests of melons, cucumbers, leeks, and onions. Thus their present state suffered greatly in comparison with the former situation in Egypt. Not content with manna, they fell to lusting for flesh to eat. When Moses heard them weeping in their tents and listened to their complaints, the burden of the people became so great that he cried unto the Lord and said:

> Wherefore hast thou afflicted thy servant . . . that thou layest the burden of all this people upon me? Have I conceived all this people? have I begotten them, that thou shouldest say unto me, Carry them in thy bosom, as a nursing father beareth the sucking child, unto the land which thou swarest unto their fathers? Whence should I have flesh to give unto all this people? . . . I am not able to bear all this people alone, because it is too heavy for me *(Num. 11:11-14).*

Every true minister has his times of mourning over those that are looking with longing eyes toward the things of the present world in utter forgetfulness of the blessings of the eternal world. And well might he mourn to God over those who are so in love with the old that they are complaining about their present state. Even today the devil seeks to sidetrack church members from their main goal. He would have them think that the homeland of heart holiness is not all that God's promise said it would be. And he even seeks to discourage God's appointed leader into thinking that the people will not follow him into the experience of entire sanctification, and to make him think that he is therefore wasting his energies in fruitless efforts as he seeks to lead them into such an experience.

HOLINESS OF HEART

Yet we must never lose sight of the fact that it is the business of the Church of the Nazarene to lead people into the land which God swore unto our fathers to give them:

> The oath which he sware to our father Abraham, that he would grant unto us, that we being delivered out of the hand of our enemies might serve him without fear, in holiness and righteousness before him, all the days of our life *(Luke 1:73-75).*

Our business is to lead people into the experience of holiness. This is our goal. We are to lead them out of . . . bondage to their actual sins into a place of justification. We are then to lead them into the experience of entire sanctification. We shall have to deal with many backsliders who, having come up to the light of holiness, have doubted and drawn back and are now wandering around in the wilderness of doubts and fears . . . longing secretly for the old life of bondage again.

Now it was at the point of his utter helplessness that God came to the help of Moses. God has two ways of helping His leaders. One is to strengthen them by His Spirit; the other is to lay the burden upon others, giving them the same Spirit which will cause them to assume responsibility and carry on the work.

> And the Lord said unto Moses, Gather unto me seventy men of the elders of Israel, whom thou knowest to be the elders of the people, and officers over them; and bring them unto the tabernacle of the congregation, that they may stand there with thee. And I will come down and talk with thee there: and I will take of the spirit which is upon thee, and will put it upon them; and they shall bear the burden of the people with thee, that thou bear it not thyself alone *(Num. 11:16-17).*

And Moses did as the Lord had commanded him

> . . . and gathered the seventy men of the elders of the people, and set them round about the tabernacle. And the Lord came down in a cloud, and spake unto him, and took of the spirit that was upon him, and gave it unto the seventy elders: and it came to pass, that, when the spirit rested upon them, they prophesied, and did not cease *(Num. 11:24-25).*

This event is an illustration of

I. *God's method of carrying on His work*

God's method is not the formal method of mere organization, but organization as the result of inspiration. I am surprised at the heartless endeavors which many of God's good people are making. They expect no results and therefore have none. They think the day of revivals is past, and for them it is. That it is hard to grapple with a lustful, pleasure-seeking, complaining, worldly people will be admitted by all, but people of strong faith will accept it as a divine challenge. We are a revival people. We stand for holiness of heart and life, and for aggressive evangelism. Such a people can never rest satisfied unless men and women are being saved and sanctified wholly. . . . God helping us, we mean to pay the price for its realization. And we will surely find that there is a price to pay for deep spirituality and for successful work in the soul-saving business. You may . . . not suffer persecution when you are not doing

HOLINESS AND EVANGELISM

any damage to the devil's kingdom, but . . . those who would injure hell's domain must suffer for it.

Now I believe that God talks to you. And I believe that you desire that I take an aggressive advance in soul-saving work. Furthermore, I have every reason to believe that you will stand shoulder to shoulder with me in this great work. We have drawn the sword and have thrown away the scabbard.

We note that Moses cried unto the Lord out of the anguish of his heart because of the burden laid upon him. It will take anguish of heart and sincere crying unto the Lord to bring people into the land of salvation. There has never been a great revival without strong crying and tears, without anguish of heart and heavy burdens. Enquire how many are thus bearing the burden, and you will find the principal reason for a lack of revivals.

Now the divine program is not that God's leader bear all the burden of the work. God calls others to shoulder their part of the burden. And as Moses gathered the elders of his people together . . . God spoke to them all and took His Holy Spirit, wherewith He had anointed Moses, and put Him upon the 70 elders, and at once they began to prophesy.

In this incident I catch a gleam of the Lord's plan for His people today. And looking down across the centuries I see the fulfillment of this prophecy in the marvelous outpouring of the Holy Spirit on the Day of Pentecost.

This event is an illustration of

II. *The divine plan for spreading scriptural holiness*

Here we have the dawning of the revelation of the plan of God for holiness evangelism. It is the first draft of God's program for the Church. It may be rough, but it is workable. It was destined to be brought to perfection in the fullness of time. It is our purpose to examine this plan and to adopt it as our own. I am sure that all of us want nothing other than the will of God.

1. The first step is *organization.* God never designed that His Church should be a one-man affair. It has leadership, to be sure, and it must be well organized. But this organization must include all the people. God sets these in the body as it pleaseth Him. So God instructed Moses to gather men to be elders and set them in their proper places around the Tabernacle.

2. The second step is *revelation.* There hovered over the Tabernacle the mighty pillar of cloud and fire, and the Shekinah dwelt upon the mercy seat. They had seen the glory . . . many times. Heretofore to them it had been silent. Only Moses, the servant of the Lord, did speak with God and hear His voice. But this morning there was something different in the Church. That mighty Presence which had awed them, and before which they had stood with bowed heads and uncovered feet, now burst forth into utterance. God came down and spoke with Moses and with *them,* as there was revealed to them the transforming vision of God himself.

DOCTRINE AND LIFE

Now the Church of the Nazarene is not founded merely upon doctrine. True it is that we hold to the old-time Pauline and Wesleyan doctrine of entire sanctification, but we hold to doctrine only as it ministers to the spiritual life. The distinguishing feature of our church is the manifestation of the divine glory. We are to see God. We are to get the glory down upon us. God is to dwell in us, and we are to stand round about the tabernacle only that He may come down and speak to us. . . . I believe that I have caught a vision of God's plan for me. I am to meet with God in His sanctuary. I am to gather out the elders, they are to stand round about the place, and the glory is to come down upon us all. We are to stand together, baptized with the mighty glory of the heavenly Shekinah.

Brothers and sisters, I am looking for the 70 elders. Seventy is a perfect number. I am looking for that number, and I believe you are here today.

THE SPIRIT'S ANOINTING

3. The third thing in this plan is *the anointing of the Holy Spirit.* "I will take of the spirit which is upon thee, and will put it upon them; and they shall bear the burden . . . with thee." We are to stand in our places round about the sanctuary, but the same Spirit is to come upon us all and we are to be actuated by the same motive, moved by the same purpose, and impelled by the same mighty power of the Spirit of God.

The great secret of power is to be found in the anointing Spirit. Human power can avail nothing. Mere organization, however perfect, will be fruitless. What the Church needs, what we need, is a mighty baptism of power, a perfect abandonment of ourselves to the Holy Ghost.

This event also suggests to us

III. *The outworkings of God's plan for the Church*

There are many who pray for the power of God, and who seem to sincerely desire the anointing of God's Spirit, who draw back when the results are seen. There is always a price to pay for deep spirituality. There is always a price to pay for every revival of the work of God. While people are going on in a merely formal way, everything seems to be pleasant. But let a servant of God be bold enough to gird on the armor and attack the devil's kingdom, and he will suffer in proportion to the damage he does to the cause of darkness.

Brethren, I have made up my mind that this life is a battle. And we need expect nothing else. Some of Dr. Bresee's sayings come to me with more force now than they did five years ago. He said at one time that he was the most hated man in the county. What he has suffered to make possible the great work of our church, no one will ever know. Yet I am convinced that we cannot rest on what he has done and suffered. We will preserve this work in the glow of holy fervor just in proportion as we are willing to do and suffer for it.

PREACHING

1. They *prophesied.* Which simply means that they preached with the attestation of divine power . . . God's message for the people.

2. There was a *continuous revival.* There was a degree of permanence. *They prophesied, and did not cease.* The Church of God is to be a revival Church. The gifts of the Spirit are to be in continuous exercise. We are not to have merely revival seasons. . . . we do believe in special revival efforts. But there is to be a continuous revival spirit. Our regular services are to be revival services. There must be a continual ingathering of souls. A great many of our own people . . . are letting down along this line. Some seem to think that the church cannot have a continuous revival. Thank God, it is not so. We can have revivals all the time. And then there will come those special seasons when the revival tide runs at its height.

3. There will be *irregularities.* There were two fellows that seemed to get out of the beaten paths and went to prophesying in the camp. Wherever there is life there will always be a leaping over the bounds of regular routine.

4. There will be *charges preferred.* Sometimes this is done by good people. There was great excitement, and a young man (notice it says a young man), one without much experience, ran and reported

that Eldad and Medad were prophesying in the camp contrary to the established order of things.

5. There was an *injunction served.* Joshua said, "*My lord Moses, forbid them.*" But Moses was a wise general superintendent who understood well the mind of God. He was gratified at the abounding life which led the people to get under the burden and share the responsibility. He was glad for a moment to feel the burden upon others. He was lifted by the Spirit of God into the realm of prophecy himself and gave utterance to the saying that was to be the culmination of the great plan of God. "*Would God that all the Lord's people were prophets!*"

IV. *This event was prophetic of the Day of Pentecost.*

The prophet Joel caught a vision of the fulfillment of this wish of Moses when he declared:

> And it shall come to pass in the last days, saith God, I will pour out of my Spirit upon all flesh: and your sons and your daughters shall prophesy, and your young men shall see visions, and your old men shall dream dreams: and on my servants and on my handmaidens I will pour out in those days of my Spirit; and they shall prophesy . . . and it shall come to pass, that whosoever shall call on the name of the Lord shall be saved *(Acts 2:17-18, 21).*
>
> And when the day of Pentecost was fully come . . . suddenly there came a sound . . . of a rushing mighty wind . . . And there appeared unto them cloven tongues like as of fire, and it sat upon each of them. And they were all filled with the Holy Ghost, and began to speak with other tongues, as the Spirit gave them utterance. . . . But Peter, standing up with the eleven, lifted up his voice, and said unto them . . . This is that which was spoken by the prophet Joel *(Acts 2:1-4, 14, 16).*

The Church is to be indwelt by the Spirit of God as the Source of her power, and she is to manifest this in prophecy. Prophecy is an utterance of the divine voice within, speaking in . . . power through the Spirit as a means of communication of blessed truth to others. Anything short of this will fail. A mere gathering together of the people is not a church. It has no more power than a club. A church is a body of people indwelt by the Holy Ghost and speaking to others under this inspiration.

"*Would God that all the Lord's people were prophets!*" Would that we all would come to our personal Pentecost! It is ready for us. . . . The fire hangs just above us. There it is like mighty pillars rising toward the skies, ready to . . . fall upon all who will take their place at the tabernacle. Oh, that God would come down and speak to us! Oh, that we might catch the vision through divine revelation! Oh, that He would take of His Spirit and put it upon us in a richer measure! Even in such a measure that all the Lord's people would at once begin to prophesy, and never cease!

True prophecy is the manifestation of the Spirit's presence and life within. It is the . . . outflow of the life within. It is a communication of the truth to others in demonstration of the Spirit and power.

"Would God that all the Lord's people were prophets!"

3

THE URGENCY OF HOLINESS

Richard S. Taylor
(1912—)

Richard S. Taylor belongs to a rare breed of men, theologians who can preach. A long, distinguished career has made him one of the best-known ministers in the holiness movement.

For 16 years he served on the faculty of Nazarene Theological Seminary as a professor of theology and missions. He also devoted some valuable years to the ministry of his church as a pastor, evangelist, and administrator.

Taylor was the founding president of Nazarene Bible College at Sydney, Australia, investing eight years of teaching and guidance there. He has preached and taught in Japan and other nations overseas from his native United States.

The discipline of one's personal life and the value of Christian culture have been dominant themes in his ministry, and he has helped hundreds of believers through his books in these areas. His theological contributions in the books *God, Man, and Salvation* and *Exploring Christian Holiness,* volume 3, *The Theological Foundations,* have been widely influential. A work in homiletics, *Preaching Holiness Today,* has been a valuable resource for those aspiring to preach the doctrine and life of holiness effectively.

Richard Taylor, through his ministry of preaching, teaching, and writing, has belonged to the entire holiness movement, highly esteemed by all its constituent churches.

"The Central Thing" expounds the sources of that love that is the essence of holiness. These sources are a pure heart, a good conscience, and an unfeigned faith. Taylor's outline simply follows the order of the text. Careful exposition and helpful illustrations inform the mind, excite the heart, and challenge the will. Like all good preaching, it leads the listener to think, to feel, and to do.

Jesse Peck advocated Christian perfection as *The Central Idea of Christianity.* But this is not an idea for the sake of mental exercise merely. The idea must become experienced reality if holiness is to be truly meaningful. "The Central Thing" is not an idea but love experienced and expressed, for "God is love." As Dr. Taylor wrote at the end of volume 3 of *Exploring Christian Holiness,* "Holiness is *knowing God* or it is an empty charade. The one controlling and continuous passion must always be to know God better."[1] This is the aim of his sermon, to enable the hearers to know God better.

---

1. *The Theological Foundations* (Kansas City: Beacon Hill Press of Kansas City, 1985), 235-36.

The Central Thing*

Now the purpose of the commandment is love from a pure heart, from a good conscience, and from sincere faith, from which some, having strayed, have turned aside to idle talk (1 Tim. 1:5-6, NKJV).

Paul has just reminded this young pastor, Timothy, of his previous instruction to see to it that his preachers in Ephesus "teach no other doctrine"; that is, that they not be permitted to go off on tangents and invent doctrinal novelties, but to stick to the basic Christian faith that Paul had taught them. The purpose of this warning to Timothy is here declared. It is that the people might not be diverted from holiness, but that they might see the *central thing,* "love from a pure heart, from a good conscience, and from sincere faith."

All sound doctrine will emphasize this; false doctrine will miss this. Paul says that when teachers and preachers stray from this central insistence, they inevitably turn aside to idle talk. "Vain jangling," the King James Version says. Satan does not care how close to the truth we come, provided we miss the center. The history of the Church down across the centuries illustrates the vain jangling that results when de-

---

*Source: Sermon manuscript.

nominations or churches emphasize ritual, gifts, miracles, prophecy, or forms of church government and miss the heart of true religion, which is love out of a pure heart, out of a good conscience, and out of sincere faith.

Love is central to the Christian religion. That is obvious to any unbiased reader of the New Testament. This verse gives an insight into love that is not always understood. It is not merely love, *period.* Even the world babbles constantly about love. But what the world means by love generally bears little relation to what the Bible means. This text is talking about Christian love. It declares that for love to be Christian, for love to be holy, it must have a threefold source: a pure heart, a good conscience, and sincere faith. Love's quality and love's expression are controlled by the heart, by the conscience, and by faith.

HOLY LOVE

It is important to be clear in our analysis of this verse, because some writers and even Bible translations associate love with a pure heart only, not with the conscience and with faith. But the *New English Bible* translates verse 5: "The aim and object of this command is the love which springs from a clean heart, from a good conscience, and from faith that is genuine." The Greek clearly supports this; therefore my message will be based on this understanding.

My outline then will be very simple: it will direct our attention to love out of a pure heart, to love out of a good conscience, and to love out of sincere faith.

I. *First, what is love out of a pure heart? It is love that is undivided in its allegiance.*

For love to be pure, it must be undivided. A young woman who is wise will not marry a man unless she is persuaded not only that he loves her but that he loves her exclusively.

1. Similarly, our love for Christ is not acceptable until it is no longer divided between Christ and *the world.* One of the saddest verses in the Bible is 1 Tim. 4:10: "Demas has forsaken me, having loved this present world" (NKJV). For some years Demas had been a member of Paul's evangelistic team. It would be presumptuous to say that Paul would use someone who had not been converted and who evidenced no love at all for Jesus. But deep in his heart, Demas' love was divided.

DOUBLE-MINDED CHRISTIANS

Paul was in prison, and the probability of his martyrdom was daily becoming more obvious. The storm clouds of persecution were extinguishing earthly hopes, and the expected return of the Lord in vengeance and power and glory had not occurred. Suddenly the world looked pretty good to Demas, and he decided he had better cut while he could. He got out. But the defection was in his heart long before it was in his heels.

While in Japan I was seeking one Monday night to instruct . . . a young Japanese woman in the doctrine of entire sanctification. She had been clearly born again some time before; but there were signs that the determined efforts of her parents to turn her from Christ were having their effect. At a certain point in the evening those of us in that little circle went to the garden and watched a full eclipse of the moon. Then I said, "Do you know why the moon is no longer shining? It is because the 'world' has come between it and its source of light." Sadly she replied, "I understand. I am afraid that I have been allowing the 'world' to come between me and Jesus and darken my soul." She too, like Demas, was double-minded. And from a double-minded heart could not flow single-minded love.

2. But neither is our love for Christ fully acceptable unless it is pure enough to be no longer divided between Christ and *self*. This probes even deeper. For it is possible to be saved from love of the world, at least in its grosser and more tawdry forms, and still not be saved from an idolatrous love of self. "My way, my rights, my plans, my feelings" can still be struggling with God's way and God's plans in my heart of hearts. The spontaneous disposition to claim my right to myself is perhaps the deepest trait in sinful human nature, and the hardest to die. A man said to E. Stanley Jones, "A dozen times a day I promise the Lord this and that, money, time—if only He will let me stay at the center."

CLEANSED FROM SELF-CENTERED LIVING

A prominent holiness leader in Holland testified that for 12 years he was a zealous Christian worker, conducting Bible studies, active in many different groups, only to find that, in his heart, he was his own lord, and Jesus Christ was his servant. This is more widespread than we suspect, perhaps even in ourselves, because the condition can be so subtle. For years Christians can hide this true state of affairs even from themselves.

Helen Temple told in a missionary book some years ago the dramatic story of David Ramirez, the Nicaraguan. After years of backsliding, in mid-life he was wonderfully reclaimed. Then at the request of a fellow worker he attended First Church of the Nazarene in Chicago to hear the pastor, H. V. Miller, who preached on total surrender. David Ramirez, a Harvard Ph.D., who understood the psychological implications of the pastor's sermon, walked out in anger and argued with his Nazarene friend. "Your pastor is wrong! No one should surrender the inner citadel of his being as completely as that, not even to God!" He went home to study the Bible in order to prove Dr. Miller wrong. But he proved himself wrong instead; and the next Sunday morning found him at the altar, dying out to self. God sanctified him and then said, "Now you are ready to go back to your own people." He became the founder of the Nazarene holiness work in Nicaragua.

COMPLETE SURRENDER

Yes, a pure heart will assure a pure love, love no longer divided in its allegiance; which means that it is no longer divided between Christ and the world and no longer divided between Christ and self.

II. *Second, what is love out of a good conscience? It is love that is uncompromising in its conduct.*

1. In order to get the picture here, we need to pause a moment to look at this faculty we call the conscience. The little boy said that conscience was that which made him tell his mother before his sister did. No, that was only prudence. Conscience is that which would prompt him to tell his mother even if he didn't have a sister. That is, the conscience is that moral faculty that perceives there is a right and there is a wrong, and that knows we ought to do the right. Furthermore, conscience is that which accuses us and makes us miserable when we do wrong, and prompts us to make it right.

But unfortunately, not every conscience is a good conscience. The Bible speaks of a "weak" conscience (1 Cor. 8:7-10); it also speaks of a "seared" conscience (1 Tim. 4:2). Many consciences are wrongly educated. A good conscience is first clear, through repentance and forgiveness; second, it is educated by the Bible. That is, our moral judgment must become a biblically trained moral judgment. This takes time beyond the new birth, even beyond entire sanctification.

Some people think some things are wrong that aren't; other people think certain things are OK that are not. They do not line up with the clear teachings of the Word. If then we are going to have a "good" conscience, in the sense of soundness in moral judgment, we must continually study the Scriptures, listen to sermons, learn to think ethically, read good books, and submit humbly and honestly to the illumination of the Holy Spirit. Only then will we be not only conscientious Christians but *wisely* conscientious Christians.

2. Now, what is love out of a good conscience? It is love that is controlled by a good conscience. Therefore, it is love that is uncompromising in its conduct. It respects law. It respects the boundaries of right and wrong. Nothing could more glaringly misinterpret the apostle Paul than *The Living Bible's* statement in Rom. 13:10 that love "is the only law you need." Love is the disposition to be fair with one's neighbor, but love alone does not always know what fairness is. Law is needed to inform love and direct its expression in ways that are pleasing to God. Love alone won't tell me to drive on the right side of the road. That is determined for me by law. In other countries it is the left side that is required.

INFORMED LOVE

3. Now let us see just how practical is the concept of love out of a good conscience:

a. Even our *love for God* needs the control of a good conscience. A lady testified in prayer meeting that for three years she had filed no IRS returns and paid no tax so that she would have more money to give to the Lord! But God doesn't want money that is given at the expense of good citizenship!

b. Certainly our *love for country* also needs to be controlled by a good conscience. If it is, we will demonstrate our love by keeping our country's laws. In many places the Bible is perfectly clear about this, in passages such as Rom. 13:1, "Let every soul be subject to the governing authorities," and verse 7, "Render therefore to all their due: taxes to whom taxes are due, customs to whom customs, fear to whom fear, honor to whom honor" (both NKJV).

c. What about our *love for the church*? Surely we should not have to be reminded that Bible Christians are conscientious church members. We will keep our church vows. We will avoid causing "divisions and offences contrary to the doctrine," as Paul puts it in Rom. 16:17; and the writer to the Hebrews says, "Obey them that have the rule over you, and submit yourselves" (13:17).

d. Then there is the *love of friends*. Will Christian love lie to protect a friend from the proper consequences of his wrongdoing? Will Christian love compromise ethical standards in order to "win" a friend? A young Christian woman was seeking to reach an unsaved, worldly-minded friend for Christ. One day the friend challenged: "Now, to be fair, since I have gone to church with

ETHICS

you, you go to the movies with me. You say you love me, now prove it!" The Christian said, "No, I will not violate my conscience." For two weeks the friend badgered her, then finally said, "I was just testing you. If you had gone with me, you would have no further influence over me." The world knows the line for Christians, even if Christians don't always seem to!

e. Even *parental love* needs the guidance of a good conscience. When disciplining me as a child, my father quoted one verse so often that I memorized it without trying! It was the second half of Rom. 14:22: "Happy is he that condemneth not himself in that thing which he alloweth." My father said, "If I allow your misbehavior by not punishing you, I will bring condemnation on myself, for I must give an account at the Judgment for the way I raise you." Fair enough! I didn't like the strappings, but I never could force myself to get very mad at a father whom I knew was seeking to be conscientious before God.

It is high time that parents—including some Christians—understand that love for children not shaped by a good conscience is not love at all, but the cruelest kind of child abuse. An Oregon law requires small children to be strapped into a protective seat while riding in cars. A huge billboard for many months showed a careless young mother driving with her small child standing in the seat beside her, unrestrained and unprotected. The caption on the billboard was, "Is this love?" Good question!

f. And certainly *love between the sexes* should be governed by a good conscience. An informed conscience knows that both premarital and extramarital sex are wrong. What could be clearer than this passage: "For this is the will of God, your sanctification: that you should abstain from sexual immorality; that each of you should know how to possess his own vessel in sanctification and honor, not in passion of lust, like the Gentiles who do not know God; that no one take advantage of and defraud his brother in this matter, because the Lord is the avenger of all such, as we also forewarned you and testified. For God did not call us to uncleanness, but in holiness. Therefore he who rejects this does not reject man, but God, who has also given us His Holy Spirit" (1 Thess. 4:3-8, NKJV).

DISCIPLINED DESIRES

As far as premarital sex is concerned, the *Revised Standard Version* understands verses 4 and 5 to be referring precisely to that: "that each one of you know how to take a wife for himself in holiness and honor, not in the passion of lust like heathen who do not know God."

So far we have sought to pinpoint the kind of love that is out of a pure heart, and the kind that is out of a good conscience. But we must not miss the equally important third member of this textual triad.

III. *Third, what is love out of sincere faith? It is love that is unhindered in its flow.*

1. Let us not forget that love is not a reservoir; it is a flow out toward others and up toward God, a flow of affection, of goodwill, of holy desire.

2. But we need to remember also that this flow is a product of sincere faith. For, you see, this love is not something we can generate within ourselves; it is a gift of grace. It is the love that is "poured out in our hearts by the Holy Spirit who was given to us" (Rom. 5:5, NKJV). It is poured out into our hearts in order that it might flow out of our hearts.

3. Our faith is the key to our love in two ways:

a. First, it is by our faith that our conscience is cleansed from condemnation through the forgiveness of our sins. But it is also by faith that we obtain a pure heart. We must believe in Christ as Sanctifier as well as Pardoner. We must believe in the power and faithfulness of the Holy Spirit to purify us from our double-mindedness—now. Our faith must be so firm and strong that it will bring the inner assurance that the work is done.

SANCTIFICATION BY FAITH

b. But second, not only are a pure heart and a good conscience dependent on faith, but faith is equally dependent on a good conscience and a pure heart, if it is to remain vital and real. That is, our faith becomes "insincere" when we begin to entertain impurity in our heart and when we begin to tamper with our conscience. When we compromise with sin, faith curls up and withers. And when faith withers, love withers too. To continue to profess faith after once being saved, when we begin to violate our conscience, is to deceive ourselves. The very chapter in which our text is located has something important to say about this. In verse 19 we are warned to keep our faith and a good conscience together. If we surrender a good conscience, we will make "shipwreck," Paul says, of our faith. But, as John Wesley says, "They who retain this"—that is, a good conscience—"do not make shipwreck of their faith."

COMPROMISE WITHERS FAITH

The process of extinguishing the light of faith can be very slow, almost imperceptible. In 1965 I held two revivals for H. E. Hegstrom in Stockholm, Sweden, one in June and the other in August. They were both held in the old YMCA auditorium. In June the room was dark and depressing. In August it was bright and cheery. What made the difference? Simply that between the two meetings Hegstrom had insisted on helping the maintenance man replace the burned-out bulbs. The room was illuminated by a single chandelier, hung many years before, with 64 bulbs. After a while a bulb burned out. Nobody noticed—can you tell the difference between the light of 64 bulbs and 63? Then another—again unnoticed. Over the years all but 4 expired. But the process was so gradual that the darkness crept up on the users of the room, stealthily, quietly, until suddenly people began to complain of the terribly poor lighting. They could scarcely see to sing a hymn or read their Bibles.

GRADUAL BACKSLIDING

What a graphic picture this is of the gradual process by which once-bright Christians, with strong and vital faith, slip into darkness, their faith finally only a name. They surrender a matter of conscience at this point, then at that point. They trim the corners here a little and there a little. They gradually let down in their prayer life, their testifying, their church attendance, their Bible reading; then next they compromise their convictions and begin watching TV shows that in their spiritual prime they would have abhorred, and going places that formerly would have held no appeal for them at all. And each time a backward step is taken, it is like a single light out of 64: The difference is so slight they hardly notice, and in each case the change is defended by an abundance of excuses and rationalizations. But finally they come to the sudden, shocking realization that their love is cold, because their heart is impure, their conscience seared, and their faith only an empty profession.

It is forever true that pure love, Christian love, the love that wins and overcomes, can only exist when it flows out of a pure heart and out of a good conscience and out of a faith that is genuine and sincere.

Let us take heart. All of us may enjoy this full blessing if we will. If we are ashamed of our lack of love, or its feebleness, or its impurity and its double-mindedness, let us come to Jesus for thorough cleansing. Let us confess our desperate depravity. If our conscience accuses us, let us repent and be forgiven. If our hearts are still divided, in their secret allegiance, between Christ

INVITATION TO HOLINESS

and the world or between Christ and self, let us confess that sad, defeated, powerless condition and allow God to so break us that He can baptize us truly with His Spirit. Then we will experience the central thing—the holiness that consists of love out of a pure heart, out of a good conscience, and out of sincere faith.

Ted E. Martin

(1911—)

Ted Martin (really *Theodore* Martin, but who knows him by that name?) combines eloquence and imagination in a way reminiscent of great Scottish and Welsh preachers after whom I have read, a few of whom I have heard. It has been my privilege to hear Martin often, and never was I disappointed in the content or delivery of his sermons. Always he challenged my thinking and my living.

He served as a pastor for 36 years, ministering to some of the largest and most exciting churches in his denomination, the Church of the Nazarene. For several years he did their radio preaching on "Showers of Blessing." He has been a frequent speaker in conventions and camp meetings.

A native of Indiana, his ministry has had international dimensions, for he labored in Canada both as a pastor and a district superintendent.

Preaching has been in the Martin blood. Ted's father, brother, and son were preachers, each of them serving with distinction, but none of them surpassing his own rich contributions to the church.

Ted retired a few years ago. His last official post was director of Nazarene News at the international headquarters of his church. He continues to bless the minds and lives of all who hear him preach.

"A Double Portion of Thy Spirit" was preached when Ted Martin pastored First Church of the Nazarene in Nashville. It reflects a concern that all of us who preach have shared or will share as we come nearer the end of our careers: how to keep a church vital and growing when it ages a few generations beyond the vision, faith, and zeal of those who founded it as a mission. How do we avoid what would seem to be, viewed in the light of history, an inevitable decline? "There must be a way to keep a movement alive though God buries His workmen." From the Old Testament and the New, from the wisdom of Elijah and Christ, Martin finds the one answer to our problem—"the personal Pentecost that awaits every believer." "There, in a crucified and Spirit-filled people, lies the hope of an ever-burning flame upon the altar of the church."

Ted Martin's preaching brings to mind something Richard Taylor wrote: "At the heart of sanctification is an emancipation from slavish dependence on the opinions of others and a confirmation of independent personhood." Martin is his own man, by the grace of Jesus Christ and in the power of the Holy Spirit.

A Double Portion of Thy Spirit*

I pray thee, let a double portion of thy spirit be upon me (2 Kings 2:9).

If the Spirit would take us today to view two scenes in very different places and at very different times, we might hear a common prayer that would express for each of us the needs of our hearts.

Are you ready to ride the magic carpet of thought, propelled by the Spirit? Well, a swish and here we are—or, where are we?

Though the landscape and mode of living seem very strange, we are at once aware of a very ordinary dialogue between an old man and a young man as they walk along the road together. This is as it ought to be, the old and young together. This is not an old man's world nor a young man's world. There is a place for both—the common ground of everyday living. The old can draw upon the ideals and courage of youth, and the young can learn from the experience and wisdom of age. The dialogue is familiar, for the old man seems to recognize that his time is short, and a deep weariness has forced him to muster his

---

*Source: Revised manuscript, first published in a local church paper, the *Nashville Weekly*.

strength to say the final things and be gone. The young man, too, seems to recognize the note of farewell and sense the weight of responsibility that will soon come upon him.

The conversation is interesting and relevant to us because it is the dialogue of change—one age about to die and another to be born. The haunting fear that something valuable will be lost in the transfer fills their hearts and ours. It has been repeated often, but is ever true, that spiritual movements scarcely outlive two or three generations. We are particularly conscious of this, for many think they can see ample evidence of erosion among us. Some even contend that the tide has gone out too far to return in our generation. Our name, they sadly say, is Ichabod. We have the unenviable lot of seeing the decline of the holiness revival that shook the beginning of this century, they assert.

This dialogue is attractive to us because we feel we share the young man's hope. There must be a way to keep a movement alive though God buries His workmen. "We are the children of the prophets and of the covenant," we remind ourselves. This cause shall not fail, nor the fire die out in our generation, if we can help it. There must be a way to be the men of God in our time that our fathers were in theirs. Perhaps we can hear something or see something here that will point it up for us. So we join the old man and the young man in their journey together.

The old man talks with a faraway look in his eyes. His conversation is not only of memory but also of unrealized vision. And these are so intermingled as to be almost inseparable. It is as though there is an eternity in his mind of yesterday and tomorrow so bound together as to be always today. The young man listens eagerly so as not to miss a word. He acts like one who has this chance only once in a lifetime and wants to lodge each word, action, and feeling forever in his memory.

He will not allow the conversation to be interrupted by those who want to warn him that the old man will soon be gone. Nor will he agree to the repeated suggestion of the old man that he be allowed to go on alone. We imagine that he is saying to himself that there must be a way in which I can be a man of my time and face its demands and opportunities. There must be a way in which I can be today, in its setting, what this old man was in his time. Well, if this was not his concern, it certainly is ours today.

But I remind you that it was not until they were alone that Elijah said to Elisha, "I have told you all I can. But you are still unsatisfied, and I will soon be gone. What do you really want?" Elisha replied, "I pray thee, let a double portion of thy spirit be upon me." Elijah answered, "Thou hast asked a hard thing: nevertheless, if thou see me when I am taken from thee, it shall be so unto thee." The dialogue then continued. Oh, if we could have heard it all. But then, what was said may not be as important as the fact of the continuing dialogue.

HUNGER

Suddenly there was a whirlwind and a chariot of fire that parted them, and Elijah was gone. Elisha looked up expectantly, but nothing happened, except there fell from the departing prophet his mantle. Disappointed, he picked it up and returned to the river. Standing there, the events of the previous few hours returned to his mind. Trembling, he raised the mantle as he had seen the old man do, and cried out, "Where is the Lord God of Elijah?" And then, when he struck the waters, they parted as they had for Elijah, and he walked over. The school of prophets, who were watching from the hill and had already written off the young man as unlikely to be able to continue the spiritual revival, now shouted, "The spirit of Elijah doth rest upon Elisha." I think that the specific action and words were not as important as the insight that God will be revealed in each event if we have the spirit of the prophets.

GOD IS STILL AVAILABLE

Well, it happened once. They said it could not be done; the second or third generation of the church will conduct its spiritual funeral. But one man proved them wrong. I dare to believe our generation can do it again. One after another of our first generation, and some of the second, are disappearing to join the innumerable caravans that move to the eternal home. I would say to them, "I pray thee, let a double portion of thy spirit be upon me." Would it not be wonderful to have the church historians say of us, "The spirit of Bresee or McClurkan or Wise—or whoever you would name—doth rest upon thee"? It is a prayer earnestly to be prayed.

"If thou see me when I am taken"; whatever could Elijah mean? Well, it would seem that at least he referred to the kind of spiritual insight that enables one to see the "chariot of God" as symbolic of the fire of the Holy Spirit. Not all can. The servant boy of Elijah only saw it as an answer to his master's prayer. It has to do with heart purity, I am sure, for Jesus said, "Blessed are the pure in heart: for they shall see God" (Matt. 5:8). Ah, perhaps this is it. Spiritual insight born of purity of motive and love of truth can discern between "traditions of men" and eternal values. Such insight enables one to apply to his day truth free from prejudice and self. He will not try to be Elijah. Rather, he will have the spirit of Elijah, which is *an ordinary man filled with the Holy Spirit.* He will see that in each generation God dwells in men who are committed to Him for their day.

FILLED WITH THE SPIRIT

"If you see me when I go—because I am nothing in myself, what I am is because of the Spirit of God who has possessed me—you will have all I ever had and more," he is saying to Elisha and to us.

While we think upon this, the Spirit brings us to another scene. Once again we are in the long ago and far away. The soft breeze from the Sea of Galilee bends the heads of the ripening grain as we find ourselves among the crowd that follows a strange man. Strange because He is so understanding that children will not leave Him alone, and yet so penetrating in insight that no one feels comfortable in His presence. While many follow Him, they seem more bent on getting what they want and getting away than they are to learn of Him. But He heals the sick without favoritism. He feeds the hungry. If He exposes the hypocrite, He forgives the sinful and the outcast. He can walk on water, speak to the wind and the waves, raise the dead, and predict the future.

What manner of man is this? He is able to meet every demand; perhaps He has the answer to our search. Maybe He can tell us how we can have the spirit of our fathers in the church today. I am sure He knows. But we cannot get near Him for the crowd; there are too many ahead of us. The practical and immediate needs are too demanding to allow time for philosophical or ecclesiastical discussion. Men's bodies require attention before the battle of ideas can be fought, and things must wait their turn.

But at last He wearies. By the hundreds the crowd leaves off following Him and turns to other pursuits or to newer interests. Sadly, He looks at us and says, "Will you also go away?" Well, I cannot, any more than Peter could, for these questions demand an answer. I will not live always. The opportunity to do something worthwhile is too short to waste time. I am haunted by the hope that I may find the key to everything here with Him. Like Elisha, I shall refuse to stop now.

When He sets His face to go to Jerusalem, I must go with Him. Strange, isn't it, that the way to truth seems to lead to the city with all its denial of the eternal and its glorification of man. But I want the answer so much that if He goes to the city, I go with Him. There is excitement there for certain, and much that makes for culture, but there is also intrigue and subterfuge—and there is sin.

Before we realize it, the events of those never-to-be-forgotten days are gone, and the evening of the Passover draws near. We have learned a lot who have dared, through reading the Gospels, to walk with Him. There is so much there that speaks to us today, almost as though, when we read them, they happen for the first time. Our problems and needs seem to be clearly in His mind. Many questions are answered, but the questions with which we began the journey remain. They confuse us the more with every consideration of them. How, oh how, can we keep the church a spiritual power? How, oh how, can we be heroic fighters for truth in the battle for men's minds? How, oh how, can we escape the narrowing isolations of little concern and truly make the world our parish?

JESUS KNEW THE ANSWER

Does He see our disappointment and fear? Perhaps, for He is saying, "I have told you much, but you are unsatisfied, and I will soon be gone. What do you really want?" In a flash of insight, we reply, "I pray Thee, let a double portion of Thy spirit be upon us." He knows us and what is in our hearts and says, "Thou hast asked a hard thing; nevertheless, if thou see Me when I am taken from thee, it shall be so unto thee."

Here we are again, face-to-face with the assertion that you lose something before you gain the heart's desire and meet life's demand. Well, Peter deserted that night, and all the rest retreated in confusion and disappointment; but we shall not. We must see it through. How much is revealed to us about ourselves as we watch His trial and agony! And then we are driven out of the city by the crowd as it rejects Him and sends Him to the hill and four crosses. Yes, four—one for Him, two for the thieves, and one that is empty, which He indicates is for us. "No, not death, it is life that I want," I cry. But He replies that whoever will not suffer with Him will not reign with Him. And so, I face the cross.

CRUCIFIED WITH CHRIST

We cannot be what we want without facing the cross. We must die out to self and sin. As completely as we know how, we must join our Master in saying, "Not my will, but thine, be done" (Luke 22:42). The death of the cross is not a sudden affair, I fear. Though it may occupy only a few minutes or seconds, it involves a lifetime. It means the constant facing up to God's "What else?" until we have gone through every excuse and subterfuge, and are emptied of every sin and human purpose for life before Him, in the light of His holy will. It means the journey into the depth until nothing remains but a complete and unreserved surrender to the highest, holiest, and best.

There are some who have done this and have looked up at last to say, "All right, I have done all that I know to do, and yet nothing has happened." As though the Master expected it, He replies, "Tarry ye in the city of Jerusalem, until ye be endued with power from on high" (Luke 24:49). For the surrendered life may know the joy of Easter morning and yet have much dialogue in the ensuing days with the Master at the place of crucifixion until the Holy Spirit fully comes. And it is Pentecost, and not Easter, that makes the man of God a power in the world. Now please understand me; I do not mean that Easter is unimportant in Christian experience. Rather, it is that Easter finds its demonstration in the power of Pentecost. We find new life in dying and being raised with Christ. But the double portion of the Spirit of Christ comes to us in the personal Pentecost that awaits every believer, and without which we are less than the persons our times demand.

A PERSONAL PENTECOST

Back in 1932 Aldous Huxley, in his *Brave New World,* predicted a kind of existence in which tranquilizers denied to men pain, struggle, and discomfort. To make sure that no little irritation would creep into life, the brave new world produced a drug they called soma that took all the rough edges from life. This is how he describes it: "If by any chance something unpleasant should happen in this brave new world, there is soma to give you a holiday from the facts. There is always soma to calm your anger, to reconcile you to your enemies, to make you patient and longsuffering. We carry our virtues about with us in a bottle. Christianity without tears—that is what soma is."

Near the close of the story a new character is introduced, a savage who has come from the outer fringes of that anemic civilization. He meets the controller of the world, and the controller explains to him the nature of this society. At that point the savage breaks out in protest, saying, "But, the tears are necessary; you get rid of them. That is just like getting rid of everything unpleasant instead of learning to put up with it. You just abolish the slings and arrows. It is too easy. I don't want comfort—I want real hunger, I want freedom, I want poetry, I want goodness, I want God." And in our world, where bottled virtue fails and the church has no holiday from the facts, we would add, "I want a double portion of the Spirit that we saw in Christ."

I WANT GOD

So, if I want an increased measure of Christ's Spirit or mind within me, I must be in Him. It is not just doing what Jesus would do if He were here, but doing what He wills through me because He is here and I am in Him. "I am crucified with Christ: nevertheless I live; yet not I, but Christ liveth in me: and the life which I now live in the flesh I live by the faith of the Son of God, who loved me, and gave himself for me" (Gal. 2:20). There, in a crucified and Spirit-filled people, lies the hope of an ever-burning flame upon the altar of the church.

T. Crichton Mitchell
(1916—)

T. Crichton Mitchell is professor of history, preaching, and Wesley studies at Nazarene Bible College in Colorado Springs.

A native of Scotland, he pastored there at Paisley, and in London, England. After serving in this role for over 20 years he began a distinguished teaching ministry. For 3 years he taught at European Nazarene Bible College, and for 6 years at British Isles Nazarene College. He has served in his present assignment for 10 years.

Mitchell is known to all the United States colleges of his denomination, having lectured at each of them. He also served as a guest professor at Nazarene Theological Seminary on three occasions.

Beyond the campus communities Mitchell is well-known through his preaching and writing ministries. Among the books he authored are *Mr. Wesley* and *Meet Mr. Wesley.* He also edited *The Wesley Century,* which is volume 2 of this series of holiness classics. He frequently preaches in revivals and camp meetings.

Holiness has been tersely defined as "love-mastered life." Mitchell, in this sermon, goes beyond that to the Source of love itself. He makes it clear that holiness is Lord-mastered life. The holy life is, first of all, a matter of pleasing God, and this means that "daily behavior will be built on trust, loyalty, and obedience to" Jesus Christ.

Such a life, Mitchell insists, is possible for us and portrayed in Scripture. It is both commanded and promised. It is offered in grace and received by faith. It is life in the Spirit, measured not by length or breadth but by depth. It comes to expression in self-forgetful service to the needs of others. It is, in short, the sort of life that Jesus lived on earth.

Frequent appeals to Scripture make clear Mitchell's understanding of the authority that lies behind preaching. The task of the holiness preacher is to expound the Word of God.

Paul's Plea for God's Pleasure*

> *Finally, brothers, we instructed you how to live in order to please God, as in fact you are living. Now we ask you and urge you in the Lord Jesus to do this more and more. For you know what instructions we gave you by the authority of the Lord Jesus.*
>
> *It is God's will that you should be sanctified: that you should avoid sexual immorality; that each of you should learn to control his own body in a way that is holy and honorable, not in passionate lust like the heathen, who do not know God; and that in this matter no one should wrong his brother or take advantage of him. The Lord will punish men for all such sins, as we have already told you and warned you. For God did not call us to be impure, but to live a holy life. Therefore, he who rejects this instruction does not reject man but God, who gives you his Holy Spirit* (1 Thess. 4:1-8, NIV).

This is an urgent appeal. In this very first of his letters Paul reveals his passionate concern that his converts should live the life that pleases God. He sees himself as their gentle but skilled nursing mother, training and guiding them in the life of the Spirit (2:7). Changing the metaphor, he presents himself as their father in God, directing, correcting, and counseling them, encouraging and helping them to live worthily of their Heavenly Father (2:11-12).

Paul is concerned for his friends because of the pressures they feel from the immoral society surrounding them. "I beg, beseech, urge, pray, and exhort you to concentrate on living the life that pleases

*Source: Sermon manuscript.

God!" Nothing could be more important to them or to us than pleasing God. That is what holiness is: It is the life-style that pleases God. To every really born-again person this is the absolute priority of life. We just must please God!

I. *The Level of the Apostolic Appeal*

1. *The Lordship of Jesus.* "We ask you and urge you in the Lord Jesus to do this more and more" (v. 1, NIV). The sovereignty of Jesus Christ over our lives is both the incentive and the rationale for Christian purity. How can it be that He is really Lord of my life if my life is not clearly and entirely under His control? And if He is, then His life dominates my living, and my daily behavior will be built on trust, loyalty, and obedience to Him "who did no sin and in whose mouth there was found no deceit" (Isa. 53:9; 1 Pet. 2:22).[1]

2. *Christian Obligation.* The King James Version focuses this obligation in the phrase "ye ought to walk and to please God." Paul sees purity of heart and the pleasure of God utterly binding upon every Christian. It is not a matter of choice with an alternative; it is solemn obligation, privilege, and responsibility. It does not lie in the area of debate; it is an absolute. We must please God! It is the quality of life in Christ Jesus.

3. *Divine Authority (v. 8).* "Whoever rejects this instruction rejects not man but God." Thus does the apostle imprint his appeal with the seal of the Sovereign God. "This is the will of God" (v. 3, KJV).

II. *The Pleasure of God (vv. 1-2)*

The Scriptures everywhere teach that God's greatest pleasure lies in His people. He had great pleasure in His creation (Rev. 4:11). Day by day as He called new glories, new beauties, and new powers into being, He declared, "That's good!" But it was His supreme creature, man, in whom God found His deepest pleasure. And it was in the sin and fall of man that He found His darkest sorrow.

It is holiness and life that give God pleasure, not evil and death. "I have no pleasure," says God, "in the death of the wicked" (Ezek. 33:11, KJV); but "the Lord taketh pleasure in them that fear him" (Ps. 147:11, KJV). The most damning thing that God can say of any one of us is "I have no pleasure in you" (Mal. 1:10, KJV).

1. *The Worthy Life.* In Eph. 5:8, 10 Paul counsels Christians: "You are light in the Lord; walk as children of light . . . and try to learn

what is pleasing to the Lord" (RSV). To the Colossian Christians he wrote, "I am praying that the Lord will give you spiritual wisdom and understanding to live a life worthy of the Lord and fully pleasing to him" (1:9-10).

It was axiomatic with Paul that what the Lord does in faithful hearts is first of all for His own pleasure but consequently for our plesasure also! For "God is at work in you to will and to do of his good pleasure" (Phil. 2:13). Jesus said, "I do always the things that please the Father" (cf. John 8:29); and the response of the Father is, "This is my beloved Son, in whom I am well pleased" (Matt. 3:17, KJV; etc.). We are true followers of Christ when we "walk before him to all well-pleasing and godliness" (Col. 1:10).

To give pleasure to God is the Christian's holy calling, the highest ideal of life, and offered in grace! Paul defines it as his total objective in life: "So we speak, not to please men, but to please God who tests our hearts" (1 Thess. 2:4, RSV; cf. Amp.). "So whether we are at home or away, we make it our aim to please him" (2 Cor. 5:9, RSV), adding, "And God will one day call us to account on this head" (v. 10).

2. *The Fragrant Life.* To God the life lived to please Him is the most precious and fragrant offering He can receive (Eph. 5:2). You and I are called to holiness in order first of all to give pleasure to God. Sin stinks; holiness is fragrant to God (2 Cor. 2:14-15). As incense accompanied the old-time sacrifices, so it is the fragrance of a living sacrifice that God desires (Rom. 12:1-2).

The perfect fragrant life as exemplified in our Savior is captured in an old German carol, "Lo, How a Rose E'er Blooming":

This Flow'r, whose fragrance tender
With sweetness fills the air,
Dispels with glorious splendor
The darkness everywhere.

III. *The Desire of the Child of God*

Surely every Christian man, woman, and young person who loves the Lord supremely will fervently aspire to be "fully pleasing to him" (Col. 1:10). But how can such as we be "fully" pleasing to such as He?

1. *The Possibility.* Is it really a fact that you and I, picked up by grace from the mire of sin (Ps. 40:2), can actually live a God-pleasing life?

a. It must be possible because the Lord expects it of us. It is in fact one of God's great expectations. Throughout history He has made that clear. He said to Abraham, "Walk before me, and be thou perfect" (Gen. 17:1, KJV). He commanded His ancient people to "love Me with all your heart, soul, and strength" (cf. Deut. 6:5), and His very command veils His longing: "I will remove your hard and stony heart and transplant into you a new and clean heart of perfect love to serve Me and to love Me wholly!" (Cf. Ezek. 36:25-27.) Our Heavenly Father has ever had a dream of having a family in which every child will be just like Jesus, the Son who is daily His delight. Hear this:

> For what the law was powerless to do in that it was weakened by the sinful nature, God did by sending his own Son in the likeness of sinful man to be a sin offering. And so he condemned sin in sinful man, in order that the righteous requirements of the law might be fully met in us, who do not live according to the sinful nature but according to the Spirit. . . . the mind controlled by the Spirit is life and peace [but] . . . Those controlled by the sinful nature cannot please God *(Rom. 8:3-4, 6, 8, NIV).*

b. It must be possible because it has been done. There have been and there are now people in whom God delights and with whom He companions. We know about Enoch (Heb. 11:5): he pleased God. We know about Noah (v. 7). We know about Jesus (Luke 3:22; John 5:30; 8:29). Paul too is in the lineup of the God-pleasers (2 Cor. 2:14); he testified to possessing the witness that "through us God spreads the fragrance of his knowledge everywhere . . . we are the aroma of Christ to God!" It must be possible.

2. *The Portrait.* What kind of life gives God pleasure? Here and there in Sacred Writ the Holy Spirit pauses to focus for us the chief purpose of this ongoing flow of revelation; He provides profiles and summaries of the life that pleases God.

a. Psalm 15 is such a profile. It is a verbal picture of the kind of company God likes to keep; a snapshot of God's guests.

b. The Beatitudes of Jesus give us a composite picture of God's kind of person, or as Wesley puts it, "the portrait of a perfect Christian."

c. First Corinthians 13 is more of a full-color portrait of the kind of life that pleases God.

This is the Lord's way, for thus we get to see the life rather than to scrutinize the brushstrokes. The Lord is a great One for wrapping up His ideas in persons such as Barnabas (Acts 4:36-37), or Epaphroditus (Phil. 2:25-30), or Epaphras (Col. 1:7-8; 4:12-13). These are some of His examples of the life that pleases Him, and His evidence that such a life can really be lived by the grace of the Holy Spirit.

3. *The Particulars.* The constituents making for the life that pleases God can in a measure be isolated for meditation.

a. It is a life of trust. Not simply of belief, but of personal, intimate trust. The Lord is really greatly pleased when His people really trust Him, and grieved when they don't. That's the core of the pleasure of God found in Enoch, Noah, Abraham, Paul, and the others: they *trusted Him!* They took Him at His word, acted on His naked promise, and gambled their lives that He meant every syllable He spoke! They stuck out their necks in the trust that actually He is much greater than even His promises!

Oh, but God likes that! He is grieved by our caution, our calculating reluctance and tardiness of trust. Because a lack of trust is a vote of no confidence in our Heavenly Father. God gets great joy in them that trust Him (Rom. 4:19-25).

b. It is life lived in the third dimension. That is, it is life in the Spirit (v. 8). The life that pleases God is not to be measured by its length of years, nor even by its breadth of interest; it is measured by its depths. The Lord loves those who look to the roots, digging deep and growing roots on their souls, roots that thrust themselves toward the river of His life. Life in the Spirit is like climbing a clean mountain; life in the flesh is like rummaging in a back alley lined with garbage bins into which we toss our most precious possibilities. Life in the Spirit is life in God's third dimension: It has eyes that see the invisible, ears that hear the inaudible, hands that grasp the intangible.

c. It is the life of perfect love: the "Agape" life. The life into whom "the love of God has been poured . . . by the Holy Spirit" (Rom. 5:5, NKJV). Thus it is able to rejoice in sufferings because they produce character that produces hope that never disappoints nor is ever disappointed! It is a life of self-forgetful love such as Jesus lived (Rom. 15:3). Living for God's pleasure makes absentminded professors of us all, just as Jesus actually forgot himself in serving others.

The truth is that we cannot serve the Lord, others, and ourselves at one and the same time. The life that pleases God seeks to forget self.

d. It is the offered life. Rom. 12:1 clinches that: "Think of God's mercy, my brothers, and worship him, I beg you, . . . by offering your living bodies as a holy sacrifice, *truly pleasing to God*" (JB, italics added). That really pleases God: He is looking for people like that (John 4:23). Spiritual worship is the offering of my life in sanctified service. He who would live for God's pleasure must, like Jesus, be "numbered with the transgressors" (Isa. 53:12, KJV) and become the servant of all!

e. It is the life-style of the entirely sanctified. This life cannot be lived with sin in the heart. God hates sin and would root and rout it out of our hearts. Jesus said so: "Every plant, which my heavenly Father hath not planted, shall be rooted up" (Matt. 15:13, KJV). Sin of every sort, and all sorts, is the work of the devil; Jesus came to destroy that (1 John 3:8). God intends His people to be clean, free from sin, and possessed by the Spirit of holiness. We must please God (1 Thess. 2:4). It is not ultimately imperative that we please anyone else, although we do not desire to displease others. But we absolutely must please God; and as Paul says, we must learn to do so more and more.

IV. *Promise and Experience*

To live the life that pleases God is not merely a high ideal, something beyond the possible. It is the highest ideal, but it is offered to God's children in grace. "Offered"; spell it out slowly, letting the letters drip into your soul. The holy life is the life that gives God pleasure, therefore all the riches of His grace and power are open to turn His promises into experience. Kinship and empathy at base lie in oneness of interest and aim. The apostle Peter shows us that God's great command to be holy is really an evangelical promise to make us so: "You shall be holy, for I am holy" (1 Pet. 1:16, Amp., NEB, RSV; cf. NASB). "But just as he who called you is holy, so be holy in all you do" (v. 15, NIV). The measure of the "so" is the measure of the corresponding "as." "God is holy with an absolute holiness that knows no degrees," wrote A. W. Tozer, "and this He cannot impart to His creatures. But there is a relative and contingent holiness . . . This holiness God can and does impart to His children. He shares it with them by imputation and by impartation, and because He has made it available to them through the blood of the Lamb, He requires it of them."[2]

What are we then to do? We must trust God's promise, believe it to be ours, submit really and truly to His will, and enter into the life that pleases Him. Remember, it is offered in grace and therefore to be received by faith, and therefore we can begin now to live the life that pleases God.

---

1. All unidentified scriptures in this sermon are the author's paraphrase.
2. *The Knowledge of the Holy: The Attributes of God: Their Meaning in the Christian Life* (New York: Harper and Brothers, Publishers, 1961), 113.

William M. Greathouse
(1919—)

William M. Greathouse has distinguished himself among the scholars and preachers of the holiness movement. He has served his denomination, the Church of the Nazarene, in a variety of challenging capacities—pastor, teacher, college president, seminary president, and general superintendent, which is his present assignment, a responsibility that takes him around the world and endears him to thousands of people.

He handles all his tasks with skill and grace, but his forte is the classroom and the pulpit. As a teacher and preacher, his spirit and behavior have been convincing demonstrations of his doctrines. Those fortunate to have schooled under him will have lifelong cause for gratitude to God.

Thousands who were never privileged to attend his classes have benefited enormously from his published commentaries, expositions, articles, and sermons.

A graduate of Lambeth College, Trevecca Nazarene College, and Vanderbilt University School of Theology, he wears learning humbly as all servants of Christ must who would not betray the spirit of their Master. And he shares learning graciously, as a man who seems to feel privileged to contribute to anyone's knowledge of our Lord Jesus Christ. In the quality of his life, learning, and labors he is an elect model for ministers.

Of special interest to Greathouse through the years have been the Epistles of Paul and the theology of John Wesley. These interests are evinced in this careful and joyful exposition of "The Goal

of the Gospel," of which Paul speaks in Colossians. More important, there shines throughout the sermon a profound love for the Christ who inspired the service and sufferings of Paul and Wesley.

The sermon outline is drawn directly from the text and follows the movement of the text. It is simply worded and easily recalled. Each heading is fleshed out with sound exegesis offered in terms understandable by the hearers. All of it moves to a logical and stirring conclusion. The doctrine of Christian perfection receives the advocacy it deserves in this message. In short, here is holiness preaching as all of us could wish to do it. Alas, most of us are not capable of this standard of performance. Nevertheless, our work is improved and exalted by the ministries of those whom God has so gifted.

The Goal of the Gospel*

That we may present every man perfect in Christ Jesus (Col. 1:28).

Paul's thought here is bold. He sees his own sufferings for Christ as filling up or completing the sufferings of the Savior himself. Jesus died to save the Church; but if that atoning sacrifice is to be efficacious in converting others and building them up in Christ, if the Church is to be enlarged as His body, then to Christ's passion must be added the sufferings of those who are His servants and ministers. "I Paul am made a minister," he writes, "who now rejoice in my sufferings for you, and fill up that which is behind of the afflictions of Christ in my flesh for his body's sake, which is the church" (vv. 23-24). Again he reminds another church, "For unto you it is given in the behalf of Christ, not only to believe on him, but also to suffer for his sake" (Phil. 1:29).

And how does Paul envision his task as the suffering servant of the suffering Savior? To make known to all men the secret counsel of God which was hidden before the advent of Christ, but which is now revealed in the Church—"Christ in you, the hope of glory"—for every human being. "Whom we preach, warning every man, and teaching

---

*Source: James McGraw, comp., *The Holiness Pulpit No. 2*. Kansas City: Beacon Hill Press of Kansas City, 1974.

every man in all wisdom; *that we may present every man perfect in Christ Jesus*" (Col. 1:27-28, italics added).

"Every man perfect in Christ Jesus." What a vision! What a commission! "Every man" means there is *no limit in the scope* of our commission as Christ's ministers. "There are no heights of Christian attainment which are not within the reach of all, by the power of divine grace" (F. F. Bruce). Moreover, every one may be "perfect." This means there is *no limit in the potential* which every believer may realize. A present perfection is God's requirement and provision for all Christians, and a final perfection is assured us by Christ's return in glory. "In Christ Jesus" is the key phrase. Our perfection is not in ourselves; it is "in Christ Jesus." This assures us there is *no limit in the resources* which are available to those who receive the good news of salvation through Christ.

PRESENT PERFECTION

I. *"Every Man"—No Limit in Scope*

Paul is absolutely sure that "every man" may be made perfect in Christ. The repetition of "every man" in this passage is a challenge to the idea put forward by some teachers in the Early Church, that perfection is the exclusive privilege of an elite group within the community of believers. The apostle is challenging this snobbish idea. The gospel reserves no such exclusive privileges for the select few. *Perfection is within the reach of all, by the power of Christ!*

FOR ALL CHRISTIANS

In the Sermon on the Mount, Jesus commands us to be perfect. "You have heard that it used to be said '*Thou shalt love thy neighbor and hate thine enemy,*' but I tell you, Love your enemies, and pray for those who persecute you, so that you may be sons of your Heavenly Father. For he makes his sun rise upon evil men as well as good, and he sends his rain upon honest and dishonest men alike.

"For if you love only those who love you, what credit is that to you? Even tax collectors do that! And if you exchange greetings only with your own circle, are you doing anything exceptional? Even the pagans do that much. No, you are to be perfect, like your Heavenly Father" (Matt. 5:43-48, Phillips). Every disciple *must* be perfect. Christ's ethic is an ethic of perfection—perfection in love. It is this forgiving, merciful love, this Godlike caring for all men, which is the very badge of our discipleship. Christ makes *no exclusions* when He commands, "You are to be perfect, like your Heavenly Father." The *law* of Christ *requires* perfect love.

PERFECT LOVE

But what about the gospel of Christ? The *gospel* of Christ *promises* perfection. This is clearly Paul's argument in the third chapter of Second Corinthians, where he is showing the superiority of the new covenant over the old covenant given at Sinai. As the mediator of the old covenant, Moses ascended Mount Sinai, where he enjoyed face-to-face communion with the Lord. Coming down from the mount, he put a veil on his face to hide the glory which shone on his countenance. Moses represents a select company of Old Testament worthies who were granted the exceptional privilege of a sanctifying communion with God. Paul vividly contrasts this privileged holiness of the Old Testament with the universal holiness now available to those who worship God through Christ. *"But we all,"* he assures us who know God under the terms of the new covenant, *"we all,* beholding as in a glass the glory of the Lord, are changed into the same image from glory to glory, even as by the Spirit of the Lord" (2 Cor. 3:18, italics added).

In Old Testament times there was a spiritual aristocracy; a *few* were permitted to ascend the mount of spiritual transfiguration—Enoch, Noah, Abraham, Moses, Isaiah. But in the gospel dispensation we enjoy a spiritual democracy; *"we all"* may climb that mount of face-to-face communion and be transfigured into the likeness of Christ.

Furthermore, in contrast to the *fading* glory that eventually disappeared from Moses' countenance, we may know a *progressively increasing* glory. "We are not like Moses, who veiled his face to prevent the Israelites from seeing its fading glory. . . . But all of us who are Christians have no veils on our faces, but reflect like mirrors the glory of the Lord. We are transfigured by the Spirit of the Lord in ever-increasing splendor into his own image" (2 Cor. 3:13, 18, Phillips). Or as the *Revised Standard Version* renders verse 18, "We all, with unveiled face, beholding the glory of the Lord, are being changed into his likeness from one degree of glory to another."

The heights of Christian perfection are within the reach of *every believer,* by the power of the Spirit of Christ!

II. *"Perfect"—No Limit in Potential*

Paul is convinced that his commission from God is to present "every man perfect in Christ Jesus." The law commands and the gospel promises nothing less than *perfection.*

The Greek word for *perfect* suggests two ideas: (1) attaining to an end, (2) completeness. These ideas are interrelated in this passage. They are also intertwined in Christian experience.

Now what is the *end,* the standard or norm, the Heavenly Father has in mind for His children through Christ Jesus? We have already seen this: *that we shall be perfect in love.* Christ does not impose absolute perfection; we are not to be *as* perfect as the Heavenly Father. No. We are rather to be perfect *like* our Father. These two ideas are quite different. We are to love all men the way God loves them. That is the sum and substance of Christian perfection.

CHRISTIAN PERFECTION

Now this was precisely Paul's concern for his churches. "Owe no man any thing, but to love one another," he wrote the Romans, "for he that loveth another hath fulfilled the law. For this, Thou shalt not commit adultery, Thou shalt not kill, Thou shalt not steal, Thou shalt not bear false witness, Thou shalt not covet; and if there be any other commandment, it is briefly comprehended in this saying, namely, thou shalt love thy neighbour as thyself. Love worketh no ill to his neighbour: therefore love is the fulfilling of the law" (Rom. 13:8-10).

John Wesley rightly says, "The whole law under which we now are, is fulfilled by love. *Faith working or animated by love is all that God now requires of man.* He has substituted (not sincerity, but) love in the room of angelic perfection." You see, God does not command us to be perfect angels, but perfect men. Love, not angelic or absolute perfection, is "the just requirement of the law" (Rom. 8:4, RSV).

PERFECT LOVE

Wesley goes on to say, "Love is the end of the commandment" (1 Tim. 1:5). "It is the end of every commandment of God. It is the point aimed at by the whole and every part of the Christian institution. The foundation is faith, purifying the heart; and the end love, preserving a good conscience." Such love is a possibility in grace for every Christian; God does not require the impossible. His very commandment, as Wesley says, is a "covered promise." What the law requires the gospel provides. You can be perfect in love.

Thus perfected in love, you are a *complete* Christian. You are "complete in him" (Col. 2:10). Every grace needed is yours through the indwelling Spirit of Christ. Moreover, you are a complete person when you are perfected in love. Then, and not until then, you are genuinely human, fulfilling the purpose for which you were created, "to glorify God and enjoy Him forever."

WHOLENESS

Many translators render the Greek word *teleioi,* used here, "mature." We see justification for this. Wesley spoke of the fully sanctified as "full grown men in Christ," "fathers," or "adult sons of God." Paul uses *teleioi* in this sense in First Corinthians. He urged those who were making a toy out of the gift of tongues (14:20), . . . along with other carnal and immature attitudes and actions, "In malice be ye children, but in understanding be *men.*"

FAITH

This does not mean, however, that we grow into perfection. It is not a matter of time, but of faith. As P. T. Forsyth says in his little volume on *Christian Perfection, "Faith* is the condition of spiritual maturity in the sense of adultness, of entering on the real heritage of the soul. It is the soul coming to itself, coming of age, feeling its feet, entering on its native powers. Faith is perfection in this sense. It is not ceasing to grow, but entering on the normal region of growth." He continues, *"Our perfection, therefore, is not to be flawless, but to be in tune with our redeemed destiny in Christ."*

"In tune with our redeemed destiny in Christ"! That destiny is to be finally perfected in Christlikeness—glorified with Christ. In this sense every Christian must confess with Paul, "Not that I have already attained, or am already perfected" (Phil. 3:12, Wesley). When we think of our final destiny in Christ, we know we are but "Christians in the making." "Let us therefore, as many as be perfect [or mature], be thus minded" (Phil. 3:15). Let each of us say,

I'm a person God is making,
Like a statue God is shaping;
God is changing me, correcting;
God's intent on my perfecting!

Cleansed from the inner antagonisms occasioned by double-mindedness, and filled with the Holy Spirit, I say, "This one thing I do, forgetting those things which are behind, and reaching forth unto those things which are before, I press toward the mark for the prize of the high calling of God in Christ Jesus" (Phil. 3:13-14). Thus cleansed from sin and filled with the Spirit, I *am* in tune with my redeemed destiny in Christ!

III. *"In Christ Jesus"—No Limit in Resources*

"There are no heights of Christian attainment which are not within the reach of all, by the power of divine grace." The possibilities of perfection are resident "in Christ Jesus," and in Him alone. Immediately after penning our text, Paul exhorts the Colossians:

"May your spiritual experience become richer as you see more and more fully God's great secret, Christ himself! For it is *in him,* and in him alone, that men will find all the treasures of wisdom and knowledge. I write like this to prevent you from being led astray by someone or other's attractive arguments. . . . Just as you received Christ Jesus the Lord, so go on living in him—in simple faith. Grow out of him as a plant grows out of the soil it is planted in, becoming more and more sure of the faith as you were taught it, and your lives will overflow with joy and thankfulness.

"Be careful that nobody spoils your faith through intellectualism or high-sounding nonsense. Such stuff is at best founded on men's ideas of the nature of the world, and disregards Christ! Yet it is in him that God gives a full and complete expression of himself (within the physical limits that he set himself in Christ). Moreover, your own completeness is only realized in him, who is the authority over all authorities, and the supreme power over all powers" (Col. 2:2-4, 6-10, Phillips).

POWER

You need not live a defeated, unfulfilled life. "In Christ Jesus" you may realize your completeness, be fulfilled! "In Christ Jesus" you were "circumcised with the circumcision made without hands," so that you may now love God with all your heart (Col. 2:11; cf. Deut. 30:6). "In Christ Jesus" you have the promise of the outpoured Holy Spirit. To you He says, "Come to me and drink. He who believes in me, as the scripture has said, 'Out of his heart shall flow rivers of living water'" (John 7:37-38, RSV).

"In Christ Jesus" we have heart-circumcision! "In Christ Jesus" we have the fullness of the Spirit! "In Christ Jesus" we may be made perfect in love and completed in grace! "In Christ Jesus," and in Him alone, we realize fulfillment. All the riches of God's grace are now resident "in Christ Jesus." We do not go *beyond* Christ to be made perfect; *we go deeper in Him.*

CHRISTLIKENESS

Dr. Charles Trumbull attended the first world missionary conference in Edinburgh. He was quite intrigued by the subject announced by a Sunday afternoon preacher: "The Resources of the Christian Life." He went to the service expecting to get some sound, practical advice. But when the preacher stood, he paused a moment and then said, "The resources of the Christian life, my friends, are simply—Jesus Christ." As F. E. Marsh puts it, "We have no inherent holiness. We are holy as we are possessed by the Holy Presence. We are holy in His holiness, loving in His love, strong in His strength, tender in His tenderness, patient in His patience, calm in His peace, and consecrated in His consecration."

Jesus Christ is made to me
All I need, all I need. . . .
Wisdom, Righteousness, and Power,
Holiness forevermore,
My Redemption full and sure—
He is all I need!

"There are no heights of Christian attainment which are not within the reach of all, by the power of divine grace." Possess your possessions *now!*

James Earl Massey

(1930—)

James Earl Massey is dean of the chapel at Tuskegee University, where he has provided a highly respected ministry of teaching and preaching.

His preaching assignments have ranged from large city pulpits to college chapels and have been marked by a gracious but uncompromising proclamation of the Word.

A minister in the Church of God (Anderson), Massey is a man gifted for many avenues of service. He is an accomplished musician. He was the speaker for his church's radio program, "The Christian Brotherhood Hour," for several years. Over 80 educational institutions have utilized his knowledge and skills as a lecturer. His pastoral ministry has enriched and developed the lives of individuals and congregations. He has authored numerous books, and his articles and sermons have often appeared in *Vital Christianity.*

Among his books is *Designing the Sermon,* one of the volumes in the Abingdon Preacher's Library. Addressed to seminarians and to working ministers, it emphasizes "story preaching," at which Massey excels. The book calls for "real preaching," which roots in the fact of God, helps people to experience His grace, and therefore "takes seriously the moral and spiritual climate of the times."

"What Sanctification Means" reflects Massey's concern for "real preaching." The meaning of sanctification is discussed, not as an abstract doctrine, but in terms of a cleansing power that

enables us to "handle ourselves rightly in the give-and-take of daily contacts with others."

God desires and effects our holiness. "Self-effort cannot sanctify us. . . . Sanctification is God at work in our lives: shaping our characters, tutoring our minds, strengthening our wills, and enabling us to satisfy His demands and fulfill our potential . . ." But His grace is not given unconditionally. "Your responsibility is to give God your consent and steady cooperation. . . . This promised life awaits only your full surrender."

Accenting God's grace and our responsibility, the sermon underscores what Massey has said in his book *The Hidden Disciplines:* "The most stupendous fact in Christian experience is our opportunity to change in the direction of what we view in the person and life of Jesus."

What Sanctification Means*

For this is the will of God, your sanctification (1 Thess. 4:3, RSV). *May the God of peace himself sanctify you wholly* (1 Thess. 5:23, RSV).

The congregation Paul established at Thessalonica began after strategic planning and in the face of great odds. When Paul went there to preach, he knew that he would be placing the gospel message in a large and important city, and carrying it farther westward than the gospel had ever gone before. He was intent to stay in the city as long as necessary, so he went to the local synagogue and introduced himself. He also began to ply his trade as a tentmaker, working to support himself and his associates.

Unfortunately, Paul's stay in Thessalonica was shorter than he had hoped. His ministry there was so successful in the first three weeks that major opposition formed against him; some opposers even sought to do him bodily harm. The believers advised Paul to leave, and they aided him in doing so.

Not long after leaving, Paul wrote back to the new church. He wanted to see the new work continue. Paul knew that those who had intended harm against him would seek to trouble the young church,

*Source: Sermon manuscript.

so he wrote with deep concern for their welfare. In the letter Paul reminded them about certain truths he had taught while with them, and he went deeper into some matters that his shortened stay among them had not allowed time to explore. Such is the background of First Thessalonians, the first of many letters Paul would write to congregations across the empire.

This also explains the setting of these textual passages, which are about Christian living and how sanctification relates to it. Let us join in looking at how Paul used the word and understood the experience about which it witnesses.

I. *Sanctification has to do with spiritual behavior.*

The first use Paul makes of the word "sanctification" is in the passage 4:1-7. Paul was explaining "how you ought to live and to please God" (v. 1, RSV), so he stated: "For this is the will of God, your sanctification: that you abstain from unchastity; that each one of you know how to take a wife for himself in holiness and honor, not in the passion of lust like heathen who do not know God; that no man transgress, and wrong his brother in this matter, because the Lord is an avenger in all these things, as we solemnly forewarned you. For God has not called us for uncleanness, but in holiness" (vv. 3-7, RSV). Paul's first use of this word tells us plainly that *sanctification has to do with spiritual behavior.*

This is but one of the many passages in Scripture that relate sanctification to moral and spiritual behavior. The passages are too numerous to list here, but again and again the Bible tells us that God is pleased only when His people live right and practice godly living.

But godly living does not just happen; it is generated. Spiritual behavior needs something more working in us than mere willpower and positive thinking. Thus Paul's second use of the word "sanctification" in 5:23-24. "May the God of peace himself sanctify you wholly . . . He who calls you is faithful, and he will do it" (RSV).

As Paul taught it, sanctification is the realization of godliness in our lives. Paul explained that true godliness shows itself in moral and spiritual behavior. He also explained that this godliness is generated within us by the direct action of God himself upon the total self. "For this is the will of God," he declared, "your sanctification." His meaning should have been clear to all from the moral distinctives he listed for Christian life.

GODLINESS

II. *God desires and effects the sanctification of our lives.*

God wants us all to know the full influence of His presence and power in our living. God wants to share His high and holy character with us and help us handle ourselves rightly in the give-and-take of daily contacts with others.

GOD'S WILL FOR US

Paul's illustration of how sanctification applies to life was most practical. He told his readers—and us—that sanctification of our lives rules out moral laxity, and that it honors and grants us ethical and moral control when tempted. Paul underscored God's will as the right use of ourselves in marriage or out of it. Sanctification of life involves more than this, of course, but it does include this, and Paul was both thoughtful and wise to state it.

Considered from the standpoint of our times, what better way could Paul have found to illustrate what sanctification of life means? The home setting is still the place of our most sensitive contacts. And the social arena is still the great testing ground for our morals. The sanctification of our lives influences the way we relate to a wife or husband—how that relationship *begins, continues,* and *matures.* The heart in which God freely works will not allow itself to act and react in selfishness, nor will it allow itself to be victimized by lust. While others in the world around us will continue to "take" or "seize" someone else in the spirit of unbridled passion, disregarding God's rules against promiscuity and lust, we Christians must not. We *will* not when our "spirit and soul and body [are] kept sound and blameless" (5:23, RSV) by the help of God working His will within us. Others living in our society will use, misuse, and abuse one another, transgressing rights and wronging each other, but the Christian must not. "For God has not called us for uncleanness, but in holiness" (4:7, RSV). Paul was most practical in explaining the sanctification of life, and his word seems shaped with our lives and times in view. What he wrote to the Thessalonians about sanctification is a fundamental description of the experience for all time.

ETHICS

God desires the sanctification of our lives. He promised to do the sanctifying. He wants to give us holiness, that is, wholeness in His will. God wants to grant that moral and spiritual condition of mind and heart by which we can do His will with all constancy and joy. Paul was pointing to this in 3:13 in his words about the heart being established "in holiness." He was pointing to it as well in 3:2 in his words about the believer being established "in . . . faith."

WHOLENESS

In both instances, Paul had the godly life in view, a life filled with moral and spiritual evidences of God's touch upon the soul.

It takes God to sanctify us. Self-effort cannot sanctify us. Holiness of life is something more than mere morality. Sanctification of life includes high morals, but it is a greater, higher life than mere morality. As Henry Ward Beecher once said, "Shoes, staff, and raiment are indispensable to a journey; but shoes, staff, and raiment are not a journey." Sanctification involves moral commitment, but sanctification is something more than morals and commitment. Sanctification is God at work in our lives: shaping our characters, tutoring our minds, strengthening our wills, and enabling us to satisfy His demands and fulfill our potential as His children. Thus Paul's prayer for his readers as he closed this letter, "May the God of peace himself sanctify you wholly; and may your spirit and soul and body be kept sound and blameless at the coming of our Lord Jesus Christ. He who calls you is faithful, and he will do it" (5:23-24, RSV).

GOD AT WORK IN US

Sanctification is the conditioning God grants to help us be like Him. That conditioning is for the whole self, and it is to continue across the entire span of our lives. God handles the conditioning; our part is to stay surrendered to that conditioning.

III. *We enter into sanctification through full surrender to God.*

I have been speaking about sanctification. I have pointed to the meaning of that experience as Paul explained it to the new Christians at Thessalonica. More could be said on the subject if we draw from Paul's letters to other churches, but we have here the basic statement about sanctification. Paul considered this statement entirely adequate to help his readers make the needed surrender.

Like Paul, I will offer no additional explanations because enough has been said about what sanctification means. I now urge you to enter into the experience by answering God's call to holiness. "For this is the will of God, your sanctification."

FOR YOU

Surrendering the self to God allows Him to begin conditioning us in holiness. That conditioning does not make us odd but normal; it does not alter our humanity but augments it. John Wesley called this the experience of "perfect love." Some others have described it as the "second blessing." The descriptions are many, and most are helpful, but the experience is more than any of us can fully explain. Those who obey God's call to holiness will discover far more than they will ever be able to fully describe.

Every believer needs the steady conditioning God gives if life is to be at its highest and best. The highest and best is a holy life. It is full conformity to the will and character of God. That is what Paul called "sanctification," and this benefit begins in all who make the necessary surrender to God.

God wants to condition you for holy living. He wants to make you ready for life and labor in His will. God wants to work His purpose *in* you, so that He can work out His purpose *for* you. Your responsibility is to give God your consent and steady cooperation. It is your privilege to have His help. It should be your longing to have His holiness. This promised life awaits only your full surrender.

4

SEEKING AND FINDING

Benjamin T. Roberts
(1823-93)

Benjamin T. Roberts led a protest against slavery, Masonry, and worldliness within the Methodist Episcopal church while serving as a pastor in the Genesee Conference of western New York.

Roberts was a graduate of Wesleyan University and a convert to what Charles E. Jones terms "Palmer-type perfectionism." Many holiness sympathizers within Methodism found his strictures unacceptable. Upshot of the controversy was the expulsion of Roberts and some like-minded believers.

In 1860, to quote Jones again, "Roberts and his 'Nazirite' associates institutionalized their criticism by forming the Free Methodist Church." ("Nazirites" was a nickname given the group because of their strict discipline. Their opponents applied to them scornfully what is an honored designation in Scripture.)

To his death in 1893, Roberts sincerely believed that he was merely restoring true Wesleyan doctrine and discipline. Freed by historical developments from further need to attempt reform of the parent church, Roberts and his colleagues pushed to expand the influence and numbers of the new denomination. His contribution to the holiness movement was undeniably great. Ironically, so was that of some of the men within Methodism who opposed him. In fact, the splintering away of the "Frees" resulted in a closing of ranks among holiness advocates in the Methodist Episcopal church, and their labors increased, chiefly through the National Holiness Association.

The message printed here was not published as a sermon, strictly speaking. It was a pamphlet issued by Roberts as a guide to holiness. Its clear outline and exposition, however, lend themselves readily to preaching, and Roberts probably preached it in this form.

Roberts differed from most holiness advocates in one respect. His editorial writings, compiled by his son and published as *Holiness Teachings,* clearly show that he viewed Christian perfection, not as synonymous with entire sanctification, but as a lifelong process embracing both purity and maturity. However perfect at the various stages of his development, the Christian is not perfect if growth is arrested at any stage short of his full development.

This difference notwithstanding, Roberts' "How Sanctified?" is a choice and helpful message for anyone seeking to enter into the experience of entire sanctification.

How Sanctified?*

> *Then will I sprinkle clean water upon you, and ye shall be clean: from all your filthiness, and from all your idols, will I cleanse you* (Ezek. 36:25).

Andrew Fuller says, "Divine truth is like chain shot; let one link get into the soul and it draws all the other links with it." One step taken in the right direction leads to another step in the same direction. So, when in one passage of Scripture we are said to be sanctified by the use of one means, and in another passage the same work is said to be done by the use of other means, there is no contradiction. The one implies the other.

The Bible plainly teaches that God alone can sanctify a human soul. He only can make a fallen being holy.

The first step in holiness is forgiveness. "Who can forgive sins but God only?" (Mark 2:7).

---

*Source: Benjamin T. Roberts, *How Sanctified?* North Chili, N.Y.: *Earnest Christian* office, n.d.

That God sanctifies the soul is taught in the promise, "Then will I sprinkle clean water upon you, and ye shall be clean: from all your filthiness, and from all your idols, will I cleanse you." Here God says that He will do the work. It is because He undertakes to do it that sanctification is possible. To deny the possibility is to charge the Almighty with promising what He cannot perform. How far does this fall short of blasphemy?

CLEANSING

In harmony with this is our Lord's prayer. "Sanctify them through thy truth: thy word is truth" (John 17:17). They were already converted. They had been assured that their names were written in heaven. Now God is asked to sanctify them. They had power over sin, power to work miracles, but they were not yet made holy. Jesus prays the Father to effect this work in them.

So the apostle prays: "And the very God of peace sanctify you wholly" (1 Thess. 5:23). They were already sanctified in part. They were ensamples to believers. Now the apostle prays for God to complete the glorious work.

SECOND BLESSING

"But if God sanctifies the soul, why does He not sanctify everyone, and especially every Christian?"

We reply. If it is God who "filleth thee with the finest of the wheat" (Ps. 147:14), why does He not so fill everyone, and especially every farmer? Because the conditions are not met. For the same reason, many who profess to be Christians are not sanctified wholly. *They do not meet the conditions.*

God is no respecter of persons. He is severely impartial. Whoever meets the conditions on which any grace is promised, always obtains that grace. There is never a failure on the part of God. The failure always is in meeting the conditions.

Let us notice some of these conditions.

I. *Belief of the truth.*

"God hath from the beginning chosen you to salvation through sanctification of the Spirit and belief of the truth" (2 Thess. 2:13). The agent of sanctification is the Spirit; the *medium* through which He works is *the truth.* But if one does not believe the truth, it does not save him. He who does not believe that he can be sanctified cannot be sanctified. Error leads men into bondage; truth sets them free and keeps them free. "And ye shall know the truth, and the truth shall make you free" (John 8:32). But to be effective, the truth must be so firmly held that it will produce appropriate action. Hence,

II. *It is another condition of sanctification that we wholly, and forever, abandon all unclean habits and utterly renounce and strive against all unholy tempers, desires, and affections.*

"Having therefore these promises, dearly beloved, let us cleanse ourselves from all filthiness of the flesh and spirit, perfecting holiness in the fear of God" (2 Cor. 7:1).

The end to be secured is, *perfecting holiness.*

The spirit in which this is to be done is, *in the fear of the Lord.*

The means to be employed is the *cleansing of ourselves from all filthiness of the flesh and spirit.* We are to do this ourselves.

It is of no use to pray against our corruptions while we are indulging these corruptions. If we would have God remove the depravity from our hearts, we must cease yielding to this depravity. He must quit smoking, and quit drinking, who would have God destroy the appetite for these sinful indulgences. The woman who would have the grace of humility must, herself, remove from her person the displays of pride. He who holds on to his corrupt practices until the love of them is destroyed will die in his sins. God will not do for us what we can do for ourselves. If we would have Him do what we cannot do, we must do what we can toward it. If we cannot make the corn grow, we can prepare the ground and plant good seed. It is to him who diligently uses the grace he has that more shall be given.

RENOUNCE WHAT GOD CONDEMNS

We must be severe with ourselves. Not a single wrong disposition must be spared. "Mortify therefore your members which are upon the earth; fornication, uncleanness, inordinate affection, evil concupiscence, and covetousness, which is idolatry."

"But now ye also put off all these; anger, wrath, malice, blasphemy, filthy communication out of your mouth" (Col. 3:5, 8).

John Wesley says: "Both repentance, rightly understood, and the practice of all good works, works of piety, as well as works of mercy, (now properly so called, since they spring from faith), are, in some sense, necessary to sanctification.

"I say, repentance rightly understood; for this must not be confounded with the former repentance. The repentance consequent upon justification is widely different from that which is antecedent to it. This implies no guilt, no sense of condemnation, no consciousness of the wrath of God. It does not suppose any doubt of the favor of God, or any 'fear that hath torment.' It is properly a conviction, wrought by the Holy

CONVICTION FOR CARNALITY

Ghost, of the *sin* which still *remains* in our heart; *the carnal mind,* which 'does still *remain . . . even* in them that are regenerate.' . . .

"It is a conviction of our proneness to evil, of a heart bent to backsliding, of the still continuing tendency of the flesh to lust against the Spirit. Sometimes, unless we constantly watch and pray, it lusteth to pride, sometimes to anger, sometimes to love of the world, love of ease, love of honor, or love of pleasure more than of God. It is a conviction of the tendency of our heart to self-will, to atheism or idolatry, and, above all, to unbelief, whereby, in a thousand ways, and under a thousand pretences, we are ever departing, more or less, from the living God."

III. *Another condition of entire sanctification is the giving up, in detail, of ourselves, our property, our influence, and all that we control, to do and suffer the will of God.*

It is true that no one can become truly converted without a full surrender to God. This our Savior plainly teaches. "So likewise, whosoever he be of you that forsaketh not all that he hath, he cannot be my disciple" (Luke 14:33). But the mind does not at first take in *all* that is implied in *forsaking all* we have. As new temptations and new duties present themselves, a great increase of faith, and love, and patience, and all the Christian graces is demanded. To those already converted, the apostle wrote: "I beseech you therefore, brethren, by the mercies of God, that ye present your bodies a living sacrifice, holy, acceptable unto God, which is your reasonable service. And be not conformed to this world: but be ye transformed by the renewing of your mind, that ye may prove what is that good, and acceptable, and perfect, will of God" (Rom. 12:1-2).

CONSECRATION

(1) *The sacrifice.* This is not expiatory. None such is needed, or permitted. Christ died for our sins. He has offered *one sacrifice for sins* for ever (Heb. 10:12). It is a thank offering. Christ has redeemed us from death and hell; in return we are to offer ourselves, soul and body, to Him, to do His will. Our *bodies* are to be placed at His disposal. They are to be fed, and dressed, and worked for Him. All that we have earned, all that we can earn is to be used as He directs. The body is to be kept well and strong, that it may do effective work for God.

(2) *The separation.* We are not to be conformed to this world in our spirit, our manners, our aims, or our appearance. Everywhere we go, we are to manifest the Christ who reigns within.

In short, we are to make what is commonly called an *entire conse-*

cration of our all to God, without the slightest reservation as to its extent or its duration. No friend, however near, is to be allowed to come between us and God. As Charles Wesley says:

If with my all I cannot part,
Cannot a child or friend forgo,
In vain I would disguise my heart,
My heart and treasure are below.

But this is all. There is to be no penance, no bodily suffering voluntarily inflicted to atone, either in whole, or in part, for our sins. It is *by grace we are saved,* and not by self-inflicted tortures. This is a point that the gospel guards with the utmost jealousy. Anything to which we ascribe merit hinders rather than helps us, in the way of salvation.

IV. *If we would be sanctified wholly, we must believe in Christ for the accomplishment of the work.*

From beginning to end, salvation is *by grace, through faith.* All who are saved are saved in this way and in no other. "And put no difference between us and them, purifying their hearts by faith" (Acts 15:9). "For with the heart man believeth unto righteousness; and with the mouth confession is made unto salvation" (Rom. 10:10).

FAITH

Whatever else one does, he can never be fully saved till he trusts in Christ to sanctify him wholly. As John Wesley says: "Though it be allowed, that both this repentance and its fruits are necessary to full salvation; yet they are not necessary either in the same sense with faith, or in the same degree: not in the *same degree;* for these fruits are necessary *conditionally,* if there be time and opportunity for them; otherwise a man may be sanctified without them.

"But he cannot be sanctified without faith. Likewise, let a man have ever so much of this repentance, or ever so many good works, yet all this does not at all avail: he is not sanctified till he believes: but the moment he believes, with or without those fruits, yea, with more or less of this repentance, he is sanctified. Not in the *same sense;* for this repentance and these fruits are only *remotely* necessary, necessary in order to the continuance of his faith, as well as the increase of it; whereas faith is *immediately* and *directly* necessary to sanctification. It remains, that faith is the only condition, which is *immediately* and *proximately* necessary to sanctification.

"'But what is that faith whereby we are sanctified? saved from sin, and perfected in love?' It is a divine evidence and conviction, first, that God hath promised it in the holy Scripture. Till we are thoroughly satisfied of this, there is no moving one step farther. And one would imagine there needed not one word more to satisfy a reasonable man of this than the ancient promise, 'Then will I circumcise thy heart and the heart of thy seed, to love the Lord thy God with all thy heart, and with all thy soul, and with all thy mind.' How clearly does this express the being perfected in love! How strongly imply the being saved from all sin! For as long as love takes up the whole heart, what room is there for sin therein?

SCRIPTURAL

"It is a divine evidence and conviction, secondly, that what God hath promised He is able to perform. Admitting, therefore, that 'with men it is impossible' to 'bring a clean thing out of an unclean,' to purify the heart from all sin, and to fill it with all holiness; yet this creates no difficulty in the case, seeing 'with God all things are possible.' And surely no one ever imagined it was possible to any power less than the Almighty! But if God speaks, it shall be done. God saith, 'Let there be light; and there is light!'

"It is, thirdly, a divine evidence and conviction that He is able and willing to do it now. And why not? Is not a moment to Him the same as a thousand years? He cannot want more time to accomplish whatever is His will. And He cannot want or stay for any more *worthiness* or *fitness* in the person He is pleased to honor. We may therefore boldly say, at any point of time, 'Now is the day of salvation!' 'Today, if ye will hear his voice, harden not your hearts!' 'Behold, all things are now ready, come unto the marriage!'

IN A MOMENT

"To this confidence, that God is both able and willing to sanctify us now, there needs to be added one thing more, a divine evidence and conviction that He doeth it. In that hour it is done: God says to the inmost soul, 'According to thy faith be it unto thee!' Then the soul is pure from every spot of sin; it is clean 'from all unrighteousness.' The believer then experiences the deep meaning of those solemn words, 'If we walk in the light, as he is in the light, we have fellowship one with another, and the blood of Jesus Christ his Son cleanseth us from all sin.'"

ASSURANCE

The faith through which we are sanctified implies the fulfillment of the conditions previously mentioned. Unless we are conscious that we heartily surrender all to God, it is impossible for us to believe He saves us. For we know He cannot lie, neither can He be deceived. He looks through all disguises. Christ says, "How can ye believe, which receive honour one of another, and seek not the honour that cometh from God only?" (John 5:44). As long as you hold on to your reputation, you cannot be saved fully.

Beloved, are you now sanctified wholly? If not, make no delay. The call of God is urgent. He calls *you* to holiness. His command is plain: *Be ye holy.* Willful disobedience to this command, as of any other, brings condemnation. If you would keep the grace you have, you must walk in the light of God. And that light leads directly to full salvation.

NOW IS THE TIME

If you would be more useful, you must be sanctified wholly. Many can do nothing toward saving others because their own experience is so unsatisfactory. Time is short. Eternity is at the door. Opportunities are passing away, never to return. If you are content with the grace you have, you are in danger of losing that grace. Unless you bestir yourself, the crown you would wear will never be placed upon your head. Unless you bestir yourself, souls will perish whom you might save. Awake, awake, and put on thy strength. Delay no longer. Turn yourself over deliberately to God, and trust in Him with all your heart. Plead in faith until the work in you is accomplished and you have the witness of the Spirit that it is done.

John S. Inskip
(1816-84)

In 1867 a group of Methodist ministers, eager to promote the doctrine, experience, and life of holiness, formed a National Camp Meeting Association. The first national camp meeting was held in Vineland, N.J., that same year. The first president of this association was John S. Inskip, then serving as a pastor in the New York Conference.

Other camp meetings followed at Manheim, Pa., in 1868, and at Round Lake, N.Y., in 1869. Inskip's sermon, "Three Inquiries," was the opening address of this third national camp meeting. It is taken from a quaint book titled *Penuel; or Face to Face with God,* a report of the camp meetings, including sermons and testimonies.

Many denominations were represented, as these believers subdued their differences without surrendering them, finding a unity in their hunger for, quest after, and experience of entire sanctification.

In the introduction to this book, Bishop Matthew Simpson of the Methodist Episcopal church, who ardently participated in the camp meetings, wrote, "The style of preaching is direct and hortatory. Present results are aimed at; present success is looked for."

Such preaching is demonstrated in this simple, earnest, pleading sermon. According to the editors, numbers sought heart cleansing at the close of the message. "Thus at the commencement of the meeting was God's power present, giving assurance to believers that, through all the services to come, the fire of the

Holy Ghost should burn mightily . . . as it did, consuming sin and setting many hearts on fire with love and zeal."

Inskip's sermon contains doctrinal elements, but in a simple and summary manner. Theological elaboration yields to practical exhortation, as was frequently the case in these meetings.

The sermon appears untitled in the book. I took the liberty of christening it myself, adopting the most obvious of choices.

Three Inquiries*

And the very God of peace sanctify you wholly (1 Thess. 5:23).

We may with profit inquire: (1) What is it to be sanctified wholly? (2) How this state may be attained? (3) The benefits that accrue from it?

I do not propose to give this theme a dogmatic discussion, and yet there are one or two points which . . . all should understand with regard to the nature of this work, for we think that many have been in some measure mistaken in their interpretation of our views and doctrines upon this subject. We wish, therefore, at the outset, to state in a plain way what we understand it is to be wholly sanctified.

NAMES

The phrases and terms perfect love, purity, perfection, entire sanctification, and holiness we shall employ as synonyms in this discussion. And now, let us proceed to the subject.

I. *What Is It to Be Sanctified Wholly?*

To be sanctified wholly is to attain to something beyond and above, and different from, that which we experienced at the time we were converted to God. . . .

We are often asked, "Is this difference one of kind, or of degree only?" We do not choose . . . to dwell upon this question, for the end we have in view is a practical one. When the sinner cries out to God, when under conviction for sin and under the condemnation of sin, his cry is for deliverance from that condemnation, and this he receives, together with a new heart and adoption into the divine family; and to

*Source: A. McLean and J. W. Eaton, eds., *Penuel; or Face to Face with God*. New York: W. C. Palmer, Jr., Publisher, 1870.

the regenerate there is no condemnation, and yet every such one who follows the Spirit soon begins to press the cry of the Psalmist, "Create in me a clean heart, O God; and renew a right spirit within me" (Ps. 51:10). There is not a Christian man . . . but is deeply anxious that his soul may be made entirely clean; for if a Christian is not interested in this, he must be a backslidden Christian. But there is in every believing heart this desire to be pure.

HUNGER

I do not say that when the soul is first saved it is not brought into a new life, for we all believe it is; but after thus experiencing to some extent the sanctifying grace of God, every Christian feels at times uprisings within his soul which clearly indicate that he is not *entirely* sanctified, and it is this that leads us to cry out with the Psalmist, "Create in me a clean heart, O God!" . . .

You know, my brother, or my sister, how there linger within the heart pride and passion, kept under control it is true, but yet not destroyed. They live there yet. But we may have these things all destroyed and cast out, so that the nature within us may be radically revolutionized, and the bias of our hearts may be all in the right direction. And oh, when a man has reached this state, how great is the advantage he has gained, and how much more easily does he triumph over his foes, for they are all without now, and none within. And this attainment is within the reach of every Christian, and is so taught by all our Methodist theology, and, better than all, by the Bible.

SCRIPTURAL

I will not call attention particularly now to the teaching of our catechism, our discipline, our hymns, and our fathers upon this subject. I will only say that our whole ritual, and all our theological course as ministers, and our whole book of discipline combine with the Word of God in holding up something above and beyond regeneration as the possibility and duty of every believer. This is what the apostle prays for in the text: "The very God of peace sanctify you *wholly*."

HOLY SPIRIT

We must not forget that this is a work to be done by the Holy Ghost. . . . It is not wrought by human power, nor can it be, but it is by the power of the Holy Ghost that we come to a state of entire purity. In this state the soul loves God with all its strength; faith is not mixed with doubt; love is never mingled with hate; humility is not discounted by pride; patience is never paralyzed by petulance. In short, the whole nature is brought into perfect harmony with the divine will; and all this mighty work is to be wrought in us by the power of the Holy Ghost.

There have been two extreme views upon this subject, both of which have led many astray. The first is the gradual theory, which teaches that we are to grow into this blessing, and which . . . ignores the fact . . . that this is a work to be done, if done at all, by divine power.

The second view seems to make this agency to be a certain intellectual exercise, by which we are able to say that, having done certain things, we are therefore wholly sanctified. I pray that no such ideas as these may be promulgated here. We are here to teach that we are to be sanctified by the power of Almighty God.

It is sometimes said that justification is an act, or change in the mind of God toward us; while sanctification is a work wrought in us whereby we are changed. But this does not change the truth of what we have just said, for what God does in us is as much His work as what He does for us.

II. *How May We Secure It?*

This, then, is God's work; but if you or I would have this power exercised in us and for us, we must put ourselves into the right relation to God. The sinner will not be pardoned unless he repents and believes in the Lord Jesus Christ, nor will the believer be entirely sanctified unless in humble penitence he believes in Jesus—trusts Him for the work.

No uninspired man ever taught more correctly and clearly with regard to sin and repentance in believers than did John Wesley, and we shall do well to remember those teachings. He declares clearly what the Scriptures also teach, that if the Christian would be fully saved, he must come into that position where he will see and abhor the remains of sin that are still in him. And you, my brother, have reason to thus abhor yourself when you come to see the pride, and self-will, and love of the world, and movings of anger that you find still within. It will not serve the purpose to turn back to your religious life when it commenced, and try to satisfy yourself with this. No, no! How is it with you *now,* today? And when you have found out this, then repent, for the good old doctrine of repentance is to be received and practiced by believers as well as by sinners, though not in the same sense.

CONVICTION FOR CARNALITY

But this is not enough. When you have had a look within and abhorred yourself, and repented sincerely before God, then go a step further. First look *at* yourself, not *to* yourself, and then . . . thoroughly consecrate yourself to the service of God. There is much that the Christian must give up if he would be entirely the Lord's. You cannot be as frivolous as are many professed Christians, nor as gay in dress as they are, for you must speak, and act, and dress to please Jesus, if you would be entirely His. You must be willing to be marked and known by your appearance, but more by your spirit, as entirely Christ's. And do not entertain the idea that on this question you can be here today and yonder tomorrow. You must be steadily and constantly Christ's. Between you and worldliness there must be a great gulf fixed that can never be passed. This matter of entire consecration means much. God help us to be thus consecrated. We cannot do this without divine help, but that help will be with us at every step if we trust it. If, then, you want full salvation, make a full consecration, and make it now. This you may do; this it is your duty to do, and to do now, cost what it may.

CONSECRATION

It takes some courage to do this; more, it may be, than most of us have; more, perhaps, than I should have possessed, had not God put me into a very close corner, where I could not retreat without being inconsistent with myself. I was in my pulpit preaching to my people, and urging upon them the necessity of consecrating all to God. I knew that a man's perceptions of religious truth never get much beyond his experience, and that his experience is bounded by his consecration. I was urging this upon my people, and urging them to do it now, when God said to me . . . *"Do this yourself!"* And I did it. I made the consecration, and I knew that I made it, and I would rather have died that hour . . . in the pulpit than not to have done it. I had no time to confer with flesh and blood, but I said at once, "Here goes for God and full salvation." I was not long then in taking hold upon Christ, and I still cling to Him, and all hell cannot break the grasp.

A TESTIMONY

When I made this consecration, I knew full well what I had done, and I knew my people understood it. There I stood in the pulpit, looking earnestly for a spot where to put my foot down next, but all was dark, and I could not see. But I said, "Here goes; in the name of God, I will not go back," and I put my foot down in the darkness, and,

Oh, hallelujah! there was a rock under it.

THE TIME IS NOW

Oh, brother, come out, *come out,* **come out** on the Lord's side! Put your flag up today, and leave it there, and put no halyards to it with which to pull it down! And I tell you, my brother, if you do this today, the power of God will take hold of you, and you will be saved.

Not by your reason and logic, saying, I have done this or that, and therefore I am saved. That will not do. What we want is the fire of God that will burn up sin, and the pure flame of love that will burn on forever and forever.

We teach the people, then, not that they are sanctified because they believe they are sanctified. It is not faith in what we are, or what we have been, or what we have done, or what has been done for us, but faith in the Almighty Christ that brings us where we cry out with joy—

'Tis done, the great transaction's done;
I am my Lord's and He is mine.

This is done in answer to faith in Jesus, and this faith should be reached at the moment of full consecration. Consecrate, and then believe. But believe what? That you are sanctified? No! But believe that the blood of Christ cleanseth from all sin. . . .

Many, and especially ministers, want to understand the philosophy of the work before they [seek it]; but if you wait till you understand that, you will never take any step toward it at all. . . .

Pride also keeps many away. We want the blessing but are too proud to seek it in God's way and cry unto Him from the valley of humiliation. Some of you will quite likely be required to come to this altar to seek this blessing. God forbid that you should be too proud to do so.

But when may you have this blessing?

I answer, just when you dare believe that the Blood cleanseth. And when shall this be? Why, *now,* if your consecration is complete; if you have digged this impassable gulf between your soul and sin. See that you do it today. . . .

III. *The Results*

The results of this will be that Jesus will put . . . His arm around you, and His mind into you. He puts His mind into you so that you have no mind of your own. Men sometimes say of another, "That man has no mind of his own, but he must do always just as his friend says." So let it be said of us, "They can do nothing only as Jesus bids them. They have no mind but His."

In this state you will do right because it is a luxury to do as God would have you to do, and you will find so much of the Divine in you as to lift you up and hold you above the power of temptation.

POWER

You will be tempted still; but let the whole of your nature be made pure, and though the enemy may come and howl around you, you will feel just as easy and secure when he roars as when he is quiet. Before I received this eternal tranquillity there were frequent and terrible storms; but now all is calm and peaceful as were the Galilean waves when He had said, "Peace, be still!" (Mark 4:39).

Troubles and trials still will come, but Christ is mightier than all. You will be thrust into the furnace still, it may be, but you are better off there with one like the Son of Man with you, than out of the furnace without Him.

If we would have the world converted to God, we must get the Church wholly saved. I know it is said that "these holiness people say nothing about the conversion of sinners," and yet sinners somehow get converted among them. . . .

And now, what have we come here for? Is it to see these fine grounds, or this beautiful lake? No! No! I trust not; we have higher ends and holier aims. All the beautiful lakes of this beautiful world are worthless when compared with the lake of salvation.

We came to wash in this fountain; to lead souls to it; to get good and to do good, as a brother here on the stand says. Oh, let us begin today and now. Seek earnestly, all you who are not

FULL SALVATION

now conscious of full salvation, that this glorious work may now be wrought in you; that, wholly sanctified yourselves, you may lead others to this great blessing.

Alexander McLean

(1826-1910)

A camp meeting crowd on Saturday afternoon is a tough challenge. Hot weather, sleepy people, and the weariness that settles upon those who have been in several services daily throughout the week do not lend themselves to gaining and holding attention.

Under these circumstances Alexander McLean preached this sermon at Landisville, Pa., in 1873, during the 16th National Camp Meeting for the Promotion of Holiness. A storm broke over the camp, and afternoon trains "filled the avenues with new arrivals," making the situation even more difficult. Adam Wallace, who reported the meeting and sermon, said, "Nothing but an all-controlling energy, aided by the Holy Spirit, could have prevented general confusion at the time." Nevertheless, "One after another made the surrender," crowning the service with blessed victory.

Alexander McLean, of the Methodist Episcopal church, had been involved with the National Holiness Association from its inception. Indeed, with J. W. Eaton, he furnished the published record of the first two national camp meetings in 1867 and 1868. At the historic General Holiness Assembly that met in Chicago in 1901, he was one of the preachers who addressed that fire-baptized group of holiness leaders.

Important to their work, and to McLean, was the unity and peace of this interdenominational effort to spread the message of holiness everywhere. At the Chicago gathering, McLean preached on "Union in Holiness" from the prayer of Christ, "That they all may be one" (John 17:21). He declared, "Whoever drops a firebrand of dissension, whoever seeks to scatter the power of the holy people by any process, is as directly hostile to Jesus Christ as possibly he can be."

The spirit of unity evidenced by Alexander McLean can only result from the crucifixion of the will, which was the burden of his message at Landisville. Our wills, when harmonized with God's will, share the desires of the Savior for His people. The need for renewed emphasis on this theme is too obvious to require elaboration.

Like so many sermons from that period, the outline is simple, logical, and progressive. The application of truth is pointed but loving. Doctrinal elements are placed in the service of practical results. The preacher aims at implementing experience, not winning arguments.

The sermon appears untitled; this editor supplied one.

The Crucified Will*

Not my will, but thine, be done (Luke 22:42).

The words of my text were those of Jesus, the Son of God, in that great struggle preceding His betrayal, agony, and crucifixion.

He had gone to an accustomed place of prayer, with three of His disciples, on the Mount of Olives. When there He retired a stone's throw apart from them and engaged in earnest prayer. Returning, He found them fast asleep. . . . Again He left them and prayed to His Father, saying: "If it be possible, let this cup pass from me [Matt. 26:39]: nevertheless not my will, but thine, be done."

COMPLETE SUBMISSION TO GOD

I need not dwell longer on the strange, sad fact, or raise the inquiry as to how it was that the dear Jesus suffered thus; nor yet, whether the human or divine nature was most affected; but rather, let us turn to a few practical thoughts on the will, [and] its submission, entire and com-

---

*Source: Adam Wallace, ed., *A Modern Pentecost.* Philadelphia: Methodist Home Journal Publishing House, 1873.

plete, to the will of God, as instanced in the prayer offered by Jesus for himself.

The will, in its relations to the claims of God upon us, may be classified thus:

1. The will when in opposition to God: this is the sinner's condition. His own will is of the highest moment.

2. The will when in partial submission to God: this is the condition of the child of God while he is not entirely sanctified.

3. The will when brought into harmony with the will of God: this is realized only in what is known as entire sanctification, or perfect love, and there fully.

WE MUST CHOOSE

The will is the mightiest power given to man. The greatest power known to men, devils, angels, or God is the will. It is this that subordinates and controls the other parts of man's nature. If you look out upon the great waters, you may with a glance at any vessel, determine what motive power was designed to propel her. From the keel up, everything indicates the motive power. So you may readily see man was built with entire reference to the kingly power of his will. It was bestowed on him that he might exercise it as a free agent, and use it he must and does, in one direction or another. There is no one who hears me but will bring his power of volition into play either for or against God, in some degree or other, this very day. God grant that it may be for Him, and in the fullest measure.

HOLY LIFE FREELY CHOSEN

I do not say that the grace of God will not reach other parts of our nature, but it will do this most effectually through the sway of the will. Nor may we by a mere volition will ourselves into the possession of any grace, but we can determine upon the means and then lay hold upon and steadily employ them. The will, under the divine assistance, can present the body a living sacrifice, holy and acceptable unto God, and then we can lay hold of Jesus by faith for the full acceptance of that gift.

I. *The will in opposition to God is the condition in which . . . the sinner is found.*

How dreadful the condition. May God help him to see that all the conflict of the universe has been a conflict of will; that it was this which turned the angels out of heaven, and our first parents out of

Eden. Sin is an open, flagrant, and persistent rebellion against God, and to Him there must be an unconditional surrender.

II. *The will in partial harmony with God is the condition of the unsanctified believer.*

This is manifested by the disposition to specify to God the manner in which He shall bless us. That the carnal mind is not wholly removed from us while the will is not wholly subdued to God, may be known by an extreme sensitiveness which is easily wounded. There may be a readiness to criticism, but a hostility to being criticized; a regret to learn the success of a rival, but a pleasure to know the fall of a foe; a faith in man, yet doubting God; a desire of goodness, yet a dread of its consequence; a longing for power, but a listlessness for purity; committed to God, yet living a life of noncommittal. The understanding admits to the fullest extent the claims of God; conscience clearly points the path to be pursued; God's Word and Spirit say: "Accept it *now*." The justified soul says, "I will," and means it, but fails to perform. He feels that his every motive should be what they are not, simply and singly for God's glory. He resolves to have them so, but does not realize his desire.

THE WILL NOT SURRENDERED

Oh, how keenly and painfully my own soul has experienced the variations to which I have alluded, while in the unsanctified condition. My will was exerted to its uttermost to abide in Christ, yet without avail. Still I deemed the fault must be in defective willing, and would gird myself for its stronger exercise. Failure followed each newly energized endeavor, until I was constrained to admit that in my will . . . there was no help. Though I regarded it as ever so mean and unworthy in me not to keep upon the high plane of Christlike living, where I saw so clearly it was my privilege to remain, yet I did not abide there, if indeed I at all gained those blessed heights.

WE CANNOT MAKE OURSELVES HOLY

I see the same sad history in your eye. I hear it in the mourning of members of all the denominations who have not yet been delivered from the bondage of sin. I read the sad strains of this experience in the hymns of the churches, and it is everywhere manifest that when we would do good, evil is present with us. The minister, class leader, deacon, or elder, seeing the young convert running on in his early zeal, admonishes him to carefulness and seeks to prepare his mind for great revulsions—as though there was no gospel plan for the entire removal of the cause of such revulsions.

III. *Yes, there is a plane of experience where these perturbations are less frequent, and where, indeed, they do not exist.*

Luke tells us that while Christ was in the agony of the garden, "There appeared an angel unto him from heaven, strengthening him" (Luke 22:43). So our will must be strengthened from on high.

What may have been impossible by our own will becomes feasible when assisted of God. Just here men stagger. They see the greatness of the work to be done, but, realizing their own feebleness, they falter, as well they might. Yet, when God enters and reinforces the will, and energizes the whole soul, how changed everything becomes. God's doing and our doing are infinitely far apart. It is God who promises, "Then will I sprinkle clean water upon you, and ye shall be clean: from all your filthiness, and from all your idols, will I cleanse you" (Ezek. 36:25). What signifies our inability, when God declares that He "will" do it for us and in us?

GOD REINFORCES THE WILL

Self-crucifixion must precede the realization of the fullest harmony between the divine and human will. Cost what it may, self must go down, all the way down, in every regard where the soul claims a separate interest from Christ. One wish, one will, one way, with Jesus in the lead, must be the soul's unvarying aspiration. John was so far from having a distaste for the fact, that his whole soul was thrilled with joy when he said of Jesus, "He must increase, but I must decrease" (John 3:30). Consent, dear hearer, to die to self. Be not satisfied with a temporary submission. If you would have a thorough work wrought, go down, down into the depths of self-abnegation.

DIE TO SELF

As an old sea captain was exhibiting a harpoon several feet in length and of considerable weight, he said, "We do not kill the whale with this; you might load the whale down with harpoons and not kill him. We fasten to the whale with this, and when he is well wearied with drawing us through the water, and comes up to breathe, we row close to him, and a strong and expert man in the bow throws a sharp lance, smaller than the harpoon, with all his force right to the spot where he lives. This is the way in which the whale is killed." Self will endure a great deal of harrowing and harpooning, but by an unreserved consecration, and faith in our Lord Jesus Christ, let us strike it where it lives. *Your will,* you will find, is the vital point; that being in entire submission to God's will, you shall find rest to your soul.

Renew my will from day to day,
Blend it with Thine, and take away
All that now makes it hard to say,
"Thy will be done."

A great change in your affections and desires will take place upon the death of self. Why should a woman, dead to sin and self, bedeck herself as though she were alive to human admiration? Do earrings, and a display of jewelry generally, well become the dead? Shall a dead woman so attest her enslavement to fashion as to still wear her golden manacles? I cannot understand how self can be fully crucified, while as yet we are so very sensitive to either the praise or censure of men; or, if we are seeking the honor which comes from men rather than the honor which comes from God only. If our feelings are wounded so easily by some reflection, remark, or supposed slight, does it not indicate the presence of the self-life? . . . Much of our discomfort and annoyance grow out of our sensitiveness. Be adamant to error and injustice, but clay on the potter's wheel to truth and righteousness.

What restfulness and soul comfort result from having our will in fullest harmony with the will of God. 'Tis yours, then, to say:

Now rest, my long divided heart;
Fixed on this blissful center, rest;
Nor ever from my Lord depart,
With Him of ev'ry good possessed.

If now you are not in the enjoyment of this grace, resolve to have it. As it is purchased for you, reach forth the hand of faith, and take it as all your own. Today let this blessed consummation be realized, and then go forward, doing everything in your power to lead others to the Cross.

Nathan Bangs

(1778-1862)

In 1858 a great spiritual awakening occurred in America. 1858 was, as Timothy Smith labels it, "Annus Mirabilis." In that same year Dr. Walter Palmer purchased the *Guide to Holiness,* and his wife, Phoebe, made it a potent instrument for uniting the holiness movement.

Among those who shared the miracles was Nathan Bangs, then just four years away from his death, but still an influential voice for holiness within Methodism. He had served his church ably and energetically as pastor, presiding elder, and editor. From his pen came the book *The Necessity, Nature, and Fruits of Sanctification,* published in 1851.

Bangs was a close friend of the Palmers, but he protested against her "altar theology," viewing it as a threat to Methodism's historic doctrine of the witness of the Spirit. Nonetheless, he agreed substantially with the Palmers and worked happily with them in the promotion of holiness.

Throughout a long ministry (he entered Methodism's "traveling connection" in 1802), Nathan Bangs preached and wrote as a constant advocate of the experience and life of holiness. Though he declined election to the bishopric, he was, as Melvin Dieter says, "one of Methodism's most highly honored leaders." Timothy Smith thinks he came close "to being the outstanding Methodist of the first half of the [19th] century."

Bangs died during the Civil War, convinced that the horrible conflict was a divine retribution "on church and state, North and South."

Historian and biographer Abel Stevens, himself a zealous holiness advocate, describes a great career in *Life and Times of Nathan Bangs, D.D.* Bangs was truly a giant in the holiness movement of his day.

"Submission to God" is a lengthy but trenchant exposition of that condition, imposed upon man by God, without which the experience and life of holiness are alike impossible. Submission to God is both a precondition and a gracious fruit of entire sanctification. Total submission is urged to God's commands, works, methods, and promises. Only by such "stillness" before the government of heaven's Sovereign can we "know" God in a personal and saving manner. In the holiness circles within which Bangs and his colleagues labored, preaching was not soft!

Submission to God*

Be still, and know that I am God (Ps. 46:10).

These words were addressed to heathen. Against the God of Israel those "heathen raged, the kingdoms were moved," even though when He "uttered his voice, the earth melted." In the midst . . . of all this frenzy and rage, the people of Israel remained unmoved by terror, because they could say . . . "The Lord of hosts is with us; the God of Jacob is our refuge." . . . To impress their minds with a suitable sense of His supreme dominion over all things, and thus to inspire them with adoration to His character, they are invited to "come, behold the works of the Lord, what desolations he hath made in the earth. He maketh wars to cease unto the end of the earth; he breaketh the bow, and cutteth the spear in sunder; he burneth the chariot in the fire" (vv. 6-9). How vain the impotent rage of these heathen, who armed themselves against the mighty God of Israel, who doeth all these terrible things! Their only safety was in a humble submission to His government; to *be still, and know that He is God.*

To *know God* is one of the primary duties of man; and the neglect

---

*Source: *The Methodist Preacher.* Auburn, N.Y.: Derby and Miller; Buffalo, N.Y.: Derby, Orton, and Mulligan, 1853.

of this duty is, therefore, one of the most prolific sources of the vices and irreligion prevalent in our world. Hence, says our Savior, "This is life eternal, that they might know thee the only true God, and Jesus Christ, whom thou hast sent" (John 17:3). The knowledge of God, however, inculcated in the Sacred Scriptures, does not suppose that we are able to "find out the Almighty unto perfection" (Job 11:7). . . . He eludes the grasp of finite minds; so that we may say, "He holdeth back the face of his throne, and spreadeth his cloud upon it" (Job 26:9). But though the "full glories of His mind" are not to be perceived by the feeble powers of man, He has condescended to make such a revelation of himself as to give us that knowledge of His perfections which is essential to our happiness and salvation.

While . . . only a small part of His ways are comprehended by us . . . it is most important for us to "acquaint [ourselves] with him" (Job 22:21). We must know Him as *our* God, who is reconciled to us through the Son of His love, and that we are reconciled to Him by faith in Jesus Christ, "in whom we have redemption . . . even the forgiveness of [our] sins" (Col. 1:14; cf. Eph. 1:7). When we thus know Him, we *feel in our hearts* that *God is love,* and that He "dwelleth in us, and . . . we dwell in him" (1 John 4:12-13). All who in this sense know God are prepared to *submit to Him in all the dispensations of His providence and grace.*

ACCEPTING GOD'S WILL

This is the duty, as I humbly conceive, taught in the text, "Be still, and know that I am God." This implies

I. *A submission to whatever God commands*

A thousand objections are perpetually urged, especially by unregenerate sinners, against the commandments of God. Though they may not array themselves in direct hostility against God and adopt the express language of the slothful servant—"Thou art an hard man" (Matt. 25:24)—yet the impious sentiment exists and rankles in their hearts, and vents itself in some form or other. When they are called upon to repent, they excuse themselves by saying they have no power to repent, thus implying that God requires an impossibility at their hands. To this, and all other objections . . . which sinners make, either expressly in . . . words or implicitly by their conduct, God furnishes them with a decisive answer in our text—*Be still, and know that I am God.* "Know thou, O man, that I, who am infinite in wisdom, power, and goodness, not only have a *right* to command thy services, but that the perfections of My nature

SUBMISSION IS WISE

preclude the possibility of commanding anything *wrong,* anything *unkind, unwise,* or even that is not for thy *highest interest* to do. Submit, therefore, to My requirements, and thou shalt live."

Others . . . excuse themselves from a prompt obedience to the commandments of God by what they suppose the text itself requires. *Be still,* say they, implies that we are to wait God's time, which He, as a Sovereign, has set for our conversion and salvation. And by this erroneous interpretation of the text, they strive to content themselves in their sins, foolishly charging them upon the sovereignty of God.

I do not deny God's sovereignty, but I deny that it furnishes any just excuse for sinners to delay . . . their repentance; or that it will in any degree lessen the criminality of their sinful conduct. The sovereignty of God is displayed in devising the plan and fixing the terms of man's salvation, and in proclaiming to him that now is the day of this salvation. The stillness, therefore, commanded in the text . . . requires them to lay aside all their unreasonable objections, to submit without reserve to the just and gracious terms of the gospel, and to surrender themselves up without delay as prisoners to the Lord Jesus Christ. . . .

God says to all those sinners who "reject . . . the counsel of God against themselves" (Luke 7:30) and strive to intrench themselves behind His sovereignty, while they are . . . trampling upon His laws, and despising the offers of His mercy in Christ Jesus, "*Be still.* Cease all your complaints and your objections; and make haste . . . to do what I, who am your God, whose 'commandment is holy, and just, and good,' have required at your hands."

There are yet others who infer from this, and other similar texts, that they are to refrain from works altogether, and especially from vocal speaking and praying, and simply rest in silence before the Lord. That this is a wrong interpretation of the meaning of such like scriptures, I think, is plainly manifest from such commands as the following: "Strive to enter in at the strait gate" (Luke 13:24); "Cry aloud, spare not, lift up thy voice like a trumpet" (Isa. 58:1); "Pray . . . with all prayer" (Eph. 6:18); "Work out your own salvation" (Phil. 2:13). So, to explain one part of Scripture as to make it contradict another, and thus destroy the harmony of its several parts, is manifestly to "wrest . . . the [holy] scriptures, unto [our] own destruction" (2 Pet. 3:16).

The meaning, therefore, is that we should silence all objections to the performance of these obvious duties; discharge them unhesitatingly, without delay; and leave the event to God, who never commands in vain, nor without a good reason. . . . The ingenious Mr. Fletcher illustrates the manner in which we may both *be still* . . . and yet move forward in the discharge of external duties at the same time, by comparing it to the mathematician when drawing a circle: while he fixes one point of the compass in the center, where it remains stationary, with the other he draws the circle. So the Christian man must fix his faith firmly and steadfastly upon the promises of God, strongly confiding in His wisdom, power, and goodness, while he cheerfully moves around in the circle of obedience to God's commands . . . fulfilling his relative and social obligations with all fidelity.

In this way he submits, with a ready cheerfulness, to whatever God has commanded, under the full conviction that He who *is God* has a right to demand the obedience of His creatures; and being infinitely powerful and good, as well as wise and just, He can require nothing of them but what is for their highest and best interest to yield. In this way they are *still* before Him.

The duty required in the text implies

II. *A submission to whatever God does*

Nothing is indeed more common than for mankind to find fault with the government of Jehovah. Not only does the professed infidel impeach the government of the God of the Bible, by saying that it is administered either in manifest injustice or with evident partiality; but even those who profess to believe in the divine authority of the Scripture, and to be governed by its precepts, very often impeach its divine Author with a want of wisdom and goodness in the dispensations of His providence and grace. Though they do not do this in so many words, yet the many complaints which are uttered on account of the hardness of their lot, the severity of their chastisements, and the cruel bereavements they are called to suffer, all imply a complaint against Divine Providence; originating, perhaps, from not duly considering that all things are under His control, and are made to serve His sovereign will. To silence all such complaints, God addresses us in the language of the text—*Be still, and know that I am God.* . . .

A HOLY GOD IS GOOD

The manifest import of this language is, "*Be still,* and know that I have a right to dispose of thee, as well as all things else, according to My own pleasure. But to silence forever thy unreasonable murmurings, and to fix, deeply to fix, in thy heart a submission to all My dispensations, *know Me;* know that My *wisdom* precludes the possibility of erring in the choice of either ends or means to accomplish them; that My *goodness* prevents Me from withholding any 'good thing' from those who 'walk uprightly'; that My *justice* secures the impartial administration of every part of My government; and if these considerations will not induce thy patient submission, nor conquer thy rebellious will, *know* that My *omnipotence* will arrest thee in thy mad career; and if thou dost continue in thy perversity, *it* will enable Me to overtake thee at last, and then 'vengeance will claim the full arrears.'

"Why, then, dost thou find fault? Canst thou resist omnipotence? Vain effort. Canst thou devise a better plan, more wise, more benevolent, better adapted to thy condition? Or if I were to resign the government of the world to thee, canst thou give any security that it shall be better administered? If not, then bow down thy will to Mine. Submit to My dispensations without murmuring, and all things shall work together for thy present and eternal good."

GOD IS WISER THAN WE

This language is particularly consoling to the pious Christian who is suffering under the unavoidable ills of life. . . . In the midst of these severe trials of his faith and patience, he may be tempted to think that his case is peculiar, and, in the language of unbelief, to say, "My judgment is passed over from my God" (Isa. 40:27). But let such remember that "all things work together for good to them that love God" (Rom. 8:28).

Be still, therefore, before the Lord; submit thy cause and thy case to Him who numbers the hairs of thy head, and He shall make "[thy life to] be clearer than the noonday" (Job 11:17) and "thy bread [and] waters shall be sure" (Isa. 33:16).

The duty inculcated in the text implies

III. *A submission to the various ways in which He is pleased to carry on His work, either in our own souls or in the souls of others*

. . . It is certainly among the many melancholy evidences of the conceitedness of the human mind, as well as the pride of the unrenewed heart, to undertake to prescribe *how,* and *when,* and *where* God shall work. The manifest design of God, in His manner of working, is to "destroy the wisdom of the wise" (1 Cor. 1:19) . . . for He "resisteth the proud, but giveth grace unto the humble" (James 4:6). And who will presume to say, in reference to God's method of bringing souls to himself, "Hitherto shalt Thou come," or, in this manner alone shalt Thou work!

This, indeed, was the great sin of the Jews. They had prescribed the manner in which the Messiah should make His appearance . . . When Jesus of Nazareth came, "meek and lowly" (Matt. 11:29), it was so opposite to their preconceived opinions, so humbling to their pride . . . that they rejected Him with scorn and derision, reproached Him as an impostor, and finally imbrued their hands in His innocent blood. All this originated from the pride of their hearts, and an unwillingness to submit to the wisdom of God, and to His ways of developing His purposes of wisdom and love to mankind.

There is in the natural heart of man a strong opposition to God's method of saving sinners. . . . It shows itself, not only in the various excuses which he invents for a neglect of his most obvious duties, but also, when convinced of his sinfulness, by the methods to which he resorts to save himself. Though struggling under the power and influence of sinful propensities, and unable to extricate himself from his sad dilemma by his own efforts, he still goes "about to establish [his] own righteousness" and will not submit to "the righteousness of God" (Rom. 10:3).

Instead of bowing with gratitude to the immutable terms of salvation which God hath proclaimed in the gospel of His Son, Jesus Christ, he vainly and proudly strives to have the terms of salvation accommodated to his narrow views, and to induce the Almighty to work according to his understanding of things.

All these, however, are vain efforts. The sinner must *submit*—he must submit to be saved by *grace* alone, through faith in the Lord Jesus, or not be saved at all. . . . Let him, therefore, *be still* before the Lord of the universe, lay aside his frivolous objections, and bow in humble submission to God, that he may be saved from his sins.

THE CARNAL MIND

There is not only an opposition to the terms of salvation, but there is also an opposition, strong and powerful, in the carnal mind, against the manner in which God works by His Holy Spirit in the heart, in order to bring the sinner to an experimental "knowledge of salvation . . . by the remission of . . . sins" (Luke 1:77). He not only struggles to free himself from the checks, the restraints, and the strivings of the Spirit of God, but he often finds a rebellious disposition rising within him, tempting him to "resist the Holy Ghost" (Acts 7:51).

And when he is at last willing to submit to be saved upon God's terms, how often does he object to the time and manner in which the work shall be completed. He either wishes God to come in a "still small voice" (1 Kings 19:12), that others may not discern the exercises of his heart, or that some great revelation may be made to him, in particular, of the love and mercy of God, that he may proclaim it aloud to his fellowmen. Now, although God often works in both of these ways, the desire itself may be, in that particular case, but the echo of a proud and deceitful heart. . . . To humble such a heart, God finds it necessary to deny its wishes and to lead the person under their influence in a way he knew not.

Whether, then, God sees fit to come in the whirlwind, or in a still small voice; whether under the word preached, or in the use of His ordinances; in answer to prayer in the closet, or in the public assembly; whether by a powerful and sudden operation of His Spirit . . . or in a more gradual method, it matters not, so that the work be *His,* and that it be done that we may *know that He has saved us and has washed us from our sins in the blood of Christ.* In this particular, also, *be still,* and know that He cannot err in the manner in which He carries on the work of thy salvation.

LIFELONG SUBMISSION

Are not professing Christians, also, frequently perplexed in a similar way? Do not they secretly, though perhaps unconsciously, resist the operation of the Holy Spirit upon their hearts? Do they not often manifest an unwillingness that . . . God should work *where,* and *when,* and *how* He pleaseth? Aye! Here is the grand secret why God's work does not more abundantly prosper. Our pride has already prescribed the manner in which the work of reformation must be carried forward; and if God see fit to deviate from our views of propriety, and of gospel order, it is all wrong; we "never saw it in this fashion, and therefore it cannot be right!" This was the sin of the Pharisees. And Pharisees exist in the church in all ages. Their spirit . . . of pride and self-sufficiency is ever opposed to the Spirit of Christ. How often, when penitent sinners, from the bitter anguish of their souls, are induced to cry aloud for mercy, saying, "Have mercy on us, O Lord, thou Son of David" (Matt. 20:30-31), do these modern Pharisees mimic the cry of those ancient opposers of Jesus Christ, and say, "Master, bid them hold their peace!" Or if, under the powerful application of divine truth to the heart, and the merciful influence of the Holy Spirit, the devout Christian is constrained to "shout aloud" unto God and praise Him for His wondrous works (Ps. 132:16), these pharisaical professors of religion . . . are offended and strive to dis-

SUBMISSION IS CHRISTLIKE

parage the work, either by speaking reproachfully of its instruments, or by vilifying its subjects!

It is sufficient, in all these cases, that we may silence all complaints, to be able to ascertain that the *work is of God. Be still,* at least for a while. "If it bear fruit, well: and if not, then . . . cut it down" (Luke 13:9). If those who profess to be subjects of this work bring forth the fruits of the Spirit—if those who are its advocates and promoters live according to the gospel in all holiness and godliness—then acknowledge and adore the hand of God. . . . Do not exalt thy wisdom against the wisdom of God. *"Stand in awe, and sin not"* (Ps. 4:4).

How many Christians, "having begun in the Spirit" (Gal. 3:3), might this day have been exulting in the enjoyment of *perfect love,* if only they had been willing to submit to *God's time and manner* of effecting this gracious and most desirable work in their souls. But, by substituting *their own ways,* they have grieved the Holy Spirit and, perhaps, have lost even their "first love" (Rev. 2:4; cf. Eph. 4:30). God says, "Be ye holy; for I am holy" (1 Pet. 1:16). Unbelief says, this is impossible, at least in this life. Our hearts are naturally so perverse, so feeble; our temptations so numerous, powerful, and constant, that we cannot obtain a victory over sin.

SUBMIT TO BE SANCTIFIED

This is the language of unbelief, which always prompts the soul to rise in opposition to God. To all such, who make these futile objections, the Lord says, *Be still, and know that I am God—know* that I, who have commanded you to be holy, am able and willing to make you so—that I, who am *your* God, have pledged . . . all the perfections of My character to defend you against all the assaults of your enemies; and when I say, respecting them, Let them be *thrust out and be destroyed,* it *shall be done.* And, in regard to your weaknesses, have I not *laid help upon One who is mighty, and able to save, even to the uttermost, all that come unto Me through Him?* What though the strength of sin in your members be great, cannot I control the monster? Am I not able to bind the strong man and cast him out—to cleanse your heart, even from all unrighteousness? Only, therefore, submit to Me. Let your willing soul bow down to My dictates—follow wheresoever I lead—walk in the light of My countenance, and these things, which seem impossible to you, shall be perfectly possible to Me; I will then accomplish *all the good pleasure of My will,* and carry on the *work of faith with power.* At last, then, *know*

GOD IS ABLE

Me; know that *I am love*—that I am *strong to save*—and that none can *pluck thee out of My hands,* so long as thou dost submit thyself to My direction."

In this way let all Christians submit themselves to their Heavenly Father, and it shall be well with them.

The duty inculcated in the text implies

IV. *A submission to God in reference to whatever He has promised*

The commands and promises of God are always inseparable. . . . Whatever God commands, there is always connected with it a promise that we shall have strength to perform it. In this respect, duties and privileges run parallel with each other. Does He command us to take up our daily cross, to deny ourselves, to walk in the light, to be and to live holy? And has He not . . . promised to give grace equal to our day; to help our infirmities; to enlighten our understandings and sanctify our natures; and to give us mercy, and enable us to "find grace to help in [every] time of need" (Heb. 4:16)? A firm reliance, therefore, on "all the promises of God," which "are yea, and . . . Amen, unto the glory of God" the Father (2 Cor. 1:20), is essential to our growth in grace, to our stability in the paths of peace, and to our being buoyed up amid the waves and billows of affliction.

BELIEVE GOD'S PROMISES

It was one of the excellencies of Abraham's character that "he staggered not at the promise of God through unbelief; but was strong in faith, giving glory to God" (Rom. 4:20). While faith is wavering, the soul is unstable and cannot receive the fulfillment of the promise. Whenever, therefore, we are tempted, from a consciousness of our own weaknesses or unworthiness, to doubt the promises of God, to question His fidelity, we may be met by the doctrine of the text, *Be still,* and know that God cannot *deny himself.* Whatever objections may originate from our past sinfulness, from our present ill deserts, or from our feebleness, they are all removed by a believing view of the infinite fullness of the "riches of his grace . . . through Christ Jesus" (Eph. 2:7). We have only to bow down before His throne, submit our wills to His will, and rely . . . upon the immutability of Him who has promised never to leave nor forsake His faithful people.

But it is chiefly under dark and afflictive dispensations that the fearful Christian is induced to question the merciful protection of his Heavenly Father. Let such, however, recollect that though "clouds and darkness are round about him: righteousness and judgment are the habitation of his throne" (Ps. 97:2). And let them also remember that . . . every stroke of His hand, however heavily it may press upon them, they abiding faithful, shall be sanctified to their present and future happiness. We may well say to them, therefore,

Judge not the Lord by feeble sense,
But trust him for his grace;
Behind a frowning providence
He hides a smiling face.

While the waves are passing over them, let them believe in Him who walketh upon the waters, who "hath gathered the wind in his fists" (Prov. 30:4), and who "taketh up the isles as a very little thing" (Isa. 40:15); and they shall be safe—they shall safely outride the storm and arrive at the haven of eternal repose at last.

In all these several ways let us *be still* before the Lord of the whole earth. Ceasing to raise objections against His commandments, His doings, or His manner of working, or the faithfulness of His promises, let us obey with cheerfulness, submit to His ways with patience and resignation, follow the openings of His providence with peaceful and steady steps, and rely upon His promises with a firm and persevering faith. Happy those who thus *submit* themselves to the government of God without murmuring!

Thrice happy all those who *know Him* as *their* God . . . who daily walk in the light of His countenance, and are joyfully anticipating that day when . . . they shall participate in that pure and perennial joy which *flows from God's right hand for evermore.* "The Lord is in his holy temple: let all the earth keep silence before him" (Hab. 2:20).

J. Rendel Harris
(1852-1941)

The inclusion of a sermon by Rendel Harris may prompt some readers to exclaim, "Is Saul among the prophets?" For Harris, according to R. E. D. Clark, was a liberal in his theological stance *(The New International Dictionary of the Christian Church).* Be that as it may, among his prolific writings are some materials rich in holiness teaching, and all the more valuable for not being mere echoes of the past.

Rendel Harris, who died in 1941, had a career as unorthodox as some of his scholarly positions. He was educated at Cambridge and taught mathematics there until he moved to the United States in 1882.

In the U.S., Harris taught at Johns Hopkins University and at Haverford College, then returned to England.

He established a reputation as a Bible scholar and an expert in oriental languages, becoming, finally, curator of manuscripts at John Rylands Library in Manchester.

Harris joined the Society of Friends in 1880. The Friends involvement in humanitarian social work found a responsive chord in his heart. Among other activities, he engaged in relief projects for survivors of the Armenian massacres in 1896.

The modern holiness movement has utilized an "Egypt to Canaan" motif in much of its hymnody and theology. Regeneration has been viewed as an exodus, and entire sanctification has been viewed as an entrance into Canaan. Whole books have been written to trace parallels between the spiritual journey of Christians and the migration of ancient Israel from Egypt to Canaan. While, at times, typology ran unbridled, the interpretation was generally sound.

Something of this shines through the sermon by Harris. We "learn the lessons of our personal sanctification out of the migration of His ancient people." To this parallel, Rendel Harris brings insight paired with imagination and clothed in splendid language. The spiritual rest that God has prepared in Christ for His people is "surveyed from a mountain of vision" and "entered upon by a passage of faith." The promised rest is so attractive that it leads to "the unreserved obedience and unlimited submission" that claims this spiritual inheritance. Harris's treatment brings to mind Wesley's admonition, that people are to be *drawn* and not driven into holiness.

The Sabbatism of the People of God*

There remaineth therefore a rest to the people of God (Heb. 4:9).

When the proposal was made for carrying a railway through some of the most beautiful scenery of the Derbyshire dales, an indignant letter was written by Mr. Ruskin to the public papers. [He asked them] to stay, if it were possible, the devastation that seemed to be impending over a country which he loved. . . . Among other arguments . . . he said that Derbyshire is "a lovely child's alphabet, an alluring first lesson in all that's admirable."

Without discussing the question of the justification of railroads in beautiful localities . . . we may recognize . . . a truth which has been closely wrought into the religious history of the race. For it has pleased God to make one small land of such importance in the spiritual progress of the people, that . . . the highest aspirations of the soul in quest of union with God have been expressed in the language of this country, of its rivers and plains, of its corn and wine and oil, of its wars and rests. . . . We may fairly say, in Ruskin's terms, that Palestine is a lovely child's alphabet, an alluring first lesson in all that's admirable.

---

*Source: J. Rendel Harris, *Union with God*. London: Hodder and Stoughton, 1896.

When we say this, we mean chiefly to draw attention to the thought expressed by the writer to the Hebrews, that out of this alphabet was spelt the truth that "there remaineth . . . a rest to the people of God."

And I suppose there is no historical student, and certainly no student of Scripture, who would dispute or deny the educational value of the land of which we speak. Nine-tenths of the good words we repeat are in Eastern language, if we only knew it; they can never be more than half translated, however progressive we may be. We shall always talk of Promised Lands, whenever God breathes into our souls the hope of good things to come; of Beulah . . . when we describe the life of abiding communion with God; of New Jerusalem . . . when we see visions and dream dreams of renewed and revised social order. . . .

LANGUAGE OF CANAAN

From the historical standpoint at all events this little land vindicates its right to be called a religious alphabet, and the smaller the land the more wonderful is it that so many lessons have been taught in terms of it. Compared with Egypt or Assyria, this land is only a strip for which they both contended; yet it is from its natural features, and not from theirs, that God taught His children their elementary lessons and is teaching them today some of their more advanced lessons. Compared with its neighbor Phoenicia, from which Western people received their secular alphabet, we may say of this land and its message to the rest of the world, that it has for its Cadmus Him that was from the beginning. For the Spirit of Truth not only made a message out of Christ's life, but also out of His environment, and made the land a talking and a teaching land for all those who have ears to hear. And so

Faith has still its Olivet,
And love its Galilee.

It was natural enough that this should have been so when Christ was on earth; for in those days all creatures found a speech, and the very birds and beasts and trees and flowers were full of oracles: the birds might say, We are created to be preached about; and the lilies, We are here to be considered; and the lambs, When in fold we are the figure of His Church, and when lost, we are the favorite text for His compassions to discourse on; and as for the trees, the fig tree when barren proclaimed His judgments, when slow of fruit, His forbearance, and in the richness of summer promise, His advent. Everything that was about Christ was vocal of Christ. But it would be a mistake to suppose that the message of the land was over when Christ ascended. For as time went by, a new lesson was framed out of the very desolations that were impending over it, and an illuminated mind made an argument, recapitulating the story of its first conquest, and saying, almost as if he were working out a string of syllogisms—

> "If they shall enter into my rest:
> They to whom it was first preached entered not;
> It remains that some must enter in;
> If Joshua had given them rest, he would not afterward have spoken of another day.
> There remaineth, therefore, a rest for the people of God."

PERSONAL SANCTIFICATION

So we conclude that it was God's will to make us learn the lessons of our personal sanctification out of the migration of His ancient people, and to say of the relation between their fortunes and ours, "The Holy Ghost this signifying . . . that there remaineth a rest to the people of God" (Heb. 9:8; 4:9).

And now let us go a step further, and with a map of Palestine before our eyes, and the story of the entrance of the children of Israel before our minds, let us say that it appears that the good land and large into which God led His people was designed (1) to be surveyed from a mountain of vision; (2) to be entered upon by a passage of faith.

We begin with vision, because eyes take possession of their inheritance before hands and feet; and as a matter of fact hands take hold and feet enter in because eyes have seen. Nothing is more important than a good perspective in the kingdom of God. Until we have a measure of vision, there is no place for footsteps of advancing and appropriating faith. Vague and general notions as to the kingdom of God are almost worthless; they never constitute the terms of a covenant between God and the soul.

GOD'S WILL FOR US

Splendor, glory, and immensity, someone has said, are great thoughts, high ideas; but a little definite happiness would be more to the purpose. We need to get some information from God himself as to what it is that He is wanting to do with us and for us; and if He opens the eyes of our heart to the knowledge of His will, and makes us strong to grasp with all saints the length and breadth and height of redeeming love, we may be encouraged to exchange the panorama for the reality, and to turn contemplation into obedience.

It is for this reason that our Lord . . . proclaimed a series of beatitudes in what we call the Sermon on the Mount. These Beatitudes are a series of instantaneous photographs of the holy life, in which the initiated soul is seen under so many successive aspects, as mourning and as merciful, as pure in heart and aspiring with divinely quickened desire; but all these detached views are only so many glimpses of what is comprehensively defined under the head of blessedness. Just as in Edison's newly invented kinetograph a succession of rapidly taken photographs may be recombined into the story of the motion of an object, so the phases of beatitude are to be combined together as beatitude, and then, seen in one combination, are to be the object of the spiritual covetousness of the soul that is ascending to the divine likeness. When, therefore, we have an intelligent conception of what blessedness is, we are on the mount of vision; and when we stand on the mount of vision it is natural to say, "I pray thee, let me go over" (Deut. 3:25).

A DESIRABLE COUNTRY

As we ascend the mountain of vision, it is a counsel of the first importance that we take our stand with our faces toward the good land and *our backs to the wilderness.* It is a panorama that lies in one direction only, and the vision depends on the attitude as well as on the altitude. For this reason the Scriptures exhort us (1) negatively, to let the dead past bury its dead, for "the time past . . . may suffice us to have wrought the will of the Gentiles" (1 Pet. 4:3); to be "forgetting those things which are behind" (Phil. 3:13), and even to be "leaving the word of the beginning of Christ" (Heb. 6:1, ASV margin), in order that (2) positively, we may "prove . . . the good and acceptable and perfect will of God" (Rom. 12:2, ERV), may reach out toward "those things which are before" (Phil. 3:13), and be carried forward "unto perfection" (Heb. 6:1).

"LET US GO ON"

This attitude implies, among other things, that we have done with legal years and have silenced vain regrets. We must exchange the obedience of the letter for "the law of the Spirit of life [which is] in Christ Jesus" (Rom. 8:2). The thought either of our own loneliness in a wide world, or of our own disappointment in a contentious world, must be eclipsed by the assurance that we shall be neither lonely nor disappointed when the kingdom of God shall be fully come.

Of the wilderness life, then, it is said, "The time past . . . may suffice"; the covenant, moreover, of God with the soul is indicated in the words [of the previous verse] with which the apostle [explains], "That he . . . should live the rest of his time . . . to the will of God"; it is a covenant with the residue of our days. And this covenant is accepted by the soul on the mountain of vision in an act of consecrating faith:

Lord, in the strength of grace,
With a glad heart and free,
Myself, my residue of days,
I consecrate to Thee.

We must not, however, forget that even on the mountain of vision, and when the soul is looking in the right direction, there are such mists as oftentimes obscure the landscape even to people who wish to see. These mists are the results, in many cases, of a false theology, which has for generation after generation insisted that God shall not do for His people, and Christ shall not be to His people, just what the Scriptures propound. It is impossible, or almost impossible, to argue with persons who are set at strife with their own blessedness by their teachers; but there is one consideration which is encouraging, and that is this: it often happens that to sincere people who are seeking the closer walk with God, there comes an experience similar to that which Wordsworth describes in the third book of his *Excursion,* when

SCRIPTURAL

a step,
A single step, that freed me from the skirts
Of the blind vapour, opened to my view
Glory beyond all glory, ever seen
By waking sense or by the dreaming soul.
. . . .
That which I saw was the revealed abode
Of spirits in beatitude!

It is a waste of time to try and fight with the blind vapor of traditional misconceptions of God and traditional misinterpretations of the Scriptures, when a single step of obedience will often set us saying and singing that "there remaineth a rest to the people of God."

OBEDIENCE

We pass on to the next thought, which is that our Lord who planned the mountain of vision planned also the passage of faith, the river which must be crossed before the good land is ours. He set Jordan on the map, and it is not for us to erase it. Here we are brought face-to-face with the fact that we are to come down out of the vision that we may go over into the reality. The vision is withdrawn as we

BY FAITH

descend to take possession of what God shows us to be most truly ours. The mystics call this deprivation which comes at a certain point in the advance of the soul the dark night of faith, when every step has to be taken in absolute dependence upon God, and assurance that the vision was truth and no lie. We drop into a lowly vale, as low as the hill was high: it is the valley of our individual nothingness, the nothingness of the creature.

Jacob is left alone, and a strange angel wrestles with him all night long, until the day of a new covenant making (that shall also be covenant keeping) dawns upon him; until the word of blessing shall be spoken, that "as a prince hast thou power with God and with men, and hast prevailed" (Gen. 32:28). The children of the patriarch are brought to the edge of the overflowing stream with which faith has to reckon; they act as though the waves were rocks, or as though the waters were dry land. And the "lovely child's alphabet" has nothing more lovely than the thought of the unreserved obedience and unlimited submission which are the characteristics of the great surrender by which such things are claimed for our own as "God hath [laid up] for them that love him" (1 Cor. 2:9).

If this be the alphabet by which God teaches, may we be the children that learn, the "obedient children" (1 Pet. 1:14), the "dear children" (Eph. 5:1), the "little children" (1 John 2:1), the "children of God" (1 John 3:1, ERV).

John H. Paul
(1877-1967)

"What God hath wrought!" would be a fitting title for a biography of John Haywood Paul. His father died when he was three, and from boyhood John Paul worked to help his widowed mother. These circumstances deprived him of the opportunity for formal education. His 7 years of schooling were all obtained before he was 15. Yet he spent years as a college teacher and administrator, in addition to a preaching and writing career of distinction.

Louisiana born and Methodist bred, he was licensed to preach in 1900. He died on the last day of 1967, having given to Christ and the church 68 years of devoted and fruitful service.

His work as a preacher included pastorates in four Southern states and evangelism throughout the United States and abroad.

He taught for five years at Meridian College in Mississippi, for six years at Asbury College in Kentucky, and was president of Taylor University in Indiana for nine years. Following this presidency he taught at Chicago Evangelistic Institute, and then became president of John Fletcher College in Iowa. His last faculty assignment was at Asbury Theological Seminary for six years.

Dr. Paul was also a prolific writer, authoring many articles and books. He served as an editor with four holiness periodicals. At the time of his death he had been associate editor of *The Herald* for 25 years.

In 1916 the *Christian Advocate,* observing the centennial anniversary of Francis Asbury's death, awarded John Paul a prize for "the best written statement of the doctrine of entire sanctification."

Paul was the founder of the Deeper Life Conference Movement in the United States. He had worked with that movement earlier in Japan.

"Wrestling Jacob" is an exposition of the surrender necessary to an experience of deliverance from inherited sin, a surrender that is reached through earnest prayer. It sets forth the human act of consecration that is the condition and prelude to the divine work of sanctification. The experience of Jacob at Peniel is a graphic paradigm of the need, struggle, and deliverance that we experience in our quest for personal holiness. It is our indifference, not God's reluctance, that necessitates the struggle. "The wrestling is not that we may subdue God, but that God may subdue us."

Wrestling Jacob: The Route to the Blessing*

I will not let thee go, except thou bless me (Gen. 32:26).

In the face of this text we discern a principle that must characterize the prayer of every successful seeker for the blessing of God, whatever that blessing may be. The principle I refer to is *resolution.* If we seek God in an unconcerned manner, as though it made but little difference whether we get His blessing or not, we are sure to miss the blessing.

BLESS ME NOW

If the blessing we seek is pardon or purity—essentials in the qualification of the soul to stand before the judgment seat of Christ—it is perfectly consistent for us to feel that we cannot get along another day without it; it is proper for us to fall into a state of scriptural recklessness and cry out, as did Jacob, substantially, I must have the blessing or die! The man who approaches the place of prayer affirming that he will never leave that sacred altar until he gets this blessing, that he will eat and drink no more until his heart receives the divine seal, is quite sure to get the blessing.

---

*Source: *The Pentecostal Pulpit.* Louisville, Ky.: Pentecostal Publishing Co., n.d.

We will first glance at the historic background of this text. Jacob was the twin brother of Esau. They had been born and reared in southern Palestine. When their father, Isaac, was old and his eyes were dim, thinking that the day of his death was near at hand, he sent Esau . . . to kill and prepare venison and spread before him a palatable meal, with the understanding that he would take that occasion to pronounce the patriarchal blessing which would put the son in line with the Messiah and give him a title to the beautiful land of Canaan.

Jacob and his mother, feeling that it was the divine plan that Jacob, who some years before purchased the birthright, should have the blessing, contrived and executed a plan to supplant Esau. Now, Esau was a rugged character, and when he discovered that his brother had stepped in before him, he swore vengeance against Jacob, declaring that he would kill him as soon as his father was dead and the days of mourning were over. When the mother heard this, she conferred with Isaac, and having some additional reasons, they sent their son Jacob away to the distant land of Mesopotamia.

With budget in hand, this celebrated character started on his distant pilgrimage. When Jacob came to a point a few miles north of Jerusalem, in the evening he lay down to sleep, pillowing his head upon a stone. While he slept he saw a vision: a ladder reaching from the earth to the skies, upon which the angels of God were ascending and descending, while the Lord stood above it proclaiming His great name and setting seal to the blessing which Isaac had bestowed.

GATE OF HEAVEN

When Jacob awoke from his sleep, he felt an awful sense of the Divine Presence, and cried out, "Surely the Lord is in this place; and I knew it not. How dreadful is this place! this is none other but the house of God, and this is the gate of heaven" (Gen. 28:16-17). His frame shook with holy fear as he arose at the dawning of the morning and took the stone that he put for his pillow, erecting it for an altar and a monument to celebrate that sacred hour in which he heard the voice of Jehovah and entered into a covenant with his father's God. From that day forward Jacob was a man of God.

Of course, as we read the sketch of his biography which lies between Bethel and Peniel, in the light of this glorious age, we see many faults in his deportment; but the severity of our judgment will be modified when we remember that he was living in an age, not only when they were without the gospel, but when they had no written law. Jacob proceeded on his journey till he reached the home of Laban, a wealthy kinsman in northern Mesopotamia.

After spending upwards of 20 years in this region, having become the head of a considerable family and the possessor of a goodly estate, he is now on his return to the land of his father, supposing that the anger of Esau has cooled. As he journeys he sends a company of his menservants to the land of Edom, hoping to form a treaty with Esau.

GOD CALLS

But the men made a speedy return and brought the sensational news that Esau seemed to be on the warpath and was coming to meet them with 400 men. Then Jacob was greatly afraid and fell into a condition of deep distress; but just at this juncture some voice of which we have no account bade him to call upon God, giving himself to prayer.

This was an ordeal that had much to do with Jacob's personal experience. It seems that in this hour of distress he got a glimpse of himself and his own needs as he never had before. Step by step the God of his fathers, who had drawn the architecture of his future estate, had led him to what we in this age call his Gethsemane—an ordeal which intervenes between each heart and the blessing of full salvation.

Jacob made his way to a place of prayer and began to pour out his soul before God. He spent a night which no human tongue could describe—the agony, the solemnity, the glory of that awful night! We have no record of the extended and varying speech, mingled with heartrending cries and groans that came from Jacob's lips that night; no doubt they would make a large book, were it not impossible for written words to express them. . . .

The keynote of his appeal was, "Bless me." He does not name the blessing he wants, but no doubt there was a sufficient understanding between God and himself. The Scriptures disclose to us the blessing that he received. It was an experience that changed his character; that work of grace which casts out fear; that blessing which endues with "power from on high" (Luke 24:49). It was not common for men of God in that day to be sanctified wholly, perfected in love, and endued with power from on high. This is a New Testament attainment; but some of the patriarchs, by means of a deep self-abasement, an importunate prayer, and a mountaintop faith, went beyond their day and partook of the experience that was thousands of years ahead of the times in which they lived.

AN OLD TESTAMENT EXPERIENCE

Like most everybody else, Jacob had inherited some unfortunate traits of character. It may be that his parents were sometimes discouraged with him, and his neighbors prophesied that no good thing would ever come of him; but God knew Jacob, and saw that beneath the rubbish of his moral character there were noble qualities which, if unalloyed and brought to the front, would bless the world.

WRONG ATTITUDES

This observation will afford hope for many a character that is beset by hopeless tempers, ungodly ambitions, and many other unhappy traits. The church may never be able to improve such a character, the colleges may dismiss him as a hopeless case, and he may spend his life unknown and underestimated; whereas if God could have had His way with that same individual, He would have brought out the beauty of his character and given him a name which would have been as ointment poured forth.

God followed Jacob. How interesting it is to see how the hand of God was with him and upon him from time to time. His case may not have seemed promising; it may be that it was a task to deal with him; but Jacob had fiber in his moral nature, and God pulled him through.

POTENTIAL UNDER GOD

No doubt there are young people who have latent in their characters the qualities of noblemen, but they go through the world unnoticed and unknown. Their influence and power are easily bounded by the limits of one county. . . . If their carnal traits were nailed to the Cross by the sanctifying Spirit, and the excellencies of their souls were brought out by the touch of the Master Workman who framed the worlds, the county could not hold them. Perhaps the state could not hold them . . . and . . . the nation and even the world itself would fail to contain the power and glory of their influence and labors.

No doubt if Jacob had not had his Peniel, we would have known but little of him; he would not have been called a prince of God, and the spiritual Church of all the ages would not have been named Israel for him as it is. The secret of his great promotion and the honor which God bestowed upon him, which is greater than the highest honors that men can bestow, and more to be appreciated than the chair of the president or the throne of an earthly king, is explained in the fact that he succeeded in letting God have His way with him.

Every human soul inherits the carnal mind, or what is called original sin. Its prominent development in Jacob was dishonesty, or a species of covetousness. This is indicated by his name, which means supplanter. Men were frequently named by inspiration according to character in those days. If you will study your own experience and the experiences of others, you will notice that in every heart the carnal mind heads up in one or two forms of besetting sin. With some it is covetousness; with some it is pride; with others an evil temper; and with others something else. The qualities may be latent in the character of a Christian, so that his nearest friends may not be able to discover the unhappy tendencies of his heart; but the individual knows. If he is a conscientious Christian, he sees himself from day to day in the mirror of God's truth, and groans inwardly because of his nonconformity to the "good and acceptable and perfect will of God" (Rom. 12:2, ASV).

THE CARNAL MIND

Jacob did not have the means of illumination that we have; he had no transparent mirror in which to examine himself from day to day as we do; it took an ordeal to reveal to him the depravity of his soul; but the ordeal has come, and with it a revelation of the possibilities of faith; and Jacob, with a holy desperation, has hurled himself upon Jehovah's altar and cried, "I will not let thee go, except thou bless me!"

We notice that notwithstanding the unfavorable surroundings and gloomy prospects, Jacob wastes no time praying over surroundings and prospects, but prays for himself. There comes a time when it is not consistent to pray for any but yourself. The difficulty with many of us is lack of definiteness. We pray all over land and sea in such a general way, until no definite results can be hoped for.

A PERSONAL ISSUE

Jacob seems to have received a revelation of the fact that when a man gets right in his heart, it improves his surroundings. There is a new brightness to the sun, there is a new music in the singing of the birds, and a new glory in all the handiwork of God. If your heart conforms to the heart of Christ and your footsteps pattern after Him, it will occur to you that the home folks are more agreeable, and the domestics more amiable. A new beauty and delight will come into your life which it will be hard for earth's turmoil to disturb.

There seems to have been a definite understanding between God and Jacob as to what he was pleading for when he said, "Bless me." We know that he had no reference to the ordinary things, which we call blessings, such as sunshine and showers and happy sensations. He had come for a work to be done in his heart, and while the language of his lips may seem to us indefinite, the cry of his heart was perfectly definite.

We may wonder why it is that Jacob prayed all night. Are we to offer long prayers in order to persuade God? No, God is always disposed to give whatever is in accordance with His will, if faith appropriates the gift. We tarry long in prayer in order that we may get on believing ground. The wrestling is not that we may subdue God, but that God may subdue us. The human heart is capable of having many desires at one time. These may be of various magnitudes. The desire for the thing for which we are praying must outshine all the other desires before we can get the blessing.

IN A MOMENT

The secret of prevailing prayer is to cherish and give vent to a certain desire in the heart until, by exercise and nourishment, this desire becomes stalwart and self-asserting, so that it can hurl all of our minor desires into the background of our natures, put its foot upon the neck of its greatest rival, and create a violent agitation throughout the soul and body of the man. There are many ways to explain the profit of long, secret prayers; we have only referred to them in their relation to prevailing prayer; but the long, secret prayer is profitable in the sense that we wait upon God, keep company with Him in a peculiar way, and thus gather strength and virtue from Him that otherwise we could not have.

Jacob could not get his blessing so long as he had other desires equally as great as the desire for the blessing, even though the other desires were legitimate. When you are seeking forgiveness of sin, or the sanctification of your soul, you must come to that extreme point where you would rather have the work of grace than anything else under heaven. If $1 million would suit you better than the forgiveness of your sins, you could not be forgiven. If the presidency of the United States would suit you as well as the inheritance of sanctification, you are not a qualified candidate for holiness. The poet had the scriptural idea when he said,

MORE THAN ANYTHING ELSE

'Tis worse than death my Lord to love,
And not my Lord alone.

We see from this sentiment, and also from the sentiment that was evidently in the heart of Jacob that night, that the desire for God's blessing must be stronger than death before we reach the climax of prevailing prayer. Physical comfort must be no consideration. We must be willing to resort to any inconvenience and suffer any degree of humiliation in order to get the blessing. The blessing is yours when the conditions are met, and you come to where you cannot do without it any longer. If there lurks in your heart an idea that you could manage to content yourself without the blessing, you cannot have the blessing.

In their approach toward the blessing of full salvation, many seekers reach a juncture where they are perplexed; they become a puzzle to themselves; conditions are met so far as they know, and they wonder why it is that they have not the blessing. Well, there is always a reason. If there were no reasons, they could have the blessing now. Of course, there is something in the way, and if the seeker will make a guess, the chances are he will locate the trouble at the first guess; but if he fails, and will hold on to God with the tenacity that is revealed in this text, the Lord will put His finger on the trouble in due time.

HINDRANCES EXPLAINED

The steps that Jacob made in order to reach the fullness of the blessing of Christ are typical of the steps that we must make today, when we seek our Pentecost. The Scriptures indicate to us the relation that Jacob's possessions held in his mind. He sent his flocks and herds and menservants across the brook; then he sent the maidservants with their children; after this, he separated himself from Leah, and her children, sending them across; this left him alone with Rachel and her babe, the dearest treasures of his heart; but he separated himself from them, and went alone to the place of prayer.

You see, it is natural for us to give up our inferior things first, consecrating our possessions according to their value until we come to some cherished ambition, valued position, or precious treasure which we idolize above all things else. Many seekers stop here, and while they may fancy that their consecration is complete according to the will of God, it is only to the limit of their wills. Such people are a long ways from the fullness of the blessing.

CONSECRATION

The separation of Jacob from his possessions and loved ones, and the lonely night of prayer, represent to our minds the fact that we must take the lone way with Jesus. The scriptural way is a narrow way. Two cannot walk side by side in the path of consecration. Your friends must go in ahead of you, or behind you . . . so the thing for you to do is to enter in today.

After Jacob had taken the initial steps and dealt with the problems around the edge of the subject, he arrives at himself. One whole night has to be spent on Jacob. People may think that their companions, their neighbors, or their peculiar circumstances in life are the greatest barriers between them and holiness, but this is usually untrue;

as a rule every man is his own worst enemy. Others may stand in our light, but we are more apt to stand in our own light.

After Jacob had passed through the season of prayer which we have already described, having to an extent prevailed with God, he arrived at the last condition. Jehovah said unto him, "What is thy name?" (Gen. 32:27). This was a final confession from the very depths of Jacob's soul. It seems that to acknowledge the doctrine of inherited depravity, and confess the Bible teaching of sin in believers, is a hard thing for some great men to do. You see, it was about the last thing that Jacob arrived at; but he made this acknowledgment and confession all in one, when with bleeding heart and anxious mind, he said, "My name is Jacob."

CARNALITY ACKNOWLEDGED

Conditions were then met. The opportunity of God had come; the man had reached his extremity; a pause of eloquent silence occurred, an exhausted and self-surrendered conqueror stood with bated breath, while an almighty Savior gave His heart the touch that told throughout the balance of Jacob's lifetime—the memory of which he celebrates today among the redeemed on high. It seems to me that there is an eloquence and a beauty clustered around this little phrase of Scripture that we seldom meet with anywhere else: "And he blessed him there" (v. 29).

God changed the patriarch's name to Israel, which means a prince, giving as His reason that Jacob had prevailed with God and with man, and was endued with power. Jacob had gained a victory by way of the throne. When he reached this mountaintop of faith and got his blessing at Peniel, he conquered all the foes for the balance of his life. Disappointment, pain, and death were beneath his feet. Once for all he had the victory, a lasting victory. No man has the victory as he ought to have it until he gets it in his soul. Disappointments will depress us, trials will irritate us, the death of loved ones will overshadow us with an undissolving cloud, and the ghost of misfortune will haunt us . . . unless we have the complete victory in our souls.

STRENGTH IN VICTORY

When Jacob met Esau, the sturdy red man broke down and wept. Jacob's battle had already been fought, and the victory won. How could Esau smite the Lord's anointed? How could he strike a man who, though physically wasted, was filled with the beauty of holiness and covered with the mantle of God?

Jacob descended from that place of prayer, not only a mightier man, but a man with a transparent character; his life told for God after that. You may discover irregularities and sins in his life up till that day, but after that he took sides with God, not only against his enemies, but against his friends; not only against his friends, but against his loved ones, and, if necessary, against himself. This fully represents to us the attitude of a man who is sanctified in Jesus Christ. Jacob had some family trouble after that, but while his own children did wrong, and showed the depravity of their natures, Jacob took sides with God in the matter.

Israel was held in high esteem by Jehovah. The last we hear of this honored patriarch, when he is ripe with age, and his hairs are bleached into a crown of glory, he is leaning upon his staff on the verge of his grave, pronouncing a blessing upon his posterity. God pulled back the curtain which veils the great future, and Jacob gazed down through the vista of ages. He saw the battles and triumphs of Zion, and said in prophetic strains, "The sceptre shall not depart from Judah, nor a lawgiver from between his feet, until Shiloh come; and unto him shall the gathering of the people be" (Gen. 49:10). God honored him with a vision of the glories of the New Testament Church, and cheered his heart with the hope of a redeemed humanity through the Lion of the tribe of Judah, and he passed to his reward.

5
THE MINISTRY OF THE HOLY SPIRIT

Jonathan Edmonson

(1766-1842)

Jonathan Edmonson began his ministry in 1786 when John Wesley appointed him to labor in the Epworth circuit. He gave himself to the itinerant ministry among the Methodists for some 50 years, and then broken health compelled him to "locate."

In the book *Wesley and His Successors,* Edmonson is described as "mild and urbane in his disposition, affectionate and steady in his attachments." He was highly respected by the Methodists and served as president of the Wesleyan Methodist Conference (Leeds).

His sermon "The Spirit May Be Quenched" is taken from a second volume of *Short Sermons,* published in the 42nd year of his ministry, when he was 62 years old. In the preface he mentions a first volume, which had been favored with "liberal reviews" in several literary journals "of considerable celebrity." The sermons sold steadily "without the aid of puffing advertisements." Having read those in volume 2, I can see why they did. His style is even plainer than John Wesley's and his sermons much briefer. He tells us that he "always endeavored, both in preaching and writing, to say as much as possible in a few well-chosen words." Simplicity of construction, urgency of tone, and patency of pastoral concern make his sermons choice models for preachers in any age.

In this particular sermon, the great themes of redemption and holiness and the practical issues of watchfulness and obedience are given lively and searching expression. Such earnest preaching, anointed by the Holy Spirit, made those early Methodists invincible. Even yellowed, brittle pages convey something of the glory that rested upon their evangelism. Such preaching can still be the catalyst of revival.

In a sermon on "The Happy Death of Believers," Edmonson wrote, "Christian believers die *in the Lord.* . . . The union of the soul and body is dissolved by death; but the union of the soul to Christ remains unbroken in that solemn hour. . . . This sacred union with Jesus, when the soul is departing hence, is the greatest blessing that can be enjoyed in that awful hour. . . . Such a death is truly happy, and is more to be desired than all the wealth and power of this world of shadows." Fourteen years after that sermon was published, the faithful preacher died, exclaiming, "Jesus is my salvation."

The Spirit May Be Quenched*

Quench not the Spirit (1 Thess. 5:19).

. . . If we examine the context, it will appear that the ordinary influences [of the Holy Spirit] are intended. For there we are commanded to rejoice evermore, to pray without ceasing, and in everything to give thanks. And these duties are binding on all Christians in every age and nation. But how can they be performed? Only by the enlightening, warming, and sanctifying influences of the Spirit; and if this holy flame be quenched, we shall neither rejoice, nor pray, nor give thanks to God. But why are the operations of the Spirit compared to fire? How may the Spirit be quenched? And what are the effects of quenching the Spirit?

I. *Why are the operations of the Spirit compared to fire?*

The comparison is frequently made both in the Old Testament and in the New. In the Old Testament the Holy Ghost is called a *Spirit*

---

*Source: Jonathan Edmonson, *Short Sermons on Important Subjects,* vol. 2. London: John Mason, 1829.

of burning, or, as Dr. Waterland reads, the *Spirit of cleansing;* and in the New Testament, His baptism is called a *baptism of fire* (Isa. 4:4; Matt. 3:11). When He came down from heaven on the Day of Pentecost, He appeared in the form of *cloven tongues like as of fire* (Acts 2:2); and this might be an intimation that He would accompany the preaching of the Word as a purifying flame, when faithfully delivered by His ministering servants.

CLEANSING

But the ordinary influences of the Spirit, like a flame of fire, *illuminate the soul* with a knowledge of the truth. When He shines on the understanding, the Scriptures are opened in their beauty and fullness, and we see wondrous things in the divine law; and when He shines on the heart, we discover our sonship, and the work of grace which He has wrought. For He witnesses with our spirits, that we are the children of God, by shining on His own work, and discovering to us our regeneration and new creation; and when this light is strong and clear, all our doubts and fears are instantly removed, and we rejoice in God our Savior.

ASSURANCE

And as fire warms and cheers the body of man, so the influences of the Holy Spirit *warm and cheer his soul,* promoting lively and active dispositions in the service of God. The soul that does not feel these influences resembles nature in the depth of winter, when all things are cold and dead, gloomy and dreary, barren and unfruitful. But when we feel the vital flame in active operation, we are like nature in the summer months, when the solar fire produces the most lively appearances in every direction, and ripens the fruits of the earth for the approaching harvest.

But the operations of the Spirit are compared to fire because He *purifies and refines the soul,* as that active and powerful [flame] purges material bodies from their dross. This is done in perfect harmony with the freedom of man as a moral agent. Thus, the warnings of the Spirit produce a fear and dread of sin; His sweet and alluring drawings produce a love of holiness; and His active influences transform the soul into the image of God. Thus He burns up the dross of sin, refines and purifies the heart, and fills the soul with a burning zeal for God.

PURIFICATION

II. *How may the Spirit be quenched?*

Everything that counteracts the work of grace in the soul quenches the Spirit of God in His hallowing influences. The whole may be comprised in two things: first, sins of omission; and, secondly, sins of commission. The first is a neglect of some known duty; and the second is a willful violation of the divine law.

We quench the Spirit by *neglecting prayer.* The reasons of this are obvious: He works in us a spirit of devotion; when we neglect prayer, we resist His workings; and that resistance damps the sacred flame. Then we feel no desire to pray, but are left to the foolish desires of our own corrupted hearts.

NEGLECT

The Spirit may be quenched by *neglecting the Word of God.* The sacred Volume was inspired by the Holy Ghost, and when we neglect it, we disregard His teachings. This is a high affront and insult offered to the Spirit, and has a direct tendency to extinguish the sacred fire in our hearts.

Many quench the Spirit by *neglecting the means of grace.* In those means, when piously attended, there is a special influence of the Holy Spirit; and he who stays at home, under any frivolous pretense, pours contempt on that influence. This damps the sacred fire in his own heart and provokes the anger of God.

It is quite certain that *vain and impure thoughts* quench the Holy Spirit. These should be hated and abhorred, because they are in direct opposition to His sanctifying influences. It was said in the days of Noah, *My spirit shall not always strive with man;* and we cannot wonder at this, because *every imagination of the thoughts of his heart was only evil continually* (Gen. 6:3, 5).

SINFUL THOUGHTS

The Spirit may be quenched by *unholy tempers.* Among these we may notice *pride,* which, as a pious writer observes, "is the master-sin, and first-born of the devil;" *covetousness,* or an inordinate love of wealth; with *anger, hatred, malice,* and *revenge.* These tempers, with many others, are so directly opposite to the pure workings of the Spirit that they cannot fail to extinguish the holy fire.

WRONG ATTITUDES

But the Spirit may be quenched by *improper conversation.* This includes foolish jesting; taking the name of God in vain; slandering absent persons; deceitful and mischievous conversation, which is like the poison of asps; and idle, trifling conversation, like that of the Athenians, who *spent their time in nothing else, but either to tell, or to hear some new thing* (Acts 17:21). Such conversation is directly opposed to the influences of the Spirit and is calculated to extinguish the holy fire of His sacred influences.

And the Spirit is quenched effectually by *wicked works.* For instance, by acts of injustice in our dealings with men; by cruelty and oppression; by gluttony and drunkenness; by fornication and all uncleanness; by turning from the living God to dumb idols; and by every open sin. These crimes quench the Spirit in a moment and leave the soul in a state of darkness and of death.

III. *What are the effects of quenching the Spirit?*

If we quench the Spirit, as an enlightening flame, we shall be left in a state of *spiritual blindness,* and in that state we may quite forget that we were once purged from our old sins by His renewing influences (2 Pet. 1:9). Apostates frequently fall into dangerous and damnable heresies. How shall we account for this dereliction of principle? We may observe, in the first place, that they put out the light which they had, by quenching the Spirit; and then, secondly, that God sent them strong delusion, as a judicial punishment, that they might believe a lie and be damned (2 Thess. 2:11-12). May we take warning and follow the illuminations of the Spirit; then we may be saved from the deadly errors of deluded men!

When we quench the Spirit, in His sanctifying influences, *sin reigns in our hearts.* Then the world comes in with all its fatal influences; corrupt nature rises up in all its strength; and the prince of the power of the air worketh in us all manner of wickedness. For when the Spirit is quenched, we have no good principle left to counteract the malignant influences of the world, the flesh, and the devil. In this deplorable state we proceed from bad to worse, till the measure of our iniquity is full, and then we sink into that death which never, never dies. Gracious Lord, save us from these abominable evils, and uphold us continually by Thy free Spirit!

HOLY SPIRIT

By quenching the Spirit, we lose the *comforts of religion.* Perhaps we retain the form; but we are cold and lifeless. The Holy Ghost is called the Comforter; and without Him there is no comfort. When He is quenched, we have no comfort in prayer, in reading the Scriptures, or in attending the means of grace. While we follow His influences, we rejoice evermore; but when we resist Him, our joy is turned to sorrow. Ask a poor backslider, who has quenched the Spirit, "Are you happy?" If he reply [honestly], he will say, "I have had no comfort since I began to resist the Holy Ghost." Then let us, as we value our peace and comfort, beware of quenching the Spirit.

We lose *spiritual gifts* by quenching the Spirit. These gifts are intended to be used for our own benefit, for the good of the church, and for the world at large; but when we lose them, we sink into a state of obscurity and spend our days in useless activity. *The manifestation of the Spirit is given to every man to profit withal* (1 Cor. 12:7). But can any man who quenches the Spirit be profited by this manifestation? Or can he profit other men? The plain fact is, that the manifestation of the Spirit in this case will cease; and the gifts, which were bestowed for holiness and usefulness, will be withdrawn forever.

Another sad effect of quenching the Spirit is *spiritual death.* By His influences we were quickened; and then we lived to God. That was a blessed state! But what is our present state? Perhaps we are *twice dead,* and *plucked up by the roots* (Jude 12). This is awful; but let us examine ourselves. We hope the life of God in our souls is not quite extinguished. Then let us *strengthen the things which remain, that are ready to die* (Rev. 3:2). If we continue to quench the Spirit, we shall entirely lose the life of God; for no man can live spiritually without His vital influences.

But the most fearful thing to be apprehended, in quenching the Spirit, is the *second death.* If we die that death, we shall be lost to all eternity. In this world the Spirit often returns, after He has been quenched, and graciously renews His work; but when He departs to return no more, our case will be hopeless, and our ruin will be inevitable. This is the final effect of apostasy. Oh, let us fear, and watch, and pray, that we may not be lost forever!

Let us nourish and cherish the heavenly influences of this sacred Spirit all the days of our life; which may God, of His infinite mercy, grant unto us all, through Jesus Christ our Lord! Amen.

Walter A. Chadwick

This sermon is another from the "Drew Sermons" based upon Golden Texts for the International Sunday School Lessons for 1908. When he wrote it, Walter Chadwick, Drew Theological Seminary alumnus, was serving as pastor of Christ Methodist Episcopal Church, Madison, N.J.

A summary of the Spirit's mission, based upon the "Paraclete" passages in John's Gospel, is a lot to ask of a sermon, but Chadwick handles it admirably.

His treatment is valuable for three special reasons: (1) He keeps the mission of the Spirit closely connected to the mission of Christ. (2) He keeps the mission of the Spirit closely allied to the Bible. (3) He keeps the mission of the Spirit closely applied to the Church. Too often the work of the Spirit has been presented in a manner almost independent of these three entities; which is to say, in a manner that is not truly biblical and not finally helpful.

Chadwick gets off on the right foot in a hurry with his opening sentence: "The mission of the Holy Spirit was to take up and carry forward the work of Jesus in the world." He continues in the right vein with the first truth he emphasizes: "At Pentecost the Holy Spirit came to abide in the Church. . . . So also the Holy Spirit dwells in the weakest and humblest believer." And his last point is still right on target: "The Comforter, as the Spirit of truth, sanctifies us through the Word." Chadwick appreciates the fact that the Spirit is not bound to the Word: "I will not say that He never leads us except by the direct teaching of some Scripture passage." Never-

theless, the Spirit does not operate contrary to the Word, but in, with, and through its message, so that "to neglect and ignore the Bible is to lose His teaching."

Life in its fullness is possible because "the Spirit presents a full Christ to your faith; trust Him fully." That key will unlock the door to unsearchable riches of sanctified living for every surrendered believer!

The Mission of the Holy Spirit*

I will pray the Father, and he shall give you another Comforter, that he may abide with you for ever (John 14:16).

The mission of the Holy Spirit was to take up and carry forward the work of Jesus in the world. He was to be to the disciples, and to those who should believe on Jesus through their word, all that Jesus had been to them; nay, to do for them and for us more than Jesus had been able to do in His bodily presence.

To take up this mission He came in His own distinctive personality, at a definite time, to abide in the world. Pentecost was the hour of His coming; the history of the Church is the evidence of His abiding. The Holy Spirit is an influence only as He is a person. Jesus constantly spoke of Him as such. Jesus had been a Comforter to His disciples, the Holy Spirit was to be another Comforter, one to stand by their side as Jesus stood, ready to respond to their call for aid as Jesus had been.

If it is asked in what sense He is in the world after Pentecost other than before, we answer, in the same sense that Jesus was in the world after the Incarnation as He had not been before. Jesus had always been in the world. The world was made by Him, and He was ever the "life [and] light" of men (John 1:4). But as the Revealer of the atoning love of the Father, He was not in the world until He came in the flesh and began that journey of obedience which ended at Calvary. So, also, the Holy Spirit was always in the world. At the Creation He brooded over the face of the deep; never a holy man spake but as he was moved by the Holy Ghost; and nowhere has God left himself

*Source: Ezra Squier Tipple, ed., *Drew Sermons on the Golden Texts for 1908*. New York: Eaton and Mains; Cincinnati: Jennings and Graham, 1907.

without His witness in human hearts. But as the Interpreter of Jesus in His saving grace, He was not in the world until at Pentecost He made the Church His habitation.

If it was His mission to take up the work of Jesus, He could not begin it until that mission was completed. If He is to interpret the life of Jesus, He could not come until Jesus was glorified.

CHRISTLIKENESS

Though the Comforter has His distinct personality, His coming is the coming of Jesus himself. This coming of the Comforter was in fulfillment of Jesus' promise, "I will come to you" (John 14:18). The Holy Spirit has no word to speak of himself. . . . His one work is to reveal Jesus, to interpret Jesus, to make the bond between Jesus and the believer a real and vital one, that Christ may dwell in our hearts by faith.

No name can better express the mission of the Holy Spirit than . . . the Comforter, if we take the divine meaning of comfort and not the world's meaning. The word itself means not only a consoler, but a helper.

The Holy Ghost was not the first Comforter. The burden of the word of the Lord to Isaiah was, "Comfort ye, comfort ye my people, saith your God" (40:1). Theirs was to be the comfort of iniquities pardoned; the comfort of human weakness exchanged for divine power. Jesus was a comforter to His disciples; never were His spirit and method better interpreted than at the very time when He gave the promise of the Spirit. "My comfort," He said to the disciples, "is not like that of the world." Now the Holy Spirit is with us as the Comforter. He is the Spirit of truth and so will comfort us in the true and not the false way. He is the Holy Spirit and so will make us realize that comfort can never be separated from holiness.

COMFORT BECAUSE OF HOLINESS

With this thought, the Holy Spirit is the Comforter even in His conviction of the world of sin. As the wise physician probes the throbbing flesh, though it hurts him to give pain, so that he may work a perfect cure, the Comforter leads us along the pathway of penitential sorrow, though He grieves to cause us bitter tears, so that He may lead us to a perfect salvation. The mission of the Comforter is fulfilled in a world saved from sin by faith in Jesus; adorned with righteousness through the grace of Jesus; delivered from judgment by the victory of Jesus. The Comforter has come that He may create and fashion a new race, even as many as have received Jesus Christ, born of the will of God, to be conformed at length to the divine likeness of their Lord.

In the mission of the Comforter I emphasize three outstanding truths:

I. *At Pentecost the Holy Spirit came to abide in the Church.*

He has never returned to heaven; He is here still and will abide forever. We are not, then, to think of His coming, or to ask for Him, as though He were absent from us. We may indeed ask for a larger manifestation of His presence, for a fuller measure of His power; but we are never to forget that He is with us.

WITH US

So also the Holy Spirit dwells in the weakest and humblest believer; the very fact that he has faith in Jesus is the evidence of the Spirit's presence, for "no man can say that Jesus is the Lord, but by the Holy Ghost" (1 Cor. 12:3). We have much to learn, and the Spirit will teach us; we may be slow of heart to believe, and the Spirit will be patient with us; we are unlike our Lord in many things, and the Spirit knows it and will correct us; but never, never let us forget that "Jesus Christ [by the Spirit] is in you, except ye be reprobates" (2 Cor. 13:5).

WITH US IN HIS FULLNESS

It is likewise true that the Holy Spirit is with us in His fullness. He is not an influence that can be given by measure; He is a person and comes to us in all the fullness of His divine personality. There is no lack in Him, and He is ever with us.

This thought of the abiding fullness and personal relationship of the Spirit has striking illustration in Bishop Thoburn's *Church of Pentecost.* He tells us that Sir Henry Baker, in seeking the sources of the Nile, camped one night on the sandy bed of a dry watercourse. At midnight he was awakened by his guide's cry, "The river! The river!" The rains had come in the mountains, and he had scarce time to escape to higher ground before the torrent was upon him. With the morning the whole surrounding scene was changed. Where there had been dry sand was a broad, deep river, flowing calm and full-banked. The birds were singing in the trees overhead; all nature rejoiced; and the peasants along the river were opening the ditches by which their fields would be irrigated from the river's fullness. The river had come for the season. So, he suggests, is the coming and abiding of the Holy Spirit.

At Pentecost, as the River of life flowing from beneath the throne of God, the Holy Spirit came. That River is flowing beside us today.

II. *The Holy Spirit comes to make us acquainted with Jesus.*

In the promise of His coming Jesus said, "He shall not speak of himself . . . He shall glorify me: for he shall receive of mine, and shall shew it unto you" (John 16:13-14). When Jesus was upon the earth, His one purpose was to glorify the Father. In His mission among men the one purpose of the Holy Spirit is to glorify Jesus. . . . Jesus glorified the Father in His person before the eyes of men; the Spirit hides himself that He may glorify the person of Jesus in the hearts of believers.

When He comes, we shall know He is in us by a new vision of Jesus; the marred face in which we saw no beauty becomes "the [fair

CHRISTLIKENESS

est] among ten thousand," and the one "altogether lovely" (Song of Sol. 5:10, 16). Not by spiritual ecstasy, nor by a thrill of the nerves, may we assure ourselves of the Spirit's presence, though in His presence there may be hours of even ecstatic joy thrilling our very body. But [assurance comes] in such a vision of Jesus as humbles us in penitent faith, leads us to commit ourselves to His care, impels us to yield ourselves in glad submission to His will, and awakens joy in His conscious presence.

Mr. F. B. Meyer, in telling of his experience at Keswick, England, spoke of attending a meeting of prayer for the filling of the Holy

TESTIMONY

Spirit. In the tense spiritual excitement of the hour he became so worn that finally he went away quietly to the mountain above the village, and there told God of his need and desire. A voice said to him, "As you took forgiveness from the hand of the dying Christ, take the Holy Ghost from the hand of the living Christ." Mr. Meyer turned to Christ and said, "Lord, as I breathe in this . . . warm night air, so I breathe into every part of me the blessed Spirit." By faith he took the gift without any conscious emotion and went down the mountain.

On his way he met a number of young men who said, "We have received the Holy Spirit; we know it, for we feel we have it," and there was some contention between them. While they were talking, a young merchant who had been listening said, "I want to say a word. You parsons have been talking a great deal about the Holy Spirit. Now, I know that I have the Holy Spirit when I have most of Jesus. In my place at Glasgow, if I miss the presence of Jesus for half an hour, I go into my counting room and kneel down and say, 'Holy Spirit, what have I done to Thee that Thou hast taken from me the presence of Christ?'"

The knowledge of the presence of Jesus—this is the touchstone of the Spirit's presence. When we have so practiced the presence of Christ that we can say with Brother Lawrence, "The hour in my kitchen among its pots and pans is as the hour of prayer in my oratory," then has the Comforter wrought His perfect work in us.

III. *The Comforter, as the Spirit of truth, sanctifies us through the Word.*

We honor George Fox and the Society of Friends for vindicating the inward light. "When the Lord God and His Son Jesus Christ," says Fox, "sent me forth into the world to preach His everlasting gospel and kingdom, I was commanded to turn men to that inward light, and grace, by which all might know the way of God; even that Divine Spirit which would lead into all truth, and would never deceive." Thank God for the inward light of the Holy Spirit, a light which will never deceive, but will guide into all truth!

GUIDED BY THE SPIRIT

But we must not magnify the inner light above the written Word. Not by inner impulse and suggestion apart from the Scriptures does the Comforter guide us into all truth. I will not say that He has no message for him who has no Bible. I will not say that He never leads us except by the direct teaching of some Scripture passage. But I will say that to neglect and ignore the Bible is to lose His teaching.

Jesus, in His prayer on the Passover night, said, "Father, sanctify them"—those whom Thou hast given me—"through thy truth: thy word is truth" (John 17:17, 11). And speaking of the relation of His disciples to himself, He said, "I am the vine, ye are the branches." "Abide in me, and I in you" (15:5, 4). A little later, as if interpreting His abiding, He said, "If ye abide in me, and my words abide in you" (v. 7), as though the abiding of His Word was the abiding of himself. Again, speaking of the Comforter, He said, "He shall bring to your remembrance the words which I have spoken unto you" (cf. 14:26). It was as the Word that Jesus made the Father known. It is by His words that the Holy Spirit will make Jesus known to us. The Word is the Sword of the Spirit. We can have no substitute for it in our conflict with the powers of evil. The Word is the Mirror reflecting to us the image of Christ, and we, "beholding as in a glass the glory of the Lord, are changed into the same image from glory to glory, even as by the Spirit of the Lord" (2 Cor. 3:18).

SANCTIFIED BY THE TRUTH

The Holy Spirit is near every one of us; open every avenue of your being to His incoming. The Bible is the Spirit's Treasury; love it, study it, obey it. The Spirit presents a full Christ to your faith; trust Him fully, that your life be not as a trickling rivulet, but as a full-banked river.

Paul S. Rees

(1900—)

Forty years ago I first heard Paul Rees preach. I can almost reproduce the message, not because my memory is exceptional but because his outline was so clear, his exposition so precise, and his manner so compelling. He is justly regarded as a prince among preachers. When you hear him, you are persuaded that he has prepared his soul as carefully as his sermon.

The son of pioneer holiness preacher Seth Cook Rees, Paul Rees comes by his preaching skill and zeal honestly. While less polished than the son, the father preached with clarity and power that were eloquent and persuasive.

Paul Rees gained international recognition as a preacher while serving as pastor of First Covenant Church of Minneapolis, an assignment he faithfully fulfilled for two decades. His pulpit, radio, and writing ministries attracted increasing numbers of people, instrumenting—under God—the conversion and sanctification of thousands.

Dr. Rees has labored fruitfully, also, with a number of parachurch ministries, including World Vision and the Billy Graham crusades. Often he has been tapped for the serious responsibility of preaching to the preachers, in the interest of deepening their spiritual lives and improving their homiletical skills.

He began his ministry in 1917 and was ordained in the Evangelical Mission Covenant Church of America. At numerous conferences, conventions, crusades, and colleges around the world his expanded ministry has borne rich fruit.

He served the National Association of Evangelicals as president, and for many years, since leaving the pastorate, has done the work of an evangelist with consummate ability.

His books, models of clarity wedded to passion, have informed and shaped the preaching of hundreds of his brothers in ministry.

Now in his 80s, he continues to travel and preach, signally honored by the Lord to whom he is utterly committed.

"The Holy Spirit and the Church's Master" expounds the ministry of the Holy Spirit in its convicting effect upon the world and its sanctifying effect upon the Church. He comes to convict of sin, to exalt the Savior, to grace the Christian, and to guide the Church, as Jesus had promised.

Placing under tribute the thoughts of other exegetes and preachers, and drawing illustrations from history and nature, Dr. Rees fleshes out a choice outline with equally choice substance.

The Holy Spirit and the Church's Master*

> *Nevertheless I tell you the truth; It is expedient for you that I go away: for if I go not away, the Comforter will not come unto you; but if I depart, I will send him unto you* (John 16:7).

Do we Christians have only the treasured memories of Christ as they are written down in a Book, or do we have the real presence of Christ as our divine Companion along the trail of life's going? The answer to that question, whether we are aware of it or not, brings us squarely up against the New Testament doctrine of the Holy Spirit.

GOOD NEWS OF THE HOLY SPIRIT

"It is expedient for you that I go away," said Jesus to those perplexed and affrighted disciples of His. It is "to your advantage," is the way Weymouth translates it. "My going is for your good," is Moffatt's rendering. That He did go away is a fact well known to all of us. But how could He say that His going would be a good thing?

---

*Source: Paul S. Rees, *Stand Up in Praise to God.* Grand Rapids: Wm. B. Eerdmans Publishing Co., 1960.

Frankly He could *not* have said it unless He had been prepared to assure them that His withdrawal in physical form was going to mean no grievous and gaping absence but rather His presence on a higher level. Earlier in this conversation He had said to them, "I will not leave you comfortless" (literally, "orphaned") (14:18). Now He assures them that the answer to their fears of loneliness will be found in the communication of the Holy Spirit. In this revelation Christ's presence will be experienced with a new and astonishing inwardness and intimacy. He shall "be in you," said the Master. He shall "abide with you for ever" (vv. 17, 16). He shall "glorify me." He shall "guide you into all truth" (16:14, 13).

Can anyone doubt that this was "good news" to those anxious and ill-equipped men upon whose ears fell the Master's words? Then it was, and is, what some have called the "gospel of the Holy Spirit." It answered certain vast and urgent needs that Jesus, more than others, understood in that hour of His approaching departure. What were those needs, and how does the Holy Spirit meet them?

I. *The world must be gripped with conviction of sin: the Holy Spirit is the Answer to that need.*

Consider the words that follow our text: "And when he is come, he will reprove the world of sin, and of righteousness, and of judgment: of sin, because they believe not on me; of righteousness, because I go to my Father, and ye see me no more; of judgment, because the prince of this world is judged."

Someone ought to set up a "Bureau of Missing Words." If we had such an institution, somewhere on the dust-laden shelves would be found the word "sin." It is the forgotten word of proud 20th-century man. We are so sure we have outgrown it that we would rather go to hell than to admit we are plagued with it. There is simply no end to the lengths we will go in building a silky vocabulary that leaves out the serpent-hissing word—sin. The quack religionists are ready to lend a hand: they smilingly remind us that sin is merely a "delusion of mortal mind." The highbrowed sociologists offer their assistance: they would sum up all that ails under the innocent-sounding phrase "the cultural lag." The superpatriots have a neat little suggestion too: they rise up self-righteously to declare that one or two madmen, like Hitler or Mussolini or Khrushchev, are to blame for all this devilishness that has loosed itself upon the world.

The one thing that most of us are stubbornly unwilling to do is to locate the troubles of human society where they really are—inside our own prideful, peevish, perverse hearts, with their subtly persistent unbelief that turns away from God's Christ and serves other gods instead. Not long before he died in the period of the Second World War, the archbishop of Canterbury said a thing that contains more moral insight and Christian wisdom than nine-tenths of the speeches and articles that are heard in Congress or published in newspaper columns.

THE SOURCE OF SIN

This terrible war, said Archbishop Temple, is simply "the latest, most violent manifestation of an all-pervasive element in the nature of unregenerate mankind." In other words, all of us are in on it in the measure that we have not allowed the redeeming Christ to save us from our self-centeredness, our callousness toward others, and our guilty failure to give God first place in our lives. It was the convicting Spirit of God that spoke through these plain words which the archbishop uttered.

In the history of the Great Wall of China there is a parable of life that you and I might well take to heart. The wall was built for reasons of security. It cost a gigantic sum in money, time, and labor. Behind the completed barrier the Chinese people felt comfortably secure; yet in the first few years after it was finished, it was breached three times by the enemy. But the thing to note is this: it was breached not by crashing the wall, but by bribing the gatekeepers. It was the human factor that failed. The wall failed to work only because the men who guarded it failed. The material massiveness was insufficient; it needed moral character to support it.

PERSONAL HOLINESS NEEDED

It is time we listened to the Holy Spirit on this matter. We have built our walls, as individuals and as nations. We have put our confidence in scientific inventions, in mass education, in industrial and commercial organization, in political and social arrangements and, latterly, in military power and superiority. Everything has failed. Nothing we have tried has given us a happier and more secure world. Nothing will until we turn our eyes in the one direction where most of us do not want to look, which is right straight down into our own spoiled hearts where our dishonesties, evasions, sensualities, hatreds, and jealousies lie coiled up like so many red-tongued serpents with pretty designs on their backs but with deadly poison in their fangs.

It is *our* sin now—not our neighbor's or our ancestors' sin—but ours—which the Holy Spirit is dragging out into the light of honest day. It isn't murder, you say. Perhaps not. Only, remember that in God's sight and in the statement of God's Word, he that "hateth his brother is a murderer" (1 John 3:15). It isn't immorality, you say. Perhaps not. Only, remember that, according to Christ, there is an immorality of the voluntary thought-life which is equivalent to adultery. It isn't racketeering, you say. Perhaps not. Only, remember that "love is the fulfilling of the law" (Rom. 13:10), and a loveless heart, though it never go criminal, is before God only a gangster in evening dress.

CONVICTION FOR INWARD SIN

So we may go on through the list of crimes from which we would fain excuse ourselves. But the Holy Spirit will not be put off so easily. Christ is not done with us until He has confronted us with this: "He will reprove the world of sin . . . of sin, because they believe not on me." Call it the top sin, if you will, or the bottom sin; in any case it is the sin of sins, this refusal to bend low before Christ and accept Him as the "Immortal Love" who suffered, died, and rose again that He might bring us to God, forgiven and transformed. When the Holy Spirit has been allowed to grip us with this conviction, we shall be ready for our next step.

II. *Christ must be glorified as a universal Savior: the Holy Spirit is the Answer to that need.*

Another area of the Spirit's activity, declares Jesus, concerns Me—My person and My work—"He shall glorify me" (v. 14). Joseph Parker, commenting on this phrase, makes the luminous remark that "what light is to the earth, the Holy Ghost is to Jesus Christ." And he adds, "The work of the Spirit is revelation, not creation. He does not make Christ, He explains Him."

As one aspect of this glorifying ministry of the Spirit of God, take the way in which He makes universally available the presence and power of the Lord Jesus Christ. The historical Jesus, whom we meet in the Gospel records, was confined within a human body. He worked within a human body. He worked within the limitations of time and space. He was on the Mount of Transfiguration with three fascinated disciples one moment, and at the foot of the mountain with a distressed father afterward. He was not accessible in both places at the same time. He was in Galilee when His friend Lazarus died and in Judea, at the graveside, four days later. He was not present in both places at the same time.

THE CHRIST OF EVERY ROAD

What was true of space was also true of time. Jesus lived 33 years. Suppose He had lived on in that body which He took to himself through the mysterious process of the Virgin Birth. By the time He was 500 years old, He would have destroyed His claim to be "in all points tempted like as we are, yet without sin" (Heb. 4:15). On the other hand, when He dies, rises again, and ascends into heaven, He must leave with men something more than the memory of His brief pilgrimage among them. Even that memory would cease to have any vivid meaning when death had removed the last man who had seen His face or heard His voice. Then we should have only a written record.

All of which argues eloquently for the Christian doctrine of the Holy Spirit. Only, be it noted, what we find in the New Testament is more than a doctrine—it is a series of glowing facts that are set on fire in the souls of men. We have, for example, Paul's profound insight. Christ, he says, "ascended up far above all heavens, that he might fill all things" (Eph. 4:10). "That he might fill all things"—all time, all space, all churches, all homes, all trusting hearts, all kingdoms and continents.

But how? Peter had the answer. He gave it to us on the Day of Pentecost, when he, too, caught sight of the glorious plan by which Jesus of Nazareth was to swing out from the cramped boundaries of little Palestine and lay hold of the souls of men under every sky to redeem them to God. "Therefore," cried Peter, concerning his ascended Lord, "being by the right hand of God exalted, and having received of the Father the promise of the Holy Ghost, he hath shed forth this, which ye now see and hear" (Acts 2:33).

You ask, What is "the gospel of the Holy Spirit"? It is the gospel of Christ, the gospel of God's redeeming love, universalized. All men need our Savior. All men may have Him—actually have Him in a living experience of His forgiveness and regeneration—through the Holy Spirit. All doors are now open. All barriers are down. All boundaries are overleaped. On a heathen temple in India is a sign that reads: "Low-castes and dogs not allowed." That is the exclusivism of paganism. It could even be found in Judaism in our Lord's time. Alas, misguided Christians sometimes duplicate it. But Calvary and Pentecost broke it forever.

And now what? In that same India it happened one day a prominent Hindu woman came to a Christian worker. She brought with her a *devidasi,* a poor, bedraggled, abused temple girl. "I bring this girl to you to be saved," said the Hindu to the Christian. Then she explained,

"I once heard my husband read a story from your sacred book, of a woman taken in adultery and what Jesus said to her and how He saved her. We have no such story in our books, so I bring the girl to you."

God be praised that we *do* have such a story in our sacred Book. But God be praised also that, because of the presence and ministry of the Holy Spirit, the story can be reproduced anywhere and everywhere, as aching hearts reach out with trusting hands to touch the Christ who died for them.

III. *Christians must be graced with Christlike qualities: the Holy Spirit is the Answer to that need.*

For, says Jesus, "he shall receive of mine, and shall shew it unto you" (v. 14). In the light of these words we can agree with Schleiermacher that "the fruits of the Spirit are the virtues of Christ." According to Paul they are: "love, joy, peace, longsuffering, gentleness, goodness, faith, meekness, temperance" (Gal. 5:22-23).

Don't dismiss that list too lightly. Don't say, "Oh, well, every Christian has these graces in his life, and all he needs to do is to take time to develop them." That is just where some of us go clean off the track. True, all Christians have these qualities of Christlikeness more or less in evidence in their lives. True, also, these plants of spiritual beauty require time for full growth. But every gardener knows that if his soil is being taken by weeds or if his plants are not healthy, he needs something besides *time* to produce a lovely garden. Something drastic, like weeding or spraying, needs to be done. Then luxuriant growth and fragrant loveliness will follow in due course.

Pentecost came to the early Christians as a definite and drastic crisis in their career as Christians. "Suddenly . . . they were all filled with the Holy Ghost" (Acts 2:2, 4). They were searched, sanctified, humbled in one high hour of meeting with the Spirit of Christ. Other blessed hours followed, but this was decisive. It moved them over from the marginal waters to the central current of the stream of the Spirit. And all of this was somehow vitally related to a certain Christlikeness of disposition that they were normally to demonstrate.

IN A MOMENT

Be sure of this, my fellow Christians: Any experience of the soul that makes us other than Christ-minded is not an experience of the Holy Spirit. It may be some other spirit—pride, hysteria, clannishness, sensualism—but it is not the Holy Comforter of whom the Master was speaking when He said, "He shall receive of mine, and shall shew it unto you" (John 16:14).

A friend of my father was one day addressing a body of ministers on "the fullness of the Holy Spirit." At the close of the message a minister came forward, deeply moved. His cheeks were wet with tears. He held one of the leading pulpits in that conference. "Your reading today broke my heart," said he, as he searched the face of the brother-preacher who had spoken. "I have been preaching Jesus, but I know I am not at all like Him. I have been cross to my wife, and to my children, and to my people. The past year has been a hard one; I cannot, I cannot try to preach Christ another year, unless I can have the 'mind' of Christ."

SURRENDER OF SELF

This, as it turned out, was the beginning of a short, sharp struggle within himself. Would he let go of himself and resign his whole being, his affairs, his future, his gifts, his family, into God's controlling hands? It was not settled easily, but it *was* settled. That day, and far into the night, the battle raged. In the small hours of the morning the flag of absolute surrender went up. The sovereign Christ, by the power of the Holy Spirit, took over. The result? Ask his wife. She testified to the new gentleness that was there. Ask his church officers. They testified to the new humility and winsomeness that were there. Ask his congregation. They testified to the new radiance and power that were there.

Here, it seems to me, in the everyday world of human relationships, is the kind of fulfillment that our Lord's promise of the Spirit requires: "He shall receive of mine"—My love and goodwill, My patience and peace, My compassion and courage—"and shall shew it unto you."

IV. *The Church must be guided into all truth: the Holy Spirit answers to that need.*

Listen again to the Master in the context: "When he, the Spirit of truth, is come, he will guide you into all truth" (v. 13).

In whatever measure any man is honest with himself and his God, in exactly that measure does he long hungrily for truth. For in the realm of truth the mind and soul of man are in commerce with reality—the underlying reality that we may easily miss if we are occupied only with the facts that appear on life's surface. A botanist, analyzing a rose, gives you all of the dry facts about the stem, the stamen, the calyx, the petals, and all the rest. When he is through, you have something about as exciting as the multiplication tables. But the *truth* regarding a rose gathers up all the subtler things of form and fragrance and color, then flings them into your beauty-ravished soul like a very gift of heaven.

Now it is the business of the Holy Spirit to make us lovers of truth and then to lead us into ever new and fuller appreciation of that incomparable One who is himself the Truth. In Christ we have the Truth—the truth about God, the truth about man, the truth about sin, the truth about salvation, the truth about the meaning and goal of life, the truth about heaven, hell, and destiny.

THE TRUTHS OF CHRIST

Does this mean that we know all there is to know about these matters that are so freighted with importance? Not at all. Christ gives the *key*. That key is in the hands of the Holy Spirit, and we, giving ourselves up to His guidance, are led into a progressive understanding of what it all means. The Spirit uses our minds; He stimulates our affections; He sharpens our intuitions; He enables us to interpret our experiences; He speaks to us through the testimony of others; He enriches us by the pooled wisdom of the whole community of believers. In all of these ways He is guiding us, slow and dull as we may be, into "all truth."

INCREASED SENSITIVITIES

Let me add one word to that last sentence. Most of us Christians are much *more* "slow and dull" about spiritual realities than we should be. It is because we have never been to Pentecost for *our* invasion and inundation by the quickening, cleansing Spirit of God. The late Dr. Jowett looked at the early Christians before Pentecost and then at those same men and women after Pentecost, and he lifted his eyes to say that one of the differences which the fullness of the Holy Spirit made was "an extraordinary power of spiritual apprehension." God was overwhelmingly real to them. Christ was so utterly dear and adequate. Eternal things were so much more important to them than the temporal. Prayer was so simple and natural. God's control of their affairs was so close and continuous and all-satisfying. Life was so radiant and conquering. And all of this in spite of innumerable privations, difficulties, and challenges.

They were being guided into all truth, and together they were being used of God to guide others. Which is precisely what the Church should be and do in this befogged and bewildered world.

The pilot of a Flying Fortress in World War II wrote to a friend of his in Texas, describing the experiences he had in bringing back his ship from many missions over Germany. He was based in England. "A striking characteristic," he wrote, "of an English landscape as seen from the air is the incredible number of churches which the country boasts. These churches have tall, stately spires and they afford excellent landmarks. When the weather is bad, we use these churches as guides to lead us home. We have become so familiar with them that when we let down through an overcast and see a church beneath us, we can immediately determine whether or not we are on our course. Believe me, it is a very comforting sight to see them appear out of the mists."

What suggestiveness in that sentence. "When the weather is bad, we use these churches as guides to lead us home"! Ah, my friends, in a far deeper and wider sense than that lieutenant meant it, the weather of this morally befogged world *is* bad. And the Church of Jesus Christ, under the guidance of the Holy Spirit, is the signpost of the eternal God, pointing, ever pointing, the way Home!

Come, Holy Spirit, come,
Let Thy bright beams arise;
Dispel all sorrow from our minds,
All darkness from our eyes.

'Tis Thine to cleanse the heart,
To sanctify the soul;
To pour fresh life in every part,
And new-create the whole.

Dwell therefore in our hearts,
Our minds from bondage free;
Then we shall know, and praise, and love
The Father, Son, and Thee.

Robert W. McIntyre
(1922—)

Robert McIntyre is a former general superintendent in The Wesleyan Church, having retired in June 1988.

Prior to this assignment, his administrative skills were exercised as executive secretary of the youth department of the Wesleyan Methodist church.

He served during those same years as editor of his denomination's youth magazine. After leaving this post, he gained additional editorial experience as general editor of The Wesleyan Church.

Behind the work of his pen were graduate studies in journalism at Ball State University. He is an alumnus of Marion College, also.

McIntyre began his ministry in the pastorate, serving local churches for 11 years before he was summoned to administrative and supervisory duties on a denominational level.

He has contributed articles to a number of periodicals and has authored various doctrinal studies and biblical commentaries.

McIntyre is first of all a preacher. In "The Prayer Christ Prayed for You" he deals with John 17, one of the most magnificent passages of the Bible. His approach to our Lord's high-priestly prayer is different from any I have encountered before. At its heart he sees three chief petitions, (1) that the Son might glorify the Father, (2) that the Father might glorify the Son, (3) that the Church might be cleansed, kept, and used in order to vindicate and extend the

mission of Christ in the world. The first and the second can be stamped "Accomplished," but the third awaits the consent of our wills and the trust of our hearts.

"What of the third petition?" is the spearpoint on this sermon. It brings the prayer of Jesus from an ancient upper room to the hearts of those who hear the sermon, and demands response. Like the Gospel of John from which the text is taken, the message is not truth for its own sake but truth for life's sake. "These are written, that ye might believe . . . and that believing ye might have life" (John 20:31). Concern for *realized* theology, for experienced truth, has always marked the holiness movement. Such urgency must continue to invest our preaching if we are to be God's instruments and change agents when we proclaim His Word.

The Prayer Christ Prayed for You*

Sanctify them through thy truth: thy word is truth (John 17:17).

Recently I received this letter from a man in Arizona:

"After seeing your name in a book I'm reading I decided to write you to see if you could enlighten me on receiving the Holy Ghost. I have read the Scriptures and heard many sermons, but somehow I've never been able to grasp, from what men say and what I read, an introduction until I feel like I've met Him.

"I think I understand about Jesus, for He was a man; I feel I have some understanding about God, for He was and is our Father; but to grasp a Spirit escapes me.

"About my background, I grew up in Indiana and my neighbors were Spiritualists. Frankly, I never understood their talking to spirits, yet Christians say the Spirit talks to them. I wonder if they mean they have impressions to go or do certain things.

"One man I know says God talks to his heart as much as I talk to you, but he can't explain it. I also know the Bible talks about the Holy Spirit guiding us and teaching us.

"This must be the most wonderful thing in the world—to be

---

*Source: James McGraw, comp., *The Holiness Pulpit No. 2*. Kansas City: Beacon Hill Press of Kansas City, 1974.

filled with and taught by the Holy Ghost—but for myself there seems to be a vagueness about it.

"I'll appreciate it if you can enlighten me on what the world of the Spirit is all about. I certainly want to be filled with the Spirit."

A day or two later, in a magazine dedicated to recognizing and encouraging the work of the Holy Spirit, I read this in a testimony: "I was shocked after I thought I had experienced the baptism with the Holy Spirit to find I was capable of violently losing my temper (on more than one occasion I smashed things against the floor in a fit of anger), was afflicted with lust, and occasionally even tempted to renounce my faith. Now I understand that God was exposing my defects and flaws."

WE NEED THE HOLY SPIRIT

These two men—the one earnestly seeking, the other unconsciously acknowledging that he had not yet found an inner experience that met the full need of his life—represent a vast and virtually universal human hunger. Jesus prayed about this need in an upper room one day, and then died himself in order to satisfy it.

Christian believers everywhere recognize that the prayer which begins, "Our Father which art in heaven," usually called "The Lord's Prayer," might better be called "The Prayer Christ Taught His Disciples," while here in the 17th chapter of John is Christ's own high-priestly prayer. . . .

It must be acknowledged that any prayer is more appreciated when it is viewed against the background of the circumstances in which it is uttered. The prayer of Christ here recorded issues forth from the very shadow of the Cross. It was wrung from the anguished lips of One who has apparently failed in His mission upon earth. It bleeds from the broken heart of a Son who has tried to glorify His Father, only to be charged with the crime of blasphemy. One disciple had betrayed Him; others are about to fail Him and then forsake Him.

But now He prays! Standing only moments away from Calvary and the tomb, what concerns will He express? And will His petition be answered?

An analysis of this prayer seems to indicate three specific concerns expressed by Christ as He faced Gethsemane and Calvary. The first two are clearly stated in the very first verse of the chapter: (1) "That thy Son . . . may glorify thee"; (2) "Glorify thy Son"; and (3) a general petition embracing His followers and their relationship to the world.

I. *The record is clear that the Son's concern that He might glorify the Father was more than fully met.*

No Christian should be surprised when he finds himself becoming part of the answer to his own prayer. A smile-provoking anecdote relates the experience of a man who took a run-down, weed-overgrown garden and by dint of many hours of labor turned it into a fruitful, well-dressed beauty spot. A friend commented, "You and the Lord certainly have produced a lovely garden." To which the response was, "Yes, but you should have seen it when the Lord had it all by himself." . . .

The fulfillment of Christ's concern that He should glorify the Father began in the Incarnation itself, when "the Word was made flesh, and dwelt among us" (John 1:14). A sinful and idolatrous world saw God in Christ even though many failed to recognize Him.

The Son glorified the Father when in cruel temptation He denied himself and denounced His satanic foe.

He glorified God when He made service a standard of greatness, teaching by precept and example that the great should be servants of the lowly.

He glorified God when in humble submission to the will of the Father He went the full route to the Cross.

II. *The record is also clear that the Son's concern that the Father might glorify Him was more than fully met.*

It is difficult to see how one could look upon the events of the day of Christ's crucifixion and fail to realize that no ordinary man was dying upon the center tree. The very laws of nature were contravened to do Him honor. At high noon the sun hid its face in shame, as though unable to look upon the spectacle of the Sun of Righteousness dying at the hands of cruel men. When the Cross, with the Creator hanging upon it, was plunged into its bosom, the earth beneath rocked and trembled in the grip of a compulsive agony. In the Temple, an invisible hand rent asunder the impregnable curtain, forever vanquishing the wall of separation and opening an unobstructed way of approach to God for His people.

But even before this, through the mysterious alchemy of divine power, God had chosen to glorify His Son by turning even the words of His enemies into an acknowledgment of His uniqueness as Son of God and Son of Man.

It is John who reports, with a controlled elation which must be read between the lines, how on an occasion when many of the people were coming to believe on Him, "the Pharisees and the chief priests sent officers to take him" (John 7:32). Hesitating to rush in boldly to make their capture, the men waited for an appropriate time. It was the last great day of the feast, the day when Jesus stood and cried, "If any man thirst, let him come unto me, and drink. He that believeth on me, as the scripture hath said, out of his . . . [innermost being] shall flow rivers of living water. (But this spake he of the Spirit, which they that believe on him should receive: for the Holy Ghost was not yet given; because that Jesus was not yet glorified)" (vv. 37-39).

THE SPIRIT'S WORK PREDICTED

Overawed and empty-handed, the armed officers who had been sent to arrest the mild-mannered Teacher returned to their superiors. Perhaps the impact of His words on them was as evident as their failure to apprehend Him. At any rate, when the officers [were asked,] "Why have ye not brought him?" their futile and inadequate defense was at the same time a profound commentary on Jesus' ministry: "Never man spake like this man" (vv. 45-46).

But other enemies, too, could speak only well of Him.

Judas said, "I have betrayed the *innocent* blood" (Matt. 27:4).

Pilate's final verdict was, "I find *no* fault in him" (John 19:4, 6; cf. 18:38).

Pilate's wife referred to Him as "that *just* man" (Matt. 27:19; all italics mine).

Even the wicked thief in his dying hour acknowledged Him as Lord: "Lord, remember me . . ." (Luke 23:42).

An ungodly Roman centurion, long accustomed to the sight of flowing blood and the agonies of the dying, exclaimed, "Truly this was the Son of God" (Matt. 27:54; cf. Mark 15:39).

Not only did God glorify His Son by the forces of nature and the voices of men, but as though to personally add honor to honor He has extended and enlarged that glory until it is a river which flows over and out of the pages of the New Testament to transform the lives of men even today.

Seizing upon the hated Cross, God transformed it from a cruel instrument of sorrow, shame, and execution to the sacred symbol of the Christian faith, and bathed it in a glory which heralds its message of triumph over sin wherever it is seen.

He glorified the blood of Christ, recognizing it as a cleansing stream, and immediately confirmed its efficacy in the salvation of the repentant, dying thief.

He glorified the body of His Son, so that it never saw corruption, and on the third day brought it forth from the tomb to place the rainbow of the assurance of immortality over the grave of every Christian.

He glorified the name of His Son, making it a name to which every knee will bow and which one day every tongue will confess—the only name in which there is salvation.

The instruments of Christ's suffering became instruments of glory: the Cross crushed the head of the serpent; the thorns became a crown on the head of a King; Pilate's mocking superscription, "This is Jesus the King of the Jews" (Matt. 27:37), will one day be proved to have been a factual title.

III. *Two petitions were answered: The Son glorified the Father and the Father glorified the Son; but what of the third petition?*

Christ's third concern there in the Upper Room embraced the relationship of His followers to the "world." Nineteen times in this short prayer the word comes to His lips. His deep concern is evident and the lines are clear: His glory, which is eternal, predated the world. The world itself is not eternal; it will pass away and so will the lust thereof. But while men are in this world which is not eternal, He has saved them and put the eternal glory of the Father within them. Now these men have a quality of life which will continue even beyond the existence of the very world into which they were born.

"Keep . . . those whom thou hast given me," He prays, ". . . that they might have my joy fulfilled in themselves" (17:11, 13).

SANCTIFY THEM

Then, "Sanctify them," that they might accomplish the mission for which they are sent. "As thou hast sent me into the world, even so have I also sent them into the world . . . that the world may believe" and "that the world may know that thou hast sent me" (vv. 18, 21, 23). "I pray for them: I pray not for the world, but for them which thou hast given me; for they are thine" (v. 9).

POWER

The Book of Acts records how Christ's fervent prayer for His early followers was fully answered. Pentecost marked a striking and dramatic change in that band of early believers. Swept by a spirit of love and filled with a spirit of power, their attitudes toward each other so impressed unbelievers that they are reported to have candidly exclaimed, "Behold, how they love one another!" When they journeyed to Thessalonica the over-the-back-fence grapevine reported, "These that have turned the world upside down are come hither also" (17:6). Of the fervency of their commitment to their beliefs it was reported that they "filled Jerusalem" with their "doctrine" (5:28). And when that fervency ran them afoul of the authorities, and their commitment to Christ's glory led them to martyrdom, they were sustained right up to the gates of death, to come shining triumphantly through on the other side.

But the picture is incomplete unless we see that Christ's high-priestly prayer extended all the way to us. "Neither pray I for these alone, but for [all] them also which shall believe on me through their word" (v. 20).

FOR ALL MEN

As the shadow of the Cross drew nearer, Christ's prayer reached down across all the centuries to touch you and lift you to the embrace of the Father's loving provision.

His prayer was for you—are you kept from the evil one?

Is His joy fulfilled in you?

Are you sanctified through the truth?

Is your life a demonstration of Christian love? Is it an example of spiritual power? Are you fulfilling your mission, that the world may *believe,* and *know?* In short, does God find in you a response to His earnest effort to answer His Son's prayer for you?

There He stands, pleading with God that the redeemed, transformed, and sanctified lives of men in every age might be the vindication of His mission on earth.

Can you ignore the prayer He prayed for you?

Myron S. Augsburger
(1929—)

Too many people mistake the Mennonites as an isolated, even irrelevant, people. The burning issues of peace and justice have made them increasingly visible and audible in the evangelical community, indeed, in the whole world. They exercise an influence greatly disproportionate to their numbers.

Among them, no leader stands taller in the esteem of the church than Myron S. Augsburger. His has been a leading voice in many circles of ministry to human need.

Augsburger is a native of Ohio, schooled at Eastern Mennonite College, Goshen College Biblical Seminary, and Union Theological Seminary.

After earning four degrees, he was ordained and began his pastoral ministry in Florida. He later served as pastor of students at Eastern Mennonite College, and in 1965 became the president of that institution.

Augsburger has been heavily engaged in evangelistic work, conducting meetings and crusades throughout the United States and in Canada, India, the Middle East, the Far East, and the Caribbean area.

He speaks with skill and appeal to college and university students and has often preached in campus settings. It was in a college church that I first heard him, and the impression for good upon my life has been permanent.

"Resisting the Spirit" is taken from a book of messages (studies, should anyone prefer) that expound the sins against the Holy

Spirit that are specified in biblical warnings and illustrated by biblical examples. It is solid and serious fare for all who desire to be Spirit-filled disciples of Christ.

I cannot resist a personal word about the book. Having read it to the immense profit of my own spiritual life, I began marking passages to share with friends. There were so many that were so vital that I ended by simply commending the whole book to them.

Resisting the Spirit is the common sin of the world in its response to the gospel. But Augsburger also stresses resistance to the Spirit as a common sin of believers who thwart the Spirit's sanctifying work, which aims at conforming them to the image of Christ, a goal that cannot be reached apart from the crucifixion of the self-life. "We are guilty of resisting the Spirit when we defend our present level of holiness as satisfactory."

Resisting the Spirit*

You stiff-necked people, uncircumcised in heart and ears, you always resist the Holy Spirit (Acts 7:51, RSV).

One of man's chief sins is to resist God. The Holy Spirit is the Executive of the Godhead at work in the world. Through Him a sovereign God moves upon the hearts of men, that He might bring faith to birth. Resisting the Spirit is to oppose the eternal work of God as it bears upon one's own soul. This attitude is a continuation of man's revolt against God, separating man from God in a state of spiritual death. It is in this sense that man's greatest potential, the freedom to make moral decisions, becomes his greatest downfall. God has given man the power to talk back to Him, and man's sin is that he has "sassed God off."

One of the most pointed sermons in the Bible is in Acts 7, where Stephen addresses the religious men of his day and exposes their sin of resisting the Holy Spirit. These men were really not in search of truth. They had a doctrine of a sovereign God, but they would not let Him be sovereign. They had sacrificed the person of God for mere precepts about God. Their search for truth failed because they had forgotten

*Source: Myron S. Augsburger, *Quench Not the Spirit*. Scottdale, Pa.: Herald Press, 1975.

the transcendent goal. They made the mistake of looking at some immediate selfish goal rather than the eternal spiritual goal.

Their preoccupation with a minor goal reminds one of the young boy scout who met with his group. When the scoutmaster asked if all had done their good deed for the day, everyone raised his hand except one little lad. He was asked, according to their rules, to leave until the good deed was accomplished. About 20 minutes later he was back with a big smile, but his hair was tousled and his clothes torn. He told the scoutmaster that he had tried to help an old lady across the street, but she didn't want to go!

The real goal is not religious practice but the reality of His presence. Man must always remember that God is larger than any system of thought or doctrine. Man's mind is closed to the truth as it was revealed in Christ because the sinfulness of man's heart reacts to the person of His holiness. The man who hates divine truth does so because of the evil in his own life. Wrapped up in our religious program, we do not realize that what is really important is what happens inside us, not outside us. As Stephen summed up his message to the resisting Pharisees, "You always resist the Holy Spirit." They had closed their minds to God's unfolding revelation.

CARNALITY RESISTS HOLINESS

Resisting the Spirit is a common sin in the experience of mankind, among both the irreligious and the religious. To resist means to oppose, to stand against, or to withstand. It is man's opposition to God's redemptive measures on his behalf. It is man's refusal to share in full reconciliation to God. It is man's choice to retain sin even at the cost of losing fellowship with God. Resisting the Spirit is to stand in opposition to God's program of making saints out of sinners.

I. *Rejecting the Spirit's Convicting Call*

God's evangelist in the world is the Holy Spirit. He is using many believers as channels through whom He works. Believers testify to the reality of grace, but it is the Spirit who transforms one through divine grace. Man may convince the mind through building a case for Christian faith, but it is only the Spirit who convicts the man. Men may confront others with the gospel, but only the Holy Spirit can convert them to the gospel.

THE SPIRIT CONVINCES

Whenever the church magnifies its program above the person of Christ and its platform above the power of the Spirit, it has sinned against the work of Christ. The Spirit is God's Evangelist in the world, using men as tools to lift up Christ. Whenever a program or tradition displaces Christ, the Spirit is hindered in His work. For this reason God writes "Ichabod" over many doors, for the glory of the Lord has departed. We cannot expect to win souls to Christ when the church has become merely a social association with religious bylaws. The church must be a body of redeemed sinners through whom the Spirit witnesses of Christ.

One of the greatest favors God does any man is to call him by the Holy Spirit. Jesus said, "No one can come to me unless the Father who sent me draws him" (John 6:44, RSV). The Spirit of God is at work calling men to faith in Christ. Of this call Jesus said that many are called but few are chosen (Matt. 20:16). Our being chosen in Him is contingent upon our response to the Spirit's call. It is when man, by voluntary choice, responds to the call of the Spirit that he is brought into a living fellowship with Christ. God, through His foreknowledge, thus speaks of us as having been chosen "in him before the foundation of the world, that we should be holy and blameless before him" (Eph. 1:4, RSV). Man resists the Spirit when he rejects this call, and thus brings upon himself the responsibility of his lost condition outside of Christ.

THE SPIRIT CALLS

The call of the Spirit is a gracious invitation for the sinner to renounce the way of self and turn to Christ. The conscience, by its very nature of passing judgment on one's behavior on the basis of acquired knowledge, is primarily a negative voice. The call of the Spirit is primarily a positive voice. One may, as did Paul, live in harmony with his conscience in not violating his religious precepts, and yet not come to God. It is the positive call of the Spirit that leads one not only to renounce sin, but to turn to Christ.

One may have a deep feeling of conviction for his violations of conscience, and be emotionally broken up over his sin, yet not come to peace in Christ. It is only as one answers the Spirit's positive call of commitment to Christ that he has peace with God. It is not enough to confess sin; one must confess Christ as Savior and Lord. One may confess sin without confessing Christ, but one cannot truly confess Christ as Lord without also confessing sin.

The conscience is the God-given channel by which the Spirit convicts man. Convictions vary in individuals because of the many differences in their traditions and training, culture and comprehension. The conscience, however, speaks consistently to all men of every culture at one point. Regardless of the validity of their claim to know right from wrong, the conscience witnesses by its vote on the side of what they think is right, that there is something within calling them to the best. Thinking man, created in the image of God, is thereby challenged to pursue the search for truth.

The conscience is not the standard; it is to be standardized by God's Word. Conscience is really a God-given servant, not a grueling master. As Christians we dare not ignore the voice nor violate the will of conscience; but we can change the conscience by educating it in divine truth! The Holy Spirit stands ready to guide the believer in this inner renewal of the mind. Paul speaks of this in Rom. 12:2, "Do not be conformed to this world but be transformed by the renewal of your mind, that you may prove what is the will of God, what is good and acceptable and perfect" (RSV).

THE SPIRIT GUIDES

Many times a person under the conviction of the Holy Spirit is greatly troubled; but the troubled heart is due to our lack of yieldedness rather than to the nature of the Spirit's call. The Spirit is not primarily interested in making a person miserable; yet when the Spirit calls and man resists, there is the misery of a "civil war" within. The gracious call of the Holy Spirit is an invitation to the abundant life in Christ, with all its joy, peace, and spiritual pleasure. The misery in the convicted soul is due to man's resisting the Spirit and continuing his revolt against God. Peace of heart comes when man, through the Spirit, is brought into a spiritual relation with the Lord, described in Romans 6 as yieldedness.

II. *Rejecting the Spirit's Revelation of Truth*

In John 14 and 16 Jesus refers to the Holy Spirit as the "Spirit of truth." He declares that the Spirit will "guide you into all the truth" (16:13, RSV). Paul states in 1 Cor. 2:10 that what the natural man cannot perceive, the believer understands because "God has revealed [it] to us through the Spirit" (RSV). John makes clear in his First Epistle that it is by the anointing of the Holy Spirit that "we all understand spiritual things" (1 John 2:20, literal trans.). Hence, we conclude that only by the Spirit's inspiration can the mind of man comprehend spiritual things. The written Word becomes "spirit and life" again (John 6:63, RSV), as the Spirit makes it a living, pulsing, creating power within the soul.

One resists the Spirit when he refuses to exchange human opinions for heaven-sent convictions. Opinion is what a man thinks on an issue, while conviction is man's belief of truth. There is no valid conviction but that which is based on divine revelation. One who is open to the Spirit is ready to add new convictions to his life as he understands the Bible. Such a person is willing to accept new truths, even though they may contradict past ideas. One resists the Spirit when he rejects new insights in the Word because it is contrary to "what we've always thought."

SCRIPTURAL

We do not reject tradition as such but must evaluate it by divine truth. One of the great privileges of the human experience is what psychologists refer to as "time-binding power." By this is meant the ability man has to reach back into history and select those things which time has proved to be of value and channel them into our time through our lives! Ours is the privilege of selecting the best from literature, from historical data, and from traditions of any heritage and channeling it into society again through our lives. Hence, to reject tradition leaves one a pauper, but to be enslaved by tradition makes one a puppet.

Many a Christian has committed the sin of resisting the Spirit in being closed to further spiritual insights. Peter, while on the housetop at Joppa, faced the question of yielding to the Spirit or resisting Him. Peter had received the Holy Spirit, yet he was imperfect in his understanding of God's will. The Lord gave him a vision in which He let down a sheet of mixed animals three times, until He broke through Peter's race prejudice, and Peter yielded to the Spirit. (See Acts 10.) One need meditate only a moment to see how much the spread of the gospel would have been hindered if Peter had resisted the Spirit and rejected the new insight of truth.

THE SPIRIT GIVES NEW INSIGHTS

The racial tensions of our day have their roots in this same human pride in one's own cultural and ethnic background. These divisions will exist in part as long as man exists, since sinful man is servant of his own pride. However, the redeeming grace of God and the redemptive mission of the Church are to make all people one in Christ. In God's redemptive program "there is neither Greek nor Jew, . . . Barbarian, Scythian, bond nor free" (Col. 3:11). The answer to racial tension is not found in force but in spiritual freedom. The Church must rise to this challenge just as it did at Antioch, Philippi, and at the house of Philemon.

REDUCES RACIAL TENSIONS

How often Christians have failed to follow the Spirit, and have not distinguished between their cultural practices and Christian principles, thus hindering the Spirit from leading them in some further spiritual conquest. One is guilty of resisting the Spirit when he refuses to be open to more complete understanding of the Word and will of God. Confessing our imperfection and acknowledging the Spirit's work in the "perfecting of the saints" (Eph. 4:12), we resist the Spirit when we are satisfied with the status quo. A spiritual leader is one who stands both outside and above the status quo and inspires persons to follow him, as he follows Christ.

III. *Rejecting the Spirit's Sanctifying Work*

THE SPIRIT'S SANCTIFYING WORK

The Bible says, "And we all, with unveiled face, beholding the glory of the Lord, are being changed into his likeness from one degree of glory to another; for this comes from the Lord who is the Spirit" (2 Cor. 3:18, RSV). This is a significant text concerning the sanctifying work of the Spirit in the life of the believer. The Spirit reveals Christ in His Word. Numerous passages refer to the sanctification of the Spirit, meaning the way in which the Spirit works within believing hearts to conform us to the image of Christ. We are guilty of resisting the Spirit when we defend our present level of holiness as satisfactory. The Spirit works to "take every thought captive to obey Christ" (2 Cor. 10:5, RSV), and He "intercedes for us with sighs too deep for words" (Rom. 8:26, RSV). He is working to make our privileges in Christ become practical realities in daily living. We resist the Spirit when we reject His sanctifying suggestions.

SALVATION FROM ALL SIN

Many professing Christians have never been honest with themselves or with God with respect to the sin question. Some want only enough religion to give them a false security. They are like the man who wrote to the Internal Revenue Service, "I can't sleep; my conscience is bothering me. Enclosed find a check for $50.00. If I still can't sleep, I'll send you the balance!" Many want God to remove their guilt but not their graft. They want His peace but not His presence.

The term "victory" is strange to the ears of many believers. Many thank God for His forgiving grace but fail to take hold of His enabling grace. Yet, the Bible says, "This is the victory that overcomes the world, our faith" (1 John 5:4, RSV). As Christians, we are engaged in a spiritual conquest. We have a known enemy—the world, the flesh, and the devil. As assurance for our victory, in Christ we have a superior power, for "he who is in you is greater than he who is in the world" (1 John 4:4, RSV).

Victory depends upon concentration of effort on the true front. In the spiritual life we must permit the Spirit to lead us into this "singleness of heart" (Acts 2:46; Col. 3:22; cf. Eph. 6:5).

CRUCIFIED WITH CHRIST

There must be an identification with Christ that results in a crucifixion of the self, the false self that has deceived us and been untrue to God. Only when we break from the old life as definitely as death itself, can we share the new resurrection life. We can then testify with Paul, "I have been crucified with Christ; it is no longer I who live, but Christ who lives in me; and the life I now live in the flesh I live by faith in the Son of God, who loved me and gave himself for me" (Gal. 2:20, RSV).

To use our God-given personality for the glory of self rather than the glory of Christ is to resist the will of the Spirit. Paul writes, "Do you not know that your body is a temple of the Holy Spirit within you, which you have from God? You are not your own; you were bought with a price. So glorify God in your body" (1 Cor. 6:19-20, RSV). The Spirit is working to bring our entire personality into conformity with His holiness. When we retain attitude, action, or appearance that is inconsistent with the mind of Christ, we are not sinning merely against a church, creed, or custom, but against the Spirit of Christ.

Since salvation is of grace, and God working redemption in us, to resist the Spirit is to sin against the only redemptive power that functions in our lives. Paul says, "Work out your own salvation with fear and trembling; for God is at work in you, both to will and to work for his good pleasure" (Phil. 2:12-13, RSV). Here Paul says we are to work out in life's expression that which God is working into our experience! How can we express Christ, or express truly good works, unless the Spirit of Christ is permitted to work graciously in our lives? We resist the Spirit when we oppose His way of perfecting saints. We resist Him when we offer a counterfeit perfection which measures up to some prescribed order rather than to the holiness of Christ. We resist the Spirit when we withstand His perfecting work to uphold our own program.

A SIN AGAINST GRACE

During a series of evangelistic meetings I once visited a man who claimed to be an atheist. In the course of the conversation he asked, "You look at me as a sinner, don't you?" I replied that all persons outside of Christ are sinners. "You count me a lost soul who needs to be saved, don't you?" he responded. After further conversation, he said, "I want to ask you a question. I boldly say there is no God and go out and live as I please. What about all those who claim to be Christians, who say there is a God, and then go out and live as they please?" Obviously, he had pointed up the great sin of "practical atheism."

It must be acknowledged that there is a little atheism in the heart of every man when he shoves God out of the center of his life and asserts self. To resist the Spirit is to partake of this sin! It is no small wonder that Jesus said, "If any man would come after me, let him deny himself and take up his cross daily and follow me" (Luke 9:23, RSV). In this sense we must die to live! We cannot share the full life of His sanctifying grace until we are willing to share the cross. Coming to Calvary for salvation is not the end of one's experience with the cross; it is only the beginning.

RESISTING THE SPIRIT IS SIN

We have observed that the sin of resisting the Spirit is an attitude of the heart which comes from man's basic revolt against God. It is the common sin in the unbeliever which prevents him from yielding to the regenerating work of the Holy Spirit. Many are those unbelievers, in the church and out of the church, who resist the Spirit to their own damnation, never coming to know a spiritual birth through Him.

We have also noted that this sin is committed in the lives of believers, as an expression of the basic sin tendency which revolts against the Lord. Believers need to find deliverance from the self-life, with its forms of self-satisfaction, self-defense, and self-confidence, which stand as evidence of resisting the Spirit. Only a life of true yieldedness, with a dying out to self, will result in a proper relation to the Holy Spirit.

6

HOLINESS IS CHRISTLIKENESS

Sheridan Baker
(1824-90)

One of the most effective and fruitful exponents of holiness in the Methodist church was Sheridan Baker. In his meetings he prayed and preached with evident anointing, patiently wearing out the opposition, and wisely leading many into the experience of entire sanctification.

He learned from painful experience the dangers of taking any man or any group as his model for holiness. He resolved to make Jesus Christ himself the standard of his life and labors, and in doing this he found the secret of both rest and growth. This caused him to be viewed as "dangerously radical" by one class of holiness workers and as "dangerously conservative" by an opposite class. Nevertheless, he found peace and power in pursuing this pattern.

Baker was a 23-year-old college senior when he became a Christian. He was soon licensed to preach and assigned to a circuit. Hungry for holiness, he began to seek it and to preach it. John Wesley had advised his preachers to proclaim the doctrine as living witnesses if they had experienced holiness, or as earnest seekers if they had not. Baker took that admonition seriously. Because he was inadequately informed and infrequently encouraged, however, he labored for 20 years before he obtained a pure heart.

PREACHING

Following this spiritual breakthrough, he had promoted the doctrine and experience of holiness with good success for some 17 years when he published the collection of "Bible Expositions and Addresses" from which this sermon was selected. The messages, given at various camp meetings and to Christian workers, had been helpful and fruitful, warranting a larger reception through the medium of print.

The two chief points of this brief address sum up Sheridan Baker's central convictions—that every Christian should experience heart purity, and that Jesus Christ is the abiding standard of holy living.

I wish to acknowledge a personal debt to Sheridan Baker. His *Hidden Manna* was the first book on the subject of holiness that I ever read. In the providence of God it came to my hands from the discarded library of a Methodist bishop who had been promoted to glory. Occasionally I reread this book, always with benefit to mind and heart.

A Purifying Hope*

Every man that hath this hope in him purifieth himself, even as he is pure (1 John 3:3).

What hope? By a reference to the . . . context it will be seen that it is . . . a hope of seeing Christ as He is, and being like Him, based upon the consciousness that we are now the sons of God. Among the many suggestions of the text it is proposed to notice only two leading thoughts.

I. *True Christians seek purity.*

It will be noticed that the verb "purifieth" is in the present tense. It does not intimate what the believer has done, or what he will do, but what he is now doing. He may have purified himself in the past, and may continue to purify himself in the future, and certainly will if he prove faithful; but it is what he is doing now that indicates the existence of a true evangelical hope. A true hope leads to present action and effort. "[He] purifieth himself."

He cannot have an evangelical hope who is not now purifying

*Source: Sheridan Baker, *Living Waters.* New York: Phillips and Hunt, 1888.

himself but only proposes to do it at some future time. All men, with very few exceptions, however degraded, have that kind of hope which springs from a purpose of future reform. Many professors of religion have no better hope. They acknowledge that they are not doing as they ought, but they intend to mend their ways by and by, and upon that purpose they claim a Christian hope. This is "the hope of unjust men [that] perisheth" (Prov. 11:7). It is affirmed in the text that "every man" who has the hope of a true Christian "purifieth himself." It is the business of the present.

FOR ALL CHRISTIANS

But what is it to purify oneself? It can mean nothing less than a *desire* for purity. He who hopes to spend his life in mercantile pursuits must desire a qualification for that business. So he who hopes to see Christ as He is and be like Him, he who hopes to live forever with the purified citizens of heaven, must desire the purity necessary for the enjoyment of such a state and such company. His soul must hunger and thirst for righteousness. His language is, "As the hart panteth after the water brooks, so panteth my soul after thee, O God. My soul thirsteth for God, for the living God" (Ps. 42:1-2).

HUNGER

To voluntarily retain any impurity of the flesh or spirit, or indulge any sin in the life, is to forfeit the favor of God. "If I regard iniquity in my heart," says the Psalmist, "the Lord will not hear me" (66:18). Every true Christian, therefore, must desire purity of life and heart.

To purify oneself must mean more than a desire for purity. "[He] purifieth" expresses the idea of *action and effort.* The earnest Christian examines himself like an inspector of flour or other articles of traffic; to determine the quality within he pierces through himself. He proves himself, or applies tests to himself, like the alchemist applies nitric acid to gold to test its integrity. Instead of applying the gospel square and plummet to others, a very common error, he is busy with himself. He "purifieth himself."

This language can mean nothing less than that he turns away from all sin, inward and outward, and to the full extent of his light he keeps himself unspotted from the world. It is a fearful mistake, which has crept into many of the different churches of late, that Christians may indulge certain habits and practice little vices which disturb religious peace and bring condemnation upon the soul, and yet claim the possession of an evangelical hope. "Every man that hath this hope in him purifieth himself."

FREE FROM SIN

This language not only indicates a turning away from all sin, but the use of such means as God has ordained for the purification of the soul. A true Christian uses all the means of grace. He [seeks to] use all losses and reverses, all prosperity and success, all disappointment and suffering. Like the worldling who presses all events and occurrences into the service of bearing down or pushing up stocks as his interests may demand, so the true believer presses all providences into the great and primary business of his life, the purification of his nature, and the development of his Christian character.

The language indicates, moreover, that a state of purity is retained by constant activity. Purity is not something that may be obtained and locked up in the heart and called upon when we need it, like a commodity which can be stored away in warerooms, but it is the divine nature inworked into the substratum of the soul, and retained by constant fidelity, by constant watchfulness and trust, or by . . . [continually] yielding to God and receiving the Holy Ghost. It is a *holy life lived.*

GROWTH

Notice next that

II. *The true Christian accepts Christ as his standard of purity.*

"[He] purifieth himself, even as he is pure." There are some false standards of purity which every true believer must shun if he would reach what is provided for him in the Atonement. It is proper for every member of the church to examine closely the Discipline, the Confession of Faith, and the creed books of his church, and defer to their teachings, but he must not make them his ultimate standard of appeal in matters of religious experience. They may place the standard too low. The only safe rule of faith and practice is the Bible. And all true Christians desire and labor to be Bible Christians.

SCRIPTURAL

Again, the professors of religion around us must not be taken as patterns. Their spirit and lives may be very defective, and though many valuable hints and helps may be derived from their lives, yet to take them as patterns is to compare ourselves among ourselves and measure ourselves by ourselves, which, says the apostle, is not wise (2 Cor. 10:12). One of the most fatal blunders that church members are making today is patterning after the religionists around them. This has been one of their blunders in every age.

The Pharisee in one of the Savior's parables made this fatal mistake. He was evidently one of the best men of his times. He could truthfully say, "I am not as other men are, extortioners, unjust, adulterers, or even as this publican. I fast twice in the week, I give tithes of all that I possess" (Luke 18:11-12). No doubt an honest comparison of himself with others around him, even with the professedly pious of his times, placed him, so far as the eye could detect, far in advance of his fellows. This led him to feel safe and to compliment himself. But had he consulted the writings of Moses and the prophets, and inquired for the spirit which God asked for in His children, he would have discovered his defects and penitently sought with deep abasement the required grace.

USE GOD'S MEASURE

Thousands upon thousands of professed Christians are committing the same mistake today, and are hoping all will be right with them beyond the grave, because they compare favorably with what they see in the lives and spirit of their brethren.

Another false standard which many raise is what they call "more religion." He who is contented to seek "more religion" raises for his standard himself with a little accession to his graces, or raises a standard a little in advance of his present self. If it be said that by "more religion" he means a great deal more than he now has, still, if he means less than the purity of Christ, he has raised a false standard.

The standard here raised and accepted by the true Christian is practicable. The Savior's life, so far as the moral elements involved in it are concerned, was an exemplification of what the gospel proposes to do for humanity. It was not the sole purpose of [Christ in] the Incarnation to suffer and die for man, but part of the mission was to present a divine pattern of holy living; to show what the Atonement provided for the believer. The practicability of this standard of purity, and imitability of this divine pattern, was exhibited in the religious life and triumphant death of the proto-martyr Stephen. His perfect devotion to the cause of Christ, and the complete imitation of the spirit of the Master in his death—"Lord, lay not this sin to their charge," meaning his bloody murderers (Acts 7:60)—shows the imitability of this pattern by fallen men through the power of grace.

CHRISTLIKENESS

Hence, no earnest Christian, who has come to see his privilege in the gospel, can aspire to less than what the Atonement provides for him, nor can he feel satisfied with a standard of purity below that raised in the text. He will be restless until he has learned to live through faith like his divine Pattern, and with perfect purity of affections, of motives, of words, and of actions, he is assured of transparency of character. He must feel assured that, examined in the sunlight of eternity, no impurity will appear in his spirit; that it is washed and made "whiter than snow," and that he is "unblameable in holiness," and "unreprovable in his sight" (Ps. 51:7; 1 Thess. 3:13; Col. 1:22). He "purifieth himself, even as he is pure."

William H. Huff
(1874-1928)

Will Huff, a Methodist evangelist, was one of the most fruitful and respected preachers of the holiness movement in America. His ministry ended dramatically in 1928, just a month before his 54th birthday. After preaching an evening service in a revival meeting in Cincinnati, he retired to his hotel room and died there from a heart attack.

God called him to preach while he was working as a potter in his native Ohio. He was largely self-educated but did receive some college training at Asbury in Wilmore, Ky. During his ministry of evangelism he earned a reputation as an orator and a Christian gentleman who modeled the message of full salvation.

Huff was passionately interested in missionary work and labored with great success in Latin America. After his death it was learned that he had borrowed on his life insurance and had placed a second mortgage on his home for the support of Methodist missions in South America.

Most of his ministry, however, was devoted to evangelism in the United States. G. A. McLaughlin, then coeditor of *The Christian Witness,* spoke of Huff's "marvelous pulpit power." Bud Robinson once named Huff the best preacher he had ever heard. The thousands who were moved by his eloquence in revivals and camp meetings were as strongly impressed by the lofty moral quality of his daily life. John Norberry, in a tribute to him, said, "He was kind, gentle, courteous, and Christlike." His ablest sermon was his own spirit and behavior.

"The Mind of the Master" is a good sample of the simple, searching messages so typical of the evangelists of the National Holiness Association, which Huff served briefly as president. Without reducing its moral challenge an iota, these men made the doctrine and experience of holiness attractive. They generated in their listeners a hunger for the blessing, and perhaps none could do it more effectively than did Will Huff. Such appetite for holiness is whetted not by doctrine alone but by truth that has become incarnate in the lives of those who proclaim it. There is a desperate need today for preachers who will serve as convincing witnesses to the message of sanctification, who can say as did Paul, "Be ye followers of me, even as I also am of Christ" (1 Cor. 11:1).

Some of the characteristics of the mind of Christ are here described briefly and compellingly. It adds to our interest to know that evangelist George Hammond, who was sanctified after hearing Will Huff preach, said, "I never felt that any knew the mind of Christ better than he."

The Mind of the Master*

We have the mind of Christ (1 Cor. 2:16). *Let this mind be in you, which was also in Christ Jesus* (Phil. 2:5).

We have in this twofold text . . . a positive declaration and a striking injunction. It is the statement of an essential fact in salvation and the injunction to realize it in experience. Throughout Paul's Epistles he was solicitous that the church possess in experience what was provided in redemption.

Writers tell us that the word "mind" in the first passage is not identical with that of the second. The first has to do more with that spiritual intelligence or consciousness in its relation to divine things. The second has to do more with the characteristics of the mind of the Master as He came in touch with men.

It is my purpose in this message to deal with the mind of Christ as to its spiritual consciousness . . . as to its characteristics, and . . . as to the how of our fullest possession of it.

---

*Source: *Twentieth Century Holiness Sermons.* Louisville, Ky.: Pentecostal Publishing Co., n.d.

I. *The declaration—"We have the mind of Christ."*

In dealing with Christian consciousness, Paul suggests the possibility of three conditions.

He speaks of the "natural man[, who] receiveth not the things of the Spirit of God: for they are foolishness unto him: neither can he know them, because they are spiritually discerned" (1 Cor. 2:14). He further declares that in this natural condition man's understanding is darkened, that he is alienated from the life of God, and that he has a heart-blindness. . . . Man is alive physically, socially, financially, and dead spiritually. Humanity dead to deity, spends its days dealing in dust. The sinner in his natural condition can have no Christian consciousness, for Christian consciousness is vitally related to Christian experience, and Christian experience is vitally related to Christ.

Again, he speaks of the man who is "yet carnal" (3:3). He says this man is a babe in Christ, has spiritual life, some appreciation of divine things, but is hindered by something he calls carnality. This is a sort of double-minded fellow, hindered in his spiritual going, hampered in his spiritual liberty, and mixed in his Christian experience. Multitudes have started well but are dwarfed today because they have failed to go on to the fullness of the blessing.

CARNALITY

Again, he speaks of "he that is spiritual" (2:15). He says this man discerneth spiritual things, has the mind of Christ, is among them who are perfect, and to such an one he can speak wisdom. I think Paul's terms here, "he that is spiritual," "them that are perfect" (2:6), and "we [who] have the mind of Christ," refer to those who have been born again out of the natural state, cleansed from the carnal principle, and in whose life . . . the lost order is restored. This man has a God-consciousness that is not speculation, neither is it reached by logical argument, but is revealed to the spiritually minded by the Holy Ghost.

With this spiritual intelligence we know God, the essential facts of our nature have found a fitting field of operation, and we have been brought into the true environment of our life. We have fellowship with God through life's pilgrimage; we have communion with God through life's plans and pleasures; we have cooperation with God through life's services and activities. We will have a home in the city that hath foundations. And all this is ours because we have the mind of Christ, the intelligence of Christ, the consciousness of Christ, the life of Christ. No wonder Paul was emphatic in his declaration, when he had in mind this central fact of Christianity, which was purchased for us in a plenteous redemption.

FULL SALVATION

II. *The injunction—"Let this mind be in you."*

Here . . . we have one of the finest injunctions ever given to the people of God. We are not only to possess the mind of Christ in its spiritual appreciation of divine things, but we are also to manifest the mind of Christ as we come in contact with men. Of course there are many who . . . tell us that as long as we live here in a world of sin . . . we cannot walk as He walked, love as He loved, and represent Him here among men. But where unbelief would discourage, the Word of God would encourage, and what would be impossible with a worldling is possible with the genuinely spiritual.

Of course Paul did not mean we were to manifest the mind of Christ in all of its scope of wisdom, greatness, and power. Christ was infinite, we are finite. He was unlimited, we are limited. He was all-wise, we are ignorant. He never made a mistake, we have made serious ones. He never took a step in the wrong direction, we walked for years in the wrong way. So it does not mean we are to possess the mind of

CHRISTLIKE

Christ in quantity but in quality. . . . We can bring our small earthen vessel to the great ocean of divinity and there be filled in our limited capacity with that which fills the Infinite. John says, "Of his fulness have all we received, and grace for grace" (1:16). He means . . . that for every grace that grew, blossomed, and bore fruit in the life of our Lord . . . we can possess a like grace.

III. *Some of the characteristics of the mind of Christ . . .*

As we notice these characteristics of the mind of the Master, we will ask the Spirit to apply the truth to our hearts and see if we be like-minded.

1. *Humility.* He was the humble-minded Christ. If we ever have an appreciation of the significance of our Lord's humiliation, we must get a firm grasp of Paul's splendid passage to the Philippians . . . "Who, being in the form of God, thought it not robbery to be equal with God: but made himself of no reputation, and took upon him the form of a servant, and was made in the likeness of men: and being found in fashion as a man, he humbled himself, and became obedient unto death, even the death of the cross" (2:6-8).

Here we have Paul's conception of our Lord's humiliation. He takes us back through the eternities to the preexistent Christ. There he declares that Christ was in the "form of God," but in the presence of the call for earth's redemption, He took on Him the *form* of a servant, that is, He came to the level of those needing succor. Thus we have the stoop of divinity on earth's redemptive mission. He passed from Sovereign to servant; for the redemption of men He came from glory to Galilee.

He not only took on Him the form of a servant, but also "humbled himself, and became obedient unto death, even the death of the cross." So humility was the secret of our blood redemption. Humility was the warp and woof of the life of our Lord. Humility was the central thought of His teaching. If I am to possess and manifest the mind of Christ, then I must be humble before God, sincere and Christlike in my dealings with men. There is certainly no place for self-importance or self-seeking here, but a large place for the compassion of Christ in . . . service for humanity.

LESS OF SELF

2. *Purity.* He was the pure-minded Christ. He said, "Which of you convinceth me of sin?" (John 8:46). He said, "The prince of this world cometh, and hath nothing in me" (14:30). He was prophetically described as "the lily of the valley" (Song of Sol. 2:1). They are snow white. His thoughts were pure, His motives were pure, His desires were pure, His propensities were pure, His words were pure. His life was transparent, there was nothing streaked in His nature. He neither talked smut or listened to smut. If we are to be Christ-minded, then we will go forth among men as the light of the world, the salt of the earth, and be a living rebuke to the veneered devilishness of the 20th century.

3. *Patience.* He was the patient Christ. He was patient with His friends and patient with His enemies. His friends were always misunderstanding Him, and His enemies were always trying to trap Him. He held onto Simon Peter and said, "I have prayed for thee" (Luke 22:32). He never gave Judas up till Judas said, "How much will you give me for Him?" (Cf. Matt. 26:14-15.) He never went to pieces under provocation, and nothing explosive was found in His nature even under fire.

LOVE IS PATIENT

You have met that fellow who says, "Of course I get impatient, of course I get mad, but I am all over it in a minute." Well, the San Francisco earthquake was all over it in a minute, but it left things in such a bad shape that a few more like it would put the real estate men out of business in that coast town. It is not the awful outbroken sins nor the vicious, vulgar things that are spoiling so many Christians, but those little momentary heart breaks with God. If we are possessed with the Christ-mind, then patience will have its "perfect work," and we will rank among those who are "perfect and entire, wanting nothing" (James 1:4).

4. *Love.* He was the Christ of love. Back of His humility, back of His purity, back of His patience, was the great love life. Love was the impulse of His service, sorrow, and suffering. He had compassion on the multitudes, wept over the city, sought the lost sheep, prayed for His murderers, and rescued the dying thief from the jaws of unfolding damnation. "Having loved his own . . . he loved them unto the end" (John 13:1). . . . Christ was love revealed. . . . John says, "As he is, so are we in this world" (1 John 4:17). That is, as He is in His essential nature, so are we in our essential nature, if we have the mind of Christ.

LOVE IS CHRISTLIKE

The apostle John uses tremendous language when he describes this love in operation. He says, "*If any man love the world, the love of the Father is not in him.*" "But whoso hath this world's good, and seeth his brother have need, and shutteth up his bowels of compassion from him, how *dwelleth the love of God in him?*" "If a man say, *I love God, and hateth his brother, he is a liar*" (1 John 2:15; 3:17; 4:20). This characteristic of the mind of Christ delivers us from the world, saves us from stinginess, and enables us to love the rest of the family.

5. *Unselfishness.* He was the unselfish Christ. He said that He "came not to be ministered unto, but to minister" (Matt. 20:28; Mark 10:45). There is nothing more subtle than selfishness. No matter how pure our motives may be at the beginning, if we are not careful and prayerful they will become mixed. This poisonous element is manifest in self-will . . . it wants its own way and plans. It is manifest in self-indulgence, self-complacency, self-glorying, self-confidence, self-consciousness, self-importance, and self-seeking. There is no service so sacred, no calling so high, no precinct so holy but what it will contaminate if we are not possessed with the mind of Jesus Christ.

6. *Joy.* Christ had a joyful mind. I know the Bible says that He was "a man of sorrows, and acquainted with grief," that "his visage was so marred," and that He "gave [His] back to the smiters" (Isa. 53:3; 52:14; 50:6); but it also says that Jesus rejoiced in spirit. His joy broke out under the most unlikely circumstances, as if it was not dependent on outer signs but on an inner condition. This joy is the legacy He bequeathed to His followers. If His mind is ours, then His joy will be our strength.

7. *Aggressiveness.* He was the aggressive Christ. At the beginning of His life He said, "I must be about my Father's business" (Luke

2:49). At the close of His life He said, "I have finished the work which thou gavest me to do" (John 17:4). Between those two statements He lived a life of unceasing service for even those who were unappreciative. For us to be Christ-minded means that we have a blood-earnestness in service and a zeal of the Lord for work in His kingdom.

8. *Loyalty.* He was the loyal-minded Christ. He never swerved an inch from truth or duty. He was loyal to God when He was popular, He was loyal to truth when it cost Him His following. . . . He said, "Except ye eat the flesh of the Son of man, and drink his blood, ye have no life in you" (John 6:53). His disciples said, "This is an hard saying; who can hear it?" (v. 60). They left the meeting, withdrew from the society, and followed Him no more; but as they departed, He did not run after them and apologize for the truth. There was a handful left. He turned to Simon Peter and said, "Will ye also go away?" Peter looked at the crowd going over the hill, then into the eyes of Christ, and said, "Lord, to whom shall we go? thou hast the words of eternal life" (vv. 67-68). If we have the mind of Christ, we will be loyal to truth, loyal to God, loyal to holiness, even if some camp followers do leave.

9. *Victory.* He was the victorious Christ. For a while it looked as if He were a failure. When His own disciple sold Him for 30 pieces of silver, when He was arrested in the olive grove, when He stood in the presence of Pontius Pilate, when He staggered down the streets of Jerusalem and struggled up the hill, when they stripped Him of His raiment, when we listen to the sickening thud of the hammer, when we see Him hanging between two thieves—it seemed as if He had failed. Hell thought He was defeated and was jubilant, but it had been declared through the prophet of old, "*He shall not fail*" (Isa. 42:4). So amid the reeling earth and darkening sun and opening graves, there was a cry, "It is finished" (John 19:30). The world was redeemed and hell was defeated.

HIS VICTORY IS OURS

Figuratively speaking, there was a rattling at the gates of perdition, the gates were twisted from their rusty hinges, and the triumphant One walked through the ashes of damnation to the throne of darkness . . . pulled the prince from his throne and threw him in the ashes. With one foot on his neck He said, "I am he that liveth, and was dead; and, behold, I am alive for evermore, Amen; and have the keys of hell and of death. . . . [I am] he that openeth, and no man shutteth; and shutteth, and no man openeth" (Rev. 1:18; 3:7). Then 40 days after the Resurrection, He ascended "far above all principality, and power, and might, and dominion, and every name that is named . . . [and] sat down on the right hand of the Majesty on high," waiting till His enemies became His footstool (Eph. 1:21; Heb. 1:3). Victor over sin, flesh, hell, and the grave!

If we possess His mind, we will be victorious in life, triumphant in death, and outshine the sun in the kingdom of our Father.

IV. *The method of obtainment*

How may I be possessed with the mind of Christ and how may I manifest it among men? There is just one little word in the text that gives us the key. That little word is "Let." This brings us to the point of personal responsibility. The whole message culminates here for the individual. The word "let" suggests abandonment. If we ever come into the possession of this grace, there must be a wholehearted, absolute, positive, final abandonment to God to be cleansed from sin, made holy in heart, and filled with the Holy Ghost. When God speaks the second time, "Be clean," we are then conditioned to be possessed with the mind that was in Christ Jesus.

SURRENDER ALL TO GOD

This, as a theory, seems easy, but to put it into actual practice is difficult. Yet there is a hope for every struggling, hungry, discouraged life. Put the past with its failures under the Blood, put the future in God's hands, cease your doubting, abide in the will and Word of God, and *let* Him have His way with thee.

Just now, your doubtings give o'er.
Just now, reject Him no more.
Just now, throw open the door;
Let Jesus come into your heart.

John A. Knight

(1931—)

John A. Knight is a son of the parsonage and was converted in childhood. In his teens he experienced the perfection of love about which he preaches in this selected sermon. As a college student he was summoned to the ministry and has faithfully responded to the various assignments that summons has entailed.

Holding graduate degrees in philosophy and theology, it is not surprising that his ministry has involved both college teaching and college presidencies. He taught in three of the United States colleges maintained by the Church of the Nazarene, and served two of them as president.

What he taught on campus has been well tested in the grass roots church. Dr. Knight has served four churches as pastor. He has never been an ivory-tower theologian, but has vindicated the relevance and power of the gospel "where the rubber meets the road."

In 1985 he was elected a general superintendent of the Church of the Nazarene. Much of his preaching now is heard in assemblies, conventions, and camp meetings.

Dr. Knight has authored many articles and some books. He served also as editor of his denomination's official organ, the *Herald of Holiness.*

"All Loves Excelling" is an exposition of 1 John 4:10-21 and draws its title from one of Charles Wesley's best-loved and much-used hymns. The outline is simple and memorable. This divine love, perfected in human life, excels all other kinds of love (1) in the fellowship it preserves; (2) in the assurance it provides; and (3) in the service it promotes.

The fellowship preserved by love is God's gift, not man's achievement. It is based upon our mutual participation in Christ's atoning death, confessed in faith.

The assurance provided by love is also a divine gift, the indwelling Spirit, who conforms us to the likeness of Christ, removing thereby all tormenting fear.

The service promoted by love is directed to others in the church and in the world, as God's love in us comes to expression in our acts of love for them.

Knight's concern is pastoral and practical. He is not interested chiefly in the formulation of a doctrine but in the implementation of an experience and life-style. What is proclaimed as gracious possibility is urged as personal responsibility: "The question is: Has the *beauty* of this perfected love come to decorate our lives?"

All Loves Excelling*

> *Herein is our love made perfect, that we may have boldness in the day of judgment: because as he is, so are we in this world* (1 John 4:17).

God's love is the *definition* and *declaration* of pure love, by which all loves are to be evaluated and measured. It has been poured out on unworthy man, and demonstrated in the propitiation for man's sins (v. 10).

The love of God in Christ "shed abroad in our hearts by the Holy [Spirit]" (Rom. 5:5; also see Titus 3:4-6) is the example that man is to emulate in all his personal and social relationships. This love alone is the *source* and *power* of all other loves.

John Wesley equated this love of God in man with holiness and holy living. He taught that "Christian perfection," or "perfect love," is "loving God with all the heart, soul, mind, and strength, and one's neighbor as oneself."

---

*Source: General Superintendents of the Church of the Nazarene (1985-89), *Sanctify Them . . . That the World May Know: Twelve Holiness Sermons.* Kansas City: Nazarene Publishing House, 1987.

The validity of Wesley's judgment is borne out by the passage before us. The purpose of the entire Epistle is seen in such expressions as: "that ye may know that ye have eternal life" (5:13); "that ye sin not" (2:1); "that your joy may be full" (1:4). John's aim is to direct believers into the *fullness* of God's love. He does this by portraying his vision of Christian holiness, which is perfect love for God and man.

This Epistle, then, is one of love, holiness, and the victorious life. It reflects a deep, vital union with God emphasizing true holiness and righteousness. The disciple whom Jesus loved combines his understanding of *life in God* and the *life of perfect love* with the *fullness of the Spirit.*

Chapter 4, verse 17, and the surrounding verses, present to Christ's followers the biblical standard of *perfect love* revealed in and made possible by Jesus Christ. The emphasis is not so much on the stages or crises of faith and experience through which one passes to come to this degree of maturity; but rather on the quality of life that results from the divine activity exercised in saving and sanctifying grace. What we have here is a description of the life of holiness and of the possibilities of Christlikeness through the fullness of the indwelling Spirit.

HOLINESS, A QUALITY OF LIFE

Our passage of Scripture clearly describes and reflects the character of one whose love has been *made perfect.* In these 12 verses the word "love" is used 22 times. The English word "love" translates two different words in the New Testament that convey different meanings. One *(agapē)* is used primarily to refer to God's love and refers to a deep and constant love that is not dependent upon the merit of its object. The other *(philia)* represents the tender affection between two human beings. In all 22 instances *agapē* is used. Thus we are talking about God's kind of love.

Three tests of divine life or perfect love are put forward in John's Epistle:

1. Whether we believe that Jesus is the Son of God—by the commitment of our will
2. Whether we are living lives of righteousness—moral and ethical uprightness
3. Whether we have love one for another—even for our enemies

When asked, "Is there any example in Scripture of persons who have attained perfect love?" Wesley replied, "Yes, St. John and all those of whom he speaks in 1 John 4:17."

Let us look at the way the apostle of love views a "true" Christian, one who is filled with perfect love. May we ask ourselves: Do we love with a love made perfect—with the very love of Christ? And may we pray with Charles Wesley:

Love divine, all loves excelling,
Joy of heav'n, to earth come down!
Fix in us Thy humble dwelling;
All Thy faithful mercies crown.
Jesus, Thou art all compassion;
Pure, unbounded love Thou art.
Visit us with Thy salvation;
Enter ev'ry trembling heart.

I. *Perfect Love Excels in the Fellowship It Preserves* (1:3-7).

First John has all the marks of a sermon, the work of a pastor who seeks to build up his people in the faith. The author employs graphic contrasts—light and darkness, life and death, saint and sinner, love and hate, Christ and Antichrist. These contrasts are practically synonymous, and any one of them may be substituted [for] almost any other. They can all be expressed in the phrase "fellowship and alienation." John is extolling "fellowship," the immediate union of the soul with God that issues in righteousness in all the relationships of one's life. Perfect love both creates and preserves this fellowship.

A. *This Fellowship Is a Gift of God Through Jesus Christ* (4:10).

Sinful man cannot love God or have fellowship with Him ("Not that we loved God"). We were enemies to God, and yet Christ died for us. It was God's love, not our merit or our lovableness, that induced Him to devise means to accomplish our salvation.

GIFT OF GOD'S LOVE

"We love him, because he first loved us" (v. 19). God's love for man is not a response to our love. Our love depends upon, and is the result of, His love. Real love in its origin is not human but divine. Human love at best is only responsive; it is never original and spontaneous. The marvel of God's method with men is that He loves them into loving—both by His prevenient grace and by His transforming grace. In this His love excels.

B. *This Fellowship Is Made Possible by the Removal of Our Sins* (4:10).

The Father has "sent his Son to be the propitiation for our sins." The Greek word for "propitiation" is used only here and in 2:2, without reference to the one to whom it is offered. It should not be understood as an appeasement to God but as a reference to [Christ] by whom God shows mercy to those who believe on [Him]. Thus the word has been rendered an "atoning sacrifice" (NIV).

In and through Christ man finds mercy and forgiveness of his sins, pardon and peace with God. The alienation and estrangement that separated man from God are taken away. The guilt and power of sin that weighted down man and held him in bondage are gone. One is reconciled to God by Christ's death, a "new and living way" whereby we have access to the Father (Heb. 10:19-20). The pollution of sin, the spirit of selfishness that hinders growth in grace, is cleansed. In dealing effectively with the sin problem, God's perfect love excels.

C. *This Fellowship Rests upon Confession of Christ as Savior and Lord* (4:14-15).

The testimony described, "we have seen and do testify," expresses the common and abiding witness of the Church (cf. 1:1-5) as it is appropriated by the faith of each believer personally. The confession "that Jesus is the Son of God" is not merely the mental assent to, nor declaration of, a fact—even the devils have this kind of faith and "tremble" (James 2:19). Rather, it is the public recognition and acceptance of the person of Christ as the Divine Savior. It is submission to Him as Lord and trust in Him for salvation. He who with the heart thus acknowledges Him, and with the tongue confesses Him, receives Him and has eternal life (cf. Rom. 10:9-10).

"God dwelleth in him" who makes this confession, "and he in God" (1 John 4:15). This reciprocal indwelling in God and in Christ implies the most intimate fellowship of the believer with the Father and with the Son, in whom He is revealed. The conditions of this fellowship are love, confession, and obedience. The effects are fruitfulness and acceptance. The sign is the possession of the Holy Spirit, who lavishes God's love in the heart and inspires the filial feeling, so that we may pray, "Abba, Father" (Rom. 8:15; Gal. 4:6). To so recognize the Father and His working, which is a result of God's grace, certifies true sonship.

Perfect love preserves this fellowship—in this it excels.

II. *Perfect Love Excels in the Assurance It Provides* (4:7).

One cannot gain acceptance with God through good deeds or accumulated merit, by one's economic or racial background—but by grace alone through faith in Jesus Christ. The apostle Paul failed to find peace with God through his own righteousness. He was circumcised the eighth day, of the stock of Israel, of the

BY GRACE

tribe of Benjamin, a Hebrew of the Hebrews, a Pharisee. He zealously persecuted the Church, a virtue in the minds of the Jews. Regarding the law, he was blameless. His dependence upon these "virtues" only increased his guilt and magnified his spiritual paucity. But when he met Jesus Christ on the Damascus road and accepted His righteousness, his life was transformed, and he was accepted into "the beloved." He testified to the Philippians: "What things were gain to me, these I counted loss for Christ" (3:7).

A. *God Assures That We Belong to Him by Giving His Spirit of Love* (4:13).

The source of the Christian's assurance is the Gift of the Holy Spirit (see 3:24; also Rom. 8:15-16). Here is the Divine Presence whom Jesus said He would ask the Father to send His disciples and all His followers of every age (John 14:16). The Holy Spirit brings assurance to the Christian because the devil has been judged, and all who dwell in God, and God in them, share in the victory over evil (John 16:11).

HOLY SPIRIT

The Holy Spirit is the Christian's proof of acceptance with God. His presence enables him to know that he belongs to God. The Spirit is the evidence of the fellowship of the community of Christ's Body, because all experience the same Presence. While the Holy Spirit respects and enhances each one's individuality, there is a oneness about His presence that assures each member of a common fellowship through Him. That oneness is the unity of their faith in Jesus Christ. This confession is prompted by the indwelling Spirit.

It is for this reason that the Spirit centers attention upon Jesus. When we say we "feel the Spirit," we mean we are sensing the presence of Christ. When the Spirit indwells us He enables us to exalt Christ, a confirmation that we belong to Him.

B. *God Gives Assurance, or "Boldness," for the Day of Judgment—Through Christlikeness* (4:17).

To live in the love of God and have it flow out of us to others bears fruit in holy boldness. The fear of judgment fades because one sees in the person of our Judge Him who has died for us, regenerated our hearts, and fills us with himself. The writer of Hebrews expresses a virtually universal anxiety of mankind when he says that all men must die and after this face the judgment (9:27). Whether that judgment be the Great White Throne (Rev. 20:11-15), or the judgment of consequences in this life, it is a fearful thing.

The love of God in one's heart brings boldness because one knows the Judge of all is working out His purpose in one's life. This boldness comes because that one is becoming like Christ, the Standard by which all men are judged. What will be asked of the believer at the last is already occurring through the cleansing and empowering love of God in the heart and life of the child of God. The love of God makes one fearless of judgment, because judgment is that which is happening in the person in whom the love of God is perfected.

John firmly declares, "As he is"—pure, holy, loving—"so are we in this world" (1 John 4:17)—saved from our sins, made like to himself in righteousness and true holiness. The ground of our boldness, then, is present likeness to Christ. Our essential likeness to Him is not in our trials, or persecutions, or sufferings, nor even primarily in the fact that we are not of the world as He is not of the world. Rather, it is the fact that we are *righteous* as He is *righteous*. Our likeness is to Christ's character and spirit.

CHRISTLIKENESS

C. *Perfect Love Casts Out Fear* (4:18).

There is "no fear in love" because fear pulls apart, while love unites. Love that is *perfect* casts out fear. This fear has to do with God's punishment and is an aspect of His discipline—"fear hath torment." The one who fears is not perfected in love and therefore shrinks away from God.

Bengel has said there are four classes of men:

> 1. Those who have *neither fear nor love*—the unregenerate and unconverted. They have no love for God and no fear of God.
>
> 2. Those who have *fear of God* but *no love for Him*—the unregenerated but now convicted. They have caught a glimpse of their sinfulness and are afraid.
>
> 3. Those who have *both fear and love*—the newly regenerated, babes in Christ, or young converts. They love God but still fear Him because of their inner uncleanness.
>
> 4. Those who have *only love for God*—Christians in whom the love of God is perfected. They have had their heart cleansed from all inward sin and have been sanctified wholly (to use our terminology).

Someone asked Dr. J. G. Morrison: "How much religion will a man have to have to make it to heaven?" He replied, "Enough that he feels comfortable in the presence of a holy God." That requires a holy heart.

A HOLY HEART FOR A HOLY GOD

"Perfect love casteth out fear."

We must not suppose that the love of God implanted in the heart of man is ever imperfect in itself; it is only so in degree. But there may be a lesser or greater degree of what is perfect in itself. So it is with respect to the love that the followers of Christ have. We are not to imagine that the love of God casts out *every* kind of fear from the soul—[for example,] fear of falling from great heights, or fear of fire . . . But perfect love does cast out that fear that has "torment"—fear of God himself. We stand in awe of Him and with reverence, but we do not cringe before Him in fear of capricious judgment.

The more one grows in the Christian graces the more other kinds of fear are removed. Fear of failure, fear that others will betray, fear of people's opinions. Such fears distort perspective, disrupt relationships, retard growth, and inhibit development. There are fears that blind moral judgment and inflame passions.

MATURE GRACE REDUCES FEARS

Love is positive; fear is negative. These are mutually exclusive. The more one loves, the less he fears. The more he fears, the less he loves. While some fears may have value, "There is nothing that fear does for us in a constructive way that love and confidence will not do better" (T. E. Martin). Perfect love enables us to accept each day and all that it brings in confidence and boldness. In this it excels.

III. *Perfect Love Excels in the Service It Promotes* (4:7-8, 11, 20-21).

A. *Love for Others Is Rooted in Love for God, or Love from God* (4: 21).

"If God so loved us, we ought also to love one another" (v. 11). We are to love those who are a part of the fellowship of believers. However, Jesus told the disciples that if they loved only those who loved them, they would have no reward (Matt. 5:46). This includes loving one's enemies and doing good to those who persecute us (Matt. 5:43-45). Loving others, even our enemies, is not so tall an order when we see the activity of God in us. The love we have for God and others comes from the indwelling presence of God. God dwells in those who love Him, and His love is perfected in them. Perfect love is the work of God in the heart of the believer. It is the nature of God not only to love but also to bring that love to perfection or fulfillment. Christian holiness is the fruit of the love relationship with God. It is what He intends for everyone born again of the Spirit.

GOD'S LOVE IN US

The initiative, of course, is God's. We do not perfect His love in us; He does. When we open our hearts to the love of God in commitment, consecration, faith, and obedience, we are at one with the purpose for which we were created. We begin to be what we were intended to be. That intention is brought to fulfillment as His love is perfected in us. Having this perfection of love, one can see God. Jesus said, "Blessed are the pure in heart: for they shall see [enjoy] God" (Matt. 5:8). This perfection or purity of heart is an unselfish and giving love that does not love for returns, but finds its joy in giving.

GOD'S PURPOSE FOR US

B. *Hatred, or Unconcern for Others, Evidences a Lack of Perfect Love* (4:20).

John asks a pointed rhetorical question: If one does not love "his brother whom he hath seen, how can he love God whom he hath not seen?" The implication is that if a man fails in the duty of love to one with whom he is in daily interaction, he cannot perform the more difficult duty of loving one whom he has never seen, and whose existence is invisible to him except by the eye of faith. To this point, John has not directly mentioned our love for God. Now he brings it into sharp focus and insists that our love for God is validated by our love for others.

LOVING GOD MEANS LOVING OTHERS

Loving others, with a love made perfect, is not an option but [is called a] "commandment" . . . (v. 21). This may be a reference to the summary of the Mosaic law that calls for loving God with one's whole heart and one's neighbor as oneself (Lev. 19:18; Deut. 6:5; Matt. 22:37-39; Mark 12:30-31; Luke 10:27). The commandment is a commandment of love. Love, being of the very nature of God, contains its own motivation to self-expression toward others. It is of the nature of God's love in us to express itself. The proof that love is real, *perfected,* in the full Christian sense, lies in the overt action to which it leads. There is no real love for God that does not show itself in obedience to His commands—love being lived out to its "fingertips" in all segments of our society. In this perfect love excels. . . .

The *beauty* of this passage of Scripture is rivaled only by 1 Corinthians 13—the "hymn of love." "God is love" (1 John 4:16). He has made His love known to man through His Son, awakening man's echoing response, which is demonstrated in visible acts of service to others.

The question is: Has the *beauty* of this perfected love come to decorate our lives? Have we confessed our lack of love and consecrated our life to God? Do we in this moment love God with all our heart, soul, mind, and strength, and our neighbor (as well as enemies) as ourself?

If not, we can by His grace. His love can be implanted in our hearts by the fullness of the Holy Spirit. We may by faith receive Him who is Love, enabling and empowering us to love "because he first loved us."

"Herein is our love made perfect."
All other loves this love excels.

7

LIVING THE HOLY LIFE

Stephen Olin
(1797-1851)

Stephen Olin was one of the most influential Methodist ministers of his day. In *A History of Methodism in the United States,* James M. Buckley says of Olin, "To no minister of the Methodist Episcopal Church can the term 'great' be applied with more unquestionable propriety than to him, and it was equally suitable whether applied physically, intellectually, or morally."

Olin was a staunch advocate of holiness. According to Timothy Smith, Olin experienced entire sanctification under the guidance of Phoebe Palmer in the early 1840s. A decade earlier his distinguished career had taken a new turn. When Randolph and Macon College was established in Virginia in 1831, Olin was selected to head the faculty. In 1839 he became the second president of Wesleyan University in Middletown, Conn. He was serving in that office when he died in 1851.

This respected educator was involved in all aspects of his church's life and work. One of the most powerful of his published sermons, for example, is an impassioned plea for missions. His debates and appeals on various social and moral issues were frequently heard in annual conferences.

The sermon "On Prayer" is intensely practical, because prayer is indispensable to Christian living. "Upon [prayer] God has been pleased to make dependent the entire success of our religious life—all the gifts of His grace." What we must do in order to live should be well done. Effective prayer is governed by character, attitude, spirit—so Olin joins holiness and prayer in his sermon, as he did in his life, and as Paul did in the text.

It is not enough to pray. Even much prayer can be unavailing. "God prescribes the terms" of prevailing prayer, and Olin expounds them simply, frankly, and briefly. The outline is drawn from the text, not imposed upon it. The text is allowed to speak its own message, with urgent and relevant applications made to Olin's listeners. To read the sermon is to realize at once its enduring value.

This sermon was not designed for publication. Like others in the volume from which it was taken, it was found among Olin's papers after his death. It lacks the "elaborate finish" that characterized the articles he submitted to the press. Even his notes and sketches, however, are complete enough, and polished enough, to encourage excellence in those who read them as models as well as for information.

On Prayer*

> *I will therefore that men pray every where, lifting up holy hands, without wrath and doubting* (1 Tim. 2:8).

In the context, the apostle enjoins special prayer "for all that are in authority," and adverts to the connection between such prayer and the peace, piety, and honesty of the people. Pray for *them,* "that *we* may lead a quiet and peaceable life in all godliness and honesty"; a duty by many Christians coldly performed, if not totally neglected. We censure, denounce, and revile our rulers—seldom pray for them.

We are exhorted, also, to pray "for all men," because God "will have all men to be saved, and to come unto the knowledge of the truth"; and because "Christ Jesus gave himself a ransom for all." Were it not so, prayer would not only be useless, but presumptuous. This "ransom" paid by Christ—the Atonement made on the Cross for sin—is the only encouragement to pray, and the foundation for all rational expectation of obtaining the things for which we pray.

Prayer, offered in the adorable name of Jesus, is, in the gospel

---

*Source: Stephen Olin, *The Works of Stephen Olin, D.D., LL.D.* Vol. 1, *Sermons and Sketches.* New York: Harper and Brothers, Publishers, 1860.

economy, the chief of Christian duties and privileges. Upon it God has been pleased to make dependent the entire success of our religious life—all the gifts of His grace. He is more willing to bestow than parents to give good gifts to their children, but [He bestows] on "them that ask him." "Ask, and it shall be given you; seek, and ye shall find; knock, and it shall be opened unto you," are broad, free announcements of His designs and compassions (Matt. 7:11, 7).

He gives the Spirit to those who ask Him. Pardon of sin depends on prayer. "Pray God, if perhaps the thought of thine heart may be forgiven thee" (Acts 8:22). Sanctification depends on prayer. "The very God of peace sanctify you wholly; and I pray God your whole spirit and soul and body be preserved blameless unto the coming of our Lord Jesus Christ" (1 Thess. 5:23). By prayer we escape the snares of the tempter. "Pray that ye enter not into temptation" (Luke 22:40; cf. Matt. 26:41). Faith, the great instrument of justification, and an essential element of success at the throne of grace, is sustained by prayer. "Lord, increase our faith" (Luke 17:5). The success of our ministry depends on prayer. "Pray . . . for me, that utterance may be given unto me, that I may open my mouth boldly, to make known the mystery of the gospel" (Eph. 6:18-19).

HOLINESS DEPENDS ON PRAYER

Other duties are occasional, and depend on exigence, or time, or place. Not so with this. "Praying always with all prayer and supplication" (Eph. 6:18); in the congregation of saints, in the family and social circle, in the closet, in the heart. Be "instant in prayer." "Pray without ceasing." "Pray every where" (Rom. 12:12; 1 Thess. 5:17; 1 Tim. 2:8).

Prayer is encouraged by the greatest promises. "Ask, and ye shall receive" (John 16:24). "All things, whatsoever ye shall ask in prayer, believing, ye shall receive" (Matt. 21:22). "If two of you shall agree on earth as touching any thing that they shall ask, it shall be done for them of my Father which is in heaven" (Matt. 18:19).

And this duty is performed, while others are neglected. The Church and the world are vocal with prayers. Millions pray at home. Nations are prostrate, at this hour, in the courts of the Lord. Millions agree in what they ask—the salvation of men, the piety and the peace of the Church. Parents pray for the conversion of their children, wives for their husbands, sisters for brothers. . . . And these are, we know, proper objects to seek. God wills to grant such petitions. Christ died to effect these objects.

But a wonderful discrepancy is here manifest; and the great question arises, With so much prayer, how is it there is so little success? Why is it? Do the promises fail? Has God forgotten to be gracious?

Far from it, brethren; the fault is in ourselves. We do not comply with the conditions of success in prayer. God prescribes the terms. These are enumerated in our text: I. *A holy life*—"lifting up holy hands." II. *A charitable, forgiving spirit*—"without wrath." III. *Faith*—"without doubting."

I. *A Holy Life*

Religion prescribes purity of life—obedience to God. "Cease to do evil; learn to do well" (Isa. 1:16-17). "Let the wicked forsake his way, and the unrighteous man his thoughts" (Isa. 55:7). These are preliminaries to acceptance. No progress can be made in religion without a compliance with its first principles. It would dishonor God to require, and ruin man to do, less. Professors of religion often overlook, overleap, all this. They so order matters that their religion and their lives stand at variance, or, at least, are quite distinct.

HOLINESS BELONGS TO PRAYER

[Religion] runs along in its own channel: prayers, reading, profession, churchgoing . . . devotion—all earnestness and fidelity. The life is conducted on common maxims, and the man in his shop . . . differs widely from him of the closet. He is exacting, unscrupulous—follows all prudent maxims—will be rich, or honored, or something else. He is at once pious and worldly. These men carry the spirit of their business to the closet, but not the spirit of devotion to their business. Prayer would sanctify their pursuits—worldliness chills their prayers. They put asunder what God has joined, and lift up *unholy* hands before the throne of grace.

We should *live* and pray for the same thing. We pray against the world, but live for it. We pray against pride and ambition, but nurture them all the day long; against appetite, but pamper it; against temptation, but brave it. This is, in fact, an insult upon God, and acting as if we verily thought we could impose upon Him.

Many pray *for,* and live against their salvation. They call on God to sanctify, and then do whatever comes in their way to defile the Spirit's temple.

Parents pray, and beg ministers to pray, for the conversion of their children—they weep, sigh, but do not restrain or train—they leave all to God.

Christians choose for themselves and their children alliances in reference to worldly ends, and pray against the inevitable consequences of their choice. In doubtful questions, they decide on the side of indulgence, relying on grace.

We should observe what effect our ways have on our prayers. The closet is often the true test of actions. It is a kind of judgment seat, where portion after portion of our history is tried, in anticipation of the final day.

But if we would pray acceptably, it is indispensable that we cultivate

II. *A Charitable, Forgiving Spirit*

Christians who are really in earnest soon conform their habits to God's Word and pass on to the inner warfare with sinful appetites and tendencies, which constitutes their probation. Their great work is hidden from men but seen of God. Forgiveness is an express condition of acceptable prayer. We must forgive all, no matter how difficult the duty. God forbids us to pray on other terms. Bad tempers are the chief hindrances of prayer. Men of faultless lives, so far as attention to external duties is concerned, are often passionate, peevish, impatient. They grieve the Spirit. They are censorious, uncharitable. Many become the scourge and curse of the circle where they move, and mar human happiness more than the robber upon the highway. Their spirit is bitter. They see the worst of all actions and words. They go to God with this spirit, and, though rebuked nowhere else, get their rebuke then. He sends them away empty.

ATTITUDES

All strong excitements, all party strife, all wrath, suspicion, denunciation, shut the soul from the throne of grace. The reforms—the moral, social, and political agitations of the day—are full of evil. Good men, convinced themselves, grow impatient, angry, denunciatory toward their brethren. The party, the church is roused, and then God's Spirit is grieved, and the spirit of prayer lost.

PERFECT LOVE NEEDED

Religious controversies, though sometimes unavoidable, are always evil, chiefly because they provoke a spirit antagonistic to charity. None but men of deep piety should meddle with them. They ought to fast and pray for a subdued spirit—for love, patience, meekness, charity. They should choose the softest words—avoid personalities, sectarianism, selfishness. And the whole church should pray not to be led into temptation. After all, in controversies of this nature, it is hardly possible to avoid doing harm. It is an unspeakable evil to awaken uncharitable, bitter feelings in the Christian community. Bad every way, socially, morally, politically, it is most fearful in that it chills devotion and stays God's mercies. Preaching becomes vain, or nearly so. The prayer meeting is comfortless. Men come out of their closets hanging their heads, their hearts heavy. No fire consumes the sacrifice. The Church would be a great loser, even should she promote orthodoxy at the expense of charity.

III. *Faith*

I shall dwell little upon this condition of successful prayer, not because it is unimportant, but because it is not difficult when the other terms are satisfied.

The struggle so often had in trying to overcome doubt and to believe, more commonly arises from our unfaithfulness—from our attempt to overleap a barrier, which waits to be removed, rather than from any distrust of God's mercy or promises. The man who has used diligence to conform his life and heart to the will of Christ, comes up to the throne of grace boldly—none more conscious of demerit, and shortcomings, and dependence on grace, and yet none so well prepared to cast his helpless soul on God. Conscious of having done nothing to merit the divine favor, he yet has the feeling of one who has tried to obey, who has respected the conditions, who has done what he could. He has acknowledged God's right to govern. He has been "holding forth the word of life" (Phil. 2:16). He has traveled up to the Cross in the prescribed pathway. He is found where God bids him be found, and he is able to trust the Lord, whom he has acknowledged, feared, obeyed, loved. He is in a position to plead the promises, to look to the "Lamb of God"; now that he is at the end of his own resources, he may cast himself on the Helper.

CONFIDENT BEFORE GOD

He cannot doubt the faithfulness of Him whom he has already trusted so far as to submit all to His will. His prayers will surely be answered. He may ask for health, or prosperity, or joy, without direct success, because, through ignorance, he may ask amiss. These may not be the blessings he most needs. But for pardon, and grace, and strength, and light, and life, he cannot ask in vain. These God always delights to bestow on all who rightly seek them. All blessings upon the Church

CONFIDENCE FROM SUBMISSION

and on men's souls He is ready to bestow in answer to prayer, if their sins do not stay His liberality.

I will add, that it is of the very essence of faith that we rightly apprehend the true import of prayer. It is not a mere exercise by which we are disciplined and grow more pious—a routine through which, if we proceed seriously and earnestly, all is done. It is an application to God, in virtue of Christ's merits, by which we obtain what would be withholden if we did not pray. As such, we must regard it more as a means—an instrument—than as a duty. We should consider our wants, and then, "by prayer and supplication with thanksgiving let [them] be made known unto God" (Phil. 4:6), who is ready to do for us more than we can "ask or think" (Eph. 3:20). In prayer, as in all God's dealings with us, does it hold true, "according to your faith be it unto you" (Matt. 9:29).

ASK LARGELY

Ask for great things, "nothing doubting," and great things will be yours. God is most honored when we expect the greatest gifts. Christ is magnified when, in the contemplation and the pleading of His infinite merits, we quite forget our own unworthiness and confidently look for the divinest bounty. We are more likely, therefore, to obtain great things than small, when God is the Giver and Christ our plea. Covet the best gifts. Cherish large views and generous hopes.

ASK TO BE HOLY

Jesus is yours, and all things in heaven and on earth are His. Is it incredible that He who put away sin by one offering of himself on the Cross, should willingly forgive your sins? that He, who gave His blood to purge away iniquity, should wash out all the stains of His children? Call upon His name for gifts worthy of a great King to bestow. Oh, we are mean in our views—"[we] have not, because [we] ask not," or "because [we] ask amiss" (James 4:2-3). We are not straitened in Jesus, but in our own bowels. Put forth great prayers. Indulge in noble, cheering anticipations. Remember it is to God's storehouse you are come—that Christ's infinite merits are your plea and ground of acceptance.

"Lift . . . up holy hands, without wrath and doubting."

James B. Chapman
(1884-1947)

Remembered by most as a general superintendent in the Church of the Nazarene, James B. Chapman also served as a college president, pastor, evangelist, and editor. He was probably known to more people through his editorials than through his preaching.

He established a reputation for wisdom, the sound common sense that looked at problems squarely and arrived at solutions through a solid knowledge of Scripture and people.

Chapman was not an orator, but his was the eloquence of important truths clearly and urgently stated. He developed a style of preaching that was almost conversational in tone, but every sentence was on target and invited listening. Under the stimulus of great themes and profound concern, he could rise to heights of impassioned pleading, which was all the more effective for being unusual.

Addressing a group of pastors shortly before his death, Dr. Chapman confided to us that he preferred to preach to small groups, where he could have eye contact with everyone in the audience. When he spoke, each listener felt personally addressed, as if he were the only one hearing the message. That was a rare gift.

Chapman was the leading influence in the establishment of Nazarene Theological Seminary. He believed strongly in higher education in a holiness context.

When James B. Chapman died in 1947, the holiness movement lost one of the most convinced and convincing advocates who ever graced its ranks.

"Grace and Good Sense" is vintage Chapman. Every paragraph breathes good sense in plain words. He sums up the text in a single prayer-sentence, "Lord, give us more grace that we may have better judgment." He proceeds to deal with the "two things which stand in the way of good moral judgment"—lack of courage and stubbornness, both of which are "cured" by love. To be "filled with the love of God" is the "heart of Christianity," a note that has been sounded loudly and clearly from Wesley's time, and never more earnestly sounded than in Chapman's preaching and writing.

The sermon presses home the individual application, and the preacher makes it first of all to himself. He closes the message with a prayer for himself that any listener would be swift to identify with. No holier-than-thou undertones spoil the sermon. The preacher is standing with the people under the judgment and grace of the Word of God.

Grace and Good Sense*

> *This I pray, that your love may abound yet more and more in knowledge and in all judgment; that ye may approve things that are excellent; that ye may be sincere and without offence till the day of Christ* (Phil. 1:9-10).

A doctor was giving expert testimony in a New York court. The case involved mental responsibility, and the doctor finally said that in order for a man to be really sane he had to possess good health, be in easy circumstances as regarding income and expenditures, and be a man of clean moral and spiritual affections. Pressed by attorneys, he admitted that on such a basis there are probably not more than five persons out of a hundred who should be classified as truly sane.

We all know there is an inclination to justify whatever we have a desire to do, and from this we know that it is necessary to be good if

---

*Source: James B. Chapman, *Christian Living in a Modern World,* 2nd ed. Kansas City: Beacon Hill Press, 1942.

we would be wise. If a man's heart is right, so that he loves only what is pure and good, he has already passed the first test in the school of sound doctrine. The conduct of men is affected by what they believe, but what they believe is affected by what they love, and since it is the specific work of the Holy Spirit to purify the affections, the Spirit-filled man will be a wise man and a good man. If men would make progress in education there is nothing that will help them more than to become possessed of purified and exalted motives, and this makes the prayer for an increase of love as a means for promoting good sense a very fitting thing. Lord, give us more grace that we may have better judgment.

HOLINESS IMPROVES WISDOM

Sometimes men speak of "common sense" as though it were indeed a common thing. But the very fact that we remark upon it is proof that it is the exception, rather than the rule. We speak of one who is not noted as a specialist of any kind and say of him, "But he has a large amount of just good, old-fashioned common sense." Now this kind of common sense is an eclectic thing composed of choice selections from the judgment of all. The person we have credited as having common sense has himself the sense that ordinarily it would require the whole community to furnish.

There is practically no one that is not remarkable for sense of one kind or another. But the trouble is he compensates his good judgment with bad judgment until we are uncertain whether to trust his ideas or not. Now if the man of common sense has the quick discernment of one, the patient mental process of another, the dependable conclusion of a third, and that practical application of still another . . . we are bound to respect him almost as a paragon, and yet he does not show a single factor that is exactly unusual. It is our compensating follies that keep the most of us from making high marks in the school of wisdom. Solomon said, "Dead flies cause the ointment of the apothecary to send forth a stinking savour: so doth a little folly him that is in reputation for wisdom and honour" (Eccles. 10:1).

There are two things which stand in the way of good moral judgment, and love is the remedy for both: 1. Men err in judgment and practice for want of courage to do what they should. 2. Men err in moral judgment because of stubbornness and unwillingness to surrender their own way. They hold out for their preference even when they have become convinced that they are wrong.

Love, perfect love, cures the first disease by casting out slavish fear, and inspiring courage that dares to take the consequences of righteousness, whatever they are, for perfect love involves moral conviction that right is might and that victory in the final sense will come to one who does right. I speak of this as moral conviction, for I am sure it is something more intuitive than the conclusions of intellectual reasoning.

LOVE INCREASES COURAGE

But love also cures stubbornness. Backbone has two provinces. One is to give the body a reasonable rigidity, and the other is to give it a certain amount of flexibility. If the backbone becomes altogether rigid, the victim is henceforth unable to walk anywhere except on perfectly level surfaces, for it is necessary to lean forward when going uphill, and backward when going downhill. And this is as applicable to the moral as to the physical realm. Unfortunate indeed is the man who thinks that man was made for the Sabbath, and who must keep rules, even if it costs lives to do so. The legalist is no more Christian than the materialist or the formalist. [James] suggested that love is "easy to be entreated" (3:17).

LOVE INCREASES REASONABLENESS

The Bible deals with the principles of holy conduct, not very largely with rules of thumb. It exhorts us to pray, but it does not settle for us the question of the attitude of prayer—whether it should be kneeling, standing, sitting, or lying prone on the ground. And yet we need direction in the details, as well as in the principles of life.

When Israel was en route to the Promised Land they were shown the general direction they were to take by the pillar of cloud and fire. But they also accepted the services of Hobab, who was able to direct them to the water holes in the desert and act as eyes for them in setting the distance they were to go day by day. The pillar gave them the principles, but Hobab filled in with details. Likewise, the Bible gives us the principles, but we need the Holy Spirit to give us detailed direction. And this is the promise of Jesus. He said, "When he, the Spirit of truth, is come, he will guide you into all truth" (John 16:13).

THE HOLY SPIRIT GUIDES

The heart of Christianity is not its doctrines, true and dependable though these be. It is not in its sacraments, beautiful and important though these are. It is not even in its ethics, although the standards of conduct are faultless. Rather, the heart of Christianity is in having Christ crowned within the heart. It is to be filled with the love of God. It is to be baptized and filled with the Holy Ghost.

We do not like the word mysticism on account of its association with philosophy, in which connection it involves dreamy contemplation and long dwelling upon impractical unrealities. But we do not have another word to describe what we mean, so we call what we have in mind "true mysticism." God is real, and the indwelling of His Holy Spirit is a conscious fact with those who have it. And there is promise of help for our intellects in the scope of the Spirit-filled life.

It is distasteful to speak frequently of the Lord's leadings, just as it is distasteful to spread family secrets abroad. "The secret of the Lord is with them that fear him; and he will shew them his covenant" (Ps. 25:14), so that when a Christian majors on saying, "The Lord told me to do this," or "I felt led to say that," there is a deserved resentment on the part of the listeners. Nevertheless, God does have a way of directing His people, and those who are delicate and instant in "minding the checks" will have growing satisfaction in the discovery that in them is fulfilled the promise that a good man's steps are ordered by the Lord.

FOLLOWING CHRIST IMPROVES JUDGMENT

Unfortunately men have a tendency to base conclusions on too few specimens. They have known one or heard of one who was deeply religious and was unbalanced. They conclude, therefore, that one who goes in for religion is mentally inadequate. But they have observed the "sports," and not the normal examples. Even those whom they have observed might easily have been worse if they had not been religious. But the large majority of those who have found grace in Christ have found wisdom in Him also.

Sometimes it is charged against the Church that it is reactionary, and that it is the last unit of society to accept a reform or to acclaim a new idea in the social order. And there are no doubt instances in which the Church has been too slow. But the general testimony is that the Church is slow to accept that which is new because it has found a larger portion in that which is old than others have found. Take intellectual concepts: at the close of the French Revolution the French Academy listed more than 80 "scientific facts" that were inconsistent with the Bible, and which therefore proved that the Bible is not dependable. But before 100 years had passed every single one of those supposed scientific facts were abandoned by the scientists themselves.

Men anchored to no rock at all are likely to drift lightly, but that does not prove that their drifting is in the right direction. Christians do have something substantial in their Bible and their vital inner experience, and they are not ready to abandon all their gains to follow every will-o'-the-wisp that shallow thinkers offer as guides to the unwary.

But we must not generalize. The prayer of Paul is a prayer for individuals. His desire was for improved discernment on the part of everyday Christians. He wanted their intuitions as relating to things that differ to be keener and more dependable. He wanted them to know intuitively when they should shun certain companions, and when they should join in for the purpose of doing good. He wanted them to have that inner "feel" that would enable them to stop or go according to the interests of Christ's kingdom and their own influence. He wanted them to get to where they would not be asking, "Is there any harm in this?" He wanted them to come to where they would emphasize the positive qualities of a good life which would make them worthy of their Christian profession in thought, word, and deed. He wanted them to become outstanding for good and wise choosing and holy living.

GUIDANCE FOR ALL CHRISTIANS

But how could all these things be accomplished by prayer? Surely so many requirements would demand . . . seminary training and the gift of intellectual capacities of a spectacular sort. No, nothing so complicated as all that is involved. The prayer is just a petition for more spiritual grace—more inwrought love. "I pray, that your love may abound yet more and more," that your judgment may improve and your conduct be worthy of commendation.

Do such by-products come from such a source? They certainly do. Let us . . . refer to our own experiences. Is it not a fact with you and me that we are wisest when we are best? Do we not seem to be masters of sociology when we are overflowing with love for our fellowmen? Do we not exceed our teachers in matters relating to God when our souls are aflame with His holy fire? Do we not excel in that wisdom that is characteristic of the soul winner when we are melted with holy passion for bringing men to God? Do not our tongues become as the pens of ready writers when we are truly moved by the Spirit?

Before this time I have listened to a "reformer" while he told of the evils of the dictators, and of the general tendency of men to be bad, and the indications that the world is incurably sick. I have listened and been convinced by what he said. But when I have gone away I have said to myself, "This is a bad situation, and something should be done about it. But what can I do about it?" And I have not been much helped by any answer I was able to give. But when I come to a proposition so simple as the one before us, I am encouraged. I can do something about this. I can open my heart to a fuller incoming of the divine Spirit. I can lay myself liable to an increase of love. I can love God and God's people and a lost world more than hitherto, and since I have found that this will do just about all I need to see done, I am encouraged.

BE OPEN TO THE SPIRIT

I pray for myself as Paul prayed for us all: Lord, grant me an increase of love. Take out of my heart everything that is contrary to Thy love. Fill me till I want no more. Purge me until there is nothing unlike Thee left. Saturate me until there is no room for self. Make me so fully like thyself that when men see me they will think of Thee. Do this for me that I may be wise to choose, courageous to act, even when the course required is unpopular; willing to yield, even when my strong personal preferences are violated; and patient to believe and bear when there is nothing active I can do to better matters. All these things Thou canst accomplish in me by an increase of Thy love, and for this I ask in Jesus' name. Amen.

INCREASE MY LOVE!

Samuel Logan Brengle

(1860-1936)

No American preacher ever spoke and wrote about holiness with more telling effect than Commissioner Brengle of the Salvation Army. Over 2 million of his books on the subject have been sold!

His writing career began strangely. A brick thrown by an angry tough smashed Brengle's head against a doorpost. During the months it took to recuperate he began to write, and his first book, *Helps to Holiness,* resulted. Sales throughout the world were phenomenal. Brengle often said that without the little brick there would have been no little book.

Brengle's ministry began in the Methodist Episcopal church, in which he had been converted as a 12-year-old boy. Called to preach as a college student, he later entered Boston Theological Seminary. Under the influence of Daniel Steele he became convinced of entire sanctification as a present possibility. His quest for holiness was satisfied as he allowed God to crucify his pride and ambition and believed 1 John 1:9 for cleansing.

Following that personal Pentecost, his first sermon was on holiness, launching a career of holiness evangelism that never lost momentum. At the age of 70 he would testify, "Ever since that wonderful morning 45 years ago when He baptized me with the Holy Ghost and fire, purifying my heart and revealing himself within me, I have felt that He meant to win His triumphs through dead men and women—dead to sin, to the world, to its prizes and praises; and all alive to Him, filled with His Spirit, indwelt by His

presence, burning with His love, glad with His joy, enduring with His patience, thrilled with His hope, daring with His self-renunciation and courage, being consumed with His zeal; all conquering with His faith, rejoicing in 'the fellowship of his sufferings,' and gladly made 'conformable unto his death.'" That was the brand of holiness Brengle experienced and proclaimed until he was promoted to glory in 1936.

"Power" is typically Brengle—simply constructed, clearly explained, urgently offered. The Holy Spirit gives power over that historic triad of evil forces that oppose the people of God—the world, the flesh, and the devil. Brengle found that truth in his Bible and demonstrated it in his life. His biographer said, "Preaching, he lifted high standards. Teaching, he taught high truth. But behind the scenes he lived an even higher life."

Power*

Ye shall receive power, after that the Holy Ghost is come upon you (Acts 1:8).

Just before His ascension, Jesus met His disciples for the last time, and repeated His command that they should "not depart from Jerusalem, but wait for the promise of the Father," and reiterated His promise that they should be "baptized with the Holy Ghost not many days hence."

Then "they asked of him, saying, Lord, wilt thou at this time restore again the kingdom to Israel?" They were still eager for an earthly kingdom. But "He said unto them, It is not for you to know the times or the seasons, which the Father hath put in his own power," or authority. And then He added, "But ye shall receive power, after that the Holy Ghost is come upon you" (Acts 1:4-8).

POWER TO WITNESS

They wanted power, and He assured them that they should have it, but said nothing of its nature, or the work and activities into which it would thrust them, and for which it would equip them, beyond the fact that they should be witnesses unto Him "in Jerusalem, and in all Judaea, and in Samaria, and unto

*Source: Samuel Logan Brengle, *When the Holy Ghost Is Come.* 1909. Reprint. Atlanta: Salvation Army Supplies and Purchasing Department, 1982.

the uttermost part of the earth." After that the Holy Ghost himself was henceforth to be their Teacher.

And then Jesus left them. Earth had lost its power to hold Him, and while they beheld Him He began to ascend; a cloud bent low from heaven, receiving Him out of sight. They were left alone, with His promise of power ringing in their ears. His command to "wait for the promise of the Father" checked any impatience that might lead them to "go a-fishing," as Peter had done some days before, or cause an undue haste to begin their . . . witnessing for Him before God's appointed time.

PENTECOST

For 10 days they waited, not listlessly, but eagerly, as a maid for her mistress, or a servant for his master, who is expected to come at any moment. They forgot their personal ambitions; they ceased to judge and criticize one another, and in the sweet unity of brotherly love, "with one accord" they rejoiced, they prayed, they waited. . . . On the Day of Pentecost, at their early morning prayer meeting, when they were all present, the windows of heaven were opened, and such a blessing as they could not contain was poured out upon them. "And suddenly there came a sound from heaven as of a rushing mighty wind, and it filled all the house where they were sitting. And there appeared unto them cloven tongues like as of fire, and it sat upon each of them. And they were all filled with the Holy Ghost."

This was the inaugural day of the Church of God (Acts 2:2-4); the dawn of the dispensation of the Holy Spirit; the beginning of the days of power.

In the morning of that day there were only a few Christians in the world; the New Testament was not written, and it is doubtful if they had among them all a copy of the Old Testament; they had no church buildings, no colleges, no religious books and papers; they were poor and despised, unlearned and ignorant; but before night they had enrolled 3,000 converts, and they had aroused and filled all Jerusalem with questionings and amazement.

What was the secret? Power. What was the secret? God the Holy Ghost. He had come, and this work was His work, and they were His instruments.

HOLY SPIRIT

When Jesus came, a body was prepared for Him (Heb. 10:5), and through that body He wrought His wondrous works; but when the other Comforter comes, He takes possession of those bodies that are freely and fully presented to Him, and He touches their lips with grace; He shines peacefully and gloriously on their faces; He flashes beams of pity and compassion and heavenly affection from their eyes; He kindles a fire of love in their hearts, and lights the flame of truth in their minds. They become His temple, and their hearts are a holy of holies in which His blessed presence ever abides; and from that central citadel He works, enduing the man who has received Him with power.

If you ask how the Holy Spirit can dwell within us and work through us without destroying our personality, I cannot tell. How can electric impulses fill and transform a dead wire into a live one which you dare not touch? How can a magnetic current fill a piece of steel, and transform it into a mighty force which by its touch can raise tons of iron, as a child would lift a feather? How can fire dwell in a piece of iron until its very appearance is that of fire, and it becomes a firebrand? I cannot tell.

Now, what fire and electricity and magnetism do in iron and steel, the Holy Spirit does in the spirits of men who believe on Jesus, follow Him wholly, and trust Him intelligently. He dwells in them and inspires them, till they are all alive with the very life of God.

The transformation wrought in men by the baptism with the Holy Ghost, and the power that fills them, are amazing beyond measure. The Holy Spirit gives:

I. *Power over the World*

They become

Dead to the world and all its toys,
Its idle pomp and fading joys.

The world masters and enslaves people who have not the Holy Spirit. To one man it offers money. He falls down and worships; he sells his conscience and character for gold. To another it offers power. He falls down and worships; he sacrifices his principles and sears his conscience for power. To another it offers pleasure; to another learning; to another fame; they fall down and worship, and sell themselves for these things. But the man filled with the Holy Ghost is free. He can turn from these things without a pang, as he would from pebbles; or, he can take them and use them as his servants for the glory of God and the good of men.

What did Peter and James and John care for the great places in the kingdoms of this world after they were filled with the Holy Ghost? They would not have exchanged places with Herod the king or with

Caesar himself. For the gratification of any personal ambition these things were no more attractive to them now than the lordship over a tribe of ants on their tiny hill. They were now kings and priests unto God, and theirs was an everlasting Kingdom, and its glory exceeds the glory of the kingdoms of this world as the splendor of the sun exceeds that of the glowworm.

POWER OVER MONEY

The head of some great business enterprises was making many thousands of dollars every year; but when the Holy Spirit filled him, money lost its power over him. He still retained his position and made vast sums; but, as a steward of the Lord, he poured it into God's work, and has been doing so for more than 30 years.

After Pentecost the disciples in Jerusalem held all their possessions in common, so completely were they freed from the power and love of money.

A rising young lawyer got filled with the Spirit and the next day said to his client: "I cannot plead your case. I have a retainer from the Lord Jesus"; and he became one of the mightiest preachers the world has ever seen.

A popular lad got the fiery baptism and went to his baseball team and said, "Boys, you swear, and I am now a Christian; I cannot play with you anymore." God made him the wonder of all his old friends, and a happy winner of souls.

A fashionable woman got the baptism, and God gave her power to break away from her worldly set and surroundings, live wholly for Him, and gave her an influence that girdled the globe.

Paul said: "The world is crucified unto me, and I unto the world" (Gal. 6:14). Men could whip and stone and imprison his body, and cut off his head, but his soul was free. It was enslaved and driven by no unholy or inordinate ambition, by no lust for gold, by no desire for power or fame, by no fear of man, by no shame of worldly censure or adverse public opinion. He had power over the world; and this same power is the birthright of every converted man, and the present possession of everyone who is wholly sanctified by the baptism with the Holy Ghost.

II. *Power over the Flesh*

The body which God intended for a "house beautiful" for the soul, and a temple holy unto himself, is often reduced to a sty, where the imprisoned soul wallows in lusts and passions, and degrades itself below the level of beasts. But this baptism gives a man power over his body.

God has given to man such desires and passions as are necessary to secure his continued existence. Not one is in itself evil, but good and only good; and when controlled and used, but not abused, will help to develop and maintain the purest and highest manhood. The appetites for food and drink are necessary to life. Another desire is intended to secure the continuance of the human race. And so all the desires and appetites of the body have useful ends, and were given to us in love by our Heavenly Father for high and essential purposes, and are necessary to us as human beings.

But the soul, cut off from fellowship with God by sin, seeks satisfaction in sensual excesses and the unlawful gratification of these appetites, and so sinks to depths of degradation to which no beast ever falls. Thus man becomes a slave; swollen and raging passion takes the place of innocent appetites and desires.

POWER TO CONTROL IMPULSES

Now, when the Holy Spirit enters the heart and sanctifies the soul, He does not destroy these desires, but purifies and regulates them. He reinforces the soul with the fear and love of God, and gives it power, complete power, over the fleshly appetites. He restores it to its full fellowship with God and its kingship over the body.

But while these appetites and desires are not in themselves sinful, but are necessary for our welfare and our complete manhood, and while their diseased and abnormal power is cured when we are sanctified, they are still avenues through which we may be tempted. Therefore, they must be guarded with care and ruled in wisdom. Many people stumble at and reject the doctrine of entire sanctification because they do not understand these things. They mistake that which is natural and essential to a human being, for the diseased and abnormal propensity caused by sin, and so miss the blessed truth of full salvation.

POWER OVER SIN

I knew a doctor, who had used tobacco for over 60 years, delivered from the abnormal appetite instantly through sanctification of the Spirit. I knew an old man, who had been a drunkard for over 50 years, similarly delivered. I knew a young man, the slave of a vicious habit of the flesh, who was set free at once by the fiery baptism. The electric current cannot transform the dead wire into a live one quicker than the Holy Spirit can flood a soul with light and love, destroy the carnal mind, and fill a man with power over all sin.

III. *Power over the Devil*

The indwelling presence of the Holy Spirit destroys all doubt as to the personality of the devil. He is discerned, and his malice is felt and known as never before.

In the dark a man may be so skillfully attacked that his enemy is not discovered, but not in the day. Many people in these days deny that there is any devil, only evil; but they are in the dark, so much in the dark that they not only say that there is no devil, but that there is no personal God, only good. But the day comes with the Holy Spirit's entrance, and then God is intimately known and the devil is discovered. And as he assailed Jesus after His baptism with the Spirit, so he does today all who receive the Holy Ghost. He comes as an angel of light to deceive, and as a roaring lion to devour and overcome with fear; but the soul filled with the Spirit outwits the devil and, clad in the whole armor of God, overcomes the old enemy.

Power "over all the power of the enemy" (Luke 10:19) is God's purpose for all His children. Power to do the will of God patiently and effectively, with naturalness and ease, or to suffer the will of God with patience and good cheer, comes with this blessed baptism. It is power for service or sacrifice, according to God's will. Have you this power? If not, it is for you. Yield yourself fully to Christ just now, and if you ask in faith you shall receive.

"Have ye received the Holy Ghost since ye believed?" (Acts 19:2).

Kenneth E. Geiger

Kenneth E. Geiger served the United Missionary church as a general superintendent for 13 years. When that group merged with the Missionary Church Association to form the Missionary church, he was elected president of the new body. Earlier he had served pastorates in Indiana and Michigan and was also a district superintendent. The administrative offices he held indicated the high esteem in which the people of his denomination held him.

Dr. Geiger has also been active in the work of the National Association of Evangelicals and the Christian Holiness Association, serving the latter as president for several years.

Another avenue of service has been the Wesleyan Theological Society. Dr. Geiger has not only shared some of his insights and convictions with that group, but placed them all in his debt by compiling a series of scholarly papers presented by various members of WTS into three books, *Insights into Holiness, Further Insights into Holiness,* and *The Word and the Doctrine.*

"The Christian's Body and the Life of Holiness" combines the concerns of Geiger for (1) the authority of Scripture over the believer's life and (2) the expression of holiness in the believer's life. He is the advocate of a biblical holiness that demands and provides the cleansing of the heart and the discipline of the conduct.

The body is viewed as (1) a trust, for which we are accountable to God; (2) a temple, in which God dwells and through which He reveals himself; (3) a testimony, by which we present Christ to those around us. "Our testimony for God is effective when an enlivened spirit, quickened by the power and grace of God, expresses itself in a consecrated body—holy and wholly the Lord's." That is, as we say today, "the bottom line."

In an age where belief and behavior are often inconsistent to the point of contradiction, Geiger's insistence upon dedicated and disciplined physical lives is on target.

In a paper presented to the Wesleyan Theological Society, Geiger injected this personal note: "It was a happy day in my life, after a period of confusion resulting from oft repeated clichés, and so much theoretical preaching that was not Bible based, that the Bible itself began to speak to me, and its total message was fully redemptive." That fullness includes the sanctification of the body.

The Christian's Body and the Life of Holiness*

> *Let not sin therefore reign in your mortal body . . . Neither yield ye your members as instruments of unrighteousness unto sin: but yield yourselves unto God, as those that are alive from the dead, and your members as instruments of righteousness unto God* (Rom. 6:12-13).

A sacred regard for the body was enjoined upon the children of Israel in their early history as the people of God. The words *holy* and *wholly* express an Old Testament precept.

The following New Testament passages [in addition to the text already cited] place in sharp focus the human body in relation to the Christian's daily practice and witness:

"I beseech you therefore, brethren, by the mercies of God, that ye present your bodies a living sacrifice, holy, acceptable unto God, which is your reasonable service" (Rom. 12:1).

"What? know ye not that your body is the temple of the Holy Ghost which is in you, which ye have of God, and ye are not your own? For ye are bought with a price: therefore glorify God in your body, and in your spirit, which are God's" (1 Cor. 6:19-20).

---

*Source: James McGraw, comp. *The Holiness Pulpit No. 2*. Kansas City: Beacon Hill Press of Kansas City, 1974.

"And the very God of peace sanctify you wholly; and I pray God your whole spirit and soul and body be preserved blameless unto the coming of our Lord Jesus Christ" (1 Thess. 5:23).

"We have this treasure in earthen vessels . . . that the life also of Jesus might be made manifest in our mortal flesh" (2 Cor. 4:7, 11).

The following scriptural precepts are obvious:

1. The human body, though imperfect and under the curse, is not the seat of sin.

2. The human body, though distinct from man's spirit, is included in God's atoning provision, not only in terms of full, final redemption but in respect to present, victorious, Christian living.

3. Man's body is made by God the depository of a great treasure, "the life of the Lord Jesus."

4. Our bodies of clay are to become effective instruments of Christian witness; i.e., Jesus is to be seen in us.

5. Man may be *wholly* sanctified and his body, as well as his soul and spirit, may be put to holy use.

As in Paul's day, so today there are those who do not relate man's experience as a justified Christian to bodily conformity in terms of holy living. The apostle deals precisely with this irregularity in 1 Corinthians, chapter 6. "The body is not for fornication, but for the Lord; and the Lord for the body" (v. 13).

When the pace and level of holy living is established in the sixth chapter of Romans, the strongest language is used. "How shall we, that are dead to sin, live any longer therein?" (v. 2). "Henceforth we should not serve sin" (v. 6). Positively, the members of the body are to be instruments of righteousness. They are to be used for holy purposes.

A question of relevance and importance is: Can one be saved from sin while living in a body that is infirm as the result of the curse? John Wesley, in his sermon "On Perfection," offers a definite answer:

HUMANITY

> The highest perfection which a man can attain, while the soul dwells in the body, does not exclude ignorance, and error, and a thousand other infirmities. . . . And, in numberless instances, it comes short of doing the will of God, as Adam did in paradise. Hence the best of men may say from the heart, "Every moment, Lord, I need the merit of thy death." . . . Love is now the fulfilling of the law which is given to fallen men. . . . What is then the perfection of which man is capable while he dwells in a corruptible body? It is the complying with that kind

> command, "My son, give me thy heart." . . . This is the sum of Christian perfection: It is all comprised in that one word, Love.

In the same sermon Wesley speaks of the "mind of Christ," the "fruit of the Spirit," and the "new man" as they are to be evidenced in the body.

Christ's atoning work, the basis of God's sanctifying grace, makes possible a full salvation with the Christian's body serving a truly spiritual function. The human body is to be regarded as: (1) a trust from God, (2) a temple of God, and (3) a testimony for God.

I. *The Body, a Trust from God*

Jesus recognized that His human body was given Him by God (Ps. 22:9-10). He spoke of His body as a temple (John 2:21). His involvement in physical suffering and death as a part of His atoning work was clearly understood. When He prayed, "Not my will, but thine, be done" (Luke 22:42), a physical body was consecrated and dedicated to God's holy purpose.

The concept of the body as a trust was very clear to Wesley. He said,

> God has entrusted us with our bodies, (those exquisitely wrought machines, so "fearfully and wonderfully made,") with all the powers and members thereof. He has entrusted us with the organs of sense; of sight, hearing, and the rest: But none of these are given us as our own, to be employed according to our own will. None of these are lent us in such a sense as to leave us at liberty to use them as we please for a season. No: We have received them on these very terms—that as long as they abide with us, we should employ them all in that very manner, and no other, which He appoints.

STEWARDSHIP OF THE BODY

The stewardship of one's body involves a proper keeping of this priceless gift. Observing the rules of health, the conservation and utilization of talent and strength, proper attire as Christians, and many other disciplines must constantly be observed. Physical cleanliness is not foreign to holiness, but is indeed related to and springs from a right relationship with God.

The accomplishments of great men are more often than not related to the stewardship of the body. Richard S. Taylor appropriately states,

> Although the discipline of the body is of less importance, it can be indispensable to power if its object is to train the body to

> serve the mind in the attaining of worthy objectives. The ability of Thomas Edison to sleep and awaken at will and to work through grueling, unbroken stretches, undoubtedly contributed to his greatness as an inventor. . . .
>
> The fact that Moses reached the age of 120 years with his natural vitality unabated may have been due partially to the 40 years in the wilderness as a shepherd, when his body became inured to summer heat and winter frost. We do know that John Wesley ascribed his preservation to his practice of rising at four o'clock and preaching at five. Though such a routine would shorten rather than extend the life of some men, . . . it is still true that the man who learns to "keep his body under" is more likely to avoid being not only a castaway spiritually but a castaway physically (*The Disciplined Life,* 19-20).

Man has accomplished many outstanding feats in the developing of remarkable, intricate machines. This is the age of computers. However, human intelligence will never be able to duplicate the genius of the human body. The world knows nothing equal to the dynamic of a consecrated body upon which the Holy Spirit falls in anointing and empowering for service.

II. *The Body, a Temple of God*

"Know ye not that your body is the temple of the Holy Ghost?" (1 Cor. 6:19). "We have this treasure in earthen vessels" (2 Cor. 4:7). We cannot understand or comprehend it, but God lives in the bodies of Christians. What is made of earth and will eventually return to dust is hallowed to become the Holy Spirit's temple. The very life of Jesus is to be seen in the lives of Christians.

As proponents of the great truth of Christian holiness, we cannot overlook the privilege and responsibility of presenting our bodies to God in order that they may be indwelt by the Holy Spirit. The "Abiding Presence" must have an "at home" relationship to the Christian. This means simply that every area of the believer's life is opened to the occupancy and control of the Spirit.

A DEDICATED BODY

Paul makes a striking contrast between the "earthen vessel" and the "treasure" it holds. How exciting it is to realize that God has invested His Son in us! Is this not an extension of Christ's condescension? If the body becomes the window in which the life of Jesus is framed and revealed, what limitations are imposed upon the greatest undertaking in the world—revealing Christ through human personality!

How rich is the person who is indwelt by God! This treasure the body holds is God's Son. A man is rich who owns something of value for which there is demand and need and which is available. Jesus Christ, the Treasure a Christian holds and shares, meets these requirements.

At a critical point in World War II, Sir Winston Churchill decided to transport the great wealth of the British Empire in the form of gold and silver to the Dominion of Canada. No longer could they risk having this wealth fall into the hands of Hitler, whose forces seemed almost certain to invade Great Britain. One oceangoing vessel had more than a billion dollars' worth of gold in its hold as it sailed across the North Atlantic.

But the treasure the Christian holds in his "earthen vessel" is worth more than the whole world. By God's grace, he should live and walk accordingly. We have something, or rather Someone, the world needs!

III. *The Body, a Testimony for God*

The "treasure [is] in earthen vessels, that the excellency of the power may be of God" (2 Cor. 4:7). According to verse 6 of this same chapter, God "hath shined in our hearts, to give the light of the knowledge of the glory of God in the face of Jesus Christ." In two direct references to the body (vv. 10-11) the statement is made, "That the life also of Jesus might be made manifest."

OUTWARD REFLECTION OF INWARD GRACE

While for most of us the physical features with which we are endowed leave something to be desired, it is nevertheless true that a genuine experience of forgiveness and cleansing and the persistent practice of self-discipline can effect a profound change in the outer man. Real beauty is more than skin-deep. It radiates from the heart and reflects itself in Christlike attitudes. Actions and reactions become Christian. The countenance becomes a window. It was said of the sainted Fletcher, "Grace was in all his steps, heaven in his eye, in all gestures sanctity and love."

Wesley, on the occasion of Fletcher's death, spoke directly to the point of Christian witness in and through the body:

> As to his outward behavior, the upright Christian believer is blameless and unreprovable. He is holy, as Christ that has called him is holy, in all manner of conversation; ever laboring to have a conscience void of offense toward God and toward man. He not

> only avoids all outward sin, but abstains from all appearance of evil. He steadily walks in all the public and private ordinances of the Lord blameless. He is zealous of good works; as he hath time, doing good, in every kind and degree, to all men.

The chief instrument of witness is one of the smallest members of the body, the tongue. James has a practical and penetrating word for us at this point. "If any man offend not in word, the same is a perfect man, and able also to bridle the whole body. . . . Even so the tongue is a little member, and boasteth great things. Behold, how great a matter a little fire kindleth! . . . Therewith bless we God, even the Father; and therewith curse we men" (James 3:2, 5, 9).

WITNESSING

A. B. Simpson makes an interesting analogy. "A sanctified body is known, as physical health is known, by the appearance of the tongue. Your physician asks to see your tongue when he calls, and there is no surer test of a sanctified body than the condition of its tongue."

It is obvious that good health, neat and proper appearance, cleanliness, and the proper use and control of every member of the body are related to effective Christian witness.

The only Jesus the world will ever see is the Jesus they see in us. The image must not be distorted. If the body holds this treasure, the "window" into which the world looks must be clean.

One of my daughters, before the current popularity of wearing beards, once saw a man wearing a full beard. The pictures of Jesus she had seen and had been taught to identify had made such an impression upon her that she said with an excited voice, "There's Jesus!" The immature relate such matters as peculiar dress, hairstyles, and various other appearances to Christian witness. Our testimony for God is effective when an enlivened spirit, quickened by the power and grace of God, expresses itself in a consecrated body—holy and wholly the Lord's.

8

HOLINESS AND SOCIAL RIGHTEOUSNESS

John Wesley
(1703-91)

John Wesley is justly regarded as the father of the modern holiness movement. As God's chief instrument for revival in 18th-century England, he was a constant traveler, a tireless preacher, and a careful organizer. Wesley made and conserved converts on an unprecedented scale. The unintended but providential legacy of his preaching and teaching ministry was the Methodist churches and their offshoots, which now adorn the globe in all directions.

John Wesley wore many hats. He was above all, however, a preacher, and as a preacher he was first of all an evangelist. Wesley practiced a close and continuous follow-up ministry with converts and felt responsible for guiding the beliefs and behavior of "the people called Methodists." Out of this stewardship of instruction and admonition arose some of Wesley's finest sermons, of which the present selection is a worthy sample.

Industry and frugality often marked the reformed conduct of those who found Christ in the Evangelical Revival. As a result, they earned more and possessed more than they had ever dreamed of obtaining. Wesley saw this as a terrible danger to their souls. Indeed, Albert Outler has concluded that "surplus accumulation leads Wesley's inventory of sins in praxis." In his unsparing denunciation of riches used selfishly, even when they have been gained honestly, Wesley was earnestly pursuing his primary task, "the saving of souls."

Other volumes of this series have utilized several of Wesley's

doctrinal sermons, in whole or in part. (See Vol. 2.) I chose, therefore, to include an intensely ethical sermon in this collection. This particular message was selected for its relevance to our day, when the improved economy of holiness people subjects them to the same perils against which Wesley so passionately sounded an alarm. The current popularity of a pseudogospel that equates divine approval with affluence increases our danger. This baptized self-indulgence denies the Cross, mocks the poor, and blurs the identity of the Church.

Simplicity, directness, and courage marked Wesley's preaching and dominate this sermon. The structure of the sermon is not only a homiletical device but also an illustration of Wesley's understanding of the preacher's task: (1) to explain and (2) to apply the truth of Scripture. The explanation served the application, because truth was not proclaimed for truth's sake but for life's sake.

The Danger of Riches*

> *They that will be rich fall into temptation and a snare, and into many foolish and hurtful [desires], which drown men in destruction and perdition* (1 Tim. 6:9).

1. How innumerable are the ill consequences which have followed from men's not knowing, or not considering, this great truth! And how few are there even in the Christian world, that either know or duly consider it! Yea, how small is the number of those, even among real Christians, who understand and lay it to heart! Most of these too pass it very lightly over, scarce remembering there is such a text in the Bible. And many put such a construction upon it, as makes it of no manner of effect. . . .

2. The apostle does not here speak of gaining riches unjustly . . . His words are to be taken in their plain, obvious sense, without any restriction or qualification whatsoever. St. Paul does not say, "They that will be rich *by evil means,* by theft, robbery, oppression, or extortion; they that will be rich by fraud or dishonest art"; but simply,

---

*Source: John Wesley, *The Works of John Wesley,* ed. Thomas Jackson. 3rd ed. Vol. 7. London: Wesleyan Methodist Book Room, 1872. Reprint. Kansas City: Beacon Hill Press of Kansas City, 1978.

"They that will be rich" . . . supposing the means they use to be ever so innocent, [these] "fall into temptation and a snare, and into many foolish and hurtful desires, which drown men in destruction and perdition."

3. But who believes that? Who receives it as the truth of God? Who is deeply convinced of it? Who preaches this? . . . I do not remember that in threescore years I have heard one sermon preached upon this subject. And what author, within the same term, has declared it from the press? . . . I have myself frequently touched upon it in preaching, and twice in what I have published to the world . . . but I have never yet either published or preached any sermon expressly upon the subject. It is high time I should . . .

4. Oh, that God would give me to speak right and forcible words; and you to receive them in honest and humble hearts! Let it not be said: "They sit before thee as my people, and they hear thy words, but they will not do them . . . thou art unto them as . . . one that hath a pleasant voice, and can play well on an instrument: for they hear thy words, but they do them not" (Ezek. 33:31-32). . . .

In [God's] name then, and by His strength, I will endeavour,

I. *To explain the words of the apostle*

1. And, first, let us consider, what it is to be rich. What does the apostle mean by this expression?

The preceding verse fixes the meaning of this: "Having food and raiment" (literally *coverings;* for the word includes lodging as well as clothes), "let us be therewith content." "But they that will be rich"; that is, who will have more than . . . "food and coverings." It plainly follows, whatever is more than these is, in the sense of the apostle, *riches;* whatever is above the plain necessaries, or at most conveniences, of life. Whoever has sufficient food to eat, and raiment to put on, with a place where to lay his head, and something over, is *rich.*

2. Let us consider, secondly, what is implied in that expression, "They that will be rich." And does this not imply, first, they that desire to be rich, to have more than *food* and *coverings;* they that seriously and deliberately desire more than . . . the plain necessaries and conveniences of life? All, at least, who allow themselves in this desire, who see no harm in it, desire to be rich.

3. And so do, secondly, all those that calmly, deliberately, and of set purpose, *endeavour* after . . . not only so much worldly substance

as will procure them the necessaries and conveniences of life, but more than this, whether to lay it up, or lay it out in superfluities. All these undeniably prove their "desire to be rich" by their endeavours after it.

4. Must we not, thirdly, rank among those that desire to be rich, all that, in fact, "lay up treasures on earth"? a thing as expressly and clearly forbidden by our Lord, as either adultery or murder. It is allowed, (1) that we are to provide necessaries and conveniences for those of our own household; (2) that men in business are to lay up as much as is necessary for the carrying on of that business; (3) that we are to leave our children what will supply them with necessaries and conveniences after we have left the world; and (4) that we are to provide things honest in the sight of all men, so as to "owe no man any thing" (Rom. 13:8). But to lay up any more, when this is done, is what our Lord has flatly forbidden. When it is calmly and deliberately done, it is a clear proof of our desiring to be rich. And thus to lay up money is no more consistent with good conscience than to throw it into the sea.

CHRISTIAN RESPONSIBILITIES

5. We must rank among them, fourthly, all who *possess* more of this world's goods than they use according to the will of the Donor: I should rather say, of the Proprietor; for He only *lends* them to us as stewards, reserving the *property* of them to himself. . . . And together with that portion of His goods which He hath lodged in our hands, He has delivered to us a writing, specifying the purposes for which He has entrusted us with them. If, therefore, we keep more of them . . . than is necessary for the preceding purposes, we certainly fall under the charge of "desiring to be rich." Over and above [that], we are guilty of burying our Lord's talent in the earth; and on that account are liable to be pronounced "wicked," because "unprofitable servants" (Matt 25:26, 30).

SELFISHNESS

6. Under this imputation of "desiring to be rich" fall, fifthly, all "lovers of money." The word properly means those that *delight in money;* those that take pleasure in it; those that seek their happiness therein; that brood over their gold or silver, bills or bonds. . . .

LOVERS OF MONEY

7. But beside this gross sort of covetousness, the love of money, there is a more refined species of covetousness, mentioned by the great apostle—*pleonexia,* which literally means *a desire of having more;* more than we have already. . . . It is true that this desire, under proper restrictions, is innocent; nay, commendable. But when it ex-

ceeds the bounds (and how difficult is it not to exceed them!), then it comes under the present censure.

8. But who is able to receive these hard sayings? Who can believe that they are the great truths of God? Not many wise, not many noble, not many famed for learning; none, indeed, who are not taught of God. And who are they whom God teaches? Let our Lord answer: "If any man be willing to do his will, he shall know of the doctrine, whether it be of God" (cf. John 7:17). Those who are otherwise minded will be so far from receiving it that they will not be able to understand it. . . .

9. Having explained the former part of the text, "They that will be rich," and pointed out, in the clearest manner I could, the persons spoken of, I will now endeavour, God being my Helper, to explain what is spoken of them: "They fall into temptation, and a snare, and into many foolish and hurtful desires, which drown men in destruction and perdition."

RICHES ARE A SNARE

"They fall into temptation." This seems to mean much more than simply, they are tempted. They *enter into the temptation:* they fall plump down into it. The waves of it compass them about and cover them all over. Of those who thus enter into temptation, very few escape out of it. And the few that do are sorely scorched by it, though not utterly consumed. If they escape at all, it is with the skin of their teeth, and with deep wounds that are not easily healed.

10. They fall, secondly, "into a snare," the snare of the devil, which he hath purposely set in their way. I believe the Greek word properly means a . . . trap, which shows no appearance of danger. But as soon as any creature touches the spring, it suddenly closes, and either crushes its bones in pieces or consigns it to inevitable ruin.

11. They fall, thirdly, "into many foolish and hurtful desires": *anoētous, silly, senseless, fantastic;* as contrary to reason, to sound understanding, as they are to religion; *hurtful,* both to body and soul, tending to weaken, yea, destroy, every gracious and heavenly temper; destructive of that faith which is of the operation of God; of that hope which is full of immortality; of love to God and to our neighbour, and of every good word and work.

12. But what desires are these? This is a most important question and deserves the deepest consideration.

In general, they may all be summed up in one, the desiring happiness out of God. This includes directly, or remotely, every foolish and hurtful desire. St. Paul expresses it [as] loving "the creature more than the Creator" (Rom. 1:25); and by being "lovers of pleasures more than lovers of God" (2 Tim. 3:4). In particular they are (to use the exact and beautiful enumeration of St. John) "the desire of the flesh, the desire of the eyes, and the pride of life" (cf. 1 John 2:16): all of which the desire of riches naturally tends both to beget and to increase.

LOVING GOD LESS

13. "The desire of the flesh" . . . does not, as is commonly supposed, refer to one of the senses only, but takes in . . . the gratification of any of the outward senses. It has reference to the *taste* in particular. How many thousands do we find . . . in whom the ruling principle is the desire to enlarge the pleasure of *tasting!* Perhaps they do not . . . incur the imputation of intemperance; much less . . . violate health or impair their understanding by gluttony or drunkenness. But they live in . . . an elegant epicurism, which does not hurt the body, but only destroys the soul, keeping it at a distance from all true religion.

14. Experience shows that the imagination is gratified chiefly by means of the eye. Therefore "the desire of the eyes," in its natural sense, is the desiring and seeking happiness in gratifying the imagination. Now the imagination is gratified either by grandeur, by beauty, or by novelty: chiefly by the last, for neither grand nor beautiful objects please any longer than they are new.

FASCINATION WITH BEAUTY

15. Seeking happiness in *learning,* of whatever kind, falls under "the desire of the eyes"; whether it be in history, languages, poetry, or any branch of natural or experimental philosophy; yea, we must include the several kinds of learning, such as geometry, algebra, and metaphysics. For if our supreme delight be in any of these, we are herein gratifying "the desire of the eyes."

16. "The pride of life" . . . seems to imply chiefly the *desire of honour;* of the esteem, admiration, and applause of men; as nothing more directly tends both to beget and cherish pride . . . And as riches attract much admiration, and occasion much applause, they proportionably minister food for pride, and so may also be referred to this head.

17. *Desire of ease* is another of these foolish and hurtful desires; desire of avoiding every cross, every degree of trouble, danger, difficulty; a desire of . . . going to heaven (as the vulgar say) upon a feather-

bed. Everyone may observe how riches first beget and then confirm and increase this desire, making men more and more soft and delicate; more unwilling, and indeed more unable, to "take up" their "cross daily," to "endure hardship as good soldiers of Jesus Christ," and "to take the kingdom of heaven by violence" (Luke 9:23; cf. 2 Tim. 2:3; Matt. 11:12).

18. Riches, either desired or possessed, naturally lead to . . . these foolish and hurtful desires; and by affording the means of gratifying them all, naturally tend to increase them. And there is a near connection between unholy desires and every other unholy passion and temper. We easily pass from these to pride, anger, bitterness, envy, malice, revengefulness; to an headstrong, unadvisable, unreprovable spirit; indeed, to every temper that is earthly, sensual, or devilish. All these the desire or possession of riches naturally tends to create, strengthen, and increase.

UNHOLY DESIRES

19. And by so doing, in the same proportion as they prevail, they "pierce men through with many sorrows" (cf. 1 Tim. 6:10); sorrows from remorse, from a guilty conscience; sorrows flowing from all the evil tempers which they inspire or increase; sorrows inseparable from those desires themselves, as every unholy desire is an uneasy desire; and sorrows from the contrariety of those desires to each other, whence it is impossible to gratify them all. And, in the end, "they drown" the body in pain, disease, "destruction," and the soul in everlasting "perdition."

I am, in the second place,

II. *To apply what has been said*

1. And this is the principal point. For what avails the clearest knowledge, even of the most excellent things, even of the things of God . . . if it be not reduced to practice? He that hath ears to hear, let him hear! And what he hears, let him instantly put in practice. . . .

2. I ask, then, in the name of God, who of *you* "desire to be rich"? Which of *you* . . . seriously and deliberately desire . . . to have more than food to eat, and raiment to put on, and a house to cover you? Who of you desires to have more than the plain necessaries and conveniences of life? Stop! Consider! What are you doing? Evil is before you! Will you rush upon the point of a sword? By the grace of God, turn and live!

3. By the same authority I ask, who of you are *endeavouring* to be rich? to procure for yourselves more than the plain necessaries and conveniences of life? Lay . . . your hand to your heart, and seriously inquire, "Am I of that number? Am I labouring, not only for what I want, but for more than I want?" May the Spirit of God say to every one whom it concerns, "Thou art the man!"

4. I ask, thirdly, who of you are in fact, "laying up for yourselves treasures upon earth" (cf. Matt. 6:19)? increasing in goods? adding, as fast as you can, house to house, and field to field? As long as *thou* thus "doest well unto thyself, men will speak good of thee" (cf. Ps. 49:18). They will call thee a wise, a prudent man! a man that *minds the main chance.* Such is, and always has been, the wisdom of the world! "But God saith unto" thee, "Thou fool!" Art thou not "treasuring up to thyself wrath against the day of wrath and revelation of the righteous judgment of God" (cf. Rom. 2:5)?

EARTHLY GOALS

5. Perhaps you will ask, "But do not you yourself advise, to gain all we can, and to save all we can? And is it possible to do this without both *desiring* and *endeavouring to be rich?* nay, suppose our endeavours are successful, without actually laying up treasures upon earth"?

I answer, It is possible. You may gain all you can without hurting either your soul or body; you may save all you can, by carefully avoiding every needless expense, and yet never lay up treasures on earth, nor either desire or endeavour so to do.

6. Permit me to speak as freely of myself as I would of another man. I *gain all I can* (namely, by writing) without hurting either my soul or body. I *save all I can,* not willingly wasting anything, not a sheet of paper, not a cup of water. I do not lay out anything, not a shilling, unless as a sacrifice to God. Yet by *giving all I can,* I am effectually secured from "laying up treasures upon earth." Yea, and I am secured from either desiring or endeavouring it, as long as I give all I can. And that I do this, I call all that know me, both friends and foes, to testify.

7. But some may say, "Whether you endeavour it or no, you are undeniably *rich.* You have more than the necessaries of life." I have. But the apostle does not fix the charge, barely on *possessing* any quantity of goods, but on possessing more than we employ according to the will of the Donor.

ENTIRE CONSECRATION

Two-and-forty years ago, having a desire to furnish poor people with cheaper, shorter, and plainer books than any I had seen, I wrote many small tracts, generally a penny apiece; and afterwards several larger. Some of these had such a sale as I never thought of; and by this means I unawares became rich. But I never desired or endeavoured after it. And now that it is come upon me unawares, I lay up no treasures upon earth: I lay up nothing at all. . . .

8. Herein, my brethren, let you that are rich be even as I am. . . . Having *gained,* in a right sense, *all you can,* and *saved all you can;* in spite of nature, and custom, and worldly prudence, *give all you can.* I do not say, "Be a good Jew, giving a tenth of all you possess." I do not say, "Be a good Pharisee, giving a fifth of all your substance." I dare not advise you to give half of what you have; no, nor three-quarters; but all! Lift up your hearts, and you will see clearly, in what sense this is to be done. . . .

9. O ye Methodists, hear the word of the Lord! I have a message from God to all men; but to *you* above all. . . . I fear there is need to apply to some of *you* those terrible words of the apostle: "Go to, now, ye rich men! Weep and howl for the miseries which shall come upon you. . . . Your gold and silver is cankered; and the rust of them shall witness against you, and shall eat your flesh as it were fire" (cf. James 5:1, 3). Certainly it will, unless ye both save all you can and give all you can. But who of you hath considered this since you first heard the will of the Lord concerning it? Who is now determined to consider and practice it? By the grace of God begin today!

LOVERS OF MONEY MORE THAN OF GOD

10. O ye lovers of money, hear the word of the Lord! Suppose ye that money, though multiplied as the sand of the sea, can give happiness? Then you . . . believe . . . a palpable lie, confuted daily by a thousand experiments. . . . Look all around you! Are the richest men the happiest? . . . Is not the very reverse true? . . . Had not the far greater part of them more content when they had less money? Look into your own breasts. If you are increased in goods, are you proportionably increased in happiness? . . .

11. O ye that *desire* or *endeavour to be rich,* hear ye the word of the Lord! . . . Why should you anymore "fall into temptation"? . . . Why will you *enter into* it? There is no necessity for this; it is your own voluntary act and deed. Why should you anymore plunge yourselves *into a snare,* into the trap Satan has laid for you, that is ready to break your bones in pieces? to crush your soul to death? After fair warning, why should you sink anymore into "foolish and hurtful desires"? . . .

12. Have they not hurt you already . . . by slackening, if not utterly destroying, your "hunger and thirst after righteousness" (Matt. 5:6)? Have you now the same longing that you had once, for the whole image of God? Have you the same vehement desire as you formerly had, of "going on unto perfection" (cf. Heb. 6:1)? Have they not hurt you by weakening your *faith?* . . . Do you endure, in all temptations, from pleasure or pain, "seeing him that is invisible" (cf. 11:27)? Have you . . . an uninterrupted sense of His presence? Have they not hurt you with regard to your *hope?* Have you now a hope full of immortality? Are you still big with earnest expectation of all the great and precious promises? Do you now "taste the powers of the world to come" (cf. 6:5)? Do you "sit in heavenly places with Christ Jesus" (cf. Eph. 2:6)?

LOVE OF MONEY DESTROYS LOVE FOR CHRIST

13. Have they not so hurt you as to stab your religion to the heart? Have they not cooled (if not quenched) your *love to God?* . . . Have you the same delight in God which you once had? . . . And if your love of God is in any wise decayed, so is also your love of your neighbour. You are then hurt in the very life and spirit of your religion! If you lose love, you lose all.

IF YOU LOSE LOVE, YOU LOSE ALL

14. Are you not hurt with regard to your *humility?* If you are increased in goods, it cannot well be otherwise. . . .

If you are hurt in your humility, it will appear by this token: You are not so teachable as you were, not so advisable . . . not so easy to be convinced, not so easy to be persuaded; you have a much better opinion of your own judgment and are more attached to your own will. Formerly one might guide you with a thread; now one cannot turn you with a cart-rope. You were glad to be admonished or reproved; but . . . you now account a man your enemy because he tells you the truth. . . .

15. Are you not equally hurt with regard to your *meekness?* You had once learned an excellent lesson of Him that was meek as well as lowly in heart. When you were reviled, you reviled not again. You did not return railing for railing, but contrariwise blessing. . . . Is this your case now? I am afraid not. . . . How quickly are you ruffled! . . .

16. And are you not hurt in your *patience* too? Does your love now "endure all things" (cf. 1 Cor. 13:7)? Do you still "in patience possess your soul" (cf. Luke 21:19), as when you first believed? . . .

You have again learned to be frequently out of humour. You are often fretful; you feel, nay, and give way to, peevishness. . . .

17. . . . Are not you who have been successful in your endeavours to increase in substance, insensibly sunk into softness of mind, if not of body too? You no longer rejoice to "endure hardship, as good soldiers of Jesus Christ." . . . You do not cheerfully . . . deny yourselves, and take up your cross daily. You cannot deny yourself the poor pleasure of a little sleep, or of a soft bed, in order to hear the word that is able to save your souls! . . .

SELF OR OTHERS?

18. You are so deeply hurt that you have [well-]nigh lost your zeal for works of mercy, as well as of piety. You once pushed on, through cold or rain . . . to see the poor, the sick, the distressed. You went about doing good, and found out those who were not able to find you. You cheerfully crept down into their cellars, and climbed up into their garrets. . . . Do you now tread in the same steps? What hinders? Do you fear spoiling your silken coat? . . . Are you afraid of catching vermin? . . . Are you not afraid of Him that hath said, "Inasmuch as ye have not done it unto the least of these, ye have not done it unto me" (cf. Matt. 25:45)? What will follow? "Depart, ye cursed, into everlasting fire, prepared for the devil and his angels" (cf. v. 41).

19. In time past how mindful were you of that word, "Thou shalt not hate thy brother in thy heart. Thou shalt in any wise reprove thy brother, and not suffer sin upon him" (cf. Lev. 19:17). You *did* reprove, directly or indirectly, all those that sinned in your sight. And happy consequences quickly followed. . . . Many a heart was pierced. . . . But which of you now has that compassion for the ignorant, and for them that are out of the way? They may wander on . . . and plunge into the lake of fire without . . . hindrance. Gold has steeled your hearts. . . .

20. Thus have I given you, O ye gainers, lovers, possessors of riches, one more (it may be the last) warning. Oh, that it may not be in vain! May God write it upon all your hearts! Though "it is easier for a camel to go through the eye of a needle than for a rich man to enter into the kingdom of God" (Matt. 19:24; Mark 10:25; cf. Luke 18:25), yet the things impossible with men are possible with God. Lord, speak! And even the rich men that hear these words shall enter Thy kingdom!

Phineas F. Bresee
(1838-1915)

This eloquent preacher, who organized the first Church of the Nazarene in Los Angeles in 1895, knew from childhood that he was destined to preach.

Born in Franklin, N.Y., on the last day of 1838, he was converted at age 17. His family moved to Iowa, where he began his labors as a circuit preacher in the Methodist Episcopal church. While serving as a pastor at Chariton, Bresee experienced a powerful baptism with the Holy Spirit. He had been struggling with inward sin and enervating doubts. During a winter revival he became a seeker at his own altar, where the outpoured Spirit purged his "tendencies to worldliness, anger, and pride," and "removed his doubts."

He could neither define nor describe his experience theologically, but it revolutionized his ministry. His continuing labors in Iowa were marked by fruitful revivals.

Moving to California, he pastored in Los Angeles, where he became familiar with holiness doctrine. His personal experience was at last "preachable." For the rest of his life he would be an ardent exponent of entire sanctification presently obtainable by faith.

He severed his connection with Methodism, after a night in prayer and with deep sorrow, because he was denied appointment to "city mission" and "holiness" work, to which God had plainly called him.

With some like-minded friends, he organized a mission that soon became the Church of the Nazarene. The declared purpose of this mission was "preaching holiness, and carrying the gospel to the poor." At his death in 1915 Bresee was a general superintendent of a burgeoning new denomination.

Bresee's preaching was noted for its energy and eloquence. A biographer, E. A. Girvin, who often heard him, said, "Few men had such unction as he. The fire of God seemed to burn through his being, as he proclaimed with all his might the glorious message of full salvation." Bresee's temperament, as well as his spiritual and intellectual interests, drew him especially to the writings of the prophet Isaiah and the apostle Paul.

Like other evangelical and holiness groups, Bresee's church was involved in moral and social reforms. It was an inveterate foe of the liquor traffic and all kindred evils.

This sermon was chosen because it reflects both the holiness movement's crusading zeal against liquor and Phineas Bresee's personal love for Isaiah.

Holiness and Civic Righteousness*

Wherefore hear the word of the Lord, ye scornful men, that rule this people which is in Jerusalem.

Because ye have said, We have made a covenant with death, and with hell are we at agreement; when the overflowing scourge shall pass through, it shall not come unto us: for we have made lies our refuge, and under falsehood have we hid ourselves:

Therefore thus saith the Lord God, Behold, I lay in Zion for a foundation a stone, a tried stone, a precious corner stone, a sure foundation: he that believeth shall not make haste.

Judgment also will I lay to the line, and righteousness to the plummet: and the hail shall sweep away the refuge of lies, and the waters shall overflow the hiding place.

And your covenant with death shall be disannulled, and your agreement with hell shall not stand: when the over-

---

*Source: Phineas F. Bresee, *Sermons on Isaiah.* Kansas City: Nazarene Publishing House, 1926.

flowing scourge shall pass through, then ye shall be trodden down by it (Isa. 28:14-18).

Recently, at a meeting of the pastors and others of this county, in this city, the pastors of the various churches were invited to call the attention of the people to the great crime of the age—the liquor traffic—on this the last Sabbath of April. It is so often done in this church that we the more readily comply with this request.

As to the measureless iniquity of the liquor traffic, the aggregated wickedness against God and man, there is little disagreement. All know that it is a consuming blight, bringing mildew and decay to every beautiful thing it touches. Turning joy to sorrow, and hope to despair wherever it comes, emptying out, driving away prosperity, plenty, health, and love, to bring in poverty, want, sickness, and hate.

In the old time the question was asked, "Who hath woe? who hath sorrow? who hath contentions? who hath babbling? who hath wounds without cause? who hath redness of eyes?" And it was answered, "They that tarry long at the wine; they that go to seek mixed wine" (Prov. 23:29-30). It is the same today, only wine has blossomed out with hellish ferocity into every fiery thing, and the results are intensified.

DESTROYS LIFE

The liquor traffic seduces the young, insidiously attacks unformed character, sets its death traps for unwary feet, despoils the home, robs womanhood and childhood of their rights, and is deaf to their cry, and crushes out their hopes and lives. It takes away all nobility from every man it touches. It blights every beautiful thing in human life, dethrones the intellect, blasts the heart, destroys the life, and damns the soul. There is not a thing it touches but that it crushes it into blackness and despair. It eats up the wealth of the people, saps their health, weakens their intellect, dethrones the kingly power of volition, often even making man lower than the brutes.

It is that of which you can say no good thing, which has no righteous defense, which is only evil and that continually. It is the promoter of all kinds of criminality. For the hope of gain it would spread ruin everywhere and despoil every beautiful thing. It is by common consent a thief, a murderer, a robber, an assassin, a frightful outlaw in all civilization.

There is nothing known among men so merciless, so cruel, so destructive, so damning as the liquor traffic. It has long been recognized that the places of its sale are "slaughter pens" and those who deal in it are "poisoners general" of the people. It is a thing which, it would seem, it would be the intention of every decent man to hate, and which demands the skill and strength of every man to kill. This long, sad, fearful, tragic text permeated with but one ray of light and hope is in reference to the drunkards of Ephraim, and the national guilt pertaining thereto.

LIQUOR CORRUPTS EVEN THE CHURCH

The priest and the prophet have been caused to err in vision and stumble in judgment through strong drink. They accuse Isaiah of being a crank on this subject, never letting it alone. Precept upon precept, line upon line, here a little and there a little. But Isaiah says, "God will speak. You call me a stammerer, ever going over and over these commonplaces. God will stammer so you will understand."

Isaiah said to them, "You say you have an arrangement made, that you are sharp and have outwitted God. You have found a place of rest. You have found deliverances through your diplomacy. You have outwitted Assyria and are too sharp for Egypt. You will loll in your drunkenness and wallow in your debauchery and abide." Then he tells them what God said. He represents these liquor interests to be saying so long what is so preeminently true in this day, "We have made a covenant with death, and with hell are we at agreement." If there ever was a "covenant with death" and an "agreement . . . with hell," it is the attitude of the controlling forces of society in regard to the liquor traffic in this country.

Nothing which ever lifted its head where the light of Christian truth made things luminous was so abominable as the licensing of this atrocious crime, giving standing and opportunity under the law to the sum and aggregation of all criminality. As of old, it makes lies its refuge, and under falsehood it hides itself.

INNER SIN CAUSES OUTWARD EVIL

The Lord showed Isaiah that the problem was deeper than drunkenness. That drunkenness was the sore on the surface, the breaking out on the skin, while the disease was in the blood. He especially calls attention to the attitude of the priest and the prophet, to whom so largely was given the keeping of the conscience of the people. They erred in vision, they stumbled in judgment. Here seems to be the fountain of the great evil. The blood disease is the absence of holiness, and the cause is in the moral fountains of the nation.

We are trying to make less saloons, closing up one here and there.

It is like rubbing Vaseline on some of the sores of a man who has the smallpox. We believe in and work for prohibitory legislation. I am thankful for the Prohibition Party. It gives an opportunity for a Christian man to express his convictions at the ballot box. I believe in what so many churches have declared, "that the sale of liquor as a beverage cannot be licensed without sin." Believing that, I cannot vote with a whiskey-soaked party under the domination of the liquor business.

It is this error in vision and stumbling in judgment that is the fountain of the difficulty today. Occasionally the priest and prophet, in General Assemblies and General Conferences, climb up to the mount of vision, and under the pressure of the world's gaze rise to justness in judgment and utter the truth, but they come down without bringing the mountain down with them, and at once enter into a covenant with death and an agreement with hell.

A RIGHTEOUS GOD JUDGES EVIL

That judgments have not yet fallen upon the land on account of this terrible and continued villainy, the smoke of whose fires surely fills the nostrils of the God of righteousness, is a matter for great thanksgiving. Of course much of the results of poverty, crime, sorrow, and death have come. The wreck of manhood and of homes, the untold agony and untimely deaths, have been a great price to pay for our sin. That 100,000 men recruited from the boys go down to drunkard's graves each year with untold sorrow and despair, is surely a blighting scourge.

The tide of drunkenness which rolls over the land bears with it a tide of agony untold and untellable, which stifles memory and blots out hope. It forbids us to look back, it forbids us to look forward, and draws its mantle of darkness closer and closer about us.

The pressure and the agony are very great, but perhaps the iniquity is not yet full. God will find a way to hurl it to the ground and grind it to powder. God will find a way to destroy the destroyer. He will lay judgment to the line, and righteousness to the plummet. The covenant with death He will disannul, and the agreement with hell He will break up. How, I may not know. The hail that sweepeth away the refuge of lies, and the waters that overflow the hiding places, and the scourge that treadeth down, I do not know, but God has the forces in His own hands. The surprises of history are very great. Pride, power, and wickedness have been hurled down together in a day when the Lord has risen up. He found a way to deal with the giants in sin, and to blot out slavery. He will find a way to blot out this darker crime as His people cry day and night unto Him.

In the meantime what is our duty? There is one peculiarity about this utterance of the Word of God. Right between the confession of these drunkards of Ephraim that they had made a covenant with death and an agreement with hell, and the statement of the Lord that He will lay judgment to the line and righteousness to the plummet and that the hail shall sweep away the refuge of lies; right between these, He says, "Therefore . . . Behold, I lay in Zion for a foundation a stone, a tried stone, a precious corner stone, a sure foundation; he that believeth shall not make haste." There is that which in God's order precedes the breaking up of this covenant, and that is the laying in Zion for a foundation a stone, a precious cornerstone; and those who are believers build upon it. And whosoever shall be so united to Him "shall not make haste," or be ashamed or confounded. They shall not fear nor flee. What does this mean? Recognize the awful curse with which we have to deal, but preach Jesus Christ.

SPIRITUAL FOUNDATIONS

We are something more than politicians. We are something more than dealers in moral suasion. We ally ourselves with the almightiness of God, and preach Jesus Christ. Political action is as uncertain as the weathervane. It moves with the wind of public sentiment. To get abiding righteous conditions we must go down to the foundations. We must build upon the Rock of Ages. There is but one way to roll back the fearful tide of the liquor curse and save this country, and that is to meet it with the Cross—to lay deep and wide the foundations of that holiness which the blood of Jesus Christ brings.

IN THE POWER OF GOD

Before the battle, that will sweep away this curse like a tornado, is really on, the public conscience has to be aroused to a depth and intensity which nothing can accomplish but that Holy Spirit, who, when He comes, convinces men of sin and of righteousness and of judgment. An appeal to the Church of today is futile because it is already worldly, and seeks the favor and the emoluments of the world. It has turned its back upon the foe. The Church of today is already disgraced before heaven and earth in this battle. Having bows, they have turned back and thrown away their bows in the day of conflict.

How is this country to be saved? I fully believe that there is to be but one way, and that is to lay this cornerstone anew. The cry of John the Baptist must go up again, "Behold the Lamb of God, which taketh away the sin of the world" (John 1:29). The army must be reformed on a basis of experience that knows no fear or compromise. There must be a Blood-washed army of holy men and women who fear God and hate evil, who can neither be cajoled nor bought. The Huguenots, Cromwell's Ironsides, and the antislavery crusaders are our forerunners. But the time has come when it needs a clearer vision, and a stronger faith, and a more perfect spiritual discernment even than our predecessors had.

HOLY MEN HATE EVIL

We come nearer the close of the dispensation, when the battle will rage sore, when it is especially against principalities and powers in high places. We are especially in a dark hour when the knights errant are few, when men value an ass's head more than a child's heart. Jesus, today, sets the little child in the midst of our legislators and city councils, and they say, "Let the devil take the child, it is the gold coin we are after." And the multitude of the people say, "Amen." Every vote cast for the licensing of the saloon thunders, "Amen," to the covenant with death.

What are we to do? Get nigh unto God, take shelter under His wings of might, feel after and find the pillars of His strength. Get into the pavilion of His holiness. The way of battle just now is by way of the throne. The way to make voters for God is by way of the outpouring of the Holy Spirit in awakening, saving, and sanctifying power. God can depend upon a holy man to go into a voting booth and vote against the saloon. What we must have is a great, deep, wide, and mighty revival of righteousness.

A REVIVAL OF RIGHTEOUSNESS

England was saved from the darkness and blood of the revolution that swept over France by the preaching of holiness by John Wesley and his coadjutors.

This country, if saved from the overwhelming curse and disaster to which the liquor traffic is dooming it, will be saved by a mighty wave of righteousness coming down through the cross of our Lord and Savior Jesus Christ, saving and sanctifying men and women and lifting them into the clear light and power of God, who will bring on the battle, and will have no compromise, but will move heaven and earth until this covenant with death and agreement with hell is swept from us.

Alex R. G. Deasley
(1935—)

Alex Deasley is professor of New Testament at Nazarene Theological Seminary.

It was my privilege to hear him preach the sermon that I have included in this volume. He speaks with clarity and precision, with gentle humor and strong conviction, as a man who believes passionately in Christ and in the gospel that sets forth Christ as Lord and Savior. Earlier it had been my good fortune to attend Sunday School classes taught by Professor Deasley, where his warmth, openness, and compassion enabled him to temper high-level scholarship to ordinary truth-seekers like myself. The experience was mentally and spiritually enriching.

He is a native of Great Britain, where he schooled, pastored, and taught before moving to Canada. There he served as chairman of the Division of Religion at Canadian Nazarene College in Winnipeg. From that post he was summoned to the faculty of Nazarene Theological Seminary, where his work and influence have been outstanding.

"Sanctification and Service" appeals to service as "a basic instinct in the Christian soul," and affirms sanctification as "first in the qualities of the usable Christian." The sermon, structured simply and effectively, progresses from exegetical discussion to practical application.

Dr. Deasley strikes a responsive chord from the first, because every Christian has a deep-down desire to be useful in Christ's work. How can that desire be realized? Deasley shows that (1)

There are two classes of Christians, usable and unusable. (2) The difference between them is remaining sin. (3) One moves from unusable to usable through the experience of inward cleansing we call entire sanctification.

Remaining sin is no trifling matter. Deasley's metaphors are strong: Sin is "the Trojan horse," "the fifth column," "the traitor within," "the great enemy." This granted, the promise of inner cleansing "is marvelous good news . . . news of a miracle!" Anecdote, poetry, and apt quotation provide illustrations that both enforce the truth and whet the listener's appetite for personal experience of the truth proclaimed.

The message opens and closes with the text, which is, as are all other Scripture quotations in this sermon, Deasley's own translation. Between those scripture brackets is a superb model of sermonic content and style.

Sanctification and Service*

> *In a great house there are not only vessels of gold and silver, but also of wood and earthenware; some to honour, and some to dishonour. If a man will cleanse himself from these, he will be a vessel unto honour: sanctified, fit for the master's use, prepared for every good work* (2 Tim. 2:20-21).

Throughout history the idea of service has exercised a great fascination over the minds of men. The thought of being useful speaks to something deep in the human heart. Those who labor at the highest levels of our national life think of themselves, as we also think of them, as servants or secretaries of state—or in the case of my native land, as ministers of the crown. And one thought which our minds repel as intolerable is the idea that we might one day be of no use to anyone. John Milton, smitten with blindness in the middle of his career, found peace for his tormented mind only in the realization that accepting his lot with ready obedience was itself a form of divine service: "They also serve who only stand and wait." A prayer which

---

*Source: Wesley D. Tracy, ed., *The Redeemed Will Walk There: Sermons on the Life of Holiness from the Chapel of Nazarene Theological Seminary*. Kansas City: Beacon Hill Press of Kansas City, 1983.

Wesley prayed repeatedly in his last years was: "Lord, let me not live to be useless"—a prayer which God graciously answered by allowing Wesley to go on preaching to within a week of his death.

To serve God is likewise a basic instinct in the Christian soul; and our text, 2 Tim. 2:20-21, has some searching things to say about it. The passage is easily misunderstood because Paul, in very typical fashion, is not as careful as he might be to keep his metaphors straight. However, the context as a whole gives us the guidance we need. Certain preachers in the church had begun to teach that the resurrection had already taken place, meaning in effect that Christians had already received their resurrection bodies. Consequently it did not matter how they behaved with their physical bodies which they would soon be leaving: a view which was taken as a passport to licentiousness and immorality (vv. 19, 22).

Paul duly denounces them as having backslidden from the faith (v. 18) and then turns to reflecting on how such a state of affairs could arise. He gives his explanation in our text in three simple truths which lay bare the roots of effective service in the kingdom of God.

I. *There are two different types of Christians: the usable and the unusable* (v. 20).

That is a startling statement! It is most important to grasp what Paul is *not* saying. He is not saying that in a wealthy house there are gold and silver vessels for the dining room table and rough earthenware pots for the kitchen, but every house has need of both. That is true. Paul teaches it in 1 Corinthians 12. The body needs legs and feet just as much as it needs eyes and hands. Every member has a useful role to play. But that is not what Paul is talking about here. He is talking about how a cheap earthenware vessel can—miraculously—become a silver or a golden vessel. He is talking not about usefulness but about usability. And in those terms he says that there are two different types of Christians.

USABLE CHRISTIANS

That, I repeat, is a startling statement. Are not all Christians the same? "In Christ Jesus you are all sons of God through faith. . . . There is neither Jew nor Greek, slave nor free, male nor female; you are all one in Christ Jesus" (Gal. 3:28). Are not all equally loved by God, redeemed by God, sustained by God? In natural life we do not like distinctions which break us up and set us apart from each other, exalting some, debasing others. In my first day as an undergraduate at Jesus College, Cambridge, I recall well the novice's pride in being a member of Jesus College rather than any other of the 22 in the university. I also remember the shock and rebuke as the president of the college concluded his welcome address by saying loftily: "In Cambridge we do not compare one college with another. Comparisons are odious, and so are the people who make them."

It is therefore somewhat surprising and even shocking to find that the New Testament writers are making comparisons among Christians all the time. In 1 Corinthians 2—3 Paul distinguishes perfect Christians (2:6) from fleshly or carnal Christians who are embroiled in jealousy and strife, which are the negation of true spirituality (2:14—3:4). In Heb. 5:12-14 the author chides those who have been Christians long enough to be able to nurture others but still require a milk diet themselves because of their spiritual immaturity which is defined as a moral thing for which they are therefore responsible (v. 14). In Phil. 1:9-10 Paul prays for his readers that their love "may abound more and more so that they may approve what is excellent and be pure and blameless for the day of Christ"; while in Eph. 3:14-21 he prays that they may be strengthened with might by God's Spirit in the inner man; that Christ may dwell in their hearts by faith; that they may come to know in understanding and experience God's love in all its dimensions, and be filled with the fullness of God.

CARNAL CHRISTIANS

All Christians are not the same. There are two clearly definable categories; and one category is usable by God and the other is not.

II. *The difference lies in remaining sin.*

What is it that makes some Christians less usable than others? The answer lies in the next words: "If a man will cleanse himself." These simple words carry two important implications.

a. The great impediment to service is sin. "If a man will cleanse himself . . . he will be a vessel unto honour." Remaining sin in their lives is what makes Christians unusable. "Let every one who names the name of Christ depart from iniquity" (v. 19). "Shun youthful passions and follow righteousness, faith, love, peace, with them that call on the Lord out of a pure heart" (v. 22). It is sin that undermines the Christian's effectiveness. It is sin that breaks one's communion with God. It is sin that torpedoes one's power to resist temptation. Sin is the Trojan horse within the city. Sin is the fifth column within the soul which is in league with the enemy without. Sin is the traitor within the gates.

Have you heard how the preaching ministry of F. B. Meyer turned on this very thing? He was already a committed Christian, but not very constant in his experience. C. T. Studd, having recently entered into the blessing himself, was touring Britain before leaving for China as a missionary and was sharing a room one night with F. B. Meyer. Meyer watched him closely and finally asked Studd: "How can I be like you?"

KEY TO EFFECTIVE MINISTRY

Studd replied: "Have you ever given yourself to Christ, for Christ to fill you?"

"I have done so in a general way," Meyer said, "but I don't know that I have done it particularly."

Studd answered: "You must do it particularly also."

That night Meyer took time to pray. "I gave God an iron ring," he said, "with all the keys of my life on it except one little key that I kept back. I said, 'Lord, I will be so devoted in everything else, but I can't live without the contents of that closet.'" Meyer was later to say: "I believe that my whole life was just hovering in the balance, and if I had kept the key of that closet, and mistrusted Christ, He never would have trusted me with the ministry of His Word." He resolved the crisis with the words: "I am not willing, but I am willing to be made willing." That was the turning point in his life. The great impediment to service is sin.

W. E. Sangster gave memorable expression to the same truth in a poem which is also a prayer.

Lord Jesus, I am longing
From sin to be set free:
To find my deep desiring
Forever fixed on Thee.
All hope I now abandon
Myself to conquer sin;
Invade my willing nature
And come and dwell within.

The passing years oppress me,
My growth in grace so slow:
My wayward, fickle cravings
Have leagued me to the foe;
Myself to self disloyal,
I loathe yet love my sin:
Now hear my heartfelt pleading
And come and dwell within.

If Thou should'st stand close by me,
'Tis more than I deserve;
But being still outside me,
From virtue yet I swerve.
Come nearer, Lord, than near me,
My succor to begin;
Usurp the heart that craves Thee!
Oh, come and dwell within.

Remaining sin is the great enemy. But the text tells us more than this. The words, "If a man will cleanse himself . . . he will be a vessel unto honour" imply something else: namely that

b. Remaining sin can be cleansed. The word "cleanse" is not a characteristically Pauline word: it is typical rather of John and Hebrews. The remarkable thing is that, on the few occasions Paul uses it, he uses it of the cleansing of sin from the lives of Christians. (That is not always so elsewhere in the New Testament, especially in Hebrews where it has a specialized sense; and we must be careful not to make it carry more exegetical freight than it can bear.)

CLEANSING

"Having therefore these promises, dearly beloved, let us cleanse ourselves from all impurity of the flesh and spirit, perfecting holiness in the fear of God" (2 Cor. 7:1). "He gave himself for us that he might redeem us from all iniquity and cleanse for himself a people of his own, zealous of good works" (Titus 2:14). This is especially true with the intensive form of the word used here which is found elsewhere only in 1 Cor. 5:7: "Cleanse out the old leaven that you may be a new lump." Remaining sin can be cleansed!

THERE IS CLEANSING FOR ALL

That is marvelous good news! It is good news of a miracle! So many of our important capacities in life are fixed: our looks, our brains, our constitutions. But in the life of the spirit, miracles are possible, and unusable Christians can be made usable. This is where Paul's metaphor breaks down. In the natural order it is impossible for an earthen pot to be changed into a golden or silver pot; but what is impossible naturally is possible spiritually. And while it would be exegetical license to say that Paul's words were intended to convey that point, that is the point which—in spite of themselves—they convey. The greatest democracy on earth is the democracy of faith. Promotion in God's service depends not on pedigree or length of service, but on cleansing, and that is equally available to all: "If a man will cleanse himself."

Not that we can cleanse *ourselves.* But when the New Testament writers think of our responsibility to cooperate with the grace that God provides, they often speak in this way. "Every man who has this hope in him purifies himself" (1 John 3:3). And if we cleanse ourselves, we can become "vessels unto honour."

III. *The key to service is sanctification.*

"If a man will cleanse himself . . . he will be a vessel unto honour: sanctified, fit for the master's use, prepared for every good work" (v. 21).

There are three marks of the usable Christian.

a. Sanctification. You will note that the translations differ at this point. RSV has "consecrated." NEB has "dedicated." NIV has "made holy." KJV has "sanctified." . . . The Greek word "sanctify" *(hagiazō)* which is used here has as its root meaning "to set apart," that is, for God's service. However, it is a familiar feature in the New Testament for those who are sanctified in the sense of being set apart to be exhorted to be *fully* sanctified in a moral sense. In a way, that is inevitable in a truly moral religion, [because] the only thing that is fit for God's service is that which has been not merely dedicated, but that which has been cleansed. There is a point at which the distinction vanishes. The meaning in our present text is clear. Sanctification is linked directly with cleansing: "If a man will *cleanse* himself . . . he will be . . . sanctified." "Sanctified" in the moral sense is the only possible meaning here.

FULLY SANCTIFIED

The point of particular significance is that sanctification is named first in the qualities of the usable Christian. The whole chain of preparation has been finely summed up in the dictum of J. Sidlow Baxter:

> *What I give He takes;*
> *What He takes He cleanses;*
> *What He cleanses He fills;*
> *What He fills He uses.*

b. The second mark of the usable Christian, after sanctification, is *serviceability:* "Fit for the master's use." It is only when we are sanctified that we are fully serviceable. The underlying picture is that of a wealthy house in which only the best tableware is fit for the use of the master. In Britain there is an institution or custom known as royal patents. On all sorts of products from steak sauce up you will see the royal coat of arms and under it the formula: "By appointment: makers of steak sauce to Her Majesty Queen Elizabeth II." These patents are issued at the beginning of each reign; and there is fierce competition among manufacturers to gain a coveted royal patent, for this advertises to the world that their product is fit for the Queen's table.

Paul is saying, in effect, that there is another royal patent; that our lives may be so changed as to meet God's approval; and that when we are sanctified, we receive the stamp of serviceability: "By appointment: fit for the Master's use."

c. The third mark of the usable Christian is *versatility:* "Prepared for every good work." There are indeed gifts which equip specific individuals for specific tasks. But there is also a Spirit-filled versatility in the New Testament; and it is striking how frequently it is associated with the language of perfection. "Now the God of peace . . . make you perfect in every good work to do his will" (Heb. 13:21). "All scripture is given by inspiration of God . . . that the man of God may be perfect, thoroughly furnished unto every good work" (2 Tim. 3:16-17). "He gave himself for us that he might redeem us from all iniquity and purify for himself a people of his own possession, zealous of good works" (Titus 2:14). It does not matter how many gifts we have: there are some good works we shall never do and can never do until we are "sanctified, fit for the master's use, prepared for every good work." Sanctification is the fundamental qualification and the comprehensive qualification.

CHRISTIAN PERFECTION

The Christian Church in our times is greatly exercised about service, and we are exhorted on all hands—and rightly—to get involved. Peter Taylor Forsyth once said in his penetrating way: "The greatest service I owe the kingdom of God is my personal holiness." Paul is saying the same thing: The best preparation for service is sanctification. "In a great house there are not only vessels of gold and silver, but also of wood and earthenware; some to honour, and some to dishonour. If a man will cleanse himself from these, he will be a vessel unto honour: sanctified, fit for the master's use, prepared for every good work."

PERSONAL HOLINESS

David L. McKenna

(1929—)

David McKenna is an ordained elder in the Free Methodist Church of North America. He has enjoyed a highly influential career as an educator-administrator. In pursuing his own education, he has garnered five degrees in the fields of history, religion, psychology, and higher education.

As an instructor, lecturer, and professor he gained teaching experience at Spring Arbor College, the University of Michigan, and Ohio State University. In 1961 he became president of Spring Arbor College, in 1968 president of Seattle Pacific University, and in 1982 president of Asbury Theological Seminary, the post he now holds.

He has been, through these years, one of the most respected speakers and writers in evangelical circles. Among his books, *The Psychology of Jesus, Megatruth: The Church in the Age of Information,* and *The Whisper of His Grace* have established his reputation as a Christian leader with a deep concern for the personal and social struggles of Christians coping with and ministering to a complex and debased society. His volumes in *The Communicator's Commentary* on Mark and Job are used by preachers throughout the English-speaking world.

Wherever he has lived and served, McKenna has been involved in the moral, social, and educational issues of his community, an involvement that has brought him many unsought honors and awards.

"New Shoes for Beautiful Feet" is an appeal for the translation of "the power of personal holiness" into "the ethics of practical holiness." It calls for a moral motivation, moral discipline, and moral standard that will furnish challenge and hope for human society. It summons the hearers to a commitment to Christ and to humanity that will make the Christian responsive to the lost, the poor, and the despairing among us. The message addresses a perennial problem for holiness people, how to be "in the world" and "for the world" without being "of the world." McKenna's answer is apostolic and Wesleyan.

"New Shoes for Beautiful Feet" was addressed to the graduating class of Asbury Theological Seminary in 1978. Directed to those who would be ministers of the gospel, largely in pastoral and educational settings, it is equally applicable to all disciples of Christ, whatever their work, wherever their homes.

The sermon is a masterful demonstration of the effective use of historical and literary resources in the explication and application of biblical truth.

New Shoes for Beautiful Feet*

How beautiful are the feet of them that preach the gospel of peace, and bring glad tidings of good things! (Rom. 10:15).

A full generation ago I sat where you sit now. My calling was sure. As a serious teenager, God had set me apart with a personalized word: "How shall they hear without a preacher? And how shall they preach, except they be sent? . . . How beautiful are the feet of them that preach the gospel of peace, and bring glad tidings of good things!"

With the future in my eyes, I returned home the next day to begin my ministry in Christian higher education. We arrived at the parsonage of my wife's parents to be welcomed by a sainted, but semihysterical, sister of the church. Having just heard about my decision to teach rather than preach, she wrapped me in her ample arms and wept, "Oh, David, I had prayed so hard that you would be a minister."

Try as I might, I could not convince her that God may put different shoes on the feet of those who are called to preach the good tidings of the gospel of peace. Twenty-six years later, I offer no apolo-

*Source: Sermon manuscript.

gies. My ministry has been the professorship and the presidency, but I would still be equally honored if God should call me to the pastorate. The tension continues to this day. Not so much in the recognition that ministers may wear different shoes, but that we are being asked to try on new shoes that squeak and bind.

James Reston, the *New York Times* columnist, brought this home to me when he spoke at the Congress of the Laity at Los Angeles in February. Straight out, he indicted our culture as a "moral pigsty" and turned to his predominantly evangelical Christian audience with the penetrating question, "How will your personal ministry affect our public morality?" True to his art of plain speaking in journalism, he then aired his suspicion that the problem of the born-again movement was not unlike the dilemma that has always plagued Americans. "We can handle adversity, but our prosperity is killing us."

Reston's prophetic comments set me on a search through the moral crisis of our times and to the discovery of the connector between the personal morality of spiritual rebirth and the public morality of social renewal.

Time does not permit a return trip through the pigsty. It suffices to say that a review of the moral crisis of our times leaves one feeling like the father who started out on a cross-country trip with four kids in a Volkswagen. After 100 miles of traveling with them, he was convinced of original sin. Another 100 miles and he had no doubt about total depravity. Robert Heilbroner came out at the same place when he wrote *An Inquiry into the Human Prospect.* At one time, he writes, Prometheus, the Grecian god who carried fire to the top of the mountain as a symbol of human achievement, represented our society. Now Atlas has taken center stage, bearing the weight of the world in his hands, struggling to stay alive, and hoping to "rescue the future from the angry condemnation of the present."

My conclusion is simple and direct. I concur with James Reston. A secular world awaits the evidence that spiritual rebirth will lead to social renewal in our generation. Turn the coin and it comes up another way: The born-again movement needs the touch of personal and practical holiness. Here our new shoes squeak and bind.

PRACTICAL HOLINESS

Admittedly, the distinction between personal and practical holiness is artificial. I use personal holiness to identify our emphasis upon the dynamic of the purifying, enabling, sanctifying, and indwelling Spirit. May the hymn of our altars ever be,

O for a heart to praise my God,
A heart from sin set free,
A heart that always feels Thy blood
So freely shed for me!

A heart in ev'ry thought renewed,
And full of love divine;
Perfect and right, and pure and good—
A copy, Lord, of thine!

—CHARLES WESLEY

But then we must encounter the conditions of the world in which we live. At this juncture, the power of personal holiness must be translated into the ethics of practical holiness. Early Methodists used the term "practical holiness" to describe the daily dimensions of perfect love. Entire sanctification was not just doctrinal theory but an experience hammered out of biblical scholarship and personal regeneration in response to the spiritual need and the moral crisis of 18th-century England.

I. *Practical holiness begins with the moral motivation to preach the gospel to the socially poor and spiritually lost.*

Jesus gives us the example. In the glory of the Baptism, the Spirit of God descended upon Him in the form of a dove, and God sealed the indwelling presence with the witness that Jesus was His beloved Son in whom He was well pleased. The same Spirit led Him into the wilderness and guided Him through Satan's temptation. In His first public utterance, then, Jesus testified to personal holiness, "The Spirit of the Lord is upon me . . ." Without waiting for a moment to bask in the glory of that experience, He proceeds to the vocation of practical holiness:

> . . . he hath anointed me to preach the gospel to the poor; he hath sent me to heal the brokenhearted, to preach deliverance to the captives, and recovering of sight to the blind, to set at liberty them that are bruised, to preach the acceptable year of the Lord *(Luke 4:18-19).*

John Wesley, the Oxford don, Anglican churchman, and loyalist to the king, was led along the same path under the direction of the Holy Spirit. On March 31, 1739, he records in his Journal,

> In the evening I reached Bristol and met Mr. Whitefield there. I could scarce reconcile myself at first to this strange way of preaching in the fields, . . . having been all my life . . . so tenacious of every point relating to decency and order that I should have thought the saving of souls almost a sin if it had not been done in a church.

UNORTHODOX METHODS

The next day was Sunday. In church, he expounded on the Sermon on the Mount and was awakened to the fact that this was "one pretty remarkable precedent for field-preaching." Monday, the next day, made history. Wesley writes in his Journal,

> At four in the afternoon, I submitted to be more vile, and proclaimed in the highways the glad tidings of salvation. . . . The scripture on which I spoke was this: . . . "The Spirit of the Lord is upon me, because he hath anointed me to preach the gospel to the poor; he hath sent me to heal the brokenhearted, to preach deliverance to the captives, and recovering of sight to the blind, to set at liberty them that are bruised, to proclaim the acceptable year of the Lord."

Quite in contrast, the question that nags the evangelical awakening of our day is on the cover of Quebedeaux's new book, titled *The Worldly Evangelicals.* The question is, "Will success spoil born-again Christians?" Similarly, Gallup's latest poll shows that the average "born-again, Bible-believing, and witnessing Christian" is a white, middle-class, Southern woman around the age of 50.

THE BRUISED IN OUR TIMES

Who are the poor, the brokenhearted, the captives, the blind, and the bruised in our time? A few years ago, I read about the wretched of the earth. In addition to the hundreds of millions who are starving from the lack of food, there are 70 million others who are diseased and dying simply because they lack clean water. Another 30 million go blind because they do not have the most elementary medication. My heart was wrenched with compassion, and I was ready to give up everything for a "clean water" and "clean eye" crusade as my ministry to the needy of the world. But the Spirit of God checked my response by another article in the same paper. The Bureau of the Census reported a doubling of the number of unmarried men and women living together and almost a doubling of the number of divorces per 1,000 married people since 1970. I had to think again about the socially poor and the spiritually lost among us. Frankly, I am repulsed by gays, shocked by "shacking up," suspicious of divorcées, distant from singles, forgetful of the aged, threatened by Blacks, and almost oblivious to the poor.

Dare I say that I am not alone among people who profess to be born-again and Spirit-filled Christians? Practical holiness will motivate us to move from the testimony, "The Spirit of the Lord is upon me, because he hath anointed me . . ." to the task of preaching the gospel of moral regeneration to the contemporary definitions of "the poor, . . . the brokenhearted, . . . the captives, . . . the blind, [and the] bruised," not only overseas but also across the street.

II. *Practical holiness then proceeds to the moral discipline of Christian character.*

In the Early Church, new converts were surrounded by a community of love that met their needs, disciplined their conduct, and nurtured their understanding of the gospel. Their singular purpose was to create a Christian character that would stand against the temptations and the confrontations of a pagan world. How often we quote Heb. 12:14 as a proof text for the doctrine of holiness:

> Follow peace with all men, and holiness, without which no man shall see the Lord.

But how seldom we tie that verse contextually to the discipline of the Spirit that precedes it.

> We have had fathers of our flesh which corrected us, and we gave them reverence: shall we not much rather be in subjection unto the Father of spirits, and live? For they verily for a few days chastened us after their own pleasure; but he for our profit, that we might be partakers of his holiness *(Heb. 12:9-10).*

John Wesley saw the need for demonstrating the Body of Christ, the family of God, and the temple of the Holy Ghost in societies and class meetings where the new converts were physically supported, socially disciplined, and spiritually nurtured. Practical holiness was to be demonstrated in the moral character of a Spirit-filled person. Not without significance, Quebedeaux has chosen the Methodist definition of Christian character as the feature of what he calls "The new Wesleyans." In response to the inquiry, "What are the distinguishing marks of a Methodist?" John Wesley wrote:

> . . . by salvation, a Methodist means holiness of heart and life.
>
> A Methodist is a person who has the love of God in his heart . . . cares about his neighbor as much as himself. . . .
>
> God has cleaned the Methodist's heart, washing away all urge for revenge . . . envy . . . wrath . . . harm . . . unkind inclination . . . evil lust and desire . . . pride . . . haughtiness. He cannot devote him-

> self to selfish indulgence, preoccupied with making money . . . The Christian thinks, speaks, and lives according to the pattern of Jesus. I ask no further questions. Do you love God? This is enough. I give you the right hand of fellowship.

May I suggest that the definition of Christian character and the discipline of practical holiness are missing dimensions in the current evangelical awakening? There is a strong and commendable emphasis upon the Body of Christ as a loving, caring community. But we are missing what Dean Kelley, in his book *Why Conservative Churches Are Growing,* has called the "Power of the Gate." The gate swings open when converts are taken into fellowship and agree to be a part of the discipline of holy living. Within the gate, mature Christians model out the qualities of Spirit-filled living and monitor the growth of new Christians. If, however, the individuals turn from faith or reject the discipline, provision must be made for the gate to swing out in exit, but only after the patience and admonition of truth in love.

As in Wesley's time, specific temptations and sins have to be addressed. His converts were saved from profanity, drunkenness, and immorality. Their newfound industry as born-again Christians created problems of handling money and their time. Thus, the discipline of stewardship became an evidence of practical holiness before the world. Times have not changed. The moral crisis of resources again calls for the discipline of stewardship with new money and new leisure for us.

THE DISCIPLINES OF HOLINESS

Strangely enough, most evangelicals today do not have the Wesleyan heritage of a disciplined life as a Spirit-filled response to the extremes of legalism and antinomianism. Those extremes threaten us again. Some are calling for the nostalgic return to a simple life-style, others are experimenting with hybrid forms of class meetings, and still others are engaging in controversial discipling. For the good of the awakening and as a witness before the world, holiness people themselves should be leading with what William Law, in *A Serious Call to a Devout and Holy Life,* called the "devotion of the common life"—or the discipline of perfection in the business of life.

III. *Once again, practical holiness holds forth a moral standard for the renewal of society.*

Much stress is put upon the role of the Holy Spirit as Comforter and upon sanctification as rest. We cannot forget that Jesus gave equal weight to the other side of the promise, "Howbeit when he, the Spirit of truth, is come, he will guide you into all truth" (John 16:13).

John later expanded that thought in his First Epistle when he wrote: "We are of God: he that knoweth God heareth us; he that is not of God heareth not us. Hereby know we the spirit of truth, and the spirit of error" (1 John 4:6).

GOD'S HOLINESS CALLS FOR JUSTICE

Practical holiness includes the function of the Holy Spirit to raise a moral standard for the development of Christian conscience. In Wesley's time, the conscience of perfect love stood for justice against human slavery. As a logical consequence of the Arminian doctrine of unlimited atonement, Wesley preached the natural rights of all men for social as well as spiritual freedom.

If there is an issue testing Christian conscience today, it is still the confusing question of justice. In one way or another, every moral crisis touches on this issue. I suspect that our spiritual forefathers would err on the side of justice. Most of us watched the television series "Holocaust." It depicted not only the depravity of man but also the failure of the church to stand for justice. As a sequel to the film, we should hear again Martin Niemöller, the Lutheran pastor, imprisoned by the Nazis in a concentration camp where 76,000 Jews died. When Pastor Niemöller was released, he was asked, "How did the world let this happen?" He responded,

> In Germany, the Nazis first came for the Communists, and I didn't speak up because I wasn't a Communist. Then they came for the Jews, and I didn't speak up because I wasn't a Jew. They came for the trade unionists, and I didn't speak up because I wasn't a trade unionist. Then they came for the Catholics, and I didn't speak up because I was a Protestant. Then they came for me, and by that time there was no one left to speak for me.

HOLINESS REQUIRES SOME HARD CHOICES

When the Spirit of God calls us to the moral standard of a Christian conscience, it is always at a risk. Even now, I carry in my briefcase a sermon preached by a leading minister in the city of Seattle. Tomorrow he will call me and ask that I take a public stand against an initiative to repeal a city ordinance that protects the rights of fair housing and fair employment for homosexuals. It is a lose-lose situation. If I stand for the civil rights of homosexuals, I will be accused of condoning their moral choices; but if I stand against their moral choice as sin, I will be lumped with those who would deny them even their human rights. On Tuesday, our city will divide over this issue. The tragedy is that neither time, energy, nor knowledge permit me to argue that the ordinance is badly written because it forces the voter to give the homosexual privilege as well as protection. Under the surface, however, is a more pervasive question, "How does a biblical Christian influence a secular society when the moral throne is empty?" I found myself humming Wesley's hymn,

> *I want a principle within*
> *Of watchful, godly fear,*
> *A sensibility of sin,*
> *A pain to feel it near.*

Did he not mean the moral standard of a Christian conscience honed by the Spirit of truth to convince the world of sin, righteousness, and judgment? How would you vote?

IV. *Practical holiness has at least one other contribution to our moral crisis and the evangelical awakening. Often neglected is the hope of the Spirit-filled life.*

Graham Greene, in his latest novel, *The Human Factor,* concludes his novel with a telephone conversation between the double agent who has been spirited to Russia after being discovered as a traitor to England, and his wife, who has been left behind. He says, "Will I see you again?" She answers, "Keep on hoping, keep on hoping." Greene then speaks theological volumes with the concluding sentence of his book, "But the line to Moscow was dead." Most evangelical writing today is optimistic about the prospects for saving men, but pessimistic about saving society. As Michael Novak described Lindsey's book, *The Late Great Planet Earth,* "He gave up on the world before God did."

Practical holiness has more hope. John Greenleaf Whittier wrote the poem "Abraham Davenport" in response to the famous day of darkness on May 19, 1780.

PERFECT LOVE CASTS OUT FEAR

When "a horror of great darkness" fell over the land, men prayed and women wept, listening for the "doom-blast of the trumpet" and looking for the "dreadful face of Christ." In the old statehouse of Connecticut, the lawgivers trembled and said, "It is the Lord's Great Day! Let us adjourn." But then they turned to Abraham Davenport, who cleaved the intolerable hush with a steady voice:

This well may be
The Day of Judgment which the world awaits;
But be it so or not, I only know
My present duty, and my Lord's command
To occupy till He come. So at the post
Where He hath set me in His providence,
I choose, for one, to meet Him face-to-face—
No faithless servant frightened from my task,
But ready when the Lord of the harvest calls;
And therefore, with all reverence, I would say,
Let God do His work, we will see to ours;
Bring in the candles.

Then, straight to the issue and with a dry natural sense of humor, Abraham Davenport debated an amendment to an act regulating shad and alewive fisheries:

And there he stands in memory to this day,
Erect, self-poised, a rugged face, half seen
Against the background of unnatural dark,
A witness to the ages as they pass,
That simple duty hath no place for fear.

How much that sounds like Peter's call to practical holiness when he wrote, "But sanctify the Lord God in your hearts: and be ready always to give an answer to every man that asketh you a reason of the hope that is in you, with meekness and fear" (1 Pet. 3:15).

With unnatural darkness above and trembling fear below, dare we say, "Bring in the candles!"

W. W. Clow

(1853-1930)

At the time this sermon was published (1916), W. W. Clow was professor of Christian ethics and practical training at the United Free Church College in Glasgow.

Two earlier books had acquainted a wide audience with his exceptional abilities as a preacher and writer: *The Cross in Christian Experience* and *Christ in the Social Order.*

The book of sermons from which this one is selected is addressed to what Professor Clow observed as a "missing note" in the preaching of his day—"the note of persuasive urgency." The church's message had become almost exclusively sociological, suggesting that "Christianity is little more than a movement for the social betterment of the people." The "work of an evangelist" had been neglected, and Clow intended to remedy, so far as he could, that neglect. "We are busy tending the flock," he wrote, but "we are less engrossed in seeking and saving the lost. That is why the note of urgency is not heard in the preacher's voice." Urgency is the dominant note struck in Clow's sermons.

The Evangel of the Strait Gate is more than a collection of sermons. When they are read carefully in sequence, the sermons therein constitute a veritable course in the meaning and message of evangelism.

While the sermons are urgent, they are also moderate. Dr. Clow recognizes the perilous temptation of the evangelist "to exaggerate, to dramatize, even to invent." The contents of his messages are not lacking in color, but they are scrupulously factual.

"The City of Desire" deals with the age-old question, "How can a society of peace, beauty, and justice be established and sustained?" Drawing upon the visions of prophets and apostles, Clow supplies the biblical answer: experienced holiness. Only when holiness pervades human character and behavior can society realize its ideals.

He interprets the vision of Zechariah that "displays holiness in three chief spheres of human energy"—work, worship, and the home. Unless common toil is sacred, a city's life will be corrupt. Unless worship is sincere, the hypocrisy of the temple will debase all aspects of life. Unless the home is holy, no other segment of society can be or will be. What is "the secret of it all"? The cleansing of the inner life by the indwelling presence of the Lord.

Holiness in its broadest dimensions, but with its source in the purified and dedicated heart, is the burden of this sermon, eloquent with simplicity of truth and diction and illustration.

The City of Desire*

In that day shall there be upon the bells of the horses, HOLINESS UNTO THE LORD . . . (Zech. 14:20-21).

The desire for a city of ordered well-being, secure peace, and gladdening beauty, has haunted the heart of all generations. Empire builders have striven to realize their conceptions in cities built beside pleasant waters, whose stately buildings, wide streets, and lovely gardens would shelter a people dwelling in felicity. Nineveh and Babylon, Athens and Rome, with many another city of the past, were founded to embody these high ideals. Yet they all failed. From their failure daring thinkers turned to describe their conceptions of a city yet to be. From Pythagoras and Plato to Sir Thomas More and William Morris they have imagined their Utopias from which poverty and pain should be banished, and sorrow and sighing should flee away. All these dreams have been nothing but dreams. The problem of the city of desire is with us still.

To the Hebrew prophets there came also this vision and passion

*Source: W. W. Clow, *The Evangel of the Strait Gate.* New York: George H. Doran Co., n.d.

of desire for a city of order and beauty. They discerned the fatal flaw in all past endeavors, and the blot on every fair dream. They knew that no city of enduring loveliness could be built upon a secular order and a material basis. They realized the truth that in all such cities there are inherent causes of corruption and decay. Neither conquest, nor a proud dominion, nor the regimen of iron laws can build and maintain a city of strength and peace.

The Hebrew prophets struck a new note in their ideal—the note of holiness. The city yet to be must be a city of God. When holiness is the supreme passion of the people, so that there shall be nothing secular, nothing unclean, nothing profane, in their thought and life, the city of secure peace and ordered well-being shall be built. That is the note which can be heard, clear and dominant, in every prophet.

HOLINESS UNDERGIRDS RIGHTEOUSNESS

Here, in rhythmic and insistent sentences, one of these prophets has set the truth in vivid and homely images. "In that day shall there be upon the bells of the horses, Holiness unto the Lord; and the pots in the Lord's house shall be like the bowls before the altar. Yea, every pot in Jerusalem and in Judah shall be holiness unto the Lord of hosts: and all they that sacrifice shall come and take of them, and seethe therein: and in that day there shall be no more the Canaanite in the house of the Lord of hosts."

That is the vision of the city of desire. When we analyze it we find it presents three pictures. It displays holiness in three chief spheres of human energy. The first is *the sphere of work;* the second is *the sphere of worship;* and the third is *the sphere of the home.* In the concluding sentence the prophet discloses the secret which lies behind the realization of this holiness.

I. First: *In the sphere of work.* "In that day shall there be upon the bells of the horses, HOLINESS UNTO THE LORD."

Jerusalem was built on an out-jutting spur of the central range of Palestine. It stands on a rocky bluff, bare, barren, on three sides almost inaccessible. Its people were crowded together in closely packed dwellings through which there ran its narrow streets. A garden was almost unknown within the walls. It was dependent for its daily bread upon the supplies brought into it every morning.

Across the brook Kidron, along the high road that ran north from Hebron and Bethlehem, up from the great plain, there came the caravans bearing the produce of the peasants who kept the city in food. As these beasts of burden made their way through the gates, the bells on their bridles made music on the morning air.

Now this trade of the carrier was, as it still is, one of the most perilous to a wisely ordered life. Then, as now, the men who conducted this traffic were often rude in their manners and ungentle in their speech. But the prophet sees them when holiness shall have become the dominant note of the city. He sees upon the bells of the horses the inscription which was engraved only on the high priest's mitre, "Holiness unto the Lord."

What is the meaning of that declaration? The prophet is affirming that a consecration rests upon this humble toil, and that the carrier has become a priest. The same inspiring conception of the priestliness of his service, the same sure sense of the presence of God which lifted up the high priest's heart, as he ministered in the Temple, were quick and living within the breast of the man who was busy in the meanest toil of the city.

HOLINESS FOR LAYMEN

That is where holiness must always be seen. The simplest of all sanctities is the sanctity of labor. If the men and women who carry on the city's industries are dishonest in their dealing, and unjust in their weight and balance, the city cannot endure in peace. Holiness must be engraved on the bells of the horses—on the least detail of every man's toil. The manufacturer must put his conscience into his product. He must put his heart into his dealing with his employees. The merchant must be a man of unfaltering uprightness with a spirit too high for greed, and too honorable to take any man at a disadvantage. The workman must be noble in his ideal and be inspired by a sense of honor in all his service. Any sloth or shirking, any mere eye service or lip service, any craving for a wage he has not earned, should be scorned by him as the breach of a solemn obligation. Holiness should be the mark of every turn of the hand. When this spirit of entire consecration rests upon men in the daily tasks of their common toil, the city of desire shall arise in peace and splendor. But whatever may have been the hopes of those who founded it, and the prayers of those who love it, the city which loses this note of sanctity in its labor shall pass into dust and bear the reproach of its shame.

A RIGHTEOUS FOUNDATION

Ruskin has set this truth in one of his prophetlike histories. It is the message he has enshrined in *The Stones of Venice.* He describes the high ideals, the self-denying industry, and the unfailing integrity of those who founded that ancient city. He records the poverty of their beginning and the sternness of their toil as they built their homes amid the marshes of the northern Adriatic. He ascribes the solemn thoughts which inspired their leaders and took shape alike in the ordered well-being of the people and in the noble artistry of their buildings.

He traces these back to that consecration to God which lifted up the heart of the humblest craftsmen, as well as the heart of the rulers. But the years came when a mean covetousness held the people in its sway. Venice became unfaithful to its ideal. Gross passions desecrated their hearts. Then Venice, once so powerful, still so fair, fell from her high dominion. One more city of desire broke the promise of its early nobility, because the note of holiness was not heard amid the sounds of its common toil.

II. Second: *In the sphere of worship.* "And the pots in the Lord's house shall be like the bowls before the altar."

The prophet passes from the highway into the Temple. He stands before the altar. He sees the bowls of costly beauty in which the sacrifices were seethed. These bowls were kept with peculiar care. But he remembered the pots, the common pots used in the menial offices of the Temple. These often lay in neglected corners, uncleansed and uncared for. But in that day when holiness shall be the dominant note, and there shall be nothing secular, nothing common, nothing profane, the very pots shall be as fit for sacrifice as the bowls of the priest's office. "The pots in the Lord's house shall be like the bowls before the altar."

ALL IS TO BE HOLY

It may seem strange that the prophet should insist on this note of holiness in worship. There at least it might be thought that holiness would be both the law and the attainment. But there is no place where it is so easy to be unreal as in the place of prayer, and there is no hour where we are so tempted to be insincere as the hour of worship. There may be a worship which is an idle show, a mere ceremonial, a sensuous delight. When the prophet condemned the vain oblations of the Hebrew people, and when Jesus rebuked the Pharisaic fastings and washings, [both] were uttering their reproach against an easy hypocrisy in worship.

The supreme grace of worship is to "worship [the Father] in spirit and in truth" (John 4:24). The supreme temptation is to be careful of the form, and heedless of the spirit; to be scrupulous that the outside is fair, and yet unmindful though the inward be foul; to give time and thought to the public observances, and neglect the hidden devotion of the private hour. We are all tempted to have regard to the bowls before the altar, and to neglect the pots of the Lord's house. It is well, it is altogether well, to care for the costly beauty of the house of prayer, the comely order of its services, and the melody of its music. Yet it is too easy to make our vows in sentences of chastened beauty, to offer our prayers in words of selected charm, to make our confessions in tones of pathetic cadences, yet to nurse our pride and our envy and our self-will, to have no care to the poor and castaway, and no zeal for the coming of the kingdom of God.

LOVING GOD SUPREMELY

We bow our heads in the house of prayer, but we fail to bow our hearts. We care for the bowls of the altar. We are heedless of the pots. Yet only when these searching realities and inward purities are regarded, and the spirit of truth shall pervade and penetrate every act of our worship, shall this dominant note of holiness become the inspiring music of every man who bows in the house of prayer.

HOLINESS OF HEART

Carlyle has set this truth in one of his touching reminiscences. He recalls the humble place of prayer in which his first worshiping hours were spent. He describes the peasant folk who gathered for worship, their little heath-thatched building, and the simple evangelist who was their teacher and guide. Then he is stirred to his tribute.

"That poor temple of my childhood is more sacred to me than the biggest cathedral then extant could have been; rude, rustic, bare, no temple in the world was more so. But there were sacred lambencies, tongues of authentic flame, which kindled what was best in one, what has not yet gone out."

There is the note of holiness in worship, and there is the testimony to its power. When these sacred lambencies shine upon the path of life, when these tongues of authentic flame fall upon those who pray, and enkindle their spiritual passion for holiness, they pass out of the house of God to build and to maintain, with pure hearts and honest hands, the city of desire. From the worship which has been [only] a ceremonial and a sensuous delight men pass out to that life of self-pleasing, self-will, and self-indulgence which corrupts the thoughts of the people and fills even the streets with the signs of moral decay.

III. Third: *In the sphere of the home.* "Yea, every pot in Jerusalem and in Judah shall be holiness unto the Lord of hosts: and all they that sacrifice shall come and take of them, and seethe therein."

The prophet passes from the Temple into the home. The home must ever be the true holy of holies. Whenever the chancel of the place of worship is holier in men's regard than the shrine within the home, the religion of the spirit is in peril. This prophet realizes that the home is the innermost sanctuary. He is drawing a picture of the housewife in her daily service.

He marks the vessels of her simple and homely labor. He sees this woman of the holy city keep these common pots in which she cooks her children's food clean and sweet with sedulous care. He points out the significance of the clean dish. For, mark it well, the care and the cleansing of the common utensil is always the sure mark of the conscientious and scrupulous conduct of the whole life of the home. Such is the keeping of her common vessels by this woman busy in the simple tasks of her life, that when the pilgrims crowd the streets, at the time of the Passover, they can take these pots and use them as bowls for the sacrifices. "All they that sacrifice shall come and take of them, and seethe therein."

HOLINESS IN THE HOME

That homely parable needs no exposition. The sanctity of labor and the sanctity of worship cannot be attained without the sanctity of the home. The holiness which does not consecrate the lowliest tasks of the household life is not the holiness of Christ. The fulfillment of the daily duties, the wearing drudgeries, and the constant sacrifices of the home constitutes a true priesthood to God. When the unfailing loyalties, the tender patiences, the pure affections, and above all the solemn and devout recollection of God and of His will, are cherished within the home, the men and women who build the city of desire will be found coming forth in the strength of the enduement of the Spirit of God.

TO CHILDREN'S CHILDREN

How clear and how universal is the testimony to this truth! It can be found on the lips of men in all ranks of life. Take up Matthew Arnold's record of the life and intercourse of his father's household, and you will understand not only the tradition of Rugby School, but the wistful and eager devotion that never died out of the heart of his son. Read the witness to the prayerfulness of the father of John G. Paton, and mark the atmosphere of a home maintained amid the demands of a constant frugality which was nevertheless potent with the power of God's

Spirit. Acquaint yourself with the story of the home out of which John Cairns came, bearing the stamp of its tender and unfaltering goodness, so that men marked its impress in his humility of bearing, and heard the echoes of its counsels in his prayers. Remember the picture by our Scottish national poet, the most beautiful among all the transcripts of gleaming beauty that Robert Burns has written, of that home where "the priest and father" made his fireside the shrine of fellowship with God. Better still, recall that home in Nazareth where Joseph and Mary lifted up the eyes of the infant Jesus until He knew it to be the place of the presence of God.

There is no holier memory that any man here can recall than the home in whose atmosphere he inbreathed the Spirit of God. There is no higher social service for any man and woman than to build and maintain a home in which young hearts shall be brought up in the faith and fear of God, and young hands guided into an obedience to His will. The kingdom of God comes out of homes which are holy as the home of Nazareth, and without these it will never come at all. When we have attained the sanctity of the home, the city of desire will arise around us.

IV. The prophet, as he concludes, touches *the secret of it all.* "And in that day there shall be no more the Canaanite in the house of the Lord of hosts."

The word Canaanite stands here for all that is alien to God, hostile to His will, defiling to His people. The Canaanite within the house of the Lord was the open mark of degradation. The city that could receive and permit the Canaanite within its holy place was no longer loyal to God. In its heart it was a rebel to His commandments.

ALL UNHOLINESS TO BE CLEANSED

Recall the arresting proof of that truth in the story of the cleansing of the Temple by Jesus. He had come up to Jerusalem at the beginning of His ministry. He made His way to the house of the Lord. It was a place not only of peculiar sanctity, but of special delight to Him. He had called it, in His youth, "My Father's house." At a glance the disloyalty of the people and the corruption of their faith broke upon Him. He found the Canaanite in the house of the Lord. The traders had edged in from without the gate and set up their bargaining within the sanctuary. In an act prophetic of His ministry, He made His scourge of small cords. He overthrew the tables of the money changers, drove out the polluting cattle, and scourged these desecrating traffickers out of the Temple. With the Canaanite in the holy place there could be no city of God.

We have no Temple up to which men go for sacrifice. The day of the Temple has passed away, for God's holy place is the house of the soul. "[Ye are] the temple of the Holy Ghost" (1 Cor. 6:19). But there the Canaanite can still be found. There, a defiant self-will, a merciless greed, a self-indulgence which descends to baser passions, and a constant rebellion against truth and purity, still carry on their commerce. We must cast out and cleanse the temple of the soul, before holiness can be the note of our work, and our worship, and our home, and the city of desire shall be built.

UNHOLY ATTITUDES

What we need is not a new special order and more drastic statutes of reform, although these may have their place. What we need is not increased wealth, larger leisure, and more frequent pleasures. These may have their value. But all of these shall issue only in that corruption which has been the grave of every other civilization, unless the temple of the soul shall be the shrine of the Spirit of God and the Canaanite cast out from it. Then there shall be no mean streets, no base trades, no defrauded laborers, no neglected poor, no heedless pride or pitiless apathy in the face of pain and weakness and sorrow.

FILLED AND CLEANSED

In the last vision of the Book of Revelation we have another seer's vision of the city of desire. He chords in perfect harmony with the dominant note of this Old Testament prophet. We are sometimes caught by the glowing pictures and the poetic figures of his message until we forget and ignore his secret. But the truth he emphasizes is this. Not by building men's homes amid garden beauty, not by filling their mouths with bread, not by the stern rigor of laws, and not by an ascetic obedience, shall the city of God arise. The secret is set in the words, "And there shall in no wise enter into it any thing that defileth, neither whatsoever worketh abomination, or maketh a lie: but they which are written in the Lamb's book of life" (21:27).

HOLINESS BECOMETH THINE HOUSE, O LORD

Only as a moral purity shall control all life, and the source and secret of every impulse shall be a faith in God, can the city of holiness be built. To men and cities alike there comes the appeal of the impassioned Psalmist, "Lift up your heads, O ye gates; and be ye lift up, ye everlasting doors; and the King of glory shall come in" (24:7, cf. 9). When the King of Glory comes into the temple of the soul, the city of desire will be built. Then and not till then.

9

PROCLAIMING HOLINESS

James Henry Potts

(1848-1942)

When I was a very young minister, there came into my hands a set of books called *The Methodist Pulpit.* These slender volumes were authored by various Methodist preachers, some whose names were well known, but most of them men who served their generation and passed into obscurity—as most of us will. To me, this enhanced the importance of reading what they had preached, gathering the wheat into the granary, and leaving the chaff on pages to which I never returned.

Among them, Potts' sermon on the purpose of preaching had a salutary and encouraging effect upon my own ministry. However, I have not included it in this collection out of sentiment, but for better reasons.

It is addressed to those who are responsible for preaching the Word of God, and it exhorts them plainly and earnestly to make the holiness of their people the object of their task.

While Potts was specifically addressing colleagues in the ministry of the Methodist church, his message is relevant to all of us who labor in what is generally termed "the holiness movement."

"The great purpose of preaching," says Potts in his opening statement, "is to perfect Christian character." Those who follow Christ are commanded to "be perfect by having [their] hearts emptied of sin and filled with love." In pursuing a ministry that stresses the possibility of holiness, we imitate Paul, who "desired

that all his parishioners be sanctified wholly," and who "regarded this wonderful doctrine as the crowning glory of the gospel."

That a holy heart and life are now possible, Potts insists, is the teaching of Scripture and of historic Methodism. "There never would have been a Methodist church, but for the Bible doctrine and experience of perfect love." Those who scoff at the doctrine must be warned, but those who proclaim it must not be intimidated by any measure of opposition.

In a manner reminiscent of John Wesley's insistence upon "living witnesses," Potts closes the message by citing the experiences of a Northern Methodist, Alfred Cookman, and a Southern Methodist, W. B. Godbey; both became notable figures in the promotion of holiness.

Potts closes with direct application and appeal: "As ministers we need this experience. It will make our preaching effective." A revival of the holiness pulpit is a consummation devoutly to be wished!

The Purpose of Preaching*

> *Whom we preach, warning every man, and teaching very man in all wisdom; that we may present every man perfect in Christ Jesus* (Col. 1:28).

The great purpose of preaching is to perfect Christian character. "He gave some, apostles; and some, prophets; and some, evangelists; and some, pastors and teachers; for the perfecting of the saints" (Eph. 4:11-12).

The faithful preacher warns every sinner and instructs every believer that each may be delivered from sin and fully established in grace. Sometimes we talk about ministers being called to preach, but the real call is to save men by preaching. Evangelism is the supreme business of the Christian life. . . .

A test of the Church's vigor is its power to propagate itself. It must win friends from its foes, regenerate their hearts, transform their lives, and set them to work to win others. A vigorous church is a

---

*Source: James Henry Potts, *The Upward Leading,* in *The Methodist Pulpit, Second Series.* Cincinnati: Jennings and Graham; New York: Eaton and Mains, 1905.

growing church, a church allied to God, consecrated to His truth, and united with Him in works of mercy and love.

By the church we mean the ministers as well as members, and the members as well as ministers. There are no ranks or orders in grace. . . . You remember that when Paul gave instruction to Timothy, he told him to look out for his character first, and then to his beliefs. "Take heed unto thyself, and unto the doctrine; continue in them: for in doing this thou shalt both save thyself, and them that hear thee" (1 Tim. 4:16). Ministers need to save themselves as well as to save others, and the minister who is himself abundantly saved is the one most likely to inspire other believers to seek an uttermost salvation.

UTTERMOST SALVATION

The mission of Jesus Christ into this world is to save men. "Thou shalt call his name Jesus: for he shall save his people from their sins" (Matt. 1:21); not *in* their sins but *from* their sins.

"Ye know that he was manifested to take away our sins; and in him is no sin" (1 John 3:5). Pilate examined Jesus closely and said, "I find no fault in this man" (Luke 23:4). His bitterest enemies were obliged to conjure up objections to His character that they might have pretext for putting Him to death.

Jesus was sinless. "Which of you convinceth me of sin?" (John 8:46). Yet . . . He lived a life of prayer . . . and was humbly dependent on His Father. Having set such an example, He said, "Follow me." "Every one that is perfect shall be as his master" (Luke 6:40). "Be ye therefore perfect, even as your Father which is in heaven is perfect" (Matt. 5:48). Be perfect by having your hearts emptied of sin and filled with love. . . . He does not command us to attain to divine perfection, nor to angelic perfection, nor even to ideal perfection as men, but to have the love of God so enthroned within our hearts that our characters and lives will exemplify it in all relations. Jesus commanded us to love God with *all our hearts,* and our neighbors as ourselves. This is perfect love.

PERFECT LOVE

Jesus said to the young man . . . "If thou wilt be perfect, go and sell [all] that thou hast, and give to the poor" (Matt. 19:21). The particular thing in his case which was keeping him from the fullness of the divine life he was to put away. With some it is property; with others, pleasure; with others, sinful tempers; with others, acquired selfishness; but whatever may mar our perfection as disciples of the Lord Jesus we are to put away.

Many stagger at the term perfection in Christianity; because they think that what is implied in it is inconsistent with a state of probation, and savors of pride and presumption; but, as Dr. Adam Clarke says, "We must take good heed how we stagger at any word of God; and much more how we deny or fritter away the meaning of any of His sayings, lest He reprove us, and we be found liars before Him." . . . There is but one passage in all Paul's writings which can be construed as a confession that he himself was not a perfect Christian. Here it is: "Not as though I had already attained, either were already perfect; but I follow after, if that I may apprehend that for which also I am apprehended of Christ Jesus. Brethren, I count not myself to have apprehended: but this one thing I do, forgetting those things which are behind, and reaching forth unto those things which are before, I press toward the mark for the prize of the high calling of God in Christ Jesus" (Phil. 3:12-14).

CHRISTIAN PERFECTION

The meaning of this passage all turns upon what Paul considered "the prize." The context shows that . . . the glory of the resurrection life was the "prize" he was seeking. And he adds, "Let us therefore, as many as be perfect, be thus minded" (v. 15). The plain meaning of the entire passage is that, in reference to the experiences beyond his mortal career, he had not yet attained, but he "followed after," while in the present experience of grace he, with others, was "perfect." Our Lord used similar language in reference to His earthly humiliation: "I do cures to day and to morrow, and the third day I shall be perfected" (Luke 13:32).

Paul presented in his experience all the characteristics of a perfected Christian life. He had a contented mind, a humble heart, a pure conscience, a burning love for God and souls, a submissive disposition, a fruitful life, and a readiness to meet death.

There is only one recorded incident in his whole career that can be construed as contrary to the doctrine of scriptural holiness, and that incident occurred when he was on trial for his life (Acts 23:1-5). But I have never blamed him much for the spirited rebuke he administered to Ananias. This was an instance in which he could be angry and sin not. Besides, when reminded of his alleged offense, he offered his apology, thereby showing himself to be a perfect gentleman as well as a perfect Christian.

LOVE CAN APOLOGIZE

Paul did not believe in willful sinning. He declared that "all have sinned, and come short of the glory of God" (Rom. 3:23); but he speaks of believers as having been "made free from sin, and become servants to God," and as having "fruit unto holiness, and the end everlasting life" (6:22). He could say with John, "He that committeth sin is of the devil" (1 John 3:8). Hear this, ye who make light of this gracious doctrine and plead for sin as a necessity in human nature and consistent with the Christian name.

FREEDOM FROM SIN

He who deliberately sins is a servant of Satan and thereby proves that the spirit of the devil is in him, and not the Spirit of Christ, for Christ came to destroy the works of the devil. The devil sinneth from the beginning. He was the father of sin. He brought sin into the world and maintains sin by living in the hearts of those who do not resist him, leading them into transgression and persuading them that there is no deliverance from sin in this life.

Sin is the only thing which mars Christian perfection. The inevitable mistakes of frail humanity do not necessarily rob us of holiness. The innumerable temptations to which we are subject do not necessarily spot our characters. Sin is in yielding.

Yield not to temptation,
For yielding is sin.

St. Augustine defined temptation as a thought, an imagination, a delight, an assent. Temptation is easy to resist at the first two points, but difficult afterward. Sin is transgression. It is the willful, reckless violation of a known law. The true Christian does not sin. "Whosoever abideth in him sinneth not: whosoever sinneth hath not seen him, neither known him" (1 John 3:6).

Christian perfection is no more or less than deliverance from the disposition to commit sin; that is, to disobey God, and the enjoyment of that inward fullness of the blessing of the gospel of Christ which is promised to all believers. To be filled with God is a great thing; to be filled with the fullness of God is still greater; but to be filled with all the fullness of God is the greatest of all, and is the highest mark of Christian character on earth.

FOR ALL CHRISTIANS

The conception of the possibility of such a life, and the recognition of it as taught in the Scriptures, is what gave distinction to the Wesleys and the early Methodists. . . . Wesley viewed Christianity as a scheme for perfect redemption, and the doctrine of perfect love became the formal principle of his theology. "It," he says, "is the grand depositum which God has given to the people called Methodists, and chiefly to propagate this, it appears, God has raised them up." Methodism was born to propagate this truth. . . . There never would have been a Methodist church, but for the Bible doctrine and experience of perfect love. . . .

The early Methodists were as much distinguished by their earnestness in seeking sanctification by faith, as a distinct work of grace, as they were by seeking justification by faith. Holiness was pressed upon them by the preachers as their present privilege, and the preachers in turn were urged by Mr. Wesley to "preach perfection to believers constantly, urgently, and explicitly." In a letter to Mrs. Bennis he said of a certain brother: "I hope he is not ashamed to preach full salvation, receivable now by faith. This is the word which God will *always bless,* and which the devil peculiarly hates; therefore he is constantly stirring up both his own children and the weak children of God against it."

PREACHING

In a letter to another he said that "if a man is not a thorough friend to Christian perfection he will easily puzzle others, and thereby weaken, if not destroy, any select society." He said further: "If we can prove that any of our local preachers or leaders, either directly or indirectly, speak against this doctrine, let him be a local preacher or leader no longer. I doubt whether he should continue in the society; because he that can speak thus in our congregations cannot be an honest man."

In his sermons and exhortations Mr. Wesley always presented this theme in its most attractive and beautiful light. More than one-half of the hymns he composed are upon the subject of holiness. He never faltered, even to his dying day, either in public or private, in exhorting the people to expect pardon or holiness *today,* and not *tomorrow.* And I believe that, were he alive today and ministering to this great American church, he would proclaim this truth just as strongly, fearlessly, and clearly as he did in England more than a century ago. Nothing would daunt him. Opposition would only inflame his zeal, and persecution would only settle him in the conviction that men need holiness to keep them from being fiends. Mr. Wesley desired his ministers to continue to preach holiness to the end of time.

IN A MOMENT

Dr. Adam Clarke said that if the Methodists gave up preaching entire sanctification, they would soon lose their glory. "This fitness," said he, "to appear before God, and thorough preparation for eternal glory, is what I plead for, pray for, and heartily recommend to all true believers."

Bishop Asbury, writing to Henry Smith, said: "Preach sanctification directly and indirectly in every sermon." To another he exclaimed: "O, purity! O, Christian perfection! O, sanctification! It is heaven below to feel all sin removed. Preach it, whether they will hear or forbear. Preach it!"

Dr. Lovick Pierce, in a sermon before the Southern Methodist General Conference, reflected that "just so far as our church has ceased to believe in entire sanctification and to seek after it . . . just so far are we a corrupt and God-forsaken church. . . ." This is true. . . .

True, some will scoff at this doctrine. These we must "warn." Dangerous is the condition of that man who can make light of, or sneer at, a doctrine which is calculated to take us out from the grip of the devil and fit us for companionship with God and the angels. Others will listen in respectful silence, or eagerly inquire for more of the truth. These we are to "teach in all wisdom." My own experience is that all earnest Christians are waiting and hoping for fearless presentation by all ministers of the deep things of God.

TEACHING

But who is sufficient? Any minister can study this doctrine and, in Bible figure and language, present it to his people for their edification. He is best fitted, however, who knows the truth, not only in mind but in heart, and can urge forward all seekers in the path which he himself hath trod, saying, "Follow me, as I follow Christ." Wonderful is the power which this experience gives to every minister of Christ!

Let me present two witnesses, one from each of the two leading branches of Methodism.

Speaking of his sanctification, Dr. Alfred Cookman wrote: "The evidence in my case was as direct and indubitable as the witness of sonship vouchsafed at the time of my adoption into the family of heaven. Need I say that the experience of sanctification inaugurated a new epoch in my religious life? Some of the characteristics of this higher life were blessed rest in Jesus, a clearer and more abiding experience of purity through the blood of the Lamb. What a conscious union and constant communion with God; what increased power to do and to suffer the will of my Father, a steadier growth in grace; what delight in the Master's service; what fear to grieve the infinitely Holy Spirit; what love for and desire to be with those who love holiness; what access and confidence in prayer; what interest and comfort in religious conversation; what illumination and joy in the perusal of the blessed Word; what increased unction and power in the pulpit!"

ASSURANCE

Dr. W. B. Godbey, of the Kentucky Conference, Methodist Episcopal Church, South, who had a clear conversion and an unmistakable call to the ministry, says that after his conversion he wandered in the wilderness 19 years, during 15 of which he preached the gospel, his heart incessantly the scene of a terrible civil war. But in 1858 he was sent to a circuit where he found some people who enjoyed more religion than he did. He soon found they were praying for him. But he had no sympathy with the doctrine of holiness as a distinct experience, and regarded its advocates as fanatics. But the Holy Spirit led him into the light.

WITNESSING

"My weary soul," he says, "found rest, happy rest, in the arms of Jesus. And where now is the war? The battle is fought, the victory is won, the field is silent. Fifteen years have rolled away since that Pentecostal baptism, but the sacred fire still flashes from the crown of my head to the soles of my feet. My ministerial character has undergone a radical revolution. I was never before a revivalist, but since that memorable epoch 5,000 souls have professed conversion and several sanctifications at my meetings."

These testimonies are clear. They speak a tremendous fact in possible Christian experience. They argue no theory and specify no method, but they do set forth a condition happy to occupy and blessed in its convergences.

As ministers we need this experience. It will make our preaching effective. It is the basis of pulpit triumph. David prayed for it (Ps. 51:10-13), knowing that, with his own heart clean, he could teach transgressors the law and lead sinners into saving grace.

"Be ye clean, that bear the vessels of the Lord" (Isa. 52:11). Be ye innocent that warn others of guilt. Be ye rescued that lift danger signals before the eyes of the perishing.

George D. Watson

(1845-1924)

George D. Watson devoted years to the promotion of holiness as a minister in the Methodist Episcopal church, but the persistent opposition of church leaders to the doctrine, and to the movement for its spread, finally drove him to the Wesleyan Methodist Connection, where he remained for the last 28 years of his life. He died in 1924.

Watson entered into an experience of heart holiness in 1876. As God plied his soul with questions that tested his commitment, Watson was enabled to surrender completely to the will of God, whatever that might cost, wherever it might lead. He consented to do all for God's glory, to accept the poorest appointments without complaint, and to give up tobacco, with which he had fought a losing battle. From that consecration he did not retreat, and the divine response was a cleansing and energizing baptism with the Spirit that made Watson an influential holiness preacher.

It was Watson, along with William McDonald, who conducted the revival meeting in Los Angeles, in 1884, during which Phineas Bresee experienced "a transformed condition of life and blessing and unction and glory" that brought a new element of power into his ministry and eventuated in the founding of the Church of the Nazarene.

Along with his activities in the National Holiness Association, George Watson was a prolific writer, bequeathing to the holiness movement a number of influential books.

From one of them, *Love Abounding,* this message is taken.

Watson explores a Pentecostal emblem, the tongue of fire, in its relation to God, to our fellowmen, and to our personal Christian lives. He interprets the tongue of fire as the instrument of God that (1) glorifies Christ, (2) convicts sinners, and (3) strengthens believers. He is emphatic in the necessity of testimony to the experience of entire sanctification.

Against this practice much of the opposition to the work of promoting holiness was focused. As Watson points out, however, the early Christians were not martyred for living holy lives, but for speaking out as fire-baptized witnesses for Jesus Christ. Satan has not persecuted a quiet holiness that does not identify its source, but has savagely opposed holiness proclaimed and witnessed aloud and abroad. Believers must combine deeds with words in order to honor Christ as the origin of holiness and to guide others into the experience of holiness.

In our day, a declining witness to the experience gives forceful relevance to Watson's message.

Tongues of Fire*

There appeared unto them cloven tongues like as of fire, and it sat upon each of them (Acts 2:3).

The visible tongue of fire that sat upon each of the 120 in the Upper Room was but the outward badge of an inward reality, for the next verse says that they all spoke "with other tongues, as the Spirit gave them utterance."

The tongue is the most complete and powerful organ of expression with which the soul is armed. It is the chief organ through which the heart and mind reveal their contents and communicate themselves. Every form of thought, every mode of reason, every shape of passion, every emotion of pain or joy, all alike reveal themselves through the tongue. . . . It is the chief weapon of evil in the world, communicating sin, arousing sin in others, and setting "on fire the

---

*Source: George D. Watson, *Love Abounding*. Boston and Chicago: McDonald, Gill, and Co., 1891.

course of nature; and it is set on fire of hell" (James 3:6). It is the chief organ of good—preeminently the instrument of the gospel.

There have been two great epochs in the history of the human tongue; one of cursing and one of transfiguration. In Gen. 11:7 . . . God said, "Let us go down, and there confound their language, that they may not understand one another's speech." That event and this one in the second chapter of Acts stand related to each other as the frigid and torrid zones of moral character. With the tower builders the Holy Spirit was utterly rejected; with the Pentecostal company the Spirit was cordially and fully received.

In both instances we see miracles wrought on the tongue, but in both instances the reason for and the conditions of the miracle lay behind the tongue in the depths of the heart; and the same things practically occur today. When people's hearts utterly reject the divine Spirit, it is still true that upon moral and religious questions such persons speak rashly, ignorantly, incoherently, contradictorily; all their talk on religion is but a babble of nonsense and a confusion of language.

And it is still true that when the heart is purified and filled with the Holy Spirit, the tongue will speak with wonderful accuracy and unity upon religious subjects, even though the person be untutored; out of a heart full of light and love there will come forth a speech that is not contradictory, but in perfect agreement with itself and with the Word of God. So . . . the two great miracles of Babel and Pentecost are still perpetuated.

INDWELLING SIN CAUSES DIVISIONS

The reason why there are so many divergent teachings in religion, and contradictory theologies, is because they proceed from the darkness of indwelling sin. If the hearts of all religious teachers were perfectly sanctified from native depravity, and filled with the Holy Ghost, it would unify their tongues, so that, in the language of Paul, they would all speak the same things on matters of essential truth; the babbling theologies would be swept away, the scattered dialects of religious truth would come into agreement, and instead of each one speaking according to the tongue of old Adam, they would all speak with another tongue as the truth is in Christ Jesus.

This tongue of fire in all its essential power is designed to be the normal state of the Church during the Spirit's dispensation, and is essential to the vital purpose of true religion. Let us notice how this tongue of fire is related to God, to our fellowmen, and to ourselves.

I. *The tongue of fire is related to God as the chief instrument of glorifying the work of Jesus and proclaiming His wondrous work in the soul.*

It is the office of the Christian tongue to be a witness for God; a simple, straightforward, unbiased witness to the work or works that God has wrought in the soul. This does not imply that its office is always to make a set speech or take the place of a teacher, or to attempt explaining the philosophy and processes of the work of grace . . . nor is it in all cases the office of the tongue of fire to formally preach or expound Scripture. Not all of the 120 became teachers, for the Holy Ghost selected those who should teach; but all were witnesses of the marvelous facts that had transpired in their consciousness.

WITNESSING

It was only the work of God which they magnified on that occasion: there was no allusion to the mere works of man. There is nothing in creation that can so glorify God as the human tongue anointed of the Holy Ghost. The tongue of formalists, Pharisees, and backsliders invariably glorify self in a disguised manner, and if their religious talk be accurately reported, you will find very little mention of the saving power of Jesus. But the tongue of fire reports the supernatural; it tells of conscious pardon, or regeneration, of conscious cleansing from indwelling sin, of the destruction of vicious appetites; it reports the incoming of perfect peace where all was storm and disorder; it reports the incoming of light and discernment utterly beyond the natural mind; it proclaims in one and the same breath the utter weakness of self and the imparted strength from God; it minifies self and magnifies grace; it glorifies not only the work of God, but the highest work—that kind of work which other people fail to see or appreciate.

GOD'S SANCTIFYING WORK

The highest and finest work which God is carrying on is in human hearts. God's work in nature is great and marvelous, and many are the poets and philosophers who have swept their harps in praise of the wonders of external creation. God's work in judgment is sublime and terrible, and the artist has joined with the prophet in defining these judgments. But higher than all the works of external nature, higher than all the works of judgment, is the work of salvation in the soul. The transforming of a sinner into a saint; melting down the rugged mountains of sin in the heart, and turning it into a garden of Eden, where the fruit of the Spirit blooms and grows—this is a work that none can see or know so well as those who experience it; and this work is reported by the tongue of testimony. "The spirit of the Lord spake by me, and his word was in my tongue" (2 Sam. 23:2). "My tongue shall speak of thy righteousness and of thy praise all the day long" (Ps. 35:28). "While I was musing the fire burned: then spake I with my tongue" (Ps. 39:3).

The tongue of fire glorifies the blood of Jesus and praises God's work on the Cross above all His works in nature or law. . . . God's saving work is His highest work; therefore the tongue of fire has a theme more honoring to God than otherwise all the tongues of men or angels could have.

II. *The tongue of fire is related to our fellowmen. It is the divinely ordained instrument of convincing them of the reality of God's work in the soul, and of their need of it.*

The most essential thing in saving men is to convince them to the heart that God can work in them salvation from sin, and show them their need of it; and this is the sphere of power that is given to the witnessing believer. The witnessing tongue is God's chief method of saving the world. . . . A clear, truthful testimony to an inward work of God is a trumpet blast to the conscience of the hearer; it puts you on a divine vantage ground, and they have no weapon to parry that sword of the Spirit.

POWER

When we speak from the plane of our natural faculties, we are on a level with men, and they can resist with the same implements; but when we are conscious of a divine deliverance from guilt and sin, and we speak out of that supernatural experience, we are speaking from an elevated position, we are speaking in the Spirit, and such testimony is the Spirit's chosen weapon to pierce the heart of the unsaved and lead them to Christ.

WITNESS BY LIFE AND WORD

Nor can a silent life of perfect propriety and outward decorum form a substitute for the witnessing tongue of fire. The cant phrase so often heard, that we are to live holiness and say nothing about it, is a lie that Satan has palmed off on a backslidden church, right in the face of hundreds of scriptures to the contrary. A dumb Christian is a dead Christian. Were it possible to live a sort of angelic life without testimony, it would be robbing God of His due, and taking all the glory to self, for everyone would credit you with making yourself angelic; and unless you report the miracle of grace wrought in your soul, how would the world know where you got your virtues from? Jesus said, "We speak that we do know, and testify that we have seen" (John 3:11). The Pentecostal baptism was preeminently designed to make witnesses: "Ye shall receive power . . . ye shall be witnesses unto me" (Acts 1:8).

The word "martyr" means a witness; and since the world began, God's people have been persecuted and slain, not for living holy, but for testimony. The reason why Satan hates testimony . . . and the reason he stirs up the ungodly world and cold, carnal professors to hate it so, is because it is the greatest agency for tearing down his kingdom and spreading the salvation of Jesus. Every . . . objection to Christian testimony, to relating what God has done in the heart, is either directly or indirectly from the devil. . . . Christ was crucified, not for living holy, but because He testified He was the Son of God. St. John was banished to Patmos, not because he lived a saintly life, but "for the word of God, and for the testimony of Jesus Christ" (Rev. 1:9).

In the early days of Christianity, and in the great revival under Wesley, and in the modern revival of sanctification, it has been and is testimony to personal experience which has been the most powerful factor in spreading the kingdom of God.

III. *The tongue of fire sustains an intimate and essential relation with our own life and experience.*

TESTIMONY STRENGTHENS FAITH

In seeking the Lord, when the soul utters itself in vocal prayer, it soon breaks the chains that bind it. The soul is so constituted that it needs to express itself in speech. Testifying to our experience wonderfully strengthens and girds the soul, by publicly committing us to the truth we have espoused. It is the means by which we cut the shorelines and launch boldly upon a life of faith; it develops moral vertebrae, and enables us to take a firm stand, which is a wonderful factor in religion. Trying to live an experience which we are not willing to confess is the very essence of moral cowardice; it destroys the spinal column of the soul; it makes us timid, easily frightened, excessively conservative, and turns us into miserable jellyfish sort of Christians. This is the very cause of the modern church producing a mass of soft, vague sentimentalism, instead of the sturdy Christianity of . . . Pentecost. For our own self-preservation we need to run our flag to the masthead, take a bold stand, and by our testimony commit ourselves thoroughly to scriptural holiness, with all its concomitants.

Again, by a clear, definite testimony we please God and receive in return from Him wonderful effusions of His Spirit. The Holy Ghost is ever poured out upon the brave and true witness. In multitudes of cases believers have stepped out by naked faith on the promise for cleansing, and while testifying to their faith, have been filled unutterably with the Spirit of God.

Furthermore . . . testimony in some form or other constitutes the largest part of Christian life. The stale adage of "living it" without talking it is an absolute contradiction. The greater part of every life is speech. How do we know anger or gentleness, benevolence or hatred, piety or wickedness, except through the tongue? Persons often say that they were led to Christ by some pious mother or friend, not so much by what they talked as by what they lived; but such persons do not speak accurately. How could they have felt a mother's kindness or love except through the mother's words and tones of the voice? If Christians were dumb, how could their meek and patient tempers be distinguished from the tempers of the oxen or dumb brutes around us? . . . To repudiate Christian testimony is to do away with the largest part of the soul's life, so far as the expression of that life is concerned.

LIVE IT—BUT ALSO TELL IT

Finally, Christian testimony is the natural ventilator of the heart. It prevents the fires of holy love from choking. The heart is so constituted that its affections are maintained and enlarged by being expressed. Just as a fire will die unless it has a draught of air passing through it, so the fire of grace in the heart will die unless ventilated in speech. The thoughts in the mind are never perfect until shaped in some form of expression. This great law is understood by poets, philosophers, and artists. What a calamity to the Christian world that the professed children of light are not as wise in their generation as the children of this world! How many thousands have lost the experience of heart purity by failing to give God the glory in definite testimony to His work? "With the heart man believeth unto righteousness [or holiness]; and with the mouth confession is made unto salvation" (Rom. 10:10).

EXPRESSION DEEPENS EXPERIENCE

The heart and tongue are so intimately connected that the faith of the one and the testimony of the other are like the two wings to a bird; deprived of either, the soul beats itself helplessly against the ground, unable to rise into those broad, bright regions which God has so amply provided for its freedom and flight. He who attempts to testify with his mouth what is not in his heart will be but a sounding brass and tinkling cymbal, and he who attempts to live in the heart what he refuses to confess with his mouth will soon have nothing to live.

A. Wingrove Taylor
(1923—)

In 1968 the National Holiness Association held its centennial convention in Cleveland. The theme of this historic convention was "Projecting Our Heritage." Among those who addressed the convention was Wingrove Taylor, presently general superintendent of the Wesleyan Holiness church, whose office is in Barbados, West Indies.

At that time Taylor was president of Caribbean Pilgrim College, Barbados. His earlier assignments, after graduating from God's Bible School, included both pastoral and evangelistic ministries.

His message spoke directly and powerfully to church leaders facing the challenge of a chaotic period. The turbulent '60s brought to many world areas, and especially to the United States, an unprecedented revolt by the young against all forms of institutional authority. Tradition was dismissed cavalierly and violently by advocates of radical change, and their ideas and goals did not leave the church uninfluenced or unscarred.

Taylor invited the convention to face without blinking these sweeping changes, and to accept the challenge of projecting to the new generation a heritage that cannot be surrendered, because it is grounded squarely upon God's unchanging principles.

The burning eloquence of his preaching cannot be captured in print. Something of his gentle spirit and invincible faith does penetrate this medium, however, and makes this imaginative and impassioned sermon a call to resolute and believing action.

The sermon is structured simply: (1) Our challenge, which is created by "new kings" unaware of and unsympathetic with our heritage; (2) Our courage, supplied by the eternal King whose purposes, principles, promises, and power may be denied and resisted but cannot be overcome.

The simplicity of the structure and the sincerity of the preacher united to produce a telling effect.

God's Unchanging Principles*

Now a new king arose over Egypt, who did not know Joseph (Exod. 1:8, Amp.).

We are surely not so naive as to think that our holiness heritage will be effortlessly projected. There are real problems, including a group of people suggested by this scripture: "Now a new king arose over Egypt, who did not know Joseph."

The first chapter of his record is negative: he knew not Joseph. This brief statement . . . brings to mind a series of unfortunate inferences. Pharaoh did not know purity, humility, holy dreams, magnanimity, marital faithfulness, cheerfulness, patience, kindness, forgiveness, nor faith. Our hearts ought to be deeply burdened for . . . "new kings" who have no experiential knowledge of the blessed Trinity, who do not know true repentance, genuine conversion, and entire sanctification. . . .

Whatever doubts we may have concerning the implications of the new Pharaoh not knowing Joseph are completely swept away when we read the second chapter of his record, which is positive. He knew envy. Carnal comparisons burned like fire in his heart: "He said unto his people, Behold, the . . . children of Israel are more and mightier than we." He knew craftiness: "Come on, let us deal wisely [cunningly] with them." He knew suspicion: ". . . lest they multiply, and it come to pass, that, when there falleth out any war, they join also unto our enemies, and fight against us, and so get them up out of the land" (vv. 9-10). He knew malice, fear, tyranny, murder, and bestiality. The presence of such traits should not be too surprising, for in moral and

*Source: Myron F. Boyd and Merne A. Harris, comps., *Projecting Our Heritage.* Kansas City: Beacon Hill Press of Kansas City, 1969.

spiritual matters where there is a frightening negative there is most likely to be a foul positive. . . .

Such was Pharaoh's record. What was the reason for this? . . . He may have suffered historical starvation. Four hundred years or more stretched between Joseph's day and . . . the new king. How easy it is to get out of touch with the past! Against the dark background of a recent assassination [Dr. Martin Luther King, Jr.], the bold outlines of racial conflict seem more blood-red. Sociologists and other scientists struggle to find the solution. In agony of spirit, Joseph H. Smith no doubt voiced the answer. He wept over the failure of the holiness movement to minister to "our brothers in black." Without meaning to add hurt to already bleeding hearts, I might comment tenderly. It does seem that you have taken holiness to the West Indies, to Africa, and other lands, but perhaps you have not done as much as you should have for the black man in North America. . . .

FAILED PROCLAMATION

Another suggestion could be that the new king was guilty of willful rejection, that he purposely refused to be governed by the righteous principles and sound policies of the past. To Belshazzar, who persisted in debauchery although he knew his father's history, Daniel's straightforward message was, "Thou his son . . . hast not humbled thine heart, though thou knewest all this" (5:22). . . . How many mothers and fathers have been brokenhearted over sons and daughters who, knowing the God of their parents, have deliberately rejected Him!

. . . the new king may have been disillusioned by Israelitish corruption. Did the Israelites become conformed, commercial, and corrupt? If they were new kindred who knew not Joseph, then it is relatively understandable that Pharaoh should be a new king who also did not know him. Do we dare face the possibility that the appalling spiritual conditions in too many areas of the world may be due to an Ephesian and Laodicean church?

FAILURE TO LIVE HOLY LIVES

The real reasons may be buried beneath the dust of antiquity, but what is more important just now is not the reasons for the record but the representation. The new king is representative of persons, possessions, nations, denominations, and generations.

Cain, Eli's sons, Belshazzar, and a host of others make up a tragic list of persons who have turned their backs on parental or personal heritage. I was shocked and pained when a profligate son crassly said to me that if his godly father thought giving him the name of a celebrated Christian would influence him to be a saint he was sadly mistaken.

All of us can possibly cite examples of symbolical new-status kings, of sincere Christians who gained new social, financial, or educational standing, and suddenly the gains created in their lives new Pharaoh-like kings which knew not Joseph and destroyed past grace and good.

Nations, too, have gone this way. Africa, once a stronghold of early Christianity, is now a seat of Mohammedanism. Europe and England, once the seedbed of missions, are now plagued by spiritual barrenness or by noxious spiritual weeds. . . . Luther's Reformation Germany became Hitler's ruthless Germany. The reason for this is, of course, that new kings arose who did not know Joseph. America surely needs to beware lest we turn our backs on everything that made America great.

What is true of persons and nations is regrettably true of denominations. The Puritans were born out of a burden to preserve spiritual purity, but with the passing of the years new-generation Puritans themselves need . . . to be purified. . . .

My friends, I only ask each denominational group here to probe its own conscience. In doing so, let us not forget that the genius of

BACKSLIDING

backsliding is a subtle insensitivity which becomes less subtle but more insensitive with each succeeding spiritual loss. Millenniums ago, Hosea cried of Israel: "Strangers have devoured his strength, and he knows it not; yes, gray hairs are sprinkled here and there upon him, and he does not know it. And the pride of Israel testifies against him and to his face. But they do not return to the Lord their God, nor seek nor inquire of nor require Him, in spite of all this" (7:9-10, Amp.). How sternly relevant is this word!

Perhaps the most glaringly crucial representation of "a new king which knew not Joseph" is the social. There are many staggering modern phenomena. The rising generation is one of the

EVANGELIZE THIS GENERATION

most staggering. Each New Year issue of *Time* magazine highlights the person who in the estimation of *Time's* editors is "The Man of the Year." Can we miss the telling significance that *Time's* "Man of the Year, 1966" was not an individual but a generation—the New Generation: the 25-and-under age-group, which comprises half the population of the United States?

It is called the New Generation because its patterns of development are so divergent from those of other generations. It is a generation fighting amid great odds to find itself.

So, then, it is called not only the New Generation but the Now Generation. . . . This uncertainty, skepticism, and unbelief of the Now People is vividly portrayed by a young lyricist's words, "It's become out of style to lay yourself open, to approach people with your arms open . . . knowing you may get kicked." How contrary this is to the spirit of Christ's Sermon on the Mount! How damaging to faith, without which it is impossible to please God!

Ah, yes, we know, and thank God, that the devil does not possess all the young people, nor command all the youthful talent, but this fact really is an insufficient refuge from the swelling tides of rebellion. . . .

Indeed, the new social situation is so electric that significant heart-searching phrases are being born: "the third world"—new nations, former colonized peoples, on the march for self-determination and identity; "intergenerational cleavage"—the new generation in conflict with the old; "generation gap"—the old and the new generation seriously out of touch. A keen young surgeon specialist made me smart recently by his decisive comment that the Church is busily engaged in preaching to people who do not exist. . . . The tragic personal, national, and denominational representation is greatly aggravated by this exploding new generation to which, for the most part, we have not effectively introduced the God of our fathers.

Far more than one candle for this darkness is the "ahead-of-dateness" of the Bible. For instance, human-heart-transplant operations are relatively new to medical science, but the Bible declares that God has been successfully "transplanting hearts," without the headaches of rejection, ever since man fatally damaged his heart in the Fall (Ezek. 11:19). Similarly, the Bible has an ancient record of generational upheaval, a phenomenon so new and frustrating to us; it gives us a picture of this in the graphic words, "And Joseph died, and all his brethren, and all that generation. And the children [descendants] of Israel were fruitful, and increased abundantly, and . . . a new king [arose] over Egypt, which knew not Joseph" (Exod. 1:6-8).

NEW HEARTS

While our *challenge* derives from a new king who did not know Joseph, our *courage* comes from the King who "shall reign for ever and ever" (Exod. 15:18). How stabilizing that for the mad chaos of changing generations we have the majestic continuity of the unchanging God! Let us adoringly and reassuringly note some truths here.

A. Let us note the *unchanging purposes of God.* The king who knew not Joseph thought to reduce and to subject Israel, but God's

GOD'S PURPOSE

purpose is that they should inhabit the land of Canaan. In Gen. 12:7, God had said, "I will give this land to your descendants." The new king for a time victimized Israel, but he could not forever void the purposes of God.

In the light of the outworkings of God's purposes for Israel, we may think calmly of His purposes for the Church and for the individuals who comprise His Church. New kings may have revolutionary new plans similar to Pharaoh's, but all men should know that God is righteously and steadily working out His purpose, whether this affects Israel, individuals, the Church, or the universe.

B. Let us note, too, the *unchanging principles of God.* Think of His unchanging principle of *holiness.* In the Old Testament, God's

GOD'S REQUIREMENT

requirement is, "Ye shall be holy." With fuller, more personal and experiential implications, the unchanged requirement in the New Testament is, "Be holy in every department of your lives" (1 Pet. 1:15, Amp.); and throughout the glad eternities it is, "He that is holy, let him be holy still" (Rev. 22:11).

Think also of God's unchanging principle of *righteousness.* Today, in the name of truth, men teach a complete moral relativity in which standards are derived exclusively from man's desires and values. God and His standards are considered nonexistent; but God does have unchanging ethical standards. The new king Pharaoh found this out. Belshazzar, too, discovered this when, weighed in God's scales of justice, he stood condemned.

Extremely loose morals characterize modern society. Adultery and other forms of vice are commonplace, but God's "Thou shalt not commit adultery" still stands, and the morally impure who are eternally unrepentant will find themselves with the liars condemned to eternal punishment.

There is urgent need to think also of God's unchanging principle of *separation from the world.* . . . This was God's demand upon Israel

SEPARATION FROM FALSE VALUES

from the days of Abraham. His similar demand is upon the church. I must confess that I am distressed over the trends to worldly conformity in the church. God's unchanging principle is that the Christian is not to be mixed with "human society organized on wrong principles, possessing base desires, and having false values."

Neither the separation which leaves Christians secluded nor the participation which makes us polluted is the New Testament standard of separation. Jesus made the Church's relationship to the world perfectly clear when He stated that those peculiarly His own are in the world but not of it. Jesus was atoningly involved in the world but never was adversely influenced by it. He set himself up as the Standard of separation and prayed, not that we might be taken out of the world, but that we might be kept from its physical and mental lusts and from its vainglory.

C. Briefly, we may note also the *unchanging promises of God,* and the *unchanging power of God.* Our scripture context contains rich illustrations of such promises and power.

PROMISES AND POWER

When Canaan was conquered and settled, after Israel's too long, yet clearly providential, journey from Egypt, Joshua gratefully acknowledged, "There failed not aught [no part] of any good thing which the Lord had spoken unto the house of Israel; all came to pass" (Josh. 21:45). To us likewise God has given exceeding great and precious promises, and these, though often conditional, are nonetheless unchanging.

Much earlier, when the Lord saved Israel out of the hand of the Egyptians, and Israel saw the Egyptians dead upon the seashore, Moses, divinely inspired, wrote a poetic masterpiece (Exod. 15:1-19) to celebrate the victory. In verse 6, Moses sang, "Your right hand, O Lord, is glorious in power; Your right hand, O Lord, shatters the enemy" (Amp.). Centuries later the eternal Word, who is God, said to the nucleus of the Church, "All authority —all power of rule—in heaven and on earth has been given to Me. Go therefore and make disciples" (Matt. 28:18-19, Amp.).

We have considered on the one hand our changing, chaotic world and on the other the high, holy, and unchanging God. The vital, living link between the two is our prerogative to project our heritage (Exod. 1:17).

GOD HAS HOLY PEOPLE

We must let neither Pharaoh's brutal oppression of the Israelites nor their bitter cries of sorrow and suffering make us overlook a truly glorious fact: that the midwives who did not as the king of Egypt commanded were obviously contemporaries of the new king who knew not Joseph (of course, so also were Amram and Jochebed and dear little Miriam). This inspiring fact speaks eloquently for the noble army of godly persons in every age who have shared the same period of history with godless new kings.

We think, too, of sweet Samuel; of daring Daniel; of the heroic Hebrews—Shadrach, Meshach, and Abednego; of the company of overcomers, particularly the saints in Sardis, all members of "the seven churches which are in Asia" (Rev. 1:11); and even of the quiet queen, or queen mother, a rose blooming on the dunghill of Belshazzar's grossly heathen court (Dan. 5:10-12).

. . . contemporaneity can present problems: some find it difficult to be different in their day; others wonder just what stand to take; yet others keenly feel the slowness of traditional minds to keep abreast. Let us fearlessly acknowledge that there is a wholesome contemporaneity, that the new which is good and helpful should be adopted. In the light of our study, however, Christians who use the easy excuse, "Times have changed," to justify their conformity to the current that is basically worldly should conscientiously check to see if it is not more true that *they* have changed, that they themselves have become new kings who no longer know Joseph.

Oh, may we tell it out on the mountains that God requires His people to be consistently clean in the midst of the change which corrupts!

We are not surprised that these midwives, Shiphrah and Puah, were women of character. It is not necessary to make them New Testament saints, nor to stumble over their apparently disguised prevarication; the Bible says they "feared God." That is, they regarded God's law and dreaded His wrath more than they did Pharaoh's.

PROCLAIM IT

It seems that the social and spiritual pressures of our day constitute a new king more forbidding than any Pharaoh, and that we will have to possess more than ordinary mettle to stem the turbulent tides of thought sweeping all about us. The task of projecting our heritage in this generation may seem as overwhelming to us as the conquest of Canaan did to the Israelites. Their encouragement also may therefore be ours: "Be strong, courageous and firm, fear not nor be in terror. . . . It is the Lord who goes before you . . . He will not fail you or let you go, or forsake you; let there be no cowardice or flinching, but fear not, neither become depressed, discouraged and unnerved with alarm" (Deut. 31:7-8, Amp.). There is also New Testament encouragement: "Rekindle the embers, fan the flame and keep burning the gracious gift of God, the inner fire that is in you . . . For God did not give us a spirit of cowardice, of craven and cringing fear . . . but He has given us a spirit of power" (2 Tim. 1:6-7, Amp.).

I do not think we do injustice to apply to ourselves some words from Paul's victory speech, "Amid the things which confront us we too can be more than conquerors and gain a surpassing victory through Him who loves us" (Rom. 8:37, Amp.)

Bibliography

Agnew, Milton S. *Transformed Christians.* Kansas City: Beacon Hill Press of Kansas City, 1974.

Augsburger, Myron S. *Quench Not the Spirit.* Scottdale, Pa.: Herald Press, 1975.

Baker, Sheridan. *Living Waters.* New York: Phillips and Hunt, 1888.

Boyd, Myron F., and Harris, Merne A., comps. *Projecting Our Heritage.* Papers and Messages Delivered at the Centennial Convention of the National Holiness Association, Cleveland, April 16-19, 1968. Kansas City: Beacon Hill Press of Kansas City, 1969.

Brengle, Samuel Logan. *When the Holy Ghost Is Come.* 1909. Reprint. Atlanta: The Salvation Army Supplies and Purchasing Department, 1982.

Bresee, Phineas F. *Sermons on Isaiah.* Kansas City: Nazarene Publishing House, 1926.

Buckley, James M. *A History of Methodism in the United States,* vols. 1—2. New York: Harper and Brothers Publishers, 1898.

Chadwick, Samuel. *Humanity and God.* Reprint. Salem, Ohio: Schmul Publishing Co., 1982.

Chambers, Oswald. *Facing Reality.* London: Simpkin Marshall, n.d.

Chapman, James B. *Christian Living in a Modern World.* 2nd ed. Kansas City: Beacon Hill Press, 1942.

Clarke, Adam. *Discourses on Various Subjects Relative to the Being and Attributes of God and His Work in Creation, Providence, and Grace,* vol. 4. London: William Tegg, 1868.

Clow, W. W. *The Evangel of the Strait Gate.* New York: George H. Doran Co., n.d.

Dieter, Melvin Easterday. *The Holiness Revival of the Nineteenth Century.* Metuchen, N.J.: Scarecrow Press, 1980.

Douglas, J. D., ed. *The New International Dictionary of the Christian Church.* Grand Rapids: Zondervan Publishing House, 1974.

Dunning, Norman G. *Samuel Chadwick.* London: Hodder and Stoughton, 1896.

Edmonson, Jonathan. *Short Sermons on Important Subjects,* vol. 2. London: John Mason, 1829.

General Superintendents of the Church of the Nazarene (1985-89). *Sanctify Them . . . That the World May Know: Twelve Holiness Sermons.* Kansas City: Nazarene Publishing House, 1987.

Harris, J. Rendel. *Union with God.* London: Hodder and Stoughton, 1896.

Jones, Charles Edwin. *Perfectionist Persuasion: The Holiness Movement and American Methodism, 1867-1936.* Metuchen, N.J.: Scarecrow Press, 1974.

Langford, Thomas. *Practical Divinity: Theology in the Wesleyan Tradition.* Nashville: Abingdon Press, 1983.

McGraw, James, comp. *The Holiness Pulpit.* Kansas City: Beacon Hill Press, 1957.

———. *The Holiness Pulpit* No. 2. Kansas City: Beacon Hill Press of Kansas City, 1974.

McLean, A., and Eaton, J. W., eds. *Penuel; or Face to Face with God.* New York: W. C. Palmer, Jr., Publisher, 1870.

The Methodist Preacher. Auburn, N.Y.: Derby and Miller; Buffalo, N.Y.: Derby, Orton, and Mulligan, 1853.

Morrison, H. C. *Life Sketches and Sermons.* Louisville, Ky.: Pentecostal Publishing Co., 1903.

Olin, Stephen. *The Works of Stephen Olin, D.D., LL.D.* Vol. 1, *Sermons and Sketches.* New York: Harper and Brothers, Publishers, 1860.

The Pentecostal Pulpit. Louisville, Ky.: Pentecostal Publishing Co., n.d.

Potts, James Henry. *The Upward Leading.* In *The Methodist Pulpit, Second Series.* Cincinnati: Jennings and Graham; New York: Eaton and Mains, 1905.

Rees, Paul S. *Stand Up in Praise to God.* Grand Rapids: Wm. B. Eerdmans Publishing Co., 1960.

Roberts, Benjamin. *How Sanctified?* North Chili, N.Y.: Earnest Christian Office, n.d.

Shaw, S. B., ed. *Echoes of the General Holiness Assembly.* Chicago: S. B. Shaw, Publisher, 1901

Smith, Timothy L. *Revivalism and Social Reform.* New York and Nashville: Abingdon Press, 1957.

Stevens, Abel. *Life and Times of Nathan Bangs, D.D.* New York: Carlton and Porter, 1863.

Tipple, Ezra Squier, ed. *Drew Sermons on the Golden Texts for 1908.* New York: Eaton and Mains; Cincinnati: Jennings and Graham, 1907.

Tracy, Wesley D., ed. *The Redeemed Will Walk There: Sermons on the Life of Holiness from the Chapel of Nazarene Theological Seminary.* Kansas City: Beacon Hill Press of Kansas City, 1983.

Turner, George Allen. *Witnesses of the Way: The Interior Life of Some Famous Christians.* Kansas City: Beacon Hill Press of Kansas City, 1981.

Twentieth Century Holiness Sermons. Louisville, Ky.: Pentecostal Publishing Co., n.d.

Wallace, Adam, ed. *A Modern Pentecost.* Philadelphia: Methodist Home Journal Publishing House, 1873.

Watson, George D. *Love Abounding.* Boston and Chicago: McDonald, Gill, and Co., 1891.

Watson, Richard. *Sermons and Sketches of Sermons*, vol. 1. New York: B. Waugh and T. Mason, 1836.

Wesley, John. *The Works of John Wesley*. Edited by Thomas Jackson. 3rd ed. Vol. 7. London: Wesleyan Methodist Book Room, 1872. Reprint. Kansas City: Beacon Hill Press of Kansas City, 1978.

Wiley, H. Orton. *The Harps of God and Other Sermons*. Compiled and edited by Ross E. Price. Kansas City: Beacon Hill Press of Kansas City, 1971.

Author Index

Subject Index

Index of Scripture References